Pro Puppet

Second Edition

Spencer Krum

William Van Hevelingen

Ben Kero

James Turnbull

Jeffery McCune

Pro Puppet, Second Edition

ISBN-13 (pbk): 978-1-4302-6040-0

ISBN-13 (electronic): 978-1-4302-6041-7

President and Publisher: Paul Manning
Lead Editor: Michelle Lowman
Technical Reviewers: Lee Lowder and Daniele Sluijters
Editorial Board: Steve Anglin, Mark Beckner, Ewan Buckingham, Gary Cornell, Louise Corrigan, Jonathan Gennick, Jonathan Hassell, Robert Hutchinson, Michelle Lowman, James Markham, Matthew Moodie, Jeff Olson, Jeffrey Pepper, Douglas Pundick, Ben Renow-Clarke, Dominic Shakeshaft, Gwenan Spearing, Matt Wade, Tom Welsh, Steve Weiss, James T. DeWolf
Coordinating Editor: Christine Ricketts
Copy Editor: James Compton
Compositor: SPi Global
Indexer: SPi Global
Artist: SPi Global
Cover Designer: Anna Ishchenko

Distributed to the book trade worldwide by Springer Science+Business Media New York, 233 Spring Street, 6th Floor, New York, NY 10013. Phone 1-800-SPRINGER, fax (201) 348-4505, e-mail orders-ny@springer-sbm.com, or visit www.springeronline.com. Apress Media, LLC is a California LLC and the sole member (owner) is Springer Science + Business Media Finance Inc (SSBM Finance Inc). SSBM Finance Inc is a Delaware corporation.

For information on translations, please e-mail rights@apress.com, or visit www.apress.com.

Apress and friends of ED books may be purchased in bulk for academic, corporate, or promotional use. eBook versions and licenses are also available for most titles. For more information, reference our Special Bulk Sales–eBook Licensing web page at www.apress.com/bulk-sales.

Any source code or other supplementary materials referenced by the authors in this text is available to readers at www.apress.com. For detailed information about how to locate your book's source code, go to www.apress.com/source-code/.

Dedicated to my Mother and Father, who have stood strong with me through so much. I am grateful.

—Spencer Krum

This book is dedicated to those of you just beginning your journey to somewhere great.

—Ben Kero

Dedicated to my family, friends and all the CATs.

—William Van Hevelingen

Contents at a Glance

About the Authors.. xvii

About the Technical Reviewers xix

Acknowledgments xxi

Foreword xxiii

■Chapter 1: Getting Started with Puppet...1

■Chapter 2: Building Hosts with Puppet..33

■Chapter 3: Developing and Deploying Puppet 73

■Chapter 4: Scaling Puppet...97

■Chapter 5: Externalizing Puppet Configuration 141

■Chapter 6: Exporting and Storing Configuration..155

■Chapter 7: Puppet Consoles 169

■Chapter 8: Tools and Integration 191

■Chapter 9: Reporting with Puppet 217

■Chapter 10: Extending Facter and Puppet 227

■Chapter 11: MCollective 249

■Chapter 12: Hiera: Separating Data from Code...263

Index...295

Contents

About the Authors.. xvii

About the Technical Reviewers xix

Acknowledgments xxi

Foreword xxiii

■Chapter 1: Getting Started with Puppet..1

What Is Puppet? 1

    Deployment..2

    The Configuration Language and Resource Abstraction Layer 3

    The Transactional Layer 6

Selecting the Right Version of Puppet 6

Installing Puppet 7

    Installing on Red Hat Enterprise Linux and Fedora...8

    Installing on Debian and Ubuntu..9

    Installing on OpenIndiana 9

    Installing on Solaris 10 and 11 10

    Installing from Source 10

    Installing on Microsoft Windows...11

    Installing on the Mac 14

    Installing on Other Platforms 18

Configuring Puppet...19

    The site.pp File 20

    Firewall Configuration 20

    Starting the Puppet Master 21

Connecting Our First Agent 22

    Completing the Connection 23

Creating Our First Configuration Item...24

    Adding a Node Definition...25

Creating Our First Module 26

    Module Structure...27

    The init.pp file..27

    Applying Our First Configuration..29

Summary 31

Resources 31

■Chapter 2: Building Hosts with Puppet..33

Getting Started 34

    Installing Puppet...34

    Integrating and Bootstrapping Puppet with Kickstart...34

Configuring Nodes...35

    Working with Similar Hosts 36

    Using External Sources..36

    Default Node..36

    Node Inheritance 37

    Variable Scoping...37

    The *Puppet Style Guide* 40

Making (More) Magic With Modules 41

    Version-Controlling Your Modules...42

    Creating a Module to Manage SSH..44

    Creating a Module to Manage Postfix...54

    Managing MySQL with the mysql Module 58

    Managing Apache and Websites..62

    Managing Puppet with the Puppet Module..67

Summary 72

Resources 72

■**Chapter 3: Developing and Deploying Puppet** **73**

The puppet apply Command and Modes of Operation 73

Printf with Puppet...74

Testing Puppet Behavior with Notify...74

Using Puppet Apply with Manifest Files 74

Foreground Puppet Master..78

Developing Puppet with Vagrant 80

Vagrant Initial Setup 80

Booting the Vagrant Box 81

Configuring Puppet on the Vagrant Box 82

Testing Puppet with Vagrant..82

Destroying and Re-Creating the Vagrant Box 82

Environments 84

Maintenance of Modules 84

Tools for External Modules 84

Configuring Puppet Environments 85

Populating the New Environments 85

Creating a Clone 86

Making Changes to the Development Environment 87

Testing the New Environments with the Puppet Agent 89

Environment Branching and Merging..91

Setting Up a Central Repository...91

Creating a Bare Repository for the Modules..92

Making Individual Changes..92

Dynamic Puppet Environments with Git Branches 93

The Git Hook 95

Summary..96

Resources..96

■Chapter 4: Scaling Puppet 97

Identifying the Challenges 97

Running the Puppet Master with Apache and Passenger 98

Installing Apache and Passenger 98

Configuring Apache and Passenger 101

Testing the Puppet Master in Apache 105

Load-Balancing Multiple Puppet Masters 107

HTTP Load Balancing 107

Puppet Master Worker Configuration 108

Front End Load Balancer Configuration Details 111

Testing the Load Balancer Configuration 112

Scaling Further 118

Puppet Certificate Authority Service Externalization 119

Load Balancing Alternatives 130

Load Balancing with DNS Round Robin 130

Load Balancing with DNS SRV records 131

Load Balancing with a TCP Load Balancer 131

Anycast 134

Masterless Puppet 134

Measuring Performance 137

Splay Time 138

Summary 139

Going Further 139

Resources 139

■Chapter 5: Externalizing Puppet Configuration 141

External Node Classification 142

Configuring Nodes Using an External Node Classifier 143

An External Node Classifier in a Shell Script 143

Parameterized Classes in YAML 144

A Ruby External Node Classifier 144

A Perl External Node Classifier 146

Back-Ending a Node Classification 147

Storing Node Configuration in LDAP 149

Installing Ruby LDAP Libraries 149

Setting Up the LDAP Server 149

Adding the Puppet Schema 150

Configuring LDAP in Puppet 150

Summary 153

Resources 153

Chapter 6: Exporting and Storing Configuration 155

Virtual Resources 155

Declaring and Realizing a Virtual Resource 156

Applying the realize Function 157

Making Virtual Resources Real 157

Relationship-Chaining Syntax 158

Getting Started with Exported and Stored Configurations 159

Using Exported Resources 160

Automated SSH Public Host Key Management 160

Exporting Load Balancer Worker Resources 163

Automating Nagios Service Checks 164

Expiring Stale Resources 168

Summary 168

Resources 168

Chapter 7: Puppet Consoles 169

The Foreman 169

Installing Foreman 169

Importing Data from Puppet 173

Connecting Your First Client 174

Using Foreman as an ENC 176

Displaying Reports in Foreman..178

Searching for Facts in Foreman 179

Puppet Enterprise Console 180

Installing Puppet Enterprise 180

Connecting PE Agents to PE Console 181

Adding Classes to Nodes 182

Inventory Service...182

Live Management 183

Puppetboard 184

Installation 185

Reviewing the Dashboard Tabs..185

The Future of Puppetboard 188

Summary 189

Resources...189

Chapter 8: Tools and Integration 191

Puppet Forge and the Module Tool...191

Searching and Installing a Module from the Forge 192

Generating a Module 195

Managing Module Dependencies 197

Puppet Librarian 197

R10K...198

Puppet-lint...199

Testing the Modules 200

rspec-puppet..200

TravisCI 205

rspec-system..207

Developing Puppet modules With Geppetto 210

Summary 214

Resources...215

■Chapter 9: Reporting with Puppet 217

Getting Started 217

Configuring Reporting 219

Report Processors 219

    log...220

    tagmail...220

    rrdgraph...221

    http..222

    puppetdb..222

Custom Reporting...222

Other Puppet Reporters 225

Summary 225

Resources...225

■Chapter 10: Extending Facter and Puppet 227

Writing and Distributing Custom Facts...227

    Configuring Puppet for Custom Facts..227

    Writing Custom Facts 228

    Testing the Facts 231

    External Facts..231

Developing Custom Types, Providers and Functions 232

    Configuring Puppet for Types, Providers and Functions 232

    Writing a Puppet Type and Provider...233

    Writing a Parsed File Type and Provider 238

    A More Complex Type and Provider 241

    Testing Types and Providers 245

    Writing Custom Functions 245

Summary 248

Resources...248

■ **Chapter 11: MCollective** **249**

More Background on MCollective 249

Installing and Configuring MCollective 250

    Generating and Storing Certificates 252

    Verifying Permissions 253

Testing 254

Installing MCollective Plug-ins 255

    Puppet Agent MCollective Plug-ins 255

    The Facter Plug-in for MCollective 257

    The NRPE Plug-in for MCollective 258

Addressing Hosts with Metadata 260

Additional Plug-ins 261

Summary 261

Resources 262

■ **Chapter 12: Hiera: Separating Data from Code** **263**

The Power of Hiera 263

    Lists 264

Installing Hiera on Earlier Versions of Puppet 265

Initial Hiera Configuration 266

    Configuring a Hiera Data Directory 267

The Hiera Command-Line Utility 267

    Populating a Hiera Datafile 267

    Performing a Hiera Lookup 267

    Using Puppet to Perform a Hiera Lookup 268

    Exploring the Hierarchy 268

    Building Dynamic Hierarchy 269

    Hiera Lookups Using Variables 269

    Hiera Lookups Using Puppet with Variables 270

    Hierarchy Organization 271

Complex Data Structures 271

    Returning Structured Data...271

    Array Merging...272

    Hash Merges...273

Additional Backends...275

    The File Backend 277

    The JSON Backend 279

    The MySQL Backend...280

    The gpg Backend..282

Hiera Functions in Depth 285

    Other Hiera Functions 286

Module Data Bindings 287

Hiera Examples 288

    The create-resources() Function 289

    Hiera as an ENC...290

Hiera-2 292

Summary..292

Resources...292

Index..295

About the Authors

Spencer Krum is a Linux and application administrator with UTi Worldwide Inc., a shipping and logistics firm. He lives and works in Portland. He has been using Linux and Puppet for years. His interests are in DevOps and teaching the next generation of hackers. He, like William, is a product of the Computer Action Team at Portland State University. He has spoken, often with either William or Ben, at Puppet Conf, Open Source Bridge, numerous BarCamps and user groups, and at Cascadia IT Conf. Spencer participates in the Portland DevOps user group and the Portland Puppet Users group. He enjoys hacking, tennis, StarCraft, and Hawaiian food. You can find his GitHub at https://github.com/nibalizer.

William Van Hevelingen started with Linux and configuration management as part of the Computer Action Team's Braindump program at Portland State University in 2009. He worked on the Wintel, Nix, and Networking teams as a volunteer and later as a student worker helping to manage hundreds of workstations, servers, and networking infrastructure. William now works full time for the Computer Action Team (TheCAT), which provides IT for the Maseeh College of Engineering and Computer Science at Portland State University, as the Unix Team lead. He helps teach the Unix server portion of the Braindump, covering topics like web servers, databases, storage, virtualization, and Puppet. William speaks regularly at conferences including OpenSource Bridge, BeaverBarcamp, CascadiaIT, and LinuxFestNW.

Benjamin Kero is a systems administrator with Mozilla's Web Operations team, where he deals with the nuances of administrating Mozilla's *large* server infrastructure and web stacks. Previously, Ben worked as a community systems administrator for the Oregon State University Open Source Lab, where he helped to maintain the infrastructure for dozens of high-profile open source projects, including Drupal and kernel.org.

Based in Portland, Oregon, he speaks at conferences worldwide on all things DevOps and scaling large-scale systems. He also participates in many local user groups, such as the PDXPUG (Puppet User Group), Portland State University's Braindump program, and the OSU Linux User's Group.

James Turnbull is the author of seven technical books about open source software and a long-time member of the open source community. James has authored books about Docker, LogStash, and Puppet. He works for Venmo as VP of Engineering. He was previously at Puppet Labs running Operations and Professional Services.

James speaks regularly at conferences including OSCON, Linux.conf.au, FOSDEM, OpenSourceBridge, DevOpsDays, and a number of others. He is a past president of Linux Australia and a former committee member of Linux Victoria, was Treasurer for Linux.conf.au 2008, and serves on the program committee of Linux.conf.au and OSCON.

Jeff McCune is a long-time Puppet community member and open source software advocate. He started off with computers and Unix at a young age thanks to his parents' company, Summit Computer Services. Before graduating with his BS CSE degree, Jeff managed Mac OS X and Linux systems at the Mathematics Department at Ohio State University, where he got started with configuration management and Puppet.

Jeff works for Puppet Labs, hacking on code and working with customers to improve their Puppet deployments. Jeff also speaks regularly at conferences, including Apple's World Wide Developer Conference, Macworld, Open Source Bridge, Velocity, and others. He travels the world teaching and consulting on Puppet.

Jeff grew up in Ohio and currently lives in Portland, Oregon. His interests include hacking on microcontrollers, anime, photography, music, hiking, and long walks on the beach.

About the Technical Reviewers

Lee Lowder is currently a Support Engineer at Puppet Labs, where he troubleshoots and resolves issues for Puppet Enterprise customers. Prior to that, he was very active in the Puppet community and used Puppet extensively at his previous job. While his educational background is in accounting, specifically operational auditing, his professional career has consisted of technical support, retail sales management, and systems administration. The core goal of operational auditing is to improve effectiveness and efficiency, and this is the philosophy that drives him. He currently resides in Springfield, MO. "Automate All the Things!"

Daniele Sluijters was born in The Netherlands but raised for most of his childhood in Brussels, Belgium. His fascination with computers started at a very young age, not even being able to correctly pronounce the word back then. This fascination grew and grew and led him to start managing small numbers of machines for different organizations as a hobby. He eventually turned this hobby into his work and field of study.

He is an operator by trade, strongly influenced by the DevOps movement and, for the last few years, also doing more and more on the development side of things. Within the Puppet community he is probably best known for bugging people about, and speaking on the subject of, testing, testing, and testing modules at Puppet Camps and as the author of Puppetboard.

Acknowledgments

I would like to thank so many people for making this book happen. I would like to thank Mom and Dad for keeping me in the game this long; I've used up about every extra life available at this point. I'd like to thank Mamgu and Dad for getting me into computers at an early age. I'd like to thank Grandma and Grampa for making my college happen. I'd like to thank Mrs. Alderman, Ashley, Beverley, and Ryan for giving me the goal to be a writer. I want to thank Corbin for his early influence and constant aid, both in tech and in life.

I want to thank Janaka for making TheCAT. I want to thank Marut, Finch, CATastrophe, Johnj, Hunner, Jesusaurus and everyone else at TheCAT who taught me ALL THE THINGS. I want to thank Donkey for 4 am Plaid Pantry runs and for teaching me how to IP. I want to thank Greg Haynes for teaching me from the day I met him until today, and for introducing me to the tech world. I want to thank Epitrope for opening the door to this book for me.

I want to thank Gary Kilmocwiz, Mike Kinney, Scot Lambert, Charles Hill, Lance Coombs and the rest of the UTi DevOps crew for putting up with me while I did this and for being the best coworkers a guy could possibly want.

I want to thank my coauthors for being awesome enough to write this book with me. I want to thank the tech reviewers for being so helpful; couldn't have done it without you.

I want to especially thank Krinkle (Colleen Murphy) for helping to edit out all of my bad English and giving me a second read no matter what else she had to do that day. I want to especially thank Nightfly (Sage Imel) for his help around some of the trickier sections of Puppet. Without the contributions of these two, this book would be considerably worse. Both of them gave considerable donations of time and energy, and I really appreciate that.

I want to thank everyone at Puppet Labs who has done such an amazing job supporting us: Dawn, Lee, Reid, Adrien, Hunter, Ben Ford, Eric0, Thomas Halgren, Brenan, Haus, Stahnma, Nigel, Nick F, Nick L, Henrik Lindberg, Jeff McCune, Kara Sowles, Kent Bye, Charlotte, Aliza, and of course Luke Kaines. Without Puppet Labs there probably wouldn't be a Puppet, and without these individuals and their effort this book would not be what it is.

I also want to thank everyone at Apress for making this possible: Steve, Christine, Michelle, and James, you guys held our hands the whole way and we really appreciate it. Also thanks to Kevin; you've been so understanding, we promise to make up for it.

—Spencer Krum

Much love to the brilliant engineers at Puppet Labs who make a strong project to build an ecosystem around, and the Puppet community members who surprise us with all these splendid tools to write about. Without you none of this would be possible. I would like to express great praise to my esteemed co-authors, without which I would have never had the opportunity or vitality to finish it through to completion. Finally, I would like to thank Apress for their top-notch support making the publishing of this book possible.

—Ben Kero

I would like to thank my mother, who has always been there for me, and my father, for introducing me to the tech world. I would like to thank John Harris teaching me how to be a sysadmin, Scott Andrew for being my mentor, Janaka Jayawardena and Reid Vandewiele for teaching me Unix, and Spencer for pushing me farther than I thought possible. And finally, thanks to all the CATs before me and all the new CATs who keep me inspired to never stop learning.

—William Van Hevelingen

Foreword

It's my pleasure to introduce the new, updated version of *Pro Puppet*. This book has proved popular since it was published in May 2011, and it's always in demand at conferences and technology events that Puppet Labs attends we routinely run out of copies.

Things have changed a bit since the first edition of *Pro Puppet*. At that time, Puppet 2.7 had just been released, and shortly after, we launched the very first version of Puppet Enterprise, our commercial product. As I write this introduction, we're shipping Puppet Enterprise 3.1, and we're actively planning updates through 4.0.

Back in May 2011, there were about 170 modules in the Puppet Forge; today there are nearly 1,700, many contributed by our large and fast-growing community. Speaking of community, more than 30 Puppet User Groups around the world meet regularly to talk about all things Puppet; when the first edition of this book came out, PUGs didn't exist.

As a company, Puppet Labs has grown from 33 people at the time *Pro Puppet* was published to about 200 today. We're able to offer a lot more resources and services to Puppet users, including our help site, ask.puppetlabs.com, where anyone can ask or answer a question.

One of the most remarkable changes to me has been in who uses Puppet. A few years ago, Puppet users were smart, innovative sysadmins responsible for a wide range of IT functions in smaller organizations. Today, many Puppet users are smart, innovative sysadmins, developers and IT managers working in large enterprises. It's no longer unusual to see environments with 50,000-plus nodes managed by Puppet. Today, Puppet users work in a wide range of industries, including banking and finance, research science, technology, retail, e-commerce, government, telecom and Internet services, and more. Wherever a business is looking for IT to provide a competitive advantage, you're probably going to find Puppet.

I originally developed Puppet as a tool for system administrators, to allow them to focus on their goals rather than on an infinite variety of technology. Computers should do the menial repetitive work, and people should get to do the difficult (and fun) work involved in building and maintaining large-scale infrastructure. I wanted people to never have to solve the same problem twice, so code reuse was critical. I knew that what really matters to customers are the services they count on, not the nodes and technology that provide them.

I created a simple declarative language dedicated to server configuration for Puppet, so it would be quick and easy for any reasonably competent sysadmin to tell any node—whether physical server, VM, switch, or router—what its job was and how it should look, without having to know the exact steps to make that happen.

I was looking at a world of increasingly heterogeneous data centers, and wanted to push it further, to where said data centers would be treated as running software. We started by managing servers and workstations, but now we're managing switches, routers, firewalls, storage arrays, and more. The API-driven world of the cloud is shortening feedback cycles and putting time pressure on the entire technology pipeline. The best sysadmins and their management teams are riding this edge, getting better technology to their users faster, and building tight feedback cycles that turn IT into a competitive advantage.

Puppet Labs is one of the organizations driving that shift, and changes in Puppet technology over the past couple of years are our efforts to further enable it. Authors Spencer Krum, William Van Hevelingen, Ben Kero, James Turnbull, and Jeffrey McCune have done a great job of updating *Pro Puppet* for anyone who wants to take advantage of the full capabilities Puppet offers.

This new edition covers the following:

Hiera: An entirely new chapter is devoted to Hiera, a key/value lookup tool that lets you set node-specific data without repeating yourself. Hiera makes Puppet better by keeping site-specific data out of your manifests, and makes it easier to configure your own nodes by using a configurable data hierarchy. You'll find it easier to use Puppet modules with Hiera, and to publish your own modules for collaboration. This new edition contains a complete introduction to the tool, as well as its advanced merging behaviors.

Geppetto: Geppetto is an Eclipse-based IDE designed for writing Puppet code. The book has been updated to cover the latest version of Geppetto, including its integration with services such as the Puppet Forge.

MCollective: In today's highly dynamic, self-service environments, it's more necessary than ever to discover the resources you are dealing with rather than statically declaring them all. MCollective provides granular control across your entire infrastructure, whether you're doing basic service maintenance or managing complex application rollouts. You can also progressively deploy changes, so you can move quickly with a high degree of confidence. This new edition of *Pro Puppet* has been updated for MCollective 2.

Puppet 3: Puppet 3 was released in 2012 with many changes, including vastly reduced agent run time, faster catalog compilation times, and seamless integration with Hiera. This new edition has been fully updated to Puppet 3, and all examples have been tested against its new parser.

PuppetDB: With the addition of a centralized storage service named PuppetDB, you can manage twice as many nodes as before. This PostgreSQL-backed datastore for Puppet has a feature-rich API, and it has already spawned the development of derivative open source projects like Puppetboard. This new edition of *Pro Puppet* introduces you to PuppetDB and takes you step by step through installation, configuration, and use.

Puppet Enterprise Console and Puppetboard: The Puppet Enterprise Console is a graphical user interface that functions as the primary interface for managing and operating your Puppet infrastructure, with tools for reporting; error discovery and analysis; resource discovery and comparison; and much more. Puppetboard is a new web interface for PuppetDB that supplants the reporting functionality of Puppet Dashboard for open source Puppet. Both are new since the first edition of *Pro Puppet*, and this volume has been updated accordingly. Foreman, a project of RedHat in a similar space, is also discussed.

Additional Tools: There is a large set of additional tools that make Puppet useful across a wide range of operating systems, platforms, and technologies. The authors have updated this section of the book to include tools such as `puppet-lint`, `puppet-rspec`, `travis-ci` integration, `r10k` and `puppet-librarian`. The section leads with an updated, step-by-step guide to the Puppet Module tool, which allows you to search the Puppet Forge from the command line; list, upgrade, and install modules; and resolve and install module dependencies.

Scaling: Puppet and its related software are fantastically scalable. This book covers a complete example of how organizations traditionally scale Puppet, along with alternative options like running Puppet in a masterless mode. While this is rarely done with Puppet Enterprise, because of its enhanced scalability out of the box, it is particularly useful in some situations and environments.

If this is your first introduction to Puppet, welcome. We're delighted to have you on board, and I hope you'll take full advantage of our free resources, including these:

Ask.puppetlabs.com

Puppet Users Google Group (https://groups.google.com/forum/#!forum/puppet-users)

Docs.puppetlabs.com

Training at puppetlabs.com/learn

Our IRC channel (http://webchat.freenode.net/?channels=puppet). Authors of this book lurk in #puppet as nibalizer, blkperl, and bkero, should you wish to reach out to them.

For those of you who already use Puppet, I'm confident this updated version of *Pro Puppet* will help you expand your mastery. All the resources above are available to you too, and I hope you'll try out the ones you haven't used yet. May all your problems be tractable, yet enjoyably challenging.

Yours,

—Luke Kanies, Founder and CEO, Puppet Labs

CHAPTER 1

■ ■ ■

Getting Started with Puppet

Puppet is an open source framework and toolset for managing the configuration of computer systems. This book looks at how you can use Puppet to manage your configuration. As the book progresses, we'll introduce Puppet's features and show you how to integrate Puppet into your provisioning and management lifecycle. To do this, we'll take you through configuring a real-world scenario that we'll introduce in Chapter 2. In Chapter 3, we'll show you how to implement a successful Puppet workflow using version control and Puppet environments. In Chapter 4, we'll show you how to build high availability and horizontal scalability into your Puppet infrastructure. The rest of the book will focus on extending what you can do with Puppet and its ecosystem of tools, and on gaining unprecedented visibility into your infrastructure.

In this chapter, you'll find the following:

- A quick overview of Puppet, what it is, how it works, and which release to use.

- How to install Puppet and its inventory tool, Facter, on RedHat, Debian, Ubuntu, Solaris, Microsoft Windows, Mac OS X, and via RubyGems.

- How to configure Puppet and create your first configuration items.

- The Puppet domain-specific language that you use to create Puppet configuration.

- The concept of "modules," Puppet's way of collecting and managing bundles of configuration data.

- How to apply one of these modules to a host using the Puppet agent.

What Is Puppet?

Puppet is Ruby-based configuration management software, licensed as Apache 2.0, and it can run in either client-server or stand-alone mode. Puppet was principally developed by Luke Kanies and is now developed by his company, Puppet Labs. Kanies has been involved with Unix and systems administration since 1997 and developed Puppet from that experience. Unsatisfied with existing configuration management tools, Kanies began working with tool development in 2001, and in 2005 he founded Puppet Labs, an open source development house focused on automation tools. Shortly after this, Puppet Labs released its flagship product, Puppet Enterprise. Puppet has two versions available: the open source version and the Enterprise version. The Enterprise version comes with an automated installer, a web management interface, and support contract. This book will focus on the open source version of Puppet, but since the software at the core of both tools is the same, the information will be valuable to consumers of either product.

Puppet can be used to manage configuration on Unix (including OS X), Linux, and Microsoft Windows platforms. Puppet can manage a host throughout its life cycle: from initial build and installation, to upgrades, maintenance, and finally to end-of-life, when you move services elsewhere. Puppet is designed to interact continuously with your hosts, unlike provisioning tools that build your hosts and leave them unmanaged.

Puppet has a simple operating model that is easy to understand and implement (Figure 1-1). The model is made up of three components:

- Deployment Layer
- Configuration Language and Resource Abstraction Layer
- Transactional Layer

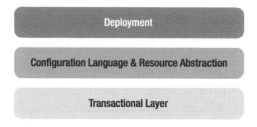

Figure 1-1. *The Puppet model*

Deployment

Puppet is usually deployed in a simple client-server model (Figure 1-2). The server is called a *Puppet master*, the Puppet client software is called an *agent,* and the host itself is defined as a *node.*

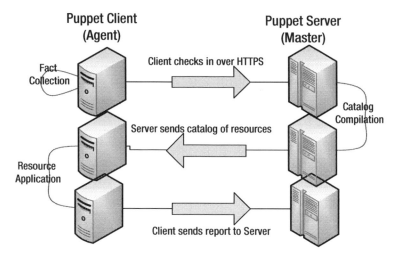

Figure 1-2. *High-level overview of a Puppet configuration run*

The Puppet master runs as a daemon on a host and contains the configuration required for the specific environment. The Puppet agents connect to the Puppet master through an encrypted and authenticated connection using standard SSL, and retrieve or "pull" any configuration to be applied.

Importantly, if the Puppet agent has no configuration available or already has the required configuration, Puppet will do nothing. Puppet will only make changes to your environment if they are required. This property is called *idempotency* and is a key feature of Puppet. The whole process is called a *configuration run.*

Each agent can run Puppet as a daemon, via a mechanism such as cron, or the connection can be manually triggered. The usual practice is to run Puppet as a daemon and have it periodically check with the master to confirm that its configuration is up-to-date or to retrieve any new configuration (Figure 1-3). However, many people find that being able to trigger Puppet via a mechanism such as cron, or manually, better suits their needs. By default, the Puppet agent will check the master for new or changed configuration once every 30 minutes. You can configure this period to suit your needs.

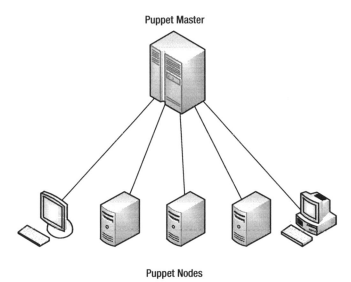

Figure 1-3. *The Puppet client-server model*

Other deployment models also exist. For example, Puppet can run in a stand-alone mode, where no Puppet master is required. Configuration is installed locally on the host and the puppet binary is run to execute and apply that configuration. We discuss this method in Chapter 4.

The Configuration Language and Resource Abstraction Layer

Puppet uses a declarative language, the Puppet language, to define your configuration items, which Puppet calls *resources*. Being declarative creates an important distinction between Puppet and many other configuration tools. A declarative language makes statements about the state of your configuration—for example, it declares that a package should be installed or a service should be started.

Most configuration tools, such as a shell or Perl script, are imperative or procedural. They describe *how* things should be done rather than the desired end state—for example, most custom scripts used to manage configuration would be considered imperative.

Puppet users just declare what the state of their hosts should be: what packages should be installed, what services should be running, and so on. With Puppet, the system administrator doesn't care *how* this state is achieved—that's Puppet's problem. Instead, we abstract our host's configuration into resources.

The Configuration Language

What does this declarative language mean in real terms? Let's look at a simple example. Suppose we have an environment with Red Hat Enterprise Linux, Ubuntu, and Solaris hosts and we want to install the vim application on all our hosts. To do this manually, we'd need to write a script that does the following:

- Connects to the required hosts (including handling passwords or keys).

- Checks to see if vim is installed.

- If not, uses the appropriate command for each platform to install vim, for example on RedHat the yum command and on Ubuntu the apt-get command.

- Potentially reports the results of this action to ensure completion and success.

▓ **Note**   This would become even more complicated if you wanted to upgrade vim (if it was already installed) or apply a particular version of vim.

Puppet approaches this process quite differently. In Puppet, you define a configuration resource for the vim package. Each resource is made up of a *type* (what sort of resource is being managed: packages, services, or cron jobs), a *title* (the name of the resource), and a series of *attributes* (values that specify the state of the resource—for example, whether a service is started or stopped).

You can see an example of a resource in Listing 1-1.

Listing 1-1. A Puppet resource

```
package { 'vim':
  ensure => present,
}
```

The resource in Listing 1-1 specifies that a package called vim should be installed. It is constructed as follows:

```
type { title:
  attribute => value,
}
```

In Listing 1-1, the resource type is the package type. Puppet comes with a number of resource types by default, including types to manage files, services, packages, and cron jobs, among others.

▓ **Note**   You can see a full list of the types Puppet can currently manage (and their attributes) at
http://docs.puppetlabs.com/references/stable/type.html. You can also extend Puppet to support additional resource types, as we'll discuss in Chapter 10.

Next is the *title* of the resource, here the name of the package we want to install, vim. This corresponds exactly to the argument to the package manager; for example, .apt-get install vim.

Last, we've specified a single attribute, ensure, with a value of present. Attributes tell Puppet about the required state of our configuration resource. Each type has a series of attributes available to configure it. Here the ensure attribute specifies the state of the package: installed, uninstalled, and so on. The present value tells Puppet we want to install the package. To uninstall the package, we would change the value of this attribute to absent.

The Resource Abstraction Layer

With our resource created, Puppet takes care of the details of managing that resource when our agents connect. Puppet handles the "how" by knowing how different platforms and operating systems manage certain types of resources. Each type has a number of *providers*. A provider contains the "how" of managing packages using a particular package management tool.

The package type, for example, has more than 20 providers covering a variety of tools, including yum, aptitude, pkgadd, ports, and emerge.

When an agent connects, Puppet uses a tool called *Facter* (see following sidebar) to return information about that agent, including what operating system it is running. Puppet then chooses the appropriate package provider for that operating system and uses that provider to check if the vim package is installed. For example, on Red Hat it would execute yum, on Ubuntu it would execute aptitude, and on Solaris it would use the pkg command. If the package is not installed, Puppet will install it. If the package is already installed, Puppet does nothing. Again, this important feature is called *idempotency.*

Puppet will then report its success or failure in applying the resource back to the Puppet master.

INTRODUCING FACTER AND FACTS

Facter is a system inventory tool, also developed principally by Puppet Labs, that we use throughout the book. It is also open source under the Apache 2.0 license. It returns "facts" about each node, such as its hostname, IP address, operating system and version, and other configuration items. These facts are gathered when the agent runs. The facts are then sent to the Puppet master, and automatically created as variables available to Puppet at *top scope*. You'll learn more about variable scoping in Chapter 2.

You can see the facts available on your clients by running the facter binary from the command line. Each fact is returned as a key => value pair:

```
$ facter
operatingsystcm => Ubuntu
ipaddress => 10.0.0.10
```

You can then use these values to configure each host individually. For example, knowing the IP address of a host allows you to configure networking on that host.

These facts are made available as variables that can be used in your Puppet configuration. When combined with the configuration you define in Puppet, they allow you to customize that configuration for each host. For example, they allow you to write generic resources, like your network settings, and customize them with data from your agents.

Facter also helps Puppet understand how to manage particular resources on an agent. For example, if Facter tells Puppet that a host runs Ubuntu, then Puppet knows to use aptitude to install packages on that agent. Facter can also be extended to add custom facts for specific information about your hosts. We'll be installing Facter shortly after we install Puppet, and we'll discuss it in more detail in later chapters.

The Transactional Layer

Puppet's transactional layer is its engine. A Puppet transaction encompasses the process of configuring each host, including these steps:

- Interpret and compile your configuration.

- Communicate the compiled configuration to the agent.

- Apply the configuration on the agent.

- Report the results of that application to the master.

The first step Puppet takes is to analyze your configuration and calculate how to apply it to your agent. To do this, Puppet creates a graph showing all resources, with their relationships to each other and to each agent. This allows Puppet to work out the order, based on relationships you create, in which to apply each resource to your host. This model is one of Puppet's most powerful features.

Puppet then takes the resources and compiles them into a *catalog* for each agent. The catalog is sent to the host and applied by the Puppet agent. The results of this application are then sent back to the master in the form of a report.

The transaction layer allows configurations to be created and applied repeatedly on the host. Again, Puppet calls this capability idempotency, meaning that multiple applications of the same operation will yield the same results. Puppet configuration can be safely run multiple times with the same outcome on your host, ensuring that your configuration stays consistent.

Puppet is not fully transactional, though; your transactions aren't logged (other than informative logging), and so you can't roll back transactions as you can with some databases. You can, however, model transactions in a "noop," or no-operation mode, that allows you to test the execution of your changes without applying them.

Selecting the Right Version of Puppet

The best version of Puppet to use is usually the latest release, which at the time of writing is the 3.2.x branch of releases; newer ones are currently in development. The biggest advantage of the 3.2.x branch of releases is improved performance and built-in Hiera integration. Hiera is Puppet's external datastore and will be extensively covered in later chapters.

The 3.1.x releases are stable, perform well, have numerous bug fixes not available in previous versions, and contain a wide of variety of new features and functions unavailable in earlier releases.

■ **Note** This book assumes you are using either a 3.1.x or later release. Some of the material will work on 2.7.x versions of Puppet, but not all of it has been tested. Specifically, information about Hiera (see Chapter 12) and functions is unlikely to be backward-compatible to version 2.7.x.

There are a variety of releases, some older than others, packaged for operating systems. The 2.7.x releases are broadly packaged. The 3.1.x releases are packaged and distributed in newer versions of operating systems and platforms. If you can't find later Puppet releases packaged for your distribution, you have the option of rolling your own packages, backporting, or installing from source (though we don't recommend the latter—see the following). Puppetlabs provides the latest rpms, deb packages, msis, and dmg files on their website and repositories.

MIXING RELEASES OF PUPPET

The most common deployment model for Puppet is client-server. Many people ask if you can have different releases of Puppet on the master and as agents. The answer is yes, with some caveats. The first caveat is that the master needs to be a later release than the agents. For example, you can have a version 2.7.20 agent connected to a version 3.1.1 master, but not a version 3.1.1 agent connected to a 2.7.20 master.

The second caveat is that the older the agent release, the less likely it will function correctly with a newer release of the master. Later versions of masters may not be so forgiving of earlier agents, and some functions and features may not behave correctly.

Finally, mixing 3.1.x and later release masters with 2.7.x and earlier agents will mean you won't get the full performance enhancements available in 3.1.x.

Installing Puppet

Puppet can be installed and used on a variety of different platforms, including the following:

- Red Hat Enterprise Linux, CentOS, Fedora, and Oracle Enterprise Linux
- Debian and Ubuntu
- OpenIndiana
- Solaris
- From source
- Microsoft Windows (clients only)
- MacOS X and MacOS X Server
- Other (that is, BSD, Mandrake, and Mandriva)

Most of these are discussed in sections that follow. On these platforms, Puppet manages a variety of configuration items, including but not limited to these:

- Files
- Services
- Packages
- Users
- Groups
- Cron jobs
- SSH keys
- Nagios configuration

For Puppet, the agent and master server installations are very similar, although most operating systems and distribution packaging systems divide the master and agent functions into separate packages. On some operating systems and distributions, you'll also need to install Ruby and its libraries and potentially some additional packages. Most good packaging systems will have most of the required packages, like Ruby, as prerequisites of the Puppet and Facter packages. For other features (including some types of reporting that we'll demonstrate later in this book), you may also need to install additional packages.

We'll also demonstrate how to install Puppet from source, but we don't recommend this approach. It is usually simpler to use your operating system's package management system, especially if you are installing Puppet on a large number of hosts.

Installing on Red Hat Enterprise Linux and Fedora

Add the Extra Packages for Enterprise Linux (EPEL) or Puppet Labs repositories to your host and then install packages, as described in the following sections. Note that at the time of writing you must use the Puppet Labs repository for Puppet 3 packages.

Installing EPEL Repositories

The EPEL repository is a volunteer-based community effort from the Fedora project to create a repository of high-quality add-on packages for Red Hat Enterprise Linux (RHEL) and its compatible spinoffs such as CentOS, Oracle Enterprise Linux, and Scientific Linux.

You can find more details on EPEL, including how to add it to your host, at http://fedoraproject.org/wiki/EPEL and http://fedoraproject.org/wiki/EPEL/FAQ#howtouse.

You can add the EPEL repository by adding the epel-release RPM (.rpm package manager)as follows:

- Enterprise Linux 5:

```
# rpm -Uvh http://dl.fedoraproject.org/pub/epel/5/i386/epel-release-5-4.noarch.rpm
```

- Enterprise Linux 6:

```
# rpm -Uvh http://dl.fedoraproject.org/pub/epel/6/i386/epel-release-6-8.noarch.rpm
```

Installing Puppet Labs Repositories

You can install the Puppet Labs repository on Linux 5 and 6 in a similar fashion:

- Enterprise Linux 5:

```
# rpm -ivh http://yum.puppetlabs.com/el/5/products/i386/puppetlabs-release-5-7.noarch.rpm
```

- Enterprise Linux 6:

```
# rpm -ivh http://yum.puppetlabs.com/el/6/products/i386/puppetlabs-release-6-7.noarch.rpm
```

Installing the EPEL and Puppet Lab Packages

On the master, you need to install the puppet, puppet-server, and facter packages from the EPEL or Puppet Labs repositories:

```
# yum install puppet puppet-server facter
```

The puppet package contains the agent, the puppet-server package contains the master, and the facter package contains the system inventory tool Facter. As mentioned earlier, Facter gathers information, or *facts*, about your hosts that are used to help customize your Puppet configuration.

On the agent, you only need to install the prerequisites and the puppet and facter packages:

```
# yum install puppet facter
```

Installing Via RubyGems

Like most Ruby-based applications, Puppet and Facter can also be installed via RubyGems. To do this, you'll need to install Ruby and the appropriate RubyGems package for your operating system. On Red Hat, CentOS, Fedora, SUSE/SLES, Debian and Ubuntu, this package is called rubygems. Once this package is installed, the gem command should be available to use. You can then use gem to install Puppet and Facter, as shown here:

```
# gem install puppet facter
```

Installing on Debian and Ubuntu

For Debian and Ubuntu, the puppet package contains the Puppet agent, and the puppetmaster package contains the master. On the master, you need to install this:

```
# apt-get install puppet puppetmaster
```

On the agent, you only need to install the puppet package:

```
# apt-get install puppet
```

▦ **Note**   Installing the puppet, puppetmaster, and facter packages will also install some prerequisite packages, such as Ruby itself, if they are not already installed.

For the latest version of Puppet you can use the following Puppetlabs repositories:

- Debian Wheezy:

```
# wget http://apt.puppetlabs.com/puppetlabs-release-wheezy.deb
# dpkg -i puppetlabs-release-wheezy.deb
# apt-gct update
```

- Ubuntu Precise:

```
# wget http://apt.puppetlabs.com/puppetlabs-release-precise.deb
# dpkg -i puppetlabs-release-precise.deb
# apt-get update
```

Replace "precise" with other code names for different versions of Debian and Ubuntu.

Installing on OpenIndiana

Installing Puppet on OpenIndiana requires installing Ruby first. Then install Puppet and Facter via a RubyGem. Start by using the pkg command to install Ruby:

```
# pkg install ruby-18
```

RubyGems is installed by default when the ruby-18 package is installed. You can use the gem command to install Puppet.

```
# gem install puppet facter
```

The puppet and facter binaries are now installed in this folder:

```
/var/ruby/1.8/gem_home/bin/
```

Installing on Solaris 10 and 11

On Solaris there are no native packages for Puppet, so you will need to install from OpenCSW packages, RubyGems or Source. OpenCSW (http://www.opencsw.org/about) is a community-led software packaging project for Solaris. They have prebuilt Puppet packages for both Solaris 10 and Solaris 11. At the time of writing there is both a puppet3 package and a puppet package. We will use the puppet3 package to get the stable 3.x version.

1. To begin we will install OpenCSW.

```
# pkgadd -d http://get.opencsw.org/now
```

2. Next install Puppet and dependencies:

```
# pkgutil --install puppet3
```

After installation Puppet will be available in /opt/csw/bin.

Installing from Source

You can also install Puppet and Facter from source tarballs. We don't recommend this approach, because it makes upgrading, uninstalling, and generally managing Puppet across many hosts difficult. To do this you'll need to ensure that some prerequisites are installed, for example Ruby and its libraries, using the appropriate packages for your host or via source again.

1. First, download the Facter tarball from the Puppet Labs site:

```
$ cd /tmp
$ wget http://downloads.puppetlabs.com/facter/facter-1.6.18.tar.gz
```

2. Unpack the tarball and run the install.rb script to install Facter:

```
$ tar -zxf facter-1.6.18.tar.gz
$ cd facter-1.6.18
# ./install.rb
```

This will install Facter into the default path for Ruby libraries on your host, for example /usr/lib/ruby/ on many Linux distributions.

3. Next, download and install Puppet using the same process:

```
$ cd /tmp
$ wget http://downloads.puppetlabs.com/puppet/puppet-3.1.1.tar.gz
$ tar -zxf puppet-3.1.1.tar.gz
$ cd puppet-3.1.1
# ./install.rb
```

Like the Facter steps, this will install Puppet into the default path for Ruby libraries on your host.

■ **Note**   You can find the latest Puppet and Facter releases at http://puppetlabs.com/misc/download-options/.

Installing on Microsoft Windows

Puppet does not currently support running a Puppet master on Microsoft Windows. You will need a Unix/Linux Puppet master for client-server, or you can run Puppet in masterless mode.

Installing on Microsoft Windows Graphically

To install on Microsoft Windows graphically, follow these steps:

1. Download the latest open source MSI from http://downloads.puppetlabs.com/windows/ (The MSI file bundles all of Puppet's dependencies, including Ruby and Facter).

2. Run the MSI as an administrator and follow the installation wizard (Figure 1-4).

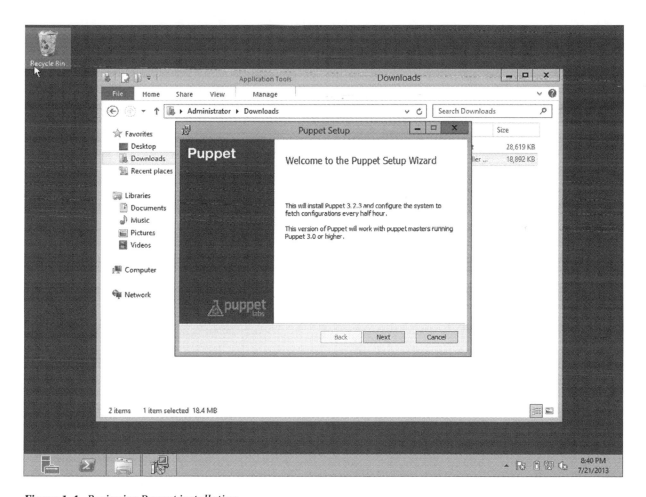

Figure 1-4. Beginning Puppet installation

3. You will need to supply the name of your Puppet master to the installer (Figure 1-5). After that, Puppet will begin running as a Windows service. When the installation is complete you will see the screen in Figure 1-6.

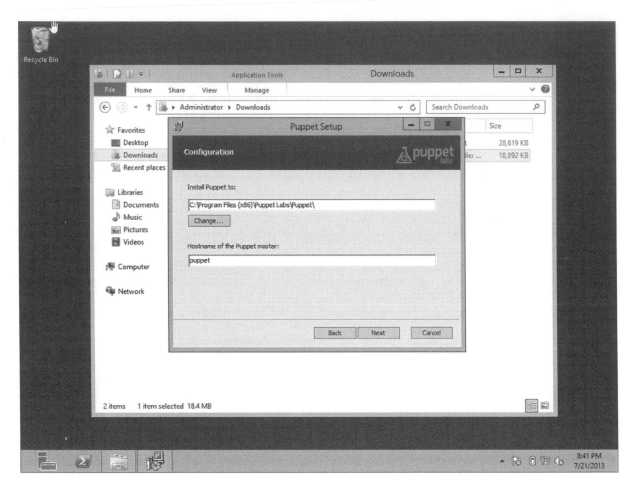

Figure 1-5. *Configuring Puppet*

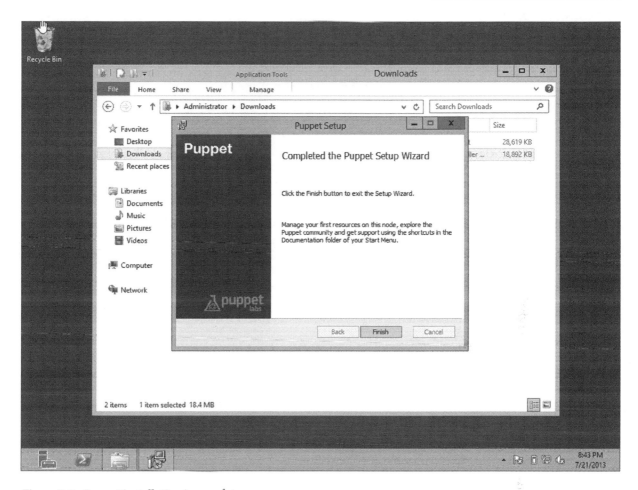

Figure 1-6. *Puppet installation is complete*

For additional information, such as automating installations, refer to the Windows installation documentation at `http://docs.puppetlabs.com/windows/installing.html.`

Installing on Microsoft Windows Using PowerShell

Many Windows administrators, particularly in cloud operations, have begun using PowerShell for remote administration and scriptable installation. To install open source Puppet, you must first download the Puppet MSI installer from Puppetlabs.com. There are two ways to do this; older PowerShell versions should use the commands in Listing 1-2, while version 3 and greater can use the command in Listing 1-3.

Listing 1-2. Downloading the Puppet MSI on Powershell versions 2 and earlier

```
$downloads = $pwd
$webclient = New-Object System.Net.WebClient
$url = http://puppetlabs.com/downloads/windows/puppet-3.2.3.msi
$file = "$downloads/puppet.msi"
$webclient.DownloadFile($url,$file)
```

13

PowerShell 3 and greater can use the `Invoke-WebRequest` commandlet to download the MSI, as shown in Listing 1-3.

Listing 1-3. Downloading the Puppet MSI on Powershell versions 3 and later

```
$url = "http://puppetlabs.com/downloads/windows/puppet-3.2.3.msi"
Invoke-WebRequest -Uri $url -OutFile puppet.msi
```

You will see a progress bar across the screen. After the MSI has been downloaded, install it using `msiexec`, as shown next. Here we actually shell out to `cmd.exe`, since `msiexec` doesn't currently work in PowerShell.

```
cmd /c "msiexec /qn /i puppet.msi /l*v install.log"
```

By using the `/qn` argument to `msiexec`, we have made the installation silent and noninteractive, meaning that no questions were asked of us and no dialog popped up. This entire exercise can be completed via remote PowerShell or script. The `/l*v install.log` argument has made the installation send its log to `install.log` in the current directory. If installation is successful, you should see "Installation Successful" at the end of the `install.log`.

We can verify that Puppet has been installed correctly by running the `puppet.bat` script as shown here:

```
& 'C:\Program Files (x86)\Puppet Labs\Puppet\bin\puppet.bat' --version
```

The MSI installer, when run in silent mode, will choose puppet as the Puppet master and CA server. If you want to override these variables, you can use the environment variables shown in Listing 1-4.

Listing 1-4. Configuring the puppet installation

```
cmd /c "msiexec /qn PUPPET_MASTER_SERVER=master.example.com
PUPPET_CA_SERVER=puppetcat.example.com /i puppet
.msi /l*v install.log"
```

Unfortunately, at the time of writing, you cannot set other configuration variables, so you would have to modify `puppet.conf` manually with notepad or another editor:

```
notepad 'C:\ProgramData\PuppetLabs\puppet\etc\puppet.conf'
```

Installing on the Mac

In this section we will cover installing Puppet on Mac OS X via the GUI and from the CLI.

Installing Puppet Open Source on Apple Mac OS X via the Graphical Installer

Download the Facter and Puppet `.dmg` files from the Puppet Labs website, `puppetlabs.com`.

Then mount the `.dmg` files and verify that you have two Apple Package installers as shown in Figure 1-7.

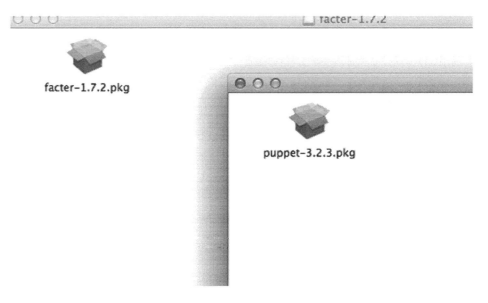

Figure 1-7. *Mac OSX pkg files*

Double-click the Facter cardboard box icon, which brings you to the welcome screen in Figure 1-8.

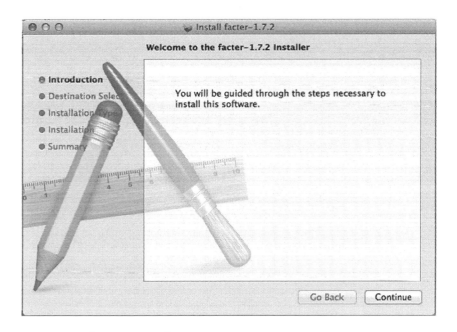

Figure 1-8. *The Facter Installer*

Assume administrator rights, as shown in Figure 1-9, and click Install Software.

Figure 1-9. Enter your administrator password

Once the installation is complete, you'll see the screen in Figure 1-10.

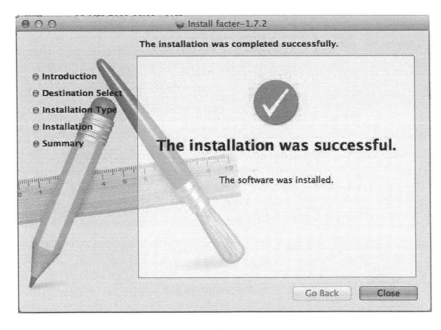

Figure 1-10. Facter installation is complete

Excellent! Facter is now installed. Now double-click the Puppet cardboard box to install it as well. The screen in Figure 1-11 will appear.

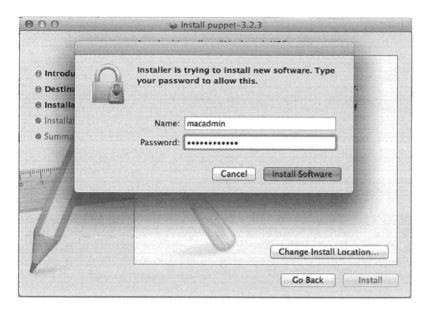

Figure 1-11. *Enter your adminstrator credentials*

Again, assume administrator rights and click the Install Software button (Figure 1-11).

Puppet is now installed! You can verify the installation with puppet –version, as shown in Figure 1-12. In this case, the Puppet installer did not prompt for a Puppet master server. If you want to use a server other than the DNS name puppet, you must create /etc/puppet/puppet.conf with server=puppet-master.pro-puppet.com.

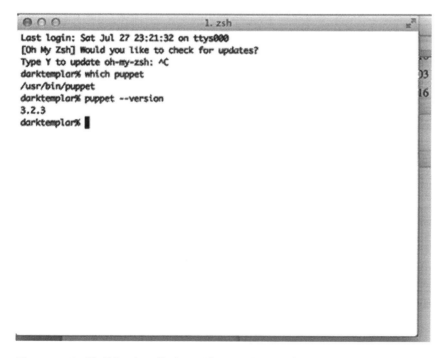

Figure 1-12. *Verifying installation with puppet –version*

Installing Puppet Open Source on Apple Mac OS X via the Command Line

Download the latest `facter` and `puppet` packages from `http://downloads.puppetlabs.com/mac/`.

Once you have downloaded the `.dmg` files, you can install them via the command line with the following instructions:

```
$ curl -0 http://downloads.puppetlabs.com/mac/facter-1.7.2.dmg
$ hdiutil mount facter-1.7.2.dmg
$ installer -package /Volumes/facter-1.7.2/facter-1.7.2.pkg/ -target /Volumes/Macintosh\ HD
$ hdutil unmount /Volumes/facter-1.7.2
```

Next install Puppet:

```
$ curl -0  https://downloads.puppetlabs.com/mac/puppet-3.2.3.dmg
$ hdiutil mount puppet-3.2.3.dmg
$ installer -package /Volumes/puppet-3.2.3/puppet-3.2.3.pkg -target /Volumes/Macintosh\ HD
$ hdutil unmount /Volumes/puppet-3.2.3/
```

At this point you can run Puppet by `cron` or with `puppet apply`. To setup a `launchd` job to run it in daemon mode, refer to the official docs:

```
http://docs.puppetlabs.com/guides/installation.html#mac-os-x
```

Installing on Other Platforms

We've just explained how to install Puppet on some popular platforms.

Puppet can also be installed on a wide variety of other platforms, including the following:

- SLES/OpenSuSE via `http://software.opensuse.org/`

- Gentoo via Portage

- Mandrake and Mandriva via the Mandriva contrib repository

- FreeBSD via ports tree

- NetBSD via pkgsrc

- OpenBSD via ports tree

- ArchLinux via ArchLinux AUR

■ **Note**   You can find a full list of additional operating systems and specific instructions at `https://puppetlabs.com/misc/download-options`.

Puppet can also work on some networks such as BIG-IP F5 devices and some Juniper network devices. F5s are an advanced configuration, configured by way of a proxy agent. Read `https://puppetlabs.com/blog/managing-f5-big-ip-network-devices-with-puppet/` to get started configuring an F5 with Puppet. Some modern Juniper devices run Puppet natively. Puppet can be installed via a Juniper package called jpuppet. Downloads and more information are available at `https://puppetlabs.com/solutions/juniper-networks/`.

Puppet's tarball also contains some packaging artifacts in the ext directory; for example, there are an RPM spec file and OS X build scripts that can allow you to create your own packages for compatible operating systems. Now that you've installed Puppet on your chosen platform, we can start configuring it.

Configuring Puppet

Let's start by configuring a Puppet master that will act as our configuration server. We'll look at Puppet's configuration files, how to configure networking and firewall access, and how to start the Puppet master. Remember that we're going to be looking at Puppet in its client-server mode. Here, the Puppet master contains our configuration data, and Puppet agents connect via SSL and pull down the required configuration (refer back to Figure 1-2).

On most platforms, Puppet's configuration will be located under the /etc/puppet directory. Puppet's principal configuration file is called puppet.conf and is stored at /etc/puppet/puppet.conf on Unix/Linux operating systems and C:\ProgramData\PuppetLabs\puppet\etc\ on Windows. It is likely that this file has already been created when you installed Puppet, but if it hasn't, you can create a simple file using the following command:

```
$ cd /etc/puppet/
$ puppet master --genconfig > puppet.conf
```

▓ **Note**   We're assuming your operating system uses the /etc/ directory to store its configuration files, as most Unix/ Linux operating systems and distributions do. If you're on a platform that doesn't, such as Microsoft Windows, substitute the location of your puppet.conf configuration file. But remember that the Puppet master cannot be run on Windows.

The puppet.conf configuration file is constructed much like an INI-style configuration file and divided into sections. Each section configures a particular element of Puppet. For example, the [agent] section configures the Puppet agent, and the [master] section configures the Puppet master binary. There is also a global configuration section called [main]. All components of Puppet set options specified in the [main] section.

At this stage, we're only going to add one entry, server, to the puppet.conf file. The server option specifies the name of the Puppet master. We'll add the server value to the [main] section (if the section doesn't already exist in your file, then create it).

```
[main]
server=puppet.example.com
```

Replace puppet.example.com with the fully qualified domain name of your host.

▓ **Note**   We'll look at other options in the puppet.conf file in later chapters.

We recommend you also create a DNS CNAME for your Puppet master host, for example puppet.pro-puppet.com, and add it to either your /etc/hosts file or your DNS configuration:

```
# /etc/hosts
127.0.0.1 localhost
192.168.0.1 puppet.pro-puppet.com puppet
```

Once we've configured appropriate DNS for Puppet, we need to add the site.pp file, which holds the basics of the configuration items we want to manage.

The site.pp File

The site.pp file tells Puppet where and what configuration to load for our clients. We're going to store this file in a directory called manifests under the /etc/puppet directory.

■ **Note** *Manifest* is Puppet's term for files containing configuration information. Manifest files have a suffix of .pp. The Puppet language is written into these files.

This directory and file is often already created when the Puppet packages are installed. If it hasn't already been created, create this directory and file now:

```
# mkdir /etc/puppet/manifests
# touch /etc/puppet/manifests/site.pp
```

We'll add some configuration to this file later in this chapter, but now we just need the file present.

■ **Note** You can also override the name and location of the manifests directory and site.pp file using the manifestdir and manifest configuration options, respectively. These options are set in the puppet.conf configuration file in the [master] section. See http://docs.puppetlabs.com/references/stable/configuration.html for a full list of configuration options. We'll talk about a variety of other options throughout this book.

Firewall Configuration

The Puppet master runs on TCP port 8140. This port needs to be open on your master's firewall (and any intervening firewalls and network devices), and your client must be able to route and connect to the master. To do this, you need to have an appropriate firewall rule on your master, such as the following rule for the Netfilter firewall:

```
$ iptables -A INPUT -p tcp -m state --state NEW --dport 8140 -j ACCEPT
```

This line allows access from everywhere to TCP port 8140. If possible, you should limit this to networks that require access to your Puppet master. For example:

```
$ iptables -A INPUT -p tcp -m state --state NEW -s 192.168.0.0/24 --dport 8140 -j ACCEPT
```

Here we've restricted access to port 8140 to the 192.168.0.0/24 subnet.

■ **Note** You can create similar rules for other operating systems' firewalls, such as pf or the Windows Firewall. The traffic between Puppet client and Puppet master is encrypted with SSL and authenticated by client x509 certificates.

Starting the Puppet Master

The Puppet master can be started via an init script or other init system, such as upstart or systemd on most Linux distributions. On Red Hat or Debian, we would run the init script with the service command, like so:

```
# service puppetmaster start
```

Other platforms should use their appropriate service management tools.

■ **Note** Output from the daemon can be seen in /var/log/messages on Red Hat–based hosts and /var/log/syslog on Debian and Ubuntu hosts. Puppet will log via the daemon facility to Syslog by default on most operating systems. You will find output from the daemons in the appropriate location and files for your operating system. On Microsoft Windows, Puppet logs go to C:\ProgramData\PuppetLabs\puppet\var\log.

Starting the daemon will initiate your Puppet environment, create a local Certificate Authority (CA), along with certificates and keys for the master, and open the appropriate network socket to await client connections. You can see Puppet's SSL information and certificates in the /var/lib/puppet/ssl directory.

```
# ls -l /var/lib/puppet/ssl/
drwxrwx--- 5 puppet puppet 4096 Apr 11 04:05 ca
drwxr-xr-x 2 puppet root   4096 Apr 11 04:05 certificate_requests
drwxr-xr-x 2 puppet root   4096 Apr 11 04:05 certs
-rw-r--r-- 1 puppet puppet  918 Apr 11 04:05 crl.pem
drwxr-x--- 2 puppet root   4096 Apr 11 04:05 private
drwxr-x--- 2 puppet root   4096 Apr 11 04:05 private_keys
drwxr-xr-x 2 puppet root   4096 Apr 11 04:05 public_keys
```

The directory on the master contains your CA, certificate requests from your clients, a certificate for your master, and certificates for all your clients.

■ **Note** You can override the location of the SSL files using the ssldir option in puppet.conf on the master. There will be much more on the Puppet internal CA in Chapter 4.

You can also run the Puppet master from the command line to help test and debug issues. We recommend doing this when testing Puppet initially. To do this, we start the Puppet master daemon like so:

```
# puppet master --verbose --no-daemonize
```

The --verbose option outputs verbose logging and the --no-daemonize option keeps the daemon in the foreground and redirects output to standard out. You can also add the --debug option to produce more verbose debug output from the daemon.

A SINGLE BINARY

All the functionality of Puppet is available from a single binary, puppet, in the style of tools like Git. This means you can start the Puppet master by running this command:

```
# puppet master
```

The agent functionality is also available in the same way:

```
# puppet agent
```

You can see a full list of the available functionality from the puppet binary by running help:

```
$ puppet help
```

And you can get help on any Puppet subcommand by adding the subcommand option:

```
$ puppet help subcommand
```

Connecting Our First Agent

Once you have the Puppet master configured and started, you can configure and initiate your first agent. On the agent, as we mentioned earlier, you need to install the appropriate packages, usually puppet and facter, using your operating system's package management system. We're going to install a client on a host called node1.pro-puppet.com and then connect to our puppet.pro-puppet.com master.

When connecting our first client, we want to run the Puppet agent from the command line rather than as a service. This will allow us to see what is going on as we connect. The Puppet agent daemon is run using puppet agent, and you can see a connection to the master initiated in Listing 1-5.

Listing 1-5. Puppet client connection to the Puppet master

```
node1# puppet agent --test --server=puppet.pro-puppet.com
Info: Creating a new SSL key for node1.pro-puppet.com
Info: Caching certificate for ca
Info: Creating a new SSL certificate request for node1.pro-puppet.com
Info: Certificate Request fingerprint (SHA256): 6F:0D:41:14:BD:2D:FC:CE:1C:DC:11:1E:26:07:4C:08:D0:C
7:E8:62:A5:33:E3:4B:8B:C6:28:C5:C8:88:1C:C8
Exiting; no certificate found and waitforcert is disabled
```

In Listing 1-5, we executed the Puppet agent with three options. The first option, --server, specifies the name or address of the Puppet master to connect to.

■ **Tip** You can also run a Puppet client on the Puppet master, but we're going to start with the more traditional client-server approach. And yes, that means you can use Puppet to manage itself!

▇ **Tip**   If we don't specify a server, Puppet will look for a host called "puppet." It's often a good idea to create a CNAME for your Puppet master, such as `puppet.pro-puppet.com`. Additionally, Puppet has the ability to query SRV records to find where the Puppet master and Puppet CA servers are. More on this in Chapter 4.

We can also specify this in the main section of the /etc/puppet/puppet.conf configuration file on the client:

```
# /etc/puppet/puppet.conf
[main]
server=puppet.pro-puppet.com
```

Your client must be able to resolve the hostname of the master to connect to (this is why it is useful to have a Puppet CNAME or to specify your Puppet master in the /etc/hosts file on your client).The --test option runs the Puppet client in the foreground, outputs to standard out, and exits after the run is complete. By default, the Puppet client runs as a daemon, and the puppet agent command forks off the Puppet daemon into the background and exits immediately.

In Listing 1-5, you can see the output from our connection. The agent has created a certificate signing request and a private key to secure our connection. Puppet uses SSL certificates to authenticate connections between the master and the agent. The agent sends the certificate request to the master and waits for the master to sign and return the certificate.

At this point, the agent has exited after sending in its Certificate Signing Request (CSR). The agent will need to be rerun to check in and run Puppet after the CSR has been signed by the CA. You can configure puppet agent not to exit, but instead stay alive and poll periodically for the CSR to be signed. This configuration is called waitforcert and is generally only useful if you are also auto-signing certificates on the master. More on that later in this chapter.

▇ **Note**   You can change the time the Puppet agent will wait by using the --waitforcert option. You can specify a time in seconds or 0 to not wait for a certificate, in which case the agent will exit.

Completing the Connection

To complete the connection and authenticate our agent, we now need to sign the certificate the agent has sent to the master. We do this using puppet cert (or the puppetca binary) on the master:

```
puppet# puppet cert list
"node1.pro-puppet.com" (SHA256) 6F:0D:41:14:BD:2D:FC:CE:1C:DC:11:1E:26:07:4C:08:D0:C7:E8:62:A5:33:E3
:4B:8B:C6:28:C5:C8:88:1C:C8
```

▇ **Tip**   You can find a full list of the binaries that come with Puppet at `http://docs.puppetlabs.com/guides/tools.html`.

The list option displays all the certificates waiting to be signed. We can then sign our certificate using the sign option:

```
puppet# puppet cert sign node1.pro-puppet.com
Notice: Signed certificate request for node1.pro-puppet.com
Notice: Removing file Puppet::SSL::CertificateRequest node1.pro-puppet.com at
'/var/lib/puppet/ssl/ca/requests/node1.pro-puppet.com.pem'
```

You can sign all waiting certificates with the puppet cert sign --all command.

■ **Note**   Rather than signing each individual certificate, you can also enable *autosign* mode. In this mode, all incoming connections from specified IP addresses or address ranges are automatically signed. This obviously has some security implications and should only be used if you are comfortable with it. You can find more details at http://docs.puppetlabs.com/guides/faq.html#why-shouldn-t-i-use-autosign-for-all-my-clients.

On the client, two minutes after signing the certificate, you should see the following entries (or you can stop and restart the Puppet agent rather than waiting two minutes):

```
# puppet agent --test
Info: Retrieving plugin
Info: Caching catalog for node1.pro-puppet.com
Info: Applying configuration version '1365655737'
Notice: Finished catalog run in 0.13 seconds
```

The agent is now authenticated with the master, and you may have another message present:

```
# puppet agent -t
Info: Retrieving plugin
Error: Could not retrieve catalog from remote server: Error 400 on SERVER: Could not find default
node or by name with 'node1.example.com, node1' on node node1.pro-puppet.com
Warning: Not using cache on failed catalog
Error: Could not retrieve catalog; skipping run
```

The agent has connected and our signed certificate has authenticated the session with the master. The master, however, doesn't have any configuration available for our puppet node, node1.pro-puppet.com, and hence we have received an error message. We now have to add some configuration for this agent on the master.

■ **Caution**   It is important for the time to be accurate on your master and agent. SSL connections rely on the clock on hosts being correct. If the clocks are incorrect, your connection may fail with an error indicating that your certificates are not trusted. You should use something like NTP (Network Time Protocol) to ensure that your host's clocks are accurate. A quick way to sync several servers is to run ntpdate bigben.cac.washington.edu on each of them. This will perform a one-time NTP sync.

Creating Our First Configuration Item

Let's get some more understanding of Puppet's components, configuration language, and capabilities. You learned earlier that Puppet describes the files containing configuration data as manifests. Puppet manifests are made up of a number of major components:

- Resources: Individual configuration items
- Files: Physical files you can serve out to your agents
- Templates: Template files that you can use to populate files

- Nodes: Specifies the configuration of each agent

- Classes: Collections of resources

- Definitions: Composite collections of resources

These components are wrapped in a configuration language that includes variables, conditionals, arrays, and other features. Later in this chapter we'll introduce you to the basics of the Puppet language and its elements. In the next chapter, we'll extend your knowledge of the language by taking you through an implementation of a multi-agent site managed with Puppet.

In addition to these components, Puppet also has the concept of a "module," which is a portable collection of manifests that contain resources, classes, definitions, files, and templates. We'll see our first module shortly.

Adding a Node Definition

Let's add our first node definition to site.pp. In Puppet manifests, agents are defined using node statements.

You can see the node definition we're going to add in Listing 1-6.

Listing 1-6. Our node configuration

```
node 'node1.pro-puppet.com' {
    package { 'vim':
      ensure => present,
    }
}
```

For a node definition we specify the node name, enclosed in single quotes, and then specify the configuration that applies to it inside curly braces { }. The client name can be the hostname or the fully qualified domain name of the client. At this stage, you can't specify nodes with wildcards (for example, *.pro-puppet.com), but you can use regular expressions, as shown here:

```
node /^www\d+\.pro-puppet\.com/ {
  ...
}
```

This example will match all nodes from the domain pro-puppet.com with the hostnames www1, www12, www123, and so on.

Next, we specify a resource stanza in our node definition. This is the same one from earlier when we were introducing the Puppet DSL. It will make sure that the vim package is installed on the host node1.pro-puppet.com.

We can run Puppet on node1 and see what action it has performed:

```
root@node1:~# puppet agent --test
Info: Retrieving plugin
Info: Caching catalog for node1.pro-puppet.com
Info: Applying configuration version '1375079547'
Notice: /Stage[main]//Node[node1]/Package[vim]/ensure: ensure changed 'purged' to 'present'
Notice: Finished catalog run in 4.86 seconds
```

We can see that Puppet has installed the vim package. It is not generally best practice to define resources at node level; those belong in classes and modules. Let's strip out our vim resource and include the sudo class instead (Listing 1-7).

Listing 1-7. Our Node Configuration

```
node 'node1.pro-puppet.com' {
  include sudo
}
```

Here we specify an `include` directive in our node definition; it specifies a collection of configurations, called a *class*, that we want to apply to our host. There are two ways to include a class:

```
node /node1/ {
  include ::sudo
}

node /node2/ {
  class { '::sudo':
    users => ['tom', 'jerry'],
  }
}
```

The first syntax is bare and simple. The second syntax allows *parameters* to be passed into the class. This feature, generally called *parameterized classes*, allows classes to be written generally and then utilized specifically, increasing the reusability of Puppet code. Notice that the syntax for including a class is very similar to the syntax for a normal Puppet resource. *Modules* are self-contained collections of Puppet code, manifests, Puppet classes, files, templates, facts, and tests, all for a specific configuration task. Modules are usually highly reusable and shareable. The double-colon syntax explicitly instructs Puppet to use top scope to look up the `sudo` module. You will learn much more about this in Chapter 2.

▓ **Note**   Puppet also has an inheritance model in which you can have one node inherit values from another node. You should avoid doing this. Refer to `http://docs.puppetlabs.com/puppet/latest/reference/lang_node_definitions.html#inheritance` for more information.

Creating Our First Module

The next step in our node configuration is to create a sudo module. Again, a module is a collection of manifests, resources, files, templates, classes, and definitions. A single module would contain everything required to configure a particular application. For example, it could contain all the resources (specified in manifest files), files, and associated configuration to configure Apache or the `sudo` command on a host. We will create a sudo module and a sudo class.

Each module needs a specific directory structure and a file called `init.pp`. This structure allows Puppet to automatically load modules. To perform this automatic loading, Puppet checks a series of directories called the *module path*. This path is configured with the `modulepath` configuration option in the `[master]` section of the `puppet.conf` file. By default, Puppet looks for modules in the `/etc/puppet/modules` and `/usr/share/puppet/modules` directories, but you can add additional locations if required:

```
[master]
modulepath = /etc/puppet/modules:/var/lib/puppet/modules:/opt/modules
```

Module Structure

Let's start by creating a module directory and file structure in Listing 1-8. We're going to create this structure under the directory /etc/puppet/modules. We will name the module sudo. Modules (and classes) must be normal words containing only letters, numbers, underscores, and dashes.

Listing 1-8. Module structure

```
# mkdir -p /etc/puppet/modules/sudo/{files,templates,manifests}
# touch /etc/puppet/modules/sudo/manifests/init.pp
```

The manifests directory will hold our init.pp file and any other configuration. The init.pp file is the core of your module, and every module should have one. The files directory will hold any files we wish to serve as part of our module. The templates directory will contain any templates that our module might use.

The init.pp file

Now let's look inside our sudo module, starting with the init.pp file, which we can see in Listing 1-9.

Listing 1-9. The sudo module's init.pp file

```
class sudo {

  package { 'sudo':
    ensure => present,
  }

  if $::osfamily == 'Debian' {
    package { 'sudo-ldap':
      ensure  => present,
      require => Package['sudo'],
    }
  }

  file { '/etc/sudoers':
    owner   => 'root',
    group   => 'root',
    mode    => '0440',
    source  => "puppet://$::server/modules/sudo/etc/sudoers",
    require => Package['sudo'],
  }
}
```

Our sudo module's init.pp file contains a single class, also called sudo. There are three resources in the class, two packages and a file resource. The first package resource ensures that the sudo package is installed, ensure => present. The second package resource uses Puppet's if/else syntax to set a condition on the installation of the sudo-ldap package.

▨ **Note**   Puppet also has two other conditional statements, a case statement and a selector syntax.
You can see more details of Puppet's conditional syntaxes at
http://docs.puppetlabs.com/guides/more_language.html#conditionals.

■ **Caution** The == comparison operator is case-insensitive. To perform a case-sensitive comparison for strings, you must use the regular expression operator =~ and you must fully root the regular expression; for example, `$osfamily =~ /^Debian$/`.

Puppet will check the value of the `operatingsystem` fact for each connecting client. If the value of the `$::osfamily` fact is Debian, then Puppet should install the `sudo-ldap` package. Operating system family is just a name Puppet uses for binary-compatible groups of distributions; for example, Debian, Ubuntu, and Mint all share the osfamily Debian.

■ **Note** We discussed Facter and its values earlier in this chapter. Each fact is available as a variable, the fact name prefixed with a $ sign, in your Puppet manifests. Facts are available at what is called *top scope*, which means we use the `$::variable` syntax. More on variable scoping in later chapters.

Last, in this resource we've also specified a new attribute, `require`.

The `require` attribute is a metaparameter. Metaparameters are resource attributes that are part of Puppet's framework rather than belonging to a specific type. They perform actions on resources and can be specified for any type of resource.

The `require` metaparameter creates a dependency relationship between the `Package["sudo-ldap"]` resource and the `Package["sudo"]` resource. In this case, adding the `require` metaparameter to the resource tells Puppet that the `Package["sudo"]` is required by the `Package["sudo-ldap"]` resource. Hence, the `Package["sudo"]` resource must and will be installed first.

Relationships are an important part of Puppet. They allow you to instantiate real-world relationships between configuration components on your hosts. A good example of this is networking. A number of resources on your hosts, such as a Web server or an MTA (Mail Transfer Agent), would rely on your network being configured and active before they can be activated. Relationships allow you to specify that certain resources, for example those configuring your network, are processed before those resources that configure your Web server or MTA.

The usefulness of relationships does not end there. Puppet can also build triggering relationships between resources. For example, if a file resource changes, you can tell Puppet to restart a service resource. This means you can change a service's configuration file and have that change trigger a restart of that service to ensure it is running with the updated configuration. We'll see a lot more of these relationships and other metaparameters in Chapter 3.

■ **Note** You can see a full list of the available metaparameters at
`http://docs.puppetlabs.com/references/stable/metaparameter.html`.

The last resource in the sudo class is a file resource, `File["/etc/sudoers"]`, which manages the `/etc/sudoers` file. Its first three attributes allow us to specify the `owner`, `group`, and permissions of the file. In this case, the file is owned by the `root` user and group and has its `mode` set to 0440 (mode is usually set using octal notation). The next attribute, `source`, allows Puppet to retrieve a file from the Puppet source and deliver it to the client. The value of this attribute is the name of the Puppet source and the location and name of the file to retrieve:

```
puppet://$::server/modules/sudo/etc/sudoers
```

Let's break down this value. The `puppet://` part specifies that Puppet will use the Puppet file server protocol to retrieve the file.

■ **Note** The Puppet file server is built into the Puppet master. Puppet clients can sync files from the Puppet master, or use HTTP or rsync to download the files from other sources.

The $::server variable contains the hostname of our Puppet server.

■ **Tip** One handy shortcut is to just remove the server name. Then Puppet will use whatever server the client is currently connected to; for example, our source line would look like puppet:///modules/sudo/etc/sudoers.

The next portion of our source value tells Puppet where to look for the file. This is the equivalent of the path to a network file share. The first portion of this share is modules, which tells us that the file is stored in a module. Next we specify the name of the module the file is contained in, in this case sudo. Finally, we specify the path inside that module to find the file.

All files in modules are stored under the files directory; this is considered the root of the module's file share. In our case, we would create the directory etc under the files directory and create sudoers in this directory.

```
Puppet# mkdir -p /etc/puppet/modules/sudo/files/etc
Puppet# cp /etc/sudoers /etc/puppet/modules/sudo/files/etc/sudoers
```

VERSION CONTROL

As your configuration becomes more complicated, you should consider adding it to a version-control system such as Subversion or Git. A version-control system allows you to record and track changes to files, and is commonly used by software developers. For configuration management, version control allows you to track changes to your configuration. This is highly useful if you need to revert to a previously known state or make changes without impacting your running configuration.

You can find information about how to use Subversion at http://svnbook.red-bean.com/ and some specific ideas about how to use it with Puppet at http://projects.puppetlabs.com/projects/puppet/wiki/Puppet_Version_Control. We'll also show you how a version control system might work with Puppet in Chapter 3.

Applying Our First Configuration

We've created our first Puppet module! Let's step through what will happen when we connect an agent that includes this module.

1. It will install the sudo package.

2. If it's an Ubuntu host, then it will also install the sudo-ldap package.

3. Finally, it will download the sudoers file and install it into /etc/sudoers.

Now let's see this in action and include our new module on the agent we've created, node1.example.com. Remember that we created a node statement for our host earlier:

```
node 'node1.pro-puppet.com' {
  include sudo
}
```

When the agent connects, it will now include the sudo module. To connect we run the Puppet agent again:

```
puppet# puppet agent --test
```

> ■ **Note** Puppet has a handy mode called *noop*. The noop mode runs Puppet but doesn't make any changes on your host. It allows you to see what Puppet would do, as a dry run. To run in noop mode, specify --noop on the command line.

Here, we've run the Puppet agent and connected to the master. We've run the agent in the foreground, in verbose mode and with the --onetime option that tells the Puppet agent to run only once and then stop.

We can see a configuration run commence on our host:

```
Info: Retrieving plugin
Info: Caching catalog for node1.pro-puppet.com
Info: Applying configuration version '1365735606'
Notice: /Stage[main]/Sudo/Package[sudo]/ensure: created
Notice: /Stage[main]/Sudo/File[/etc/sudoers]/ensure: defined content as '{md5}1b00ee0a97a1bcf9961e4
76140e2c5c1'
Notice: Finished catalog run in 25.94 seconds
```

> ■ **Tip** In Puppet, the combined configuration to be applied to a host is called a *catalog*, and the process of applying it is called a *run*. You can find a glossary of Puppet terminology at http://docs.puppetlabs.com/references/glossary.html.

Let's look at what has happened during our run. First we see that the agent has cached the configuration for the host. By default, will Puppet use this cache if it fails to connect to the master during a future run.

Next, we can see our resources being applied. First the sudo package is installed and then the /etc/sudoers file is copied across. During the copy process Puppet will back up the old file if it makes a modification, a process Puppet calls *file bucketing*. This means that if we've made a mistake and overwritten the file incorrectly, we can always recover it.

> ■ **Tip** Puppet can back up files remotely to our master using the filebucket type. See http://docs.puppetlabs. com/references/stable/type.html#filebucket for more information. We'll show you how to do this in Chapter 3.

The last line of the catalog run tells us this process took 25.94 seconds to complete. If we look on the Puppet master, we can see the results of the run logged there, too:

```
puppet# puppet master --no-daemonize --verbose --debug
Notice: Starting Puppet master version 3.1.1
[..]
Info: Caching node for node1.example.com
Debug: importing '/etc/puppet/modules/sudo/manifests/init.pp' in environment production
Debug: Automatically imported sudo from sudo into production
Notice: Compiled catalog for node1.pro-puppet.com in environment production in 0.23 seconds
```

```
Debug: Finishing transaction 70065298446380
Debug: Received report to process from node1.pro-puppet.com
Debug: Processing report from node1.example.com with processor Puppet::Reports::Store
```

Here we can see that Puppet has loaded our sudo module and compiled the catalog for node1.pro-puppet.com. This catalog is then sent down to the agent and applied on the target host. If the Puppet agent is running as a daemon, it would then wait 30 minutes and then connect to the master again to check if the configuration has changed on our host or if a new configuration is available from the master. We can adjust this run interval using the runinterval option in the /etc/puppet/puppet.conf configuration file on the agent host:

```
[agent]
runinterval=3600
```

Summary

So that's it—we've used Puppet to configure our first agent. You've also been introduced to the theoretical underpinnings of Puppet and how to:

- Install Puppet

- Configure Puppet

- Use Puppet to manage simple configuration on a single host

In the next chapter, we'll extend our Puppet configuration to multiple agents, explore Puppet's configuration language further, and build more complex configurations.

Resources

- *Introduction to Puppet*: http://docs.puppetlabs.com/guides/introduction.html

- *Installing Puppet*: http://docs.puppetlabs.com/guides/installation.html

- *Configuring Puppet*: http://docs.puppetlabs.com/guides/configuring.html

- *Configuration Reference*: http://docs.puppetlabs.com/references/stable/configuration.html

CHAPTER 2

■ ■ ■

Building Hosts with Puppet

In Chapter 1 we installed and configured Puppet, created our first module, and applied that module and its configuration via the Puppet agent to a host. In this chapter, we're going to extend this process to build some more complete modules and hosts with Puppet for a hypothetical company, Example.com Pty Ltd. Each host's functionality we build will introduce new Puppet concepts and ideas.

Example.com Pty Ltd has four hosts we're going to manage with Puppet: a web server, a database server, a mail server, and our Puppet master server, located in a flat network. You can see that network in Figure 2-1.

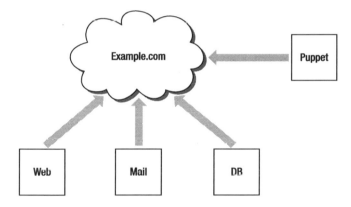

Figure 2-1. *The Example.com Pty Ltd network*

Like many organizations, however, Example.com is not a very homogenous environment, and each host uses a different operating system, as follows:

- mail.example.com: Red Hat Enterprise Linux 6

- db.example.com: Solaris 11

- web.example.com: Ubuntu 10.04

- puppet.example.com: Ubuntu 12.04

To solve this problem, we'll begin by working through how we use Puppet in a multiple operating–system environment. Be sure you've installed the base operating system on these hosts as described in Chapter 1, because we'll perform some basic configuration on the hosts. We'll start with configuring SSH for each host. Then we'll install and configure some role-specific applications for the hosts as follows:

- Postfix (`mail.example.com`)
- MySQL (`db.example.com`)
- Apache and a website (`web.example.com`)
- Puppet master (`puppet.example.com`)

As we configure each host, we'll introduce some of the different features and functions available in Puppet. By the end of the chapter you will have a firm grasp of the basics. In subsequent chapters, we will build on this knowledge and introduce some of Puppet's more advanced features.

Getting Started

Before proceeding, we must have the proper setup. Let's install the Puppet master and agent and then create node definitions for each of our hosts.

■ **Note**   As we mentioned in Chapter 1, the Puppet client software is called the *agent*. Puppet calls the definition of the host itself a *node*. The Puppet server is called the *master*.

Installing Puppet

First, we need to install the Puppet master and agent. We're going to install the Puppet master on `puppet.example.com` and the Puppet agent on all our hosts, including `puppet.example.com`. We're installing the agent on the Puppet master because we're going to use Puppet to manage itself! We then need to connect, create, and sign certificates for each host. To do this, you should follow the installation instructions for the relevant operating system from Chapter 1 on each of the four hosts. For example, for installation on the Red Hat Enterprise Linux host, use the instructions in the "Installing on Red Hat Enterprise Linux and Fedora" section there. You can then move on to configuring the nodes.

■ **Note**   If you use a provisioning tool like Kickstart or Preseed, you can also include Puppet installation and signing as part of your build process.

Integrating and Bootstrapping Puppet with Kickstart

Configure the host normally for your environment. Add the lines shown in Listing 2-1 to the %post section of your Kickstart file.

Listing 2-1. Kickstart configuration for bootstrapping Puppet

```
# Add Puppetlabs apt-repo gpg key
gpg --keyserver pgp.mit.edu --recv-keys 4BD6EC30 && gpg --export --armor 4BD6EC30 | apt-key add -
# Add Puppetlabs apt repo
cat > /etc/apt/sources.list.d/puppetlabs.list <<-EOF
```

```
# puppetlabs
deb http://apt.puppetlabs.com precise main
deb-src http://apt.puppetlabs.com precise main
EOF
# Install puppet
/usr/bin/apt-get -y install puppet
# Make puppet startable
/bin/sed -i 's/START\=no/START\=yes/' '/etc/default/puppet'
# Create a puppet.conf file
cat > /etc/puppet/puppet.conf <<-EOF
[main]
logdir=/var/log/puppet
vardir=/var/lib/puppet
ssldir=/var/lib/puppet/ssl
rundir=/var/run/puppet
factpath=$vardir/lib/facter
pluginsync=true
runinterval=1380
configtimeout=600
splay=true
report=true
server = puppet.example.com
ca_server = puppetca.example.com
EOF
```

Configuring Nodes

After installing the Puppet master and associated agents, we need to create node definitions for each of our hosts in the site.pp file. We created this file in the /etc/puppet/manifests/ directory in Chapter 1. As you can see in Listing 2-2, we've created empty node definitions for each of the nodes in our network.

Listing 2-2. Node defintions in site.pp

```
node   'puppet.example.com'
{
# Puppet code wll go here
}

node   'web.example.com'
{
# Puppet code will go here
}

node   'db.example.com'
{
# Puppet code will go here
}

node   'mail.example.com'
{
# Puppet code will go here
}
```

We haven't included any configuration on our node definitions—Puppet will just recognize the node as it connects and do nothing.

As you might imagine, if you've got a lot of nodes, the site.pp file could become quite large and complex. Puppet has some simple ways of dealing with this issue, described next.

Working with Similar Hosts

The first method works best for large number of similar hosts, such as Web servers, where the configuration of the host is largely identical. For example, if our environment had multiple hosts called web1, web2, web3, and so on, we could specify them as shown in Listing 2-3.

Listing 2-3. Multiple nodes with the same definition

```
node
 'web1.example.com',
 'web2.example.com',
 'web3.example.com'
{
# Puppet code goes here
}
```

Note that these hosts are separated by a comma, and the last host does not have a trailing comma. We can also specify these nodes in the form of a regular expression:

```
node /^web\d+\.example\.com$/
{
# Puppet code goes here
}
```

This would match any host starting with webx, where x is a digit or digits, such as web1 or web20.

Using External Sources

Puppet also has the ability to use external sources for your node data. These sources can include LDAP directories, databases, or other external repositories. This allows you to leverage existing sources of information about your environment, such as asset management systems or identity stores. This functionality is called External Node Classification, or ENC, and we'll discuss it in more detail in Chapter 5.

Default Node

You can also specify a special node called default. This is, as you'd imagine, a default node. If no other node definition exists, then the contents of this node are applied to the host. This is especially useful if you are autosigning certificates.

```
node default {
    include defaultclass
}
```

Node Inheritance

Puppet supports inheritance at the node level, but it is no longer considered best practice. Inheritance is generally discouraged in Puppet code at this point. Nonetheless, as of Puppet 3.0, node inheritance as demonstrated in Listing 2-4 is fully supported and doesn't throw any kind of deprecation warning, and there are no plans yet to remove the feature from the language. Flexible configuration is best achieved through parameterized classes and Hiera, a tool we will explore briefly later in the chapter before returning to it in Chapter 12. Especially when you are starting out with Puppet, don't be afraid to be verbose.

Listing 2-4. Node inheritance

```
node basenode {
    include  sudo
    include  mailx
}

node
  'web.example.com'
  inherits basenode {
    include apache
}
```

The base node has sudo and mailx classes, and the web.example.com node includes those as well as the apache class.

▓ **Caution**   The *Puppet Style Guide* specifically recommends against inheritance whenever possible. Setting most nodes to inherit from the base node is still a relatively common pattern. A better solution is to use parameterized classes and one glue class to define high-level behaviors at node level. See the Openstack Puppet infrastructure for an example of this pattern: https://github.com/openstack-infra/config/blob/master/manifests/site.pp.

Variable Scoping

The topic of node inheritance is a good place to talk about an important and sometimes tricky concept in Puppet: variable scoping.

▓ **Caution**   Variable scoping in Puppet has changed significantly. In Puppet versions before 3.0, variable scoping was *dynamic*. In modern Puppet, meaning versions above 3.0, scoping is not dynamic. This mostly affects class inheritance Four scopes are available: top scope, node scope, parent scope, and local scope.

Let's imagine we've decided to configure some variables in our nodes, as in this example:

```
node 'pro-puppet.example.com'
{
  $location = 'dc1'
  ...
  $location = 'dc2'
}
```

In most programming languages, the $location variable would start out with a value of 'dc1' and then, when it was next assigned, it would change to a value of 'dc2'. In Puppet, these same two statements cause an error:

```
err: Cannot reassign variable location at /etc/puppet/manifests/node.pp:4
```

Why does this happen? Puppet is a *declarative language*. Allowing variable reassignment would require us to rely on order in the file to determine the value of the variable, and order does not matter in a declarative language. The principal outcome of this is that you cannot redefine a variable inside the same *scope* it was defined in, like our node.

So what's a *scope*? Each class, definition, or node introduces a new scope, and there is also a top scope for everything defined outside of those structures. At any given time, four scopes are available to Puppet: top scope, node scope, parent scope, and local scope. Top scope is anything declared in site.pp or imported manifests. Top scope can be explicitly accessed by prepending :: to a variable. It is best practice to write fact variables as $::osfamily so as to use the fact at top scope, thus preventing the variable from being overwritten anywhere. Node scope is the scope created by the enclosing brackets of a node definition. Node scope is unfortunately anonymous, so there is no way to explicitly retrieve it. A variable set at node scope will still be available in local scope unless it is overridden at local scope or parent scope. Local scope is the scope of a single class or defined type. In Puppet 3, parent scope is the scope of a class that is explicitly inherited through use of the inherits keyword, as illustrated in Listing 2-5.

Listing 2-5. Class inheritance

```
class ssh::params {
  case $::osfamily {
  'Debian': { $sshd_package  = 'ssh' }
  'RedHat': { $sshd_package  = 'openssh-server' }
  default:  {fail("Login class does not work on osfamily: ${::osfamily}")}
  }
}

class ssh inherits ssh::params {
  package { $::ssh::params::sshd_package:
    ensure => installed,
  }
}

include ssh
```

In this example the ssh::params class is included in the local scope of the ssh class. The variable $::ssh::params::sshd_package is a way of writing the $sshd_package variable so that it can refer only to a single declaration; this is in keeping with the *Puppet Style Guide*. We also follow the style guide in giving our case statement a default that fails catalog compilation, ensuring that no unexpected behavior happens. A similar way to gain access to the ssh::params class is to use the include keyword, as shown in Listing 2-6.

Listing 2-6. The ssh class using include instead of inherits

```
class ssh::params {
  case $::osfamily {
  'Debian': { $sshd_package  = 'ssh' }
  'RedHat': { $sshd_package  = 'openssh-server' }
  default:  {fail("Login class does not work on osfamily: ${::osfamily}")}
  }
}
```

```
class ssh {
  include ssh::params
  package { $::ssh::params::sshd_package:
    ensure => installed,
  }
}

include ssh
```

■ **Tip** The *Puppet Style Guide* is available at `http://docs.puppetlabs.com/guides/style_guide.html`. It describes coding best practices and what good Puppet code should look like.

Using this method we avoid the inherits keyword, and we can include multiple classes. Where this method does not work is in *parameterized classes*. These are classes that take parameters when they are called. Let's modify our example as shown in Listing 2-7 to use a parameterized class for the ssh class.

Listing 2-7. Parameterized classes

```
class ssh::params {
  case $::osfamily {
    'Debian': {
      $sshd_package  = "ssh"
      $sshd_service  = "ssh"
    }
    'RedHat': {
      $sshd_package  = "openssh-server"
      $sshd_service  = "sshd"
    }
    default:  {fail("Login class does not work on osfamily: ${::osfamily}")}
  }
}

class ssh (
  manage_package = false,
  manage_service = false,
  package_name   = $::ssh::params::sshd_package
) inherits ssh::params  {

  if manage_package == true {
    package { $package_name:
      ensure => installed,
    }
  }

  if manage_service == true {
    service { $::ssh::params::sshd_service:
      ensure => running,
    }
  }

}
```

```
class { 'ssh':
  manage_package => true,
  manage_service  => true,
}
```

Here we have increased the complexity of the code, but we have also increased its flexibility and power. Note that parameterized classes are instantiated with the same syntax as any other resource. In this case we use ssh inherits ssh::params because that is the only way to set up scoping so that we can access variables from the ssh::params class in the default parameters of the ssh class. This is an acceptable and standard practice among Puppet module developers.

Listing 2-7 and following code samples are valid code in Puppet. However, in Puppet code, each class should be in its own file, and those files should be named and placed in a directory structure as specified in the *Puppet Style Guide*. These code samples are condensed together into one file so that the examples can be short and easy to understand. All of the code used in this book can be found at http://www.apress.com/9781430260400.

The key idea to understand is that in previous versions of Puppet, variable scoping was dynamic and often difficult to predict. In modern Puppet (3.x or greater), variable scoping is much more static and best practices require all variables to be rooted at top scope, for example $::ssh::params::sshd_package. With these two changes, it is much less important for non-core developers to know how variable scoping works in detail. Use parameterized classes, use top-scope rooted variables, and don't use inheritance.

■ **Note** You can learn more about variable scoping, workarounds, and related issues at http://docs.puppetlabs.com/puppet/3/reference/lang_scope.html.

The *Puppet Style Guide*

Puppet now has a style guide. It can be accessed at http://docs.puppetlabs.com/guides/style_guide.html. It is worth reading the whole way through at least once because it will expose you to the correct way to style your Puppet code and because the document isn't very long. A few highlights:

- Use two spaces for indentation; no literal tab characters.

- Avoid inheritance whenever possible.

- Known as hashrockets or fat commas, the => should be aligned.

- Use explicit top-scope with variables, for example $::osfamily.

Puppet also has a linter to enforce the style guide. It is called puppet-lint and can be installed from gems. Use it as shown in Listing 2-8.

Listing 2-8. Puppet lint example

```
root@pro-puppet4:~# puppet-lint parent-scope.pp
ERROR: ssh::params not in autoload module layout on line 2
ERROR: ssh not in autoload module layout on line 10
WARNING: top-scope variable being used without an explicit namespace on line 12
```

Many people install pre- or post-receive hooks to automatically puppet-lint their code as they develop. Others, for example the OpenStack infrastructure team, have integrated puppet-lint into their continuous integration and code review system.

With Puppet installed and node definitions in place, we can now move on to creating our modules for the various hosts. But first, let's do a quick refresher on modules in general.

Making (More) Magic With Modules

In Chapter 1, we learned about modules: self-contained collections of resources, classes, files, and templates for configuration files. We will use several modules to define the various facets of each host's configuration. For example, we will have a module for managing Apache on our Web server and another for managing Postfix on our mail server.

Recall that modules are structured collections of Puppet manifests. Puppet will search the module path, which is by default /etc/puppet/modules/ and /var/lib/puppet/modules, for modules and load them. These paths are controlled by the modulepath configuration option, which is set in /etc/puppet/puppet.conf. This means we don't need to import any of these files into Puppet—it all happens automatically.

▓ **Note** These paths will be different for Puppet Enterprise users. Puppet Enterprise uses a composite modulepath, bringing in standard modules from /opt/puppet/share and local modules from /etc/puppetlabs/modules.

It's very important that modules are structured properly. For example, our sudo module contains the lines shown in Listing 2-9.

Listing 2-9. Module file structure

```
sudo/
sudo/manifests
sudo/manifests/init.pp
sudo/files
sudo/templates
```

Inside our init.pp (Listing 2-10), we create a class with the name of our module.

Listing 2-10. init.pp

```
class sudo {
configuration...
}
```

Last, we can apply a module, like the sudo module we created in Chapter 1, to a node by using the include function as shown in Listing 2-11.

Listing 2-11. Snippet of site.pp

```
node 'puppet.example.com'
{
  include sudo
}
```

The include function adds the resources contained in a class or module, in this example adding all the resources contained in the sudo module here to the node puppet.example.com.

▓ **Tip** You don't have to always create your own modules. The Puppet Forge at http://forge.puppetlabs.com contains a large collection of existing modules that you can either use immediately or modify to suit your environment. This can make getting started with Puppet extremely simple and fast.

The Puppet module tool is a part of Puppet. At the time of printing, the module tool is part of Puppet core, but in the future it is expected to move out of Puppet core so that it can have tighter and faster development cycles. You won't have to do anything special to get the Puppet module tool on your system. You can generate a blank puppet module using the syntax puppet module generate *name-name*, where the first name is the name of you or your organization, and the second is the name of the service you are managing, such as propuppet-amanda in the example shown in Listing 2-12.

Listing 2-12. Generating a Puppet module template

```
root@pro-puppet4:~# puppet module generate propuppet-amanda
Notice: Generating module at /root/propuppet-amanda
propuppet-amanda
propuppet-amanda/Modulefile
propuppet-amanda/README
propuppet-amanda/manifests
propuppet-amanda/manifests/init.pp
propuppet-amanda/spec
propuppet-amanda/spec/spec_helper.rb
propuppet-amanda/tests
propuppet-amanda/tests/init.pp
```

In Chapter 8 you will learn more about the Puppet module tool and other tools to speed Puppet module development and testing.

Let's now see how to manage the contents of our modules using version control tools as recommended in Chapter 1.

Version-Controlling Your Modules

Because modules present self-contained collections of configuration, we also want to appropriately manage the contents of these modules, allowing us to perform change control. To manage your content, we recommend that you use a version control system (VCS).

Version control is the method most developers use to track changes in their application source code. Version control records the state of a series of files or objects and allows you to periodically capture that state in the form of a revision. This allows you to track the history of changes in files and objects and potentially revert to an earlier revision should you make a mistake. This makes management of our configuration much easier and saves us from issues like undoing inappropriate changes or accidentally deleting configuration data.

In this case, we are going to show you an example of managing your Puppet manifests with a tool called Git, which is a distributed version control system (DVCS). Distributed version control allows the tracking of changes across multiple hosts, making it easier to allow multiple people to work on your modules. Git is used by many large open source projects, such as the Linux kernel, and was originally developed by Linus Torvalds for that purpose. It is a powerful tool, but learning the basic steps is easy. You may use whatever version control system suits your environment. For example, many people use Subversion or CVS for the same purpose.

First, we need to install Git. On most platforms we install the git package. For example, on Red Hat and Ubuntu:

```
$ sudo yum install git
```

or

```
$ sudo apt-get install git
```

Once Git is installed, let's identify ourselves to Git so it can track who we are and associate some details with actions we take:

```
$ git config --global user.name "Your Name"
$ git config --global user.email your@email.address.com
```

Now let's version-control the path containing our modules, in our case /etc/puppet/modules. We change to that directory and then execute the git binary to initialize our new Git repository:

```
$ cd /etc/puppet/modules
$ git init
```

This creates a directory called .git in the /etc/puppet/modules directory that will hold all the details and tracking data for our Git repository.

We can now add files to this repository using the git binary with the add option:

```
$ git add *
```

This adds everything in our currently working directory to Git. You can also use git and the rm option to remove items you don't want to be in the repository:

```
$ git rm filename
```

This doesn't mean, however, that our modules are already fully tracked by our Git repository. As in Subversion and other version control systems, we need to "commit" the objects we'd like to track. The commit process captures the state of the objects to be tracked and managed, and it creates a revision to mark that state. You can also create a file called .gitignore in the directory. Every file or directory specified in this file will be ignored by Git and never added.

Before we commit, though, we can see what Git is about by using the git status command:

```
$ git status
```

This tells us that when we commit, Git will add the contents to the repository and create a revision based on that state.

Now let's commit our revision to the repository:

```
$ git commit -a -m "Initial commit"
```

The -m option specifies a commit message that allows us to document the revision we're about to commit. It's useful to be verbose here and explain what you have changed and why, so it's easier to find out what's in each revision and make it easier to find an appropriate point to return to if required. If you need more space for your commit message, you can omit the -m option, and Git will open your default editor and allow you to type a more comprehensive message.

The changes are now committed to the repository, and we can use the git log command to see our recent commit:

```
$ git log
```

We can see some information here about our commit. First, Git uses SHA1 hashes to track revisions; Subversion, for example, uses numeric numbers—1, 2, 3, and so on. Each commit has a unique hash assigned to it. We will also see some details about who created the commit and our commit message telling us what the commit is all about.

Every time you add a new module or file you will need to add it to Git using the `git add` command and then commit it to store it in the repository. We recommend you add and commit changes regularly to ensure that you have sufficiently granular revisions to allow you to easily roll back to an earlier state.

■ **Tip** If you're interested in Git, we strongly recommend Scott Chacon's excellent book *Pro Git*, also published by Apress (2009). The book is available in both paper form and online at www.apress.com and at http://progit.org/book/. Scott is also one of the lead developers of the Git hosting site, GitHub http://www.github.com, where you can find a number of Puppet-related modules.

Returning to Puppet, our simple sudo module is a good introduction to Puppet, but it only showcased a small number of Puppet's capabilities. It's now time to expand our Puppet knowledge and develop some new, more advanced modules, starting with one to manage SSH on our hosts. We'll then create a module to manage Postfix on mail.example.com, one to manage MySQL on our Solaris host, db.example.com, another to manage Apache and web sites, and finally one to manage Puppet with Puppet itself.

We'll also introduce you to some best practices for structuring, writing, and managing modules and configuration.

Creating a Module to Manage SSH

We first need to create an appropriate module structure. We're going to do this under the /etc/puppet/modules directory on our Puppet master:

```
$ cd /etc/puppet/modules
$ puppet module generate propuppet-ssh
$ mv propuppet-ssh ssh
```

The mv command here is required because the module will be referred to as the ssh module containing the ssh class, and needs to be named ssh for Puppet to correctly load it. If and when the module is pushed to the Puppet Forge or GitHub, the full name propuppet-ssh should be preserved.

Next, we create some classes inside the module and some initial resources, as shown in Listing 2-13. A stub ssh class will have already been created; you only need to modify it.

Listing 2-13. The ssh module

ssh/manifests/init.pp

```
class ssh {
 class { '::ssh::package': } ->
 class { '::ssh::config': }  ->
 class { '::ssh::service':}  ->
 Class['ssh']
}
```

ssh/manifests/install.pp

```
class ssh::install {
  package { "openssh":
    ensure => present,
  }
}
```

ssh/manifests/config.pp

```
class ssh::config {
  file { "/etc/ssh/sshd_config":
    ensure  => present,
    owner   => 'root',
    group   => 'root',
    mode    => 0600,
    source  => "puppet:///modules/ssh/sshd_config",
    require => Class["ssh::package"],
    notify  => Class["ssh::service"],
  }
}
```

ssh/manifests/service.pp

```
class ssh::service {
  service { "sshd":
    ensure     => running,
    hasstatus  => true,
    hasrestart => true,
    enable     => true,
    require    => Class["ssh::config"],
  }
}
```

In Listing 2-13, we created a functional structure by dividing the components of the service we're managing into functional domains: packages to be installed, files to be configured, and services to be executed or run.

We created a class called ssh (which we need to ensure that the module is valid) and used the include function to add all the classes to the module.

We've created three classes: ssh, ssh::install, ssh::config, and ssh::service. Modules can be made up of multiple classes. We use the :: namespace syntax as a way to create structure and organization in our modules. The ssh prefix tells Puppet that each class belongs in the ssh module, and the class name is suffixed.

■ **Tip** We also want to create a sshd_config file in the ssh/files/ directory so that our File["/etc/ssh/sshd_config"] resource can serve out that file. The easiest way to do this is to copy an existing functional sshd_config file and use that. Later we'll show you how to create template files that allow you to configure per-host configuration in your files. Without this file Puppet will report an error for this resource.

When Puppet loads the ssh module, it will search the manifests directory for files suffixed with .pp, look inside them for namespaced classes, and automatically import them. This means that ssh::config and others are automatically available.

Our ssh module directory structure looks like Listing 2-14 (most of this was printed out by the Puppet module tool on generation).

Listing 2-14. SSH Module Directory Structure

```
root@pro-puppet4:/etc/puppet/modules# find.
.
./ssh
./ssh/Modulefile
./ssh/README
./ssh/manifests
./ssh/manifests/init.pp
./ssh/manifests/service.pp
./ssh/manifests/config.pp
./ssh/manifests/package.pp
./ssh/spec
./ssh/spec/spec_helper.rb
./ssh/tests
./ssh/tests/init.pp
./ssh/files
./ssh/files/sshd_config
```

Neat and simple.

░ **Tip**　You can nest classes by another layer, for example `ssh::config::client`, and our auto-importing magic will still work by placing this class in the `ssh/manifests/config/client.pp` file.

The ssh::install Class

Now that we've created our structure, let's look at the classes and resources we've created. Let's start with the `ssh::install` class containing the `Package["openssh"]` resource, which installs the OpenSSH package.

It looks simple enough, but we've already hit a stumbling block—we want to manage SSH on all of `Example.com's` hosts, and across these platforms the OpenSSH package has different names:

- Red Hat: `openssh-server`
- Ubuntu: `openssh-server`
- Solaris: `openssh`

How are we going to ensure that Puppet installs the correctly named package for each platform? The answer lies with Facter, Puppet's system inventory tool. During each Puppet run, Facter queries data about the host and sends it to the Puppet master. This data includes the operating system of the host, which is made available in our Puppet manifests as a variable called `$osfamily`. We can now use this variable to select the appropriate package name for each platform. Let's rewrite our `ssh::package` class as shown in Listing 2-15.

Listing 2-15. Rewriting the `ssh::package` class

```
class ssh::install {

  $package_name = $::osfamily  ?
    'RedHat'  => "openssh-server",
    'Debian'  => "openssh-server",
    'Solaris' => "openssh",
    },
```

```
  package { 'ssh':
    ensure => present,
    name   => $package_name,
  }
}
```

In the preamble of the ssh::params class, we are using a conditional syntax that Puppet calls a *selector*. To construct a selector, we specify the variable containing the value we want to select on as the value of our attribute, here $::osfamily, and follow this with a question mark (?). We then list on new lines a series of selections; for example, if the value of $::osfamily is Solaris, then the value of the name attribute will be set to openssh, and so on. Note that we could have specified multiple values in the form of simple regular expressions, like /(Solaris|Ubuntu|Debian)/. However, many Puppet users believe this decreases readability, and we did not use it in Listing 2-15.

You can see that we've changed the title of our package resource to ssh and specified a new attribute called name. As we explained in Chapter 1, each resource is made up of a type, title, and a series of attributes. Each resource's attributes include a name variable, or namevar, and the value of this attribute is used to determine the name of the resource. For example, the Package and Service resources use the name attribute as their namevar, while the File type uses the path attribute as its namevar. Most of the time we wouldn't specify the namevar, as it is synonymous with the title. For example, in this resource:

```
file { "/etc/passwd":
  ...
}
```

we don't need to specify the namevar because the value will be taken from the title, "/etc/passwd". But often we're referring to resources in many places, and we might want a simple alias, so we can give the resource a title and specify its namevar this way:

```
file { "passwd":
  path => "/etc/passwd",
  ...
}
```

We can now refer to this resource as File["passwd"] as an aliased shorthand.

■ **Note** You should also read about the alias metaparameter, which provides a similar capability, at http://docs.puppetlabs.com/references/latest/metaparameter.html#alias.

In our current example, the name of the package we're managing varies on different hosts. Therefore, we want to specify a generic name for the resource and a platform-selected value for the actual package to be installed.

■ **Caution** Selector matching is case-insensitive. You can also see some other examples of regular expressions in selectors at http://docs.puppetlabs.com/puppet/latest/reference/lang_conditional.html#selectors.

We can also specify a value called `default`:

```
default => "ssh",
```

This value is used if no other listed selection matches. If we don't specify a `default` value and no selection matches, then the `name` attribute would be set to a nil value. The *Puppet Style Guide* has several requirements on defaults for `case` statements and selectors:

1. All selectors and case statements must have a default.

2. Defaults should call the `fail()` function if a default behavior is at all questionable on most platforms.

3. `default: { }` is acceptable if the author meant for a no-effect fall through.

Is the default value of `ssh` here valid? Installing `ssh` works on Ubuntu, but Ubuntu is covered by the `$::osfamily` Debian, so what other operating systems might run this code? On FreeBSD, there is no `ssh` port to install. Similarly for OSX; thus, the default is not sane. We should replace it with:

```
default => fail("Module propuppet-ssh does not support osfamily: ${::osfamily}")
```

As can you imagine, this requirement to select the appropriate value for a particular platform happens a lot. This means we could end up scattering a lot of very similar conditional statements across our Puppet code. That's pretty messy; as a best practice we recommend that you move all your conditional checks to a separate class. This greatly improves code readability.

We usually call that class *module*`::params`, so in our current case it would be named `ssh::params`. As before, we're going to store that class in a separate file. Let's create that file:

```
$ touch ssh/manifests/params.pp
```

We can see that class in Listing 2-16.

Listing 2-16. The `ssh::params` class

```
class ssh::params {
  case $::osfamily {
    Solaris: {
      $ssh_package_name = 'openssh'
    }
    Debian: {
      $ssh_package_name = 'openssh-server'
    }
    RedHat: {
      $ssh_package_name = 'openssh-server'
    }
    default: {
      fail("Module propuppet-ssh does not support osfamily: ${::osfamily}")
    }
  }
}
```

You can see that inside our ssh::params class we've created another type of conditional, the case statement. Much like a selector, the case statement operates on the value of a variable, here $::osfamily. Unlike a selector, case statements allow us to specify a block of things to do if the value of the variable matches one of the cases. In our case we're setting the value of a new variable we've created, called $ssh_package_name. You could do other operations here, such as include a class or a resource, or perform some other function.

Now we need to open up our ssh::package class and modify it for use with the ssh::params class, as shown in Listing 2-17.

Listing 2-17. SSH Package class

```
class ssh::package {
  include ssh::params
  package { 'ssh':
    ensure => present,
    name   => $::ssh::params::ssh_package_name,
  }
}
```

You can see that our namespacing is useful for other things, here using variables from other classes. We can refer to a variable in another class by prefixing the variable name with the class it's contained in, here ssh::params. In this case, rather than our messy conditional, the package name to be installed will use the value of the $::ssh::params::ssh_package_name parameter. Our resource is now much neater, simpler, and easier to read. You can refer to the earlier discussion in this chapter on variable scoping for a refresher if you need it.

■ **Tip** So how do we refer to namespaced resources? Just like other resources; for example,
Package[$::ssh::params::ssh_package_name].

■ **Note** You can read more about case statements and selectors at
http://docs.puppetlabs.com/puppet/latest/reference/lang_conditional.html.

And finally, we need to include our new class in the ssh class:

```
class ssh {
 class { '::ssh::package': } ->
 class { '::ssh::config': }  ->
 class { '::ssh::service':}  ->
 Class['ssh']
}
```

These class resources tell Puppet that when you include the ssh module, you're getting all of these classes. They also build an internal relationship using the -> syntax.

FUNCTIONS

The `include` directive we use to include our classes and modules is called a *function*. Functions are commands that run on the Puppet master to perform actions. Puppet has a number of other functions, including the `generate` function that calls external commands and returns the result, and the `notice` function that logs messages on the master and is useful for testing a configuration. For example:

```
notice("This is a notice message including the value of the $ssh_package variable")
```

Functions run only on the Puppet master and cannot be run on the client, and thus can only work with the resources available on the master.

You can see a full list of functions at `http://docs.puppetlabs.com/references/stable/function.html`, and we will introduce a variety of other functions in subsequent chapters. You can also find documentation on how to write your own functions at `http://docs.puppetlabs.com/guides/custom_functions.html`, and we will talk about developing functions in Chapter 10.

We're going to come back to the `ssh::params` class and add more variables as we discover other elements of our OpenSSH configuration that are unique to particular platforms.

The ssh::config Class

Now let's move onto our next class, `ssh::config`, which we can see in Listing 2-18.

Listing 2-18. The `ssh::config` class

```
class ssh::config {
  file { "/etc/ssh/sshd_config":
    ensure  => present,
    owner   => 'root',
    group   => 'root',
    mode    => 0440,
    source  => 'puppet:///modules/ssh/sshd_config',
    require => Class['ssh::install'],
    notify  => Class['ssh::service'],
  }
}
```

Note the `source` parameter to the `file` resource in Listing 2-18. This is Puppet's syntax for saying "copy this file over from the Puppet master." The path here says to look in the `ssh` class, and then in the `files` directory, for a file called `sshd_config`. The syntax:

```
source => 'puppet:///modules/ldap/ldap.conf',
```

says to look inside the `ldap` module, in the `files` directory, for a file called `ldap.conf`.

We know that the location of the sshd_config files will vary across different operating systems. Therefore, we're going to have to add another conditional for the name and location of that file. Let's go back to our ssh::params class from Example 2-16 and add a new variable:

```
class ssh::params {
  case $::osfamily {
    Solaris: {
      $ssh_package_name = 'cswopenssh'
      $ssh_service_config = '/etc/opt/csw/ssh/sshd_config'
    }
    Debian: {
      $ssh_package_name = 'openssh-server'
      $ssh_service_config = '/etc/ssh/sshd_config'
    }
    RedHat: {
      $ssh_package_name = 'openssh-server'
      $ssh_service_config = '/etc/ssh/sshd_config'
    }
    default: {
      fail("Module propuppet-ssh does not support osfamily: ${::osfamily}")
    }
  }
}
```

We add the $ssh_service_config variable to each of the cases in our conditional and then update our file resource in the ssh::config class:

```
include ssh::params

file { ::$ssh::params::ssh_service_config:
  ensure = > present,
  ...
}
```

Again, we have no need for a messy conditional in the resource; we can simply reference the $::ssh::params::ssh_service_config variable.

We can also see that the file resource contains two metaparameters, require and notify. These metaparameters both specify relationships between resources and classes. You'll notice here that both metaparameters reference classes rather than individual resources. They tell Puppet that it should create a relationship between this file resource and every resource in the referenced classes.

▓ **Tip** It is a best practice to establish relationships with an entire class, rather than with a resource contained within another class, because this allows the internal structure of the class to change without refactoring the resource declarations related to the class.

For example, the require metaparameter tells Puppet that all the resources in the specified class must be processed prior to the current resource. In our example, the OpenSSH package must be installed before Puppet tries to manage the service's configuration file.

The `notify` metaparameter creates a notification relationship. If the current resource (the service's configuration file) is changed, then Puppet should notify all the resources contained in the `ssh::service` class. In our current case, a "notification" will cause the service resources in the `ssh::service` class to restart, ensuring that if we change a configuration file, the service will be restarted and running with the correct, updated configuration.

■ **Tip** A shorthand method called *chaining* exists for specifying metaparameter relationships, such as `require` and `notify`. You can read about chaining at `http://docs.puppetlabs.com/guides/language_tutorial.html#chaining_resources`.

So why specify the whole `ssh::service` class rather than just the `Service['sshd']` resource? This is another best practice that allows us to simplify maintaining our classes and the relationships between them. Imagine that instead of a single package, we had twenty packages. If we didn't require the class, then we'd need to specify each individual package in our `require` statement, like this:

```
require => [ Package['package1'], Package['package2'], Package['package3']
],
```

■ **Tip** Adding square brackets [] around a list creates a Puppet array. You can specify arrays as the values of variables and many attributes; for example, you can specify many items in a single resource:

```
package { [ 'package1', 'package2', 'package3' ]: ensure => installed }
```

In addition to arrays, Puppet also supports a hash syntax, which you can see at `http://docs.puppetlabs.com/guides/language_tutorial.html#hashes`.

We would need to do that for every resource that required our packages, making our `require` statements cumbersome and potentially error-prone, and most importantly requiring that every resource that requires packages be updated with any new package requirements.

Because we've required the whole class, it doesn't matter how many packages we add to the `ssh::install` class—Puppet knows to install packages before managing configuration files, and we don't have to update a lot of resources every time we make a change. This means our classes become the public API to our modules, enhancing usability and making it possible to make minor updates without breaking compatibility.

■ **Tip** In our current example we could make use of arrays to extend the variables in the `ssh::params` class. For example, by changing `$ssh_package_name` to an array, we could specify multiple packages to be installed without needing to create another Package resource in the `ssh::install` class. Puppet is smart enough to know that if you specify a variable with a value of an array, it should expand the array; so changing the value of the `$ssh_package_name` variable to [openssh, package2, package3] would result in the `ssh::install` class installing all three packages. This greatly simplifies the maintenance of our `ssh` module, as we need to change values in only one place to manage multiple configuration items.

The ssh::service Class

Let's look at our last class, ssh::service, and update it to reflect our new practice:

```
class ssh::service {
  include ssh::params
  service { $::ssh::params::ssh_service_name:
    ensure      => running,
    hasstatus   => true,
    hasresstart => true,
    enable      => true,
    require     => Class['ssh::config'],
  }
}
```

We've added our new variable, $ssh_service_name, to the ssh::params class, too:

```
class ssh::params {
  case $::osfamily {
    Solaris {
      $ssh_package_name = 'cswopenssh'
      $ssh_service_config = '/etc/opt/csw/ssh/sshd_config'
      $ssh_service_name = 'cswopensshd'
    }
...
}
```

Let's also look at our Service[$::ssh::params::ssh_service_name] resource (at the start of this section), as this is the first service we've seen managed. You'll notice two important attributes, ensure and enable, which specify the state and status of the resource, respectively. The state of the resource specifies whether the service is running or stopped. The status of the resource specifies whether it is to be started at boot; for example, as controlled by the chkconfig or enable-rc.d commands.

Puppet understands how to manage a variety of service frameworks, like SMF and init scripts, and can start, stop, and restart services. It does this by attempting to identify the service framework a platform uses and executing the appropriate commands. For example, on Red Hat it might execute:

```
$ service sshd restart
```

If Puppet can't recognize your service framework, it will resort to simple parsing of the process table for processes with the same name as the service it's trying to manage. This obviously isn't ideal, so it helps to tell Puppet a bit more about your services to ensure that it manages them appropriately. The hasstatus and hasrestart attributes we specified in the ssh::service class offer one of the ways we tell Puppet useful things about our services. If we specify hasstatus as true, then Puppet knows that our service framework supports status commands of some kind. For example, on Red Hat it knows it can execute the following:

```
$ service sshd status
```

This enables it to determine accurately whether the service is started or stopped. The same principle applies to the hasrestart attribute, which specifies that the service has a restart command.

Now if we include our new `ssh` module in our Puppet nodes, we can see Puppet managing a full service, as shown in Listing 2-19.

Listing 2-19. Adding the `ssh` module

```
class base {
  include sudo
  include ssh
}

node 'puppet.example.com' {
  include base
}

node 'web.example.com' {
  include base
}

node 'db.example.com' {
  include base
}

node 'mail.example.com' {
  include base
}
```

Here we've created a class called base, in which we're going to place the modules that will be base or generic to all our nodes. Thus far, these are our `sudo` and `ssh` modules. We then `include` this class in each `node` statement.

Creating a Module to Manage Postfix

Let's now create a module to manage Postfix on `mail.example.com`. We start with a structure similar to our SSH module. In this case, we know which platform we're going to install our mail server on, so we don't need to include any conditional logic. However, if we had multiple mail servers on different platforms, it would be easy to adjust our module using the example we've just shown to accommodate disparate operating systems.

```
root@pro-puppet4:/etc/puppet/modules# puppet module generate propuppet-postfix
Notice: Generating module at /etc/puppet/modules/propuppet-postfix
propuppet-postfix
propuppet-postfix/Modulefile
propuppet-postfix/README
propuppet-postfix/manifests
propuppet-postfix/manifests/init.pp
propuppet-postfix/spec
propuppet-postfix/spec/spec_helper.rb
propuppet-postfix/tests
propuppet-postfix/tests/init.pp
root@pro-puppet4:/etc/puppet/modules# mv propuppet-postfix postfix
```

Then we will need to add a files directory and several files:

```
root@pro-puppet4:/etc/puppet/modules# cd postfix
root@pro-puppet4:/etc/puppet/modules# mkdir files
root@pro-puppet4:/etc/puppet/modules# mkdir templates
root@pro-puppet4:/etc/puppet/modules# touch files/master.cf
root@pro-puppet4:/etc/puppet/modules# touch manifests/package.pp
root@pro-puppet4:/etc/puppet/modules# touch manifests/config.pp
root@pro-puppet4:/etc/puppet/modules# touch manifests/service.pp
root@pro-puppet4:/etc/puppet/modules# touch templates/main.cf.erb
```

The postfix::package Class

We also have some similar resources present in our Postfix module that we saw in our SSH module. For example, in the postfix::package class we install two packages, postfix and mailx:

```
class postfix::package {
  package { [ "postfix", "mailx" ]:
    ensure => present,
  }
}
```

■ **Note** We've used an array to specify both packages in a single resource statement. This is a useful shortcut that allows you specify multiple items in a single resource.

The postfix::config Class

Next we have the postfix::config class, which we will use to configure our Postfix server.

```
class postfix::config {
  File {
    owner => 'postfix',
    group => 'postfix',
    mode  => 0644,
  }

  file { '/etc/postfix/master.cf':
    ensure => present,
    source => 'puppet:///modules/postfix/master.cf',
    require => Class['postfix::install'],
    notify  => Class['postfix::service'],
  }

  file { '/etc/postfix/main.cf':
    ensure => present,
    content => template('postfix/main.cf.erb'),
    require => Class['postfix::install'],
    notify  => Class['postfix::service'],
  }
}
```

You may have noticed some new syntax: we specified the File resource type capitalized and without a title. This syntax is called a *resource default*, and it allows us to specify defaults for a particular resource type. In this case, all File resources within the postfix::config class will be owned by the user postfix and the group postfix, and with a mode of 0644. Resource defaults only apply to the current scope.

A common use for global defaults is to define a global "filebucket" for backing up the files Puppet changes. You can see the filebucket type and an example of how to use it globally at http://docs.puppetlabs.com/references/stable/type.html#filebucket.

We have also introduced a new attribute in our File['/etc/postfix/main.cf'] resource—content. You've already seen the source attribute, which allows Puppet to serve out files, and we have used it in one of our File resources, File['/etc/postfix/master.cf']. The content attribute allows us to specify the content of the file resources as a string. But it also allows us to specify a template for our file. The template is specified using a function called template.

As previously mentioned, functions are commands that run on the Puppet master and return values. In this case, the template function allows us to specify an Embedded Ruby (ERB) template (http://ruby-doc.org/stdlib/libdoc/erb/rdoc/), from which we can create the templated content for our configuration file. We specify the template like this:

```
content => template('postfix/main.cf.erb'),
```

We've specified the name of the function, template, and placed inside brackets the name of the module that contains the template and the name of the template file. Puppet knows when we specify the name of the module to look inside the postfix/templates directory for the requisite file—here, main.cf.erb.

THE REQUIRE FUNCTION

In addition to the include function, Puppet also has a function called require. The require function works just like include, except that it introduces some order to the inclusion of resources. With the include function, resources are not included in any sequence. The only exception is individual resources, which have relationships (using metaparameters, for example) that mandate some ordering. The require function tells Puppet that all resources being required must be processed first. For example, if we specified the following:

```
class ssh {

require ssh::params

include ssh::install
include ssh::config
include ssh::service

}
```

then the contents of ssh::params would be processed before any other includes or resources in the ssh class. This is useful as a simple way to specify less granular ordering to your manifests than metaparameter relationships, but it's not recommended as a regular approach. That's because Puppet implements this feature by creating relationships between all the resources in the required class and the current class. This can lead to cyclical dependencies between resources. It's cleaner, more elegant, and simpler to debug if you use metaparameters to specify the relationships between resources that need order.

In Listing 2-20 you can see what our template looks like.

Listing 2-20. The Postfix `main.cf` template

```
soft_bounce = no
command_directory = /usr/sbin
daemon_directory = /usr/libexec/postfix
mail_owner = postfix
myhostname = <%= @hostname %>
mydomain = <%= @domain %>
myorigin = $mydomain
mydestination = $myhostname, localhost.$mydomain, localhost, $mydomain
unknown_local_recipient_reject_code = 550
relay_domains = $mydestination
smtpd_reject_unlisted_recipient = yes
unverified_recipient_reject_code = 550
smtpd_banner = $myhostname ESMTP
setgid_group = postdrop
```

You can see a fairly typical Postfix `main.cf` configuration file with the addition of two ERB variables that use Facter facts to correctly populate the file. Each variable is enclosed in `<%=` and `%>` brackets and will be replaced with the fact values when Puppet runs. You can specify any variable in a template like this. Puppet variables in the current scope are available as Ruby instance variables, `@varname`, and as Ruby local variables, `varname`. The variable `$mydomain` is a Postfix variable, since it is not enclosed in `<%=` and `%>` ERB brackets, and it will not be interpreted by Ruby.

Older templates will probably use the local variable syntax, and newer templates should use the instance variable syntax. Instance variable syntax is superior because the local variable syntax may collide with reserved keywords in the Ruby language.

This is a very simple template, and ERB has many of the same capabilities as Ruby, so you can build templates that take advantage of iteration, conditionals, and other features. You can learn more about how to use templates at `http://docs.puppetlabs.com/guides/templating.html`.

▓ **Tip** You can easily check the syntax of your ERB templates for correctness using the following command:

```
erb -x -T '-' mytemplate.erb | ruby -c
```

Replace *mytemplate*.erb with the name of the template you want to check for syntax.

The postfix::service Class

Next we have the `postfix::service` class, which manages our Postfix service:

```
class postfix::service {
  service { 'postfix':
    lensure      => running,
    hasstatus  => true,
    hasrestart  => true,
```

```
    enable       => true,
    require       => Class['postfix::config'],
  }
}
```

And finally, we have the core postfix class, where we include all the other classes from our postfix module:

```
class postfix {
  include postfix::install
  include postfix::config
  include postfix::service
}
```

We can then apply our postfix module to the mail.example.com node:

```
node 'mail.example.com' {
  include base
  include postfix
}
```

Now when the mail.example.com node connects, Puppet will apply the configuration in both the base and postfix modules.

Managing MySQL with the mysql Module

Our next challenge is managing MySQL on our Solaris host, db.example.com. To do this we're going to create a third module, called mysql. We create our module structure as follows:

```
root@pro-puppet4:/etc/puppet/modules# puppet module generate propuppet-mysql
Notice: Generating module at /etc/puppet/modules/propuppet-mysql
propuppet-mysql
propuppet-mysql/Modulefile
propuppet-mysql/README
propuppet-mysql/manifests
propuppet-mysql/manifests/init.pp
propuppet-mysql/spec
propuppet-mysql/spec/spec_helper.rb
propuppet-mysql/tests
propuppet-mysql/tests/init.pp
root@pro-puppet4:/etc/puppet/modules# mv propuppet-mysql mysql
```

And add the files:

```
mysql/files/my.cnf
mysql/manifests/install.pp
mysql/manifests/config.pp
mysql/manifests/service.pp
mysql/templates/
```

The mysql::install Class

Our first class is our `mysql` class, contained in the `init.pp` file, where we load all the required classes for this module:

```
class mysql (
  $group              = 'mysql',
  $service_enabled = true,
  $service_running = true,
  $user               = 'mysql'
){
  class { 'mysql::install':
    user  => $user,
    group => $group,
  }
  class { 'mysql::config':
    user  => $user,
    group => $group,
  }
  class { 'mysql::service':
    ensure  => $service_running,
    enabled => $service_enabled,
  }
}
```

This is our first example of a parameterized class inside a module. This type of class takes arguments when it is invoked, allowing much greater flexibility of the module and module reuse. Ideally, there will be no site-specific configuration in your brick modules, and all configuration will be exposed as parameters to the base class of the module. When just starting out, you don't need to build this level of abstraction into your module; however, when building modules to share with the world via the Puppet Module Forge or GitHub, try to make the most generic modules you can.

Notice that parameterized classes look very similar to defined types. Also note that we use the = symbol instead of the => symbol, and that the final parameter does have a trailing comma. The trailing comma on the last line fails for Puppet 2.7, but you should include it because most new code should be written for Puppet 3. By convention, required parameters (those without default values) go at the top and other parameters follow, both lists alphabetized separately. It is also worth noting that this example is somewhat contrived; it would be much more valuable to expose parameters that would make up values in a template that would create `my.conf`.

Let's quickly walk through the other classes to create, starting with `mysql::install`.

```
class mysql::install (
  $user,
  $group
){
  $mysql_pkgs = ['mysql5',
                 'mysql5client',
                 'mysql5rt',
                 'mysql5test',
                 'mysql5devel' ]

  package { $mysql_pkgs:
    ensure  => present,
    require => User[$user],
  }
```

```
user { $user:
  ensure      => present,
  comment => 'MySQL user',
  gid         => $group,
  shell       => '/bin/false',
  require     => Group[$group],
}

group { $group:
  ensure => present,
}
}
```

You can see that we've used two new resource types in our `mysql::install` class, User and Group. We also created a `mysql` group and then a user, and we added that user, using the `gid` attribute, to the group we created. We then added the appropriate `require` metaparameters to ensure that the user and group are created in the right order.

The mysql::config Class

Next, we add our `mysql::config` class:

```
class mysql::config (
  $user,
  $group,
){
  file { '/opt/csw/mysql5/my.cnf':
    ensure  => present,
    source  => 'puppet:///modules/mysql/my.cnf',
    owner   => $user,
    group   => $group,
    require => Class['mysql::install'],
    notify    => Class['mysql::service'],
  }

  file { '/opt/csw/mysql5/var':
    group   => $user,
    owner   => $group,
    recurse => true,
    require => File['/opt/csw/mysql5/my.cnf'],
  }
}
```

You can see that we've added a `File` resource to manage our `/opt/csw/mysql5` directory. By specifying the directory as the title of the resource and setting the `recurse` attribute to `true`, we are asking Puppet to recurse through this directory and all directories underneath it and change the owner and group of all objects found inside them to `mysql`.

The mysql::service Class

Then we add our mysql::service class:

```
class mysql::service (
  enabled,
  ensure,
){

  service { 'cswmysql5':
    ensure     => $ensure,
    hasstatus  => true,
    hasrestart => true,
    enabled    => $enabled,
    require    => Class['mysql::config'],
  }
}
```

It is worth noting that ensure => can take true and false values, and it interprets them as you would expect. Finally, we can apply our mysql module to the db.example.com node:

```
node 'db.example.com' {
  include base
  include mysql
}
```

Now, when the db.example.com node connects, Puppet will apply the configuration in both the base and mysql modules.

Since the mysql module has sane defaults for all parameters, we don't need to specify any parameters to it. However, if we wanted to modify its configuration or behavior, it would be as simple as modifying the node definition:

```
node 'db.example.com' {
  include base
  class { 'mysql':
    user            => 'staging-mysql',
    service_running => false,
    service_enabled => false,
  }

}
```

AUDITING

In addition to the normal mode of changing configuration (and the --noop mode of modeling the proposed configuration), Puppet has an auditing mode. A normal Puppet resource controls the state you'd like a configuration item to be in, for example:

```
file { '/etc/hosts':
  owner => 'root',
  group => 'root',
  mode  => '0660',
}
```

This file resource specifies that the /etc/hosts file should be owned by the root user and group and have permissions set to 0660. Every time Puppet runs, it will check that this file's settings are correct and make changes if they are not. In audit mode, however, Puppet merely checks the state of the resource and reports differences back. It is configured using the audit metaparameter.

Using this new metaparameter we can specify our resource as follows:

```
file { '/etc/hosts':

  audit => [ owner, group, mode ],

}
```

Now, instead of changing each value (though you can also add and mix attributes to change it, if you wish), Puppet will generate auditing log messages, which are available in Puppet reports (see Chapter 9):

```
audit change: previously recorded value owner root has been changed to owner daemon
```

This allows you to track any changes that occur on resources under management on your hosts. You can specify this audit metaparameter for any resource and all attributes, and track users, groups, files, services and the myriad other resources Puppet can manage.

You can specify the special value all to have Puppet audit every attribute of a resource, rather than needing to list all possible attributes, like so:

```
file { '/etc/hosts':

  audit => all,

}
```

You can also combine the audited resources with managed resources, allowing you to manage some configuration items and simply track others. It is important to remember, though, that unlike many file integrity systems, this method does not protect your audit state by a checksum or the like, and the state is stored on the client. Future releases plan to protect and centralize this state data.

Managing Apache and Websites

As you're starting to see a much more complete picture of our Puppet configuration, we come to managing Apache, Apache virtual hosts, and their websites. We start with our module layout:

```
root@pro-puppet4:/etc/puppet/modules# puppet module generate propuppet-apache
Notice: Generating module at /etc/puppet/modules/propuppet-apache
propuppet-apache
propuppet-apache/Modulefile
propuppet-apache/README
propuppet-apache/manifests
propuppet-apache/manifests/init.pp
propuppet-apache/spec
propuppet-apache/spec/spec_helper.rb
propuppet-apache/tests
propuppet-apache/tests/init.pp
root@pro-puppet4:/etc/puppet/modules# mv propuppet-apache apache
```

And add some additional files:

```
root@pro-puppet4:/etc/puppet/modules# mkdir apache/files
root@pro-puppet4:/etc/puppet/modules# mkdir apache/templates
root@pro-puppet4:/etc/puppet/modules# touch apache/manifests/install.pp
root@pro-puppet4:/etc/puppet/modules# touch apache/manifests/service.pp
root@pro-puppet4:/etc/puppet/modules# touch apache/manifests/vhost.pp
root@pro-puppet4:/etc/puppet/modules# touch apache/templates/vhost.conf.erb
```

■ **Note** We're introducing a lot of modules in this chapter. Several of the services we're Puppeting, especially Apache, already have excellent modules in place on the Puppet Forge. We're showing you how to create your own modules using services we hope you already have experience with so that you can learn the patterns and go on to Puppet the things that haven't already been Puppeted by the community. If you want to use Puppet to manage an Apache server, don't use the module we're building here; use the puppetlabs-apache module from the Forge. However, there are important lessons about the Puppet language in the following pages, so you should not neglect to read them.

The apache::install Class

First, we install Apache via the apache::install class:

```
class apache::install {
  package { [ 'apache2' ]:
    ensure => present,
  }
}
```

This class currently just installs Apache on an Ubuntu host; we could easily add an apache::params class in the style of our SSH module to support multiple platforms.

The apache::service Class

For this module we're going to skip a configuration class, because we can just use the default Apache configuration. Let's move right to an apache::service class to manage the Apache service itself:

```
class apache::service {
  service { "apache2":
    ensure     => running,
    hasstatus  => true,
    hasrestart => true,
    enable     => true,
    require    => Class['apache::install'],
  }
}
```

This class allows us to manage Apache, but how are we going to configure individual websites? To do that, we're going to use a new syntax, the *definition*.

The Apache Definition

Definitions are collections of resources like classes, but unlike classes they can be specified and are evaluated multiple times on a host. They also accept parameters.

■ **Tip** Remember that classes are singletons. They can be included multiple times on a node, but they will only be evaluated ONCE. A definition, because it takes parameters, can be declared multiple times, and each new declaration will be evaluated.

We create a definition using the define syntax, as shown in Listing 2-21.

Listing 2-21. The first definition

```
define apache::vhost(
  $docroot,
  $port,
  $priority,
  $ssl=true,
  $serveraliases = '',
  $template='apache/vhost.conf.erb',
){

  include apache

  file {"/etc/apache2/sites-enabled/${priority}-${name}":
    content => template($template),
    owner   => 'root',
    group   => 'root',
    mode    => '0640',
    require => Class['apache::install'],
    notify  => Class['apache::service'],
  }
}
```

We gave this definition a title (apache::vhost) and then specified a list of potential variables. Variables can be specified as a list, and any default values can be specified; for example, $ssl=true. Defaults will be overridden if the parameter is specified when the definition is used.

Inside the definition we can specify additional resources or classes; for example, here we've included the apache class to ensure that all required Apache configuration will be performed prior to our definition being evaluated. This is because it doesn't make sense to create an Apache VirtualHost if we don't have Apache installed and ready to serve content.

In addition to the apache class, we've added a basic file resource, which manages Apache site files contained in the /etc/apache2/sites-enabled directory. The title of each file is constructed using the priority parameter, and the title of our definition is specified using the $name variable.

Puppet allows only one resource of a given type and name on the system. If it finds two resources with the same type and name in the catalog, it will fail to compile the catalog and the whole Puppet run will fail. Classes are singletons, and so including the class multiple times won't cause a duplicate definition error, but defined types are not singletons and if called with the same parameters multiple times in Puppet code will cause a duplicate definition error.

■ **Tip** The $name variable contains the name, also known as the title, of a declared defined resource. This is the value of the string before the colon when declaring the defined resource. The $title variable, which usually has the same value, is also available.

Worse, and many new Puppet users are bitten by this, resources created inside a defined type can conflict with other resources. This is why we are putting the $name variable in the file resource in Listing 2-21. In addition to satisfying the implicit need to have different virtual hosts exist in different files on the filesystem, using the $name variable in the names of resources within the defined type helps us avoid a duplicate definition error. This is especially problematic when a defined type contains an exec resource. The second time the defined type is used on the system, the Puppet catalog fails to compile with a duplicate definition error. Putting the $name variable as part of the name of the exec resource will solve this problem.

This file resource's content attribute is specified by a template, the specific template being the value of the $template parameter. Let's look at a fairly simple ERB template for an Apache VirtualHost in Listing 2-22.

Listing 2-22. VirtualHost template

```
NameVirtualHost *:<%= @port %>
<VirtualHost *:<%= @port %>>
  ServerName <%= @name %>
<%if @serveraliases.is_a? Array -%>
<% @serveraliases.each do |name| -%><%= "  ServerAlias #{@name}\n" %><% end
-%>
<% elsif @serveraliases != '' -%>
<%= "  ServerAlias #{@serveraliases}" -%>
<% end -%>
  DocumentRoot <%= @docroot %>
  <Directory <%= @docroot %>>
    Options Indexes FollowSymLinks MultiViews
    AllowOverride None
    Order allow,deny
    allow from all
  </Directory>
  ErrorLog /var/log/apache2/<%= @name %>_error.log
  LogLevel warn
  CustomLog /var/log/apache2/<%= @name %>_access.log combined
  ServerSignature On
</VirtualHost>
```

Each parameter specified in the definition is used, including the $name variable to name the virtual host we're creating.

You can also see some embedded Ruby in our ERB template:

```
<%if @serveraliases.is_a? Array -%>
<% @serveraliases.each do |name| -%><%= "  ServerAlias #{@name}\n" %><% end
-%>
<% elsif @serveraliases != '' -%>
<%= "  ServerAlias #{@serveraliases}" -%>
<% end -%>
```

Here we've added some logic to the serveraliases parameter. If that parameter is an array of values, then create each value as a new server alias; if it's a single value, create only one alias.

Let's now see how we would use this definition and combine our definition and template:

```
apache::vhost { 'www.example.com':
  port          => '80',
  docroot       => '/var/www/www.example.com',
  ssl           => false,
  priority      => '10',
  serveraliases => 'home.example.com',
}
```

Here we have used our definition much the same way we would specify a resource by declaring the apache::vhost definition and passing it a name, www.example.com (which is also the value of the $name variable). We've also specified values for the required parameters. Unless a default is already specified for a parameter, you need to specify a value for every parameter of a definition. Otherwise, Puppet will return an error. We could also override parameters, for example by specifying a different template:

```
template => 'apache/another_vhost_template.erb',
```

So in our current example, the template would result in a VirtualHost definition that looks like Listing 2-23.

Listing 2-23. The VirtualHost configuration file

```
NameVirtualHost *:80
<VirtualHost *:80>
  ServerName www.example.com
  ServerAlias home.example.com
  DocumentRoot /var/www/www.example.com
  <Directory /var/www/www.example.com>
    Options Indexes FollowSymLinks MultiViews
    AllowOverride None
    Order allow,deny
    allow from all
  </Directory>
  ErrorLog /var/log/apache2/www.example.com_error.log
  LogLevel warn
  CustomLog /var/log/apache2/www.example.com_access.log combined
  ServerSignature On
</VirtualHost>
```

The final class in our module is the apache class in the init.pp file, which includes our Apache classes:

```
class apache {
  include apache::install
  include apache::service
}
```

You can see we've included our two classes but not the definition, apache::vhost. This is because of some module magic called *autoloading*. Puppet scans your module and loads any .pp file in the manifests directory that is named after the class it contains; for example, the install.pp file contains the apache::install class and so is autoloaded.

The same thing happens with definitions: The vhost.pp file contains the definition apache::vhost, and Puppet autoloads it. However, as we declare definitions, for example calling apache::vhost where we need it, we don't need to do an include apache::vhost because calling it implies inclusion.

Next, we include our classes into our www.example.com node and call the apache::vhost definition to create the www.example.com website:

```
node 'www.example.com' {
  include base

  apache::vhost { 'www.example.com':
    port          => '80',
    docroot       => '/var/www/www.example.com',
    ssl           => false,
    priority      => '10',
    serveraliases => 'home.example.com',
  }
}
```

Note that we don't need to include the apache class in the node definition, because the defined type takes care of this. We could now add additional web servers easily and create additional Apache VirtualHosts by calling the apache::vhost definition again, for example:

```
apache::vhost { 'another.example.com':
    port     => '80',
    docroot  => '/var/www/another.example.com',
    ssl      => false,
    priority => '10',
}
```

Managing Puppet with the Puppet Module

In our very last module we're going to show you Puppet being self-referential, so you can manage Puppet with Puppet itself. To do this we create another module, one called puppet, with a structure as follows:

```
root@pro-puppet4:/etc/puppet/modules# puppet module generate propuppet-puppet
Notice: Generating module at /etc/puppet/modules/propuppet-puppet
propuppet-puppet
propuppet-puppet/Modulefile
propuppet-puppet/README
propuppet-puppet/manifests
propuppet-puppet/manifests/init.pp
propuppet-puppet/spec
propuppet-puppet/spec/spec_helper.rb
propuppet-puppet/tests
propuppet-puppet/tests/init.pp
root@pro-puppet4:/etc/puppet/modules# mv propuppet-puppet puppet
```

And add the extra files we need:

```
root@pro-puppet4:/etc/puppet/modules# mkdir puppet/files/
root@pro-puppet4:/etc/puppet/modules# mkdir puppet/templates/
root@pro-puppet4:/etc/puppet/modules# touch puppet/manifests/install.pp
root@pro-puppet4:/etc/puppet/modules# touch puppet/manifests/config.pp
root@pro-puppet4:/etc/puppet/modules# touch puppet/manifests/params.pp
root@pro-puppet4:/etc/puppet/modules# touch puppet/manifests/service.pp
root@pro-puppet4:/etc/puppet/modules# touch puppet/templates/puppet.conf.erb
```

The puppet::install Class

This class does the work of installing the Puppet client software.

```
class puppet::install {
  package { 'puppet' :
    ensure => present,
  }
}
```

All of the operating systems we're installing on call the Puppet package puppet, so we're not going to use a variable here. We do, however, need a couple of variables for our Puppet module, so we add a puppet::params class.

```
class puppet::params {
  $puppetserver = "puppet.example.com"
}
```

For the moment, this class contains only a Puppet server variable that specifies the fully qualified domain name (FQDN) of our Puppet master.

Now we create our puppet::config class:

```
class puppet::config {

  include puppet::params

  file { '/etc/puppet/puppet.conf':
    ensure  => present,
    content => template('puppet/puppet.conf.erb'),
    owner   => 'puppet',
    group   => 'puppet',
    require => Class['puppet::install'],
    notify  => Class['puppet::service'],
  }
}
```

This class contains a single file resource that loads the puppet.conf.erb template. It also includes the puppet::params class to make available the variables defined in that class. Let's take a look at the contents of our template, too:

```
[main]
    user = puppet
    group = puppet
    report = true
    reports = log,store

[master]
    certname = <%= @puppetserver %>

[agent]
    pluginsync = false
    report = true
    server = <%= @puppetserver %>
```

This is a very simple template, which we can then expand upon, or you can easily modify to add options or customize it for your own purposes. You'll notice that we've included configuration for both our master and the client. We're going to manage one puppet.conf file rather than a separate one for master and client. This is mostly because it's easy and because it doesn't add much overhead to our template.

We can then add the puppet::service class to manage the Puppet client daemon.

```
class puppet::service {
  service { 'puppet':
    ensure     => running,
    hasstatus  => true,
    hasrestart => true,
    enable     => true,
    require    => Class['puppet::install'],
  }
}
```

We can then create an init.pp that includes the puppet class and the subclasses we've just created:

```
class puppet {
  include puppet::install
  include puppet::config
  include puppet::service
}
```

Just stopping here would create a module that manages Puppet on all our clients. All we need to do, then, is to include this module on all of our client nodes, and Puppet will be able to manage itself. But we're also going to extend our module to manage the Puppet master as well. To do this, we're going to deviate slightly from our current design and put all the resources required to manage the Puppet master into a single class, called puppet::master:

```
class puppet::master {

  include puppet
  include puppet::params
```

```
  package { 'puppet-server':
    ensure => installed,
  }

  service { 'puppetmasterd':
    ensure     => running,
    hasstatus  => true,
    hasrestart => true,
    enable     => true,
    require    => File['/etc/puppet/puppet.conf'],
  }
}
```

You can see that our class puppet::master includes the classes puppet and puppet::params. This means that all of the preceding Puppet configuration will be applied, in addition to the new package and service resources we've defined in this class.

Let's now return to the puppet::params class so that we can discuss another huge concept in Puppet: Hiera. The Puppet Labs project page describes this as "a simple pluggable Hierarchical Database." It provides to Puppet a separation and interface for code and data. Look again at the puppet::parameters class:

```
class puppet::params {
  $puppetserver = "puppet.example.com"
}
```

Here we have a variable that will be needed somewhere else in our Puppet manifests, $puppetserver, and the data in that variable, the string "puppet.example.com". The purpose of this class is to bring these two entities together and to provide a flat-file datastore for the key-value pair.

Hiera is a place to keep these kind of variables. It presents itself to Puppet as a function call. Hiera configuration and extension will be covered in Chapter 12, but the YAML backend is a good way to introduce its use. This is an example Hiera data file, written in YAML:

```
puppetserver = 'puppet.example.com'
```

This allows us to rewrite the puppet::params class as:

```
class puppet::params {
  $puppetserver = hiera('puppetserver')
}
```

In this example Puppet will use the hiera function to get the string value 'puppet.example.com' and place it into the $puppetserver variable. In Puppet 3, but not Puppet 2.7, there is an automatic lookup of parameters in a parameterized class. We can use this to rewrite the puppet::params class further:

```
class puppet::params (
  $puppetserver,
){
}
```

When this is called with no arguments, Puppet 3 will attempt to look up thc puppct::params::puppetserver key in Hiera and populate it accordingly. It will not fail unless the Hiera lookup fails. Hiera has multiple backends and an entire system of hierarchal lookups, which will be discussed in Chapter 12. The important thing to understand now is that Hiera helps us separate configuration from data. It helps us create modules that are interchangeable library-like blocks that can be used to implement any configuration by placing the details of that configuration, the data, into Hiera and leaving the logic of the module in the Puppet manifests.

We can now add the puppet module to our nodes, leaving them looking like this:

```
class base {
  include sudo
  include ssh
  include puppet
}

node 'puppet.example.com' {
  include base
  include puppet::master
}

node 'web.example.com' {
  include base
  include apache

  apache::vhost { 'www.example.com':
    port         => '80',
    docroot      => '/var/www/www.example.com',
    ssl          => false,
    priority     => '10',
    serveraliases => 'home.example.com',
  }
}

node 'db.example.com' {
  include base
  include mysql
}

node 'mail.example.com' {
  include base
  include postfix
}
```

We've added the puppet module to the base class we created earlier. This will mean it's added to all the nodes that include base. We've also added the puppet::master class, which adds the additional resources needed to configure the Puppet master, to the puppet.example.com node.

Summary

In this chapter, you've been introduced to many of Puppet's basic features and language elements, including:

- How to structure modules, including examples of modules to manage SSH, Postfix, MySQL, Apache and Puppet itself

- How to use language constructs like selectors, arrays and case statements

- A greater understanding of files and templates

- Definitions that allow you to manage configuration, such as Apache VirtualHosts

- Variable scoping

- Parameterized classes

- A brief example using Hiera

You've also seen how a basic Puppet configuration in a simple environment might be constructed, including some simple modules to manage your configuration. Also, Puppet Forge contains a large collection of existing modules that you can either use immediately or modify to suit your environment.

In the next chapter, we'll look at how to scale Puppet beyond the basic Webrick server, using tools like Passenger and Unicorn and allowing you to manage larger numbers of hosts.

Resources

- Puppet Documentation: `http://docs.puppetlabs.com`

- Puppet Forge: `http://forge.puppetlabs.com`

CHAPTER 3

■ ■ ■

Developing and Deploying Puppet

We've introduced you to installing Puppet and the basics of the Puppet language. In this chapter, we'll show you how to develop new Puppet code, test it, and deploy it. This will allow you to use Puppet to make changes and manage your infrastructure in a logical and stable way.

To do this, we are going to introduce and develop a number of new Puppet concepts, including environments, the puppet apply tool, and running the master in debug mode.

Environments allow you to define, maintain, and separate your infrastructure into appropriate divisions. In most organizations, you already have some of these divisions: development, testing, staging, preproduction, and others. Just like a set of production, testing, and development systems, which are separated from one another to effectively isolate risky changes from production services, Puppet environments are designed to isolate changes to the configuration and prevent them from impacting critical production infrastructure.

Puppet apply is the standalone version of the Puppet software. It directly reads manifest files and makes changes. Developing and testing using puppet apply is an important part of speedy Puppet development.

Most organizations will have one or more centralized Puppet masters for all the nodes in their ecosystem, but when developing Puppet it can be useful to run a Puppet master process locally on the development machine. We'll explore how to do this and how to get productivity gains from it. Chapter 4 will show how to set up a production-ready Puppet master installation.

We'll then show how to use a local Puppet master and the Vagrant virtualization tool to do even more development and testing of Puppet code. In this chapter we also build upon the concept of modules, which we introduced in Chapters 1 and 2. We show you how to configure environments on your Puppet masters and how to control which agents connect to which environment. Each agent can connect to a specific environment that will contain a specific configuration.

Finally, we exercise the workflow of making changes using our version control system (VCS), testing small development changes in a safe and easy way, and then deploying the tested changes to the production environment in Puppet. We will gradually increase the flexibility and complexity of our environment infrastructure, as well as its integration with VCS.

Instead of beginning with configuration changes to our new test mail server, we are going to start out, as developers do, on our local workstation. We're going to use puppet apply to do our initial module development.

The puppet apply Command and Modes of Operation

Puppet has several subcommands. You've already seen the agent and master subcommands in Chapter 1. The apply subcommand combines the catalog-compilation logic of the master subcommand with the state-ensuring behavior of the agent subcommand.

Printf with Puppet

To begin we'll use the apply subcommand to do the Puppet equivalent of a printf or echo statement in Listing 3-1, which shows two alternative approaches.

Listing 3-1. Printf with puppet apply

```
root@pro-puppet:~# puppet apply -e 'notify {"Hello World": }'
Notice: Hello World
Notice: /Stage[main]//Notify[Hello World]/message: defined 'message' as 'Hello World'
Notice: Finished catalog run in 0.05 seconds

root@pro-puppet:~# puppet apply -e 'notice ("Hello World")'
Notice: Scope(Class[main]): Hello World
Notice: Finished catalog run in 0.04 seconds
```

These two examples both produce output. The first does so by creating a notify resource, a dummy resource that merely sends a message to the output log. The second creates output by calling the notice() function, which writes output to the log. The differences are that the first example will show a resource being run in a report of the run, and the notify function is much more forgiving about its inputs.

Testing Puppet Behavior with Notify

Most Puppet experts are very comfortable using puppet apply on the command line to test syntax. The Puppet language is full of little gotchas, and testing is the best way to verify behavior and build experience. For example, take the simple test in Listing 3-2.

Listing 3-2. Testing Puppet behavior with puppet apply

```
root@pro-puppet5:~# puppet apply -e 'if "Puppet" == "puppet" { notify { "true!?": } }'
Notice: true!?
Notice: /Stage[main]//Notify[true!?]/message: defined 'message' as 'true!?'
Notice: Finished catalog run in 0.04 seconds
```

The == operator in Puppet is not case-sensitive. We used puppet apply to check the behavior of the operator.

Using Puppet Apply with Manifest Files

We can also use puppet apply to evaluate short Puppet manifests. In the following manifest we write two file resources. We are testing the autorequires property of file resources. That is, we're checking whether file resources underneath a managed directory will automatically require that directory. Listing 3-3 shows the code and Listing 3-4 the output.

Listing 3-3. Code to test autorequire behavior

```
[root@pro-puppet ~]# cat autorequires.pp

file { '/tmp/redshirt':
  ensure => directory,
}

file { '/tmp/redhsirt/logan':
  ensure => file,
}
```

Listing 3-4. Testing autorequires

```
[root@pro-puppet ~]# puppet apply autorequires.pp
Notice: /Stage[main]//File[/tmp/redshirt]/ensure: created
Notice: /Stage[main]//File[/tmp/redshirt/logan]/ensure: created
Notice: Finished catalog run in 0.06 seconds
```

Because this Puppet code works without a require => File['/tmp/redshirt'] on the '/tmp/redshirt/logan'
file resource, we can be assured that the autorequire behavior is in fact functional. Note that explicitly requiring state
is always better than letting autorequires take care of things.

We can use the puppet apply command with modules as well. First let's bring down puppetlabs-stdlib from
GitHub, and then we'll use one of the functions it provides. Listing 3-5 shows the process of pulling down the module
from GitHub, and Listing 3-6 shows the contents of our test manifest using this tool.

Listing 3-5. Pulling down a module from GitHub

```
[root@pro-puppet testing]# git clone https://github.com/puppetlabs/puppetlabs-stdlib
Cloning into 'puppetlabs-stdlib'...
remote: Counting objects: 4313, done.
remote: Compressing objects: 100% (2485/2485), done.
remote: Total 4313 (delta 1676), reused 3883 (delta 1293)
Receiving objects: 100% (4313/4313), 746.01 KiB | 325 KiB/s, done.
Resolving deltas: 100% (1676/1676), done.
[root@pro-puppet testing]# ls
puppetlabs-stdlib
[root@pro-puppet testing]# mv puppetlabs-stdlib/ stdlib
```

Listing 3-6. Testing a manifest using a function from the stdlib module

```
 [root@pro-puppet testing]# ls
puppet_example.pp   stdlib
[root@pro-puppet testing]# cat puppet_example.pp

$array1 = ['one','two','three']
$array2 = ['four','five','six']

$concatenated_array = concat($array1, $array2)

notify { $concatenated_array: }
```

The Puppet code in Listing 3-6 uses the concat function from the puppetlabs-stdlib module. We need to load
that module by setting –modulepath on the puppet apply command line as shown in Listing 3-7.

Listing 3-7. puppet apply using a modulepath

```
[root@pro-puppet testing]# puppet apply --modulepath=/root/testing puppet_example.pp
Notice: five
Notice: /Stage[main]//Notify[five]/message: defined 'message' as 'five'
Notice: six
Notice: /Stage[main]//Notify[six]/message: defined 'message' as 'six'
Notice: one
```

```
Notice: /Stage[main]//Notify[one]/message: defined 'message' as 'one'
Notice: four
Notice: /Stage[main]//Notify[four]/message: defined 'message' as 'four'
Notice: three
Notice: /Stage[main]//Notify[three]/message: defined 'message' as 'three'
Notice: two
Notice: /Stage[main]//Notify[two]/message: defined 'message' as 'two'
Notice: Finished catalog run in 0.03 seconds
[root@pro-puppet testing]#
```

Note that Puppet's evaluation order is random. We created six notify resources, but they appeared in a random order. The only way to be sure of ordering is to use require, before, subscribe, and notify metaparameters. Also note the behavior in Puppet that passing an array of items to a type like notify (or any other type, including user-defined types) produces one resource of that type for every element in the array.

We can also use puppet apply and a modulepath option to develop modules. Assuming we are working on an ssh module, we can set up a development environment as shown in Listing 3-8.

Listing 3-8. Creating a module testing environment

```
 [root@pro-puppet development]# ls
site.pp  ssh
[root@pro-puppet development]# cat site.pp

node default {

  class { 'ssh': }

}
[root@pro-puppet development]# cat ssh/manifests/init.pp
class ssh {

  package { 'ssh':
    ensure => present,
  }

}
```

This example has a very bare ssh class and an example site.pp file. We can use the Puppet line in Listing 3-9 to test the code.

Listing 3-9. Testing a Puppet module

```
[root@pro-puppet development]# puppet apply --modulepath=. --noop site.pp
Notice: /Stage[main]/Ssh/Package[ssh]/ensure: current_value absent, should be present (noop)
Notice: Class[Ssh]: Would have triggered 'refresh' from 1 events
Notice: Stage[main]: Would have triggered 'refresh' from 1 events
Notice: Finished catalog run in 0.30 seconds
```

So what's going on here? We've made a very bare-bones site.pp file that simply includes the ssh class. Then we ran Puppet against the site.pp file in noop, or simulation, mode. This mode didn't make any changes to our system. We can now go back into the ssh class and make additional changes, run Puppet in noop mode again, and repeat that cycle until our development goals are satisfied. Listing 3-10 demonstrates the process.

Listing 3-10. Changes to the ssh class

```
[root@pro-puppet development]# cat ssh/manifests/init.pp
class ssh {

  package { 'ssh':
    ensure => present,
  }

  service { 'ssh':
    ensure  => running,
    enabled => true,
  }

}
```

Then we can run puppet apply again in noop mode as shown in Listing 3-11.

Listing 3-11. Running puppet apply in noop mode

```
[root@pro-puppet development]# puppet apply --modulepath=. --noop site.pp
Error: Invalid parameter enabled at /root/development/ssh/manifests/init.pp:10 on node
box1.pro-puppet.com
Error: Invalid parameter enabled at /root/development/ssh/manifests/init.pp:10 on node
box1.pro-puppet.com
```

The puppet apply run has errored out. The parameter enabled is incorrect; the correct value is enable. We can make that change (Listing 3-12) and then run the code again (Listing 3-13).

Listing 3-12. Changes to the ssh class

```
...
  service { 'ssh':
    ensure => running,
    enable => true,
  }
...
```

Listing 3-13. Testing the ssh class

```
[root@pro-puppet development]# puppet apply --modulepath=. --noop site.pp
Notice: /Stage[main]/Ssh/Package[ssh]/ensure: current_value absent, should be present (noop)
Notice: /Stage[main]/Ssh/Service[ssh]/ensure: current_value stopped, should be running (noop)
Notice: Class[Ssh]: Would have triggered 'refresh' from 2 events
Notice: Stage[main]: Would have triggered 'refresh' from 1 events
Notice: Finished catalog run in 0.31 seconds
```

Since the code ran successfully in noop mode, we can be reasonably sure that it is good. Advanced testing using rspec-puppet and rspec-system will be covered in Chapter 8. We could also have found the syntax error using puppet parser validate, which can be integrated into prereceive or precommit hooks. This coding/testing development cycle is a tight iterative loop that can be performed totally offline. This procedure, or one very similar to it, is behind most Puppet manifest development.

Foreground Puppet Master

It is also possible to run a Puppet master process locally on the development machine. This is very useful for making changes and testing behavior for your wider collection of Puppet code. Let's look at a possible scenario in Listing 3-14. This scenario has a Hiera component; Hiera will be fully covered in Chapter 12, and you may read that chapter now if you wish. First verify that you have set an alias for the Puppet DNS name in /etc/hosts as follows:

```
127.0.0.1 puppet localhost
```

Listing 3-14. Layout of /etc/puppet

```
root@pro-puppet-dev:/etc/puppet# ls
data  environments  hiera.yaml  puppet.conf
root@pro-puppet-dev:/etc/puppet# ls environments/
development  production  staging
root@pro-puppet-dev:/etc/puppet# ls environments/development/
manifests  modules
root@pro-puppet-dev:/etc/puppet# ls environments/development/modules/
apache  collectd  concat  nrpe  postfix  stdlib  sudo
root@pro-puppet-dev:/etc/puppet# ls environments/production/modules/
apache  collectd  concat  nrpe  postfix  stdlib  sudo
root@pro-puppet-dev:/etc/puppet# ls environments/staging/modules/
apache  collectd  concat  nrpe  postfix  stdlib  sudo
root@pro-puppet-dev:/etc/puppet# ls environments/development/manifests/site.pp
environments/development/manifests/site.pp
root@pro-puppet-dev:/etc/puppet# ls data/
common.yaml  env
root@pro-puppet-dev:/etc/puppet# ls data/env/
development.yaml  production.yaml  staging.yaml
```

This is a pretty typical layout for /etc/puppet on a Puppet master. We're using Puppet environments here, a feature that will be fully explained later in this chapter. For now, just note that we have a full copy of the site.pp and all modules in each environment subdirectory. These modules are often source-control checkouts, and they represent different points on the timeline of development: development, where code is actively worked on; staging, where code is put through quality control and performance testing; and production, where code is live and maintaining production services. You are, of course, welcome to delineate these environments however you see fit.

Since we have the code set up on the developer's workstation, we can run the master in debug mode (Listing 3-15), and connect to it with an agent in a different window (Listing 3-15).

Listing 3-15. Output of foreground Puppet master

```
root@pro-puppet-dev:/etc/puppet# puppet master --no-daemonize --verbose
dnsdomainname: Name or service not known
Info: Creating a new SSL key for ca
Info: Creating a new SSL certificate request for ca
```

```
Info: Certificate Request fingerprint (SHA256):
98:B2:A7:07:0B:55:F7:04:B2:72:DE:7E:B6:83:95:E9:AE:C9:C2:09:6C:64:7E:63:
3D:FA:25:EE:B2:87:3C:DE
Notice: Signed certificate request for ca
Notice: Rebuilding inventory file
Info: Creating a new certificate revocation list
Info: Creating a new SSL key for pro-puppet-dev
Info: Creating a new SSL certificate request for pro-puppet-dev
Info: Certificate Request fingerprint (SHA256):
DA:F9:16:08:8F:63:40:01:80:54:57:FD:54:15:46:21:D0:13:3C:70:83:54:BC:E4:
8A:55:D8:C1:42:BA:0F:98
Notice: pro-puppet-dev has a waiting certificate request
Notice: Signed certificate request for pro-puppet-dev
Notice: Removing file Puppet::SSL::CertificateRequest pro-puppet-dev.hsd1.or.comcast.net at
'/etc/puppet/ssl/ca/requests
/pro-puppet-dev'
Notice: Removing file Puppet::SSL::CertificateRequest pro-puppet-dev.hsd1.or.comcast.net at
'/etc/puppet/ssl/certificate
_requests/pro-puppet-dev'
Notice: Starting Puppet master version 3.1.1
```

This does not terminate; instead, it will print output as we connect to it, including any errors. Note that on the first run the master sets up its own certificate chain. This is fine for development. For production deployments, refer to Chapter 4.

Next, in another window, run the puppet agent command (Listing 3-16).

Listing 3-16. puppet agent connecting to localhost

```
root@pro-puppet-dev:/etc/puppet# puppet agent --test --server=puppet
Info: Retrieving plugin
Info: Loading facts in /etc/puppet/environments/production/modules/stdlib/lib/facter/puppet_vardir.rb
Info: Loading facts in /etc/puppet/environments/production/modules/stdlib/lib/facter/root_home.rb
Info: Loading facts in /etc/puppet/environments/production/modules/stdlib/lib/facter/facter_dot_d.rb
Info: Loading facts in /etc/puppet/environments/production/modules/stdlib/lib/facter/pe_version.rb
Info: Loading facts in /etc/puppet/environments/production/modules/concat/lib/facter/concat_basedir.rb
Info: Loading facts in /var/lib/puppet/lib/facter/concat_basedir.rb
Info: Loading facts in /var/lib/puppet/lib/facter/puppet_vardir.rb
Info: Loading facts in /var/lib/puppet/lib/facter/root_home.rb
Info: Loading facts in /var/lib/puppet/lib/facter/facter_dot_d.rb
Info: Loading facts in /var/lib/puppet/lib/facter/pe_version.rb
Info: Caching catalog for pro-puppet-dev.hsd1.or.comcast.net
Info: Applying configuration version '1382354758'
Notice: Puppet is running
Notice: /Stage[main]//Node[default]/Notify[Puppet is running]/message: defined 'message' as
'Puppet is running'
Notice: Finished catalog run in 0.05 seconds
```

The puppet agent run syncs facts and other pluginsync artifacts as usual, and then outputs a Puppet run precisely as expected. The other windows, containing the Puppet master running in –no-daemonize mode, will have some output relating to the successful Puppet run:

```
Notice: Compiled catalog for pro-puppet-dev in environment production in 0.01 seconds
```

Running the Puppet master like this is useful because it makes cloning the settings in place on your Puppet master trivial. Cloning can be as simple as an `rsync` of `/etc/puppet` or as complicated as you would like. Some organizations have separate version control repositories for every module, the manifests, and sometimes multiple repositories for Hiera data, as well as tooling and orchestration around all of it.

The second reason to run a local Puppet master is to streamline development with virtual machines.

Developing Puppet with Vagrant

When you are developing Puppet code, it is good to test your code as you move forward. One of the best ways to do this is to run your Puppet manifests against a fresh virtual machine regularly. There are two tools we'll combine to make this painless and effective.

We've already seen how to run a Puppet master locally on the development machine. When this is in place, you can write and modify Puppet manifests on your own machine without any external dependencies. You can also use your own customized development environment (such as vim, emacs, geppetto, or .gitconfig). When it's time to push the code to a centralized code repository, you can do this directly; you won't have to push trust into an untrusted virtual machine.

The second tool we're going to use is Vagrant (http://www.vagrantup.com/), a virtualization middleware that makes starting, logging into, destroying, and repeating the process smooth. Vagrant is a collection of Ruby scripts that wrap software hypervisors such as VirtualBox and VMware. Vagrant workflow starts with downloading or creating a vagrant virtual machine template called a base box. Then a virtual machine is created from this template, booted, and eventually destroyed.

The overall pattern with these two tools is as follows:

1. Set up the Puppet master on a local development machine.

2. Check out the organization's Puppet code.

3. Download a Vagrant base box that is representative of your production server load.

4. Make changes to the Puppet code.

5. Boot the Vagrant machine.

6. Log into the Vagrant machine and perform a test Puppet run.

7. Evaluate the results.

8. Destroy the Vagrant machine.

9. Repeat steps 4-8 until satisfied.

We will assume that you have steps 1 and 2 completed, as they were demonstrated earlier in this chapter. However, we will make one change by setting the Puppet master to autosigning mode:

```
root@pro-puppet-dev:/etc/puppet# echo '*' > autosign.conf
```

Then add the key/value pair `autosign = true` to either the `[main]` or `[master]` section of `puppet.conf`.

Vagrant Initial Setup

Use Vagrant to download a box prototype. There are standard builds for most common Linux utilities. Your site can use tools like Packer and Veewee to build customized Vagrant boxes to represent your environment. For now we'll just use a default Ubuntu Precise box as shown in Listing 3-17.

Listing 3-17. Adding a template in Vagrant

```
PS C:\Users\skrum> vagrant box add precise64
http://puppet-vagrant-boxes.puppetlabs.com/ubuntu-server-12042-x64-vbox4210.box
.box
Downloading or copying the box...
Extracting box...ate: 5495k/s, Estimated time remaining: --:--:--)
The box you're attempting to add already exists:

Name: precise64
Provider: virtualbox
```

Note that the Vagrant commands in this section are being run from Windows. Vagrant is platform-agnostic and behaves exactly the same across Windows, Mac, and Linux. This is one of the reasons it is such a popular and powerful aid to development.

Next we will use the vagrant init command to create a basic Vagrant file. This file can be modified to allow multiple-VM setups and advanced configuration. The vagrant init command creates a very simple file to get us underway (Listing 3-18).

Listing 3-18. Creating an instance in Vagrant

```
PS C:\Users\skrum\Documents> vagrant init precise64
A `Vagrantfile` has been placed in this directory. You are now
ready to `vagrant up` your first virtual environment! Please read
the comments in the Vagrantfile as well as documentation on
`vagrantup.com` for more information on using Vagrant.
```

Booting the Vagrant Box

In Listing 3-19 we will start the virtual machine with vagrant up.

Listing 3-19. Starting the Vagrant machine

```
PS C:\Users\skrum\Documents> vagrant up
Bringing machine 'default' up with 'virtualbox' provider...
[default] Clearing any previously set forwarded ports...
[default] Fixed port collision for 22 => 2222. Now on port 2200.
[default] Creating shared folders metadata...
[default] Clearing any previously set network interfaces...
[default] Preparing network interfaces based on configuration...
[default] Forwarding ports...
[default] -- 22 => 2200 (adapter 1)
[default] Booting VM...
[default] Waiting for machine to boot. This may take a few minutes...
[default] Machine booted and ready!
[default] Mounting shared folders...
[default] -- /vagrant
```

Vagrant has booted the virtual machine and set up a port forward from a local port on the host to the SSH port on the virtual machine. Vagrant also has a simple vagrant ssh command to connect to the machine—no passwords, no fuss; it "just works." This is demonstrated in Listing 3-20.

Listing 3-20. Logging into the machine

```
PS C:\Users\skrum\Documents> vagrant ssh
Welcome to Ubuntu 12.04.2 LTS (GNU/Linux 3.5.0-23-generic x86_64)

 * Documentation:  https://help.ubuntu.com/
Last login: Mon Oct 21 12:15:04 2013 from 10.0.2.2

vagrant@ubuntu-server-12042-x64-vbox4210:~$
```

We start out logged in as the vagrant user, an unprivileged user. Assume superuser permissions as follows:

```
vagrant@ubuntu-server-12042-x64-vbox4210:~$ sudo -i
```

Configuring Puppet on the Vagrant Box

Next we must inform the client where the Puppet master is. In our example setup, the Puppet master is running on the host machine. It could also be running on a separate, more long-lived virtual machine. What we need to do is alias the name puppet to the IP address of the Puppet master. We will do this by configuring the hosts file of the Vagrant box:

```
root@ubuntu-server-12042-x64-vbox4210:~# echo '192.168.134.131 puppet' >> /etc/hosts
```

Testing Puppet with Vagrant

Next we will perform a Puppet test run in Listing 3-21.

Listing 3-21. Perform a test Puppet run.

```
root@ubuntu-server-12042-x64-vbox4210:~# puppet agent --test
Info: Retrieving plugin
Info: Caching catalog for ubuntu-server-12042-x64-vbox4210.hsd1.or.comcast.net
Info: Applying configuration version '1382954099'
Notice: puppet is running
Notice: /Stage[main]//Node[vbox]/Notify[puppet is running]/message: defined 'message' as
'puppet is running'
Info: Creating state file /var/lib/puppet/state/state.yaml
Notice: Finished catalog run in 0.06 seconds
```

We see that the Puppet manifests ran, and we can look around the filesystem and process table to evaluate our handiwork.

Destroying and Re-Creating the Vagrant Box

The next step in the iterative cycle is to log out of the Vagrant box, destroy it, and create a new one (see Listings 3-22 through 3-24).

Listing 3-22. Logging out of the Vagrant box

```
root@vagrant-ubuntu-precise-64:~# exit
logout
vagrant@vagrant-ubuntu-precise-64:~$ exit
logout
Connection to 127.0.0.1 closed.
```

Listing 3-23. Destroying the Vagrant box

```
PS C:\Users\skrum\Documents> vagrant destroy
Are you sure you want to destroy the 'default' VM? [y/N] y
[default] Forcing shutdown of VM...
[default] Destroying VM and associated drives...
```

Listing 3-24. Creating the Vagrant box anew

```
PS C:\Users\skrum\Documents> vagrant up
Bringing machine 'default' up with 'virtualbox' provider...
[default] Clearing any previously set forwarded ports...
[default] Fixed port collision for 22 => 2222. Now on port 2200.
[default] Creating shared folders metadata...
[default] Clearing any previously set network interfaces...
[default] Preparing network interfaces based on configuration...
[default] Forwarding ports...
[default] -- 22 => 2200 (adapter 1)
[default] Booting VM...
[default] Waiting for machine to boot. This may take a few minutes...
[default] Machine booted and ready!
[default] Mounting shared folders...
[default] -- /vagrant

PS C:\Users\skrum\Documents> vagrant ssh
Welcome to Ubuntu 12.04.2 LTS (GNU/Linux 3.5.0-23-generic x86 64)

 * Documentation:  https://help.ubuntu.com/
Last login: Mon Oct 21 12:15:04 2013 from 10.0.2.2

vagrant@ubuntu-server-12042-x64-vbox4210:~$
```

■ **Note**   You can use a Vagrant snapshotting plug-in like `https://github.com/scalefactory/vagrant-multiprovider-snap` to decrease the time you spend spinning up and down Vagrant boxes.

Automated testing of modules, through the tools `rspec-puppet` and `rspec-system`, is demonstrated in Chapter 8.

Environments

In order to demonstrate environments, we create another host for the Example.com Pty Ltd organization we first introduced in Chapter 1. This new host is called mailtest.example.com and has been introduced to allow Example.com to test changes to their email server without impacting the production mail server. You can see the new node in Figure 3-1.

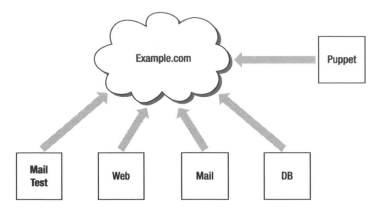

Figure 3-1. *The Example.Com Pty Ltd network*

To get started, we've installed the RedHat Enterprise Linux operating system on mailtest.example.com in order to match the operating system Puppet already manages on mail.example.com. Because we already have configuration to manage the mail.example.com host, we don't need to create any new manifests—we can reuse the existing ones to configure our new mailtest.example.com host.

■ **Note**   This chapter starts to demonstrate the power of Puppet for reusing configuration: rather than starting a new configuration from scratch, we can use existing Puppet manifests to create a new mail server.

Maintenance of Modules

In a typical production setup your modules will be placed in a version control system. How exactly you do this is up to you, but there are two competing popular models. Both of them have merits.

- The first method is to have each module be its own repository.

- The second method is to have a single repository for the entire modules/ directory.

Tools for External Modules

If you're going to be reusing modules from external sources (and you probably should), there are several tools that you should know about.

The first is called Puppet-Librarian. It will download a module from the Puppet Forge, calculate all the dependencies, and then install those in your modules/ directory as well. This sometimes creates problems, which is why r10k was created.

R10k is like Puppet-Librarian but does not attempt to do such smart behavior. Instead, it leaves you to figure out dependency installation. Many people prefer this tool because of its simplicity and predictable success. Much work has also gone into making r10k a fast tool for deployment. R10k is covered in Chapter 8.

Configuring Puppet Environments

To configure Puppet environments, you need to add them to the Puppet master's configuration. If you add each environment to the Puppet master, then each Puppet agent can request a specific environment when requesting a catalog from the master.

The first step in configuring your Puppet master and agents to use environments is to add a stanza in the /etc/puppet.conf configuration file on the Puppet master for each environment you want to support. Let's do this now, by creating the three environments shown in Listing 3-25.

Listing 3-25. Puppet master environments in puppet.conf

```
[production]
 modulepath = $confdir/modules
 manifest = $confdir/manifests/site.pp

[development]
 modulepath = $confdir/environments/development/modules
 manifest = $confdir/environments/development/manifests/site.pp

[testing]
 modulepath = $confdir/environments/testing/modules
 manifest = $confdir/environments/testing/manifests/site.pp
```

As you can see, each environment section of the Puppet configuration file defines two settings, modulepath and manifest. The modulepath setting defines the path to the modules that will apply to each environment, and manifest specifies the site.pp file that applies to that environment. Recall from Chapter 1 that site.pp is the file that tells Puppet which configuration to load for our clients. These settings allow each environment to have a distinct set of modules and configuration.

■ **Note**   When setting up environments, you should restart the Puppet master process in order to activate configuration changes. As described in Chapter 1, the restart process depends on how Puppet is installed on the master. Most systems include an init script to accomplish this task.

In Chapters 1 and 2, we introduced you to building modules to store your Puppet configuration. In order to fully utilize environments, your Puppet manifests should be organized into modules. In this chapter, we use the modules we've created to manage our production environment, the production environment defined in Listing 3-25.

Populating the New Environments

Once you've defined the multiple environments on the Puppet master server, you need to populate these new search paths with the Puppet modules and manifests you've already created in production. In the "Version-Controlling Your Modules" section of Chapter 2, our hypothetical company configured Puppet modules using the Git version control system. We'll expand on the file organization and introduce a strategy to manage and migrate changes between Puppet environments.

▓ **Note**   If you have not yet installed Git and would like to do so now, please refer back to the Git installation information in Chapter 2.

We will use Git to make sure each of our three new environments, main (or production), development, and testing, will receive an identical copy of our production environment. The version control system will also allow us to easily keep these three environments synchronized when necessary, while also allowing them to diverge when we want to try out new changes. Three environments with identical modules and manifests will allow us to quickly make changes in the development or testing environment without impacting the production environment. If we're satisfied, we can easily merge the changes into production.

▓ **Note**   Many organizations with multiple people committing changes to the Puppet configuration will benefit from a code review process. Information about the code review process used by the Puppet development community is available at https://github.com/puppetlabs/puppet/blob/master/CONTRIBUTING.md.

In Chapter 2, we initialized the /etc/puppet/modules directory as a Git repository. Once a Git repository exists, it may be cloned one or more times. Once there are multiple clones, changes to any of the repositories may be fetched and merged into any other repository.

Creating a Clone

Let's create a clone of the /etc/puppet/modules Git repository for the development and testing environments now.

First, you need to create the directory structure necessary to contain the new module search path in Listing 3-26.

Listing 3-26. Creating the development and testing environments

```
$ cd /etc/puppet
$ mkdir -p environments/development
$ mkdir -p environments/testing
```

Next, clone the original module repository you created in Chapter 2 into your development environment (Listing 3-27).

Listing 3-27. Copying the code in

```
$ cd /etc/puppet/environments/development
$ git clone ../../modules
Initialized empty Git repository in
/etc/puppet/environments/development/modules/.git/
```

This command makes a new copy of the Git repository, called a "clone," and automatically sets up a reference to the repository we cloned from. This reference, named "origin," refers to the original repository this repository was cloned from. The origin is actually the repository in the production Puppet environment, so you can add another name to be clear when you fetch updates, as shown in Listing 3-28.

Listing 3-28. Working with Git remotes

```
$ cd /etc/puppet/environments/development/modules
$ git remote add production /etc/puppet/modules
$ git remote -v
production       /etc/puppet/modules (fetch)
production       /etc/puppet/modules (push)
```

As you can see, we've added a remote reference to the production environment module repository in the development environment's module repository. This remote reference allows Git to fetch changes.

Similar to the development environment you just set up, you'll also clone the production environment modules into a testing environment in Listing 3-29.

Listing 3-29. Cloning production to a testing environment

```
$ cd /etc/puppet/environments/testing
$ git clone ../../modules
Initialized empty Git repository in
/etc/puppet/environments/testing/modules/.git/
$ cd modules
$ git remote add production /etc/puppet/modules
$ git remote add development /etc/puppet/environments/development/modules
```

Notice that we've also added the development repository as a remote in the testing environment repository. This will allow you to fetch changes you make in the development repository to the testing repository.

▓ **Tip**   For additional information on a branch-and-merge strategy using environments and Subversion rather than Git, please see `http://projects.puppetlabs.com/projects/1/wiki/Branch_Testing`.

Making Changes to the Development Environment

Now that you have your three environments populated with the same Puppet modules, you can make changes without affecting the production environment. We're going to use a basic workflow of editing and committing changes in the development branch first. This mirrors the common development life cycle of moving from development to testing and finally to production.

We'll start by running a Puppet agent in the development environment to test the change we've made. Then, if everything goes well in the development environment, you can merge this change into testing or production.

▓ **Tip**   In large Puppet setups where changes from multiple groups of people need to be managed, it is common to run a selection of hosts against the testing environment. Periodically, the production environment repository will be synchronized against the testing environment.

We're going to edit the `postfix` configuration file template we created in Chapter 2 to explore how Puppet isolates the three environments we've created. We'll edit the file `main.cf.erb` in the development environment and then run the Puppet agent in this environment to see the change. We'll also run the Puppet agent in the `production` environment, which we have not changed yet, and make sure our changes do not have any effect on it.

To start, edit the file init.pp in /etc/puppet/environments/development/modules/postfix/manifests/ using your favorite text editor and add a new line at the very top of the file so that it looks like Listing 3-30.

Listing 3-30. Syntax error in Puppet code

```
This is a syntax error, since it is clearly not puppet code.

class postfix {
  include postfix::install
  include postfix::config
  include postfix::service
}
```

The line at the top is an error because it is just plain English, not Puppet code.

Now that you've made a change to the development environment, Git will let you know that the status of the repository has changed, as shown in Listing 3-31.

Listing 3-31. Using git to show status

```
$ git status
# On branch master
# Changed but not updated:
#   (use "git add <file>..." to update what will be committed)
#   (use "git checkout -- <file>..." to discard changes in working
directory)
#
#       modified:    init.pp
#
no changes added to commit (use "git add" and/or "git commit -a")
```

Git has noticed that you've made a change to the main.cf.erb file and tells you this on the modified line. As you learned in Chapter 2, we must add files changed in the working directory to the index, and then commit the index to the repository. Before you do this, you should double-check to make sure the line you modified is what will be added in the new commit (Listing 3-32).

Listing 3-32. Using git to show a diff

```
$ git diff
diff --git a/postfix/manifests/init.pp b/postfix/manifests/init.pp
index 3331237..2be61e0 100644
--- a/postfix/manifests/init.pp
+++ b/postfix/manifests/init.pp
@@ -1,3 +1,4 @@
+This is a syntax error, since it is clearly not puppet code.

class postfix {
  include postfix::install
  include postfix::config
```

Notice the line beginning with the single plus sign. This indicates that you've added one line and this addition will be recorded when we commit the change, as we will with the git commit command in Listing 3-33.

Listing 3-33. Commiting changes (checking in)

```
$ git commit -a -m 'Updated postfix class'
[master 0fb0463] Updated postfix class
 1 files changed, 1 insertions(+), 1 deletions(-)
```

You've now successfully changed the development environment. But before testing the change on our mailtest.example.com system, let's review the environment configuration changes you've made to the Puppet master.

- puppet.conf on the master now contains a development and testing section.

- The Puppet master process has been restarted to activate the change to puppet.conf.

- You updated modulepath and manifest in the development and testing section.

You cloned the modules VCS repository to /etc/puppet/environments/{testing,development}/modules.

- You updated the postfix module and committed the change to the development repository.

Testing the New Environments with the Puppet Agent

Now that you have multiple environments configured on the Puppet master system and have made a change to the development environment, you're able to test this change using the Puppet agent. In order to tell Puppet to use an environment other than production, use the environment configuration parameter or command line option:

```
# puppet agent --noop --test --environment=testing
```

▓ **Tip**   Up through Puppet 3.0, the Puppet configuration on a node configures the environment that the node uses. The Puppet master does not directly control which environment a machine connects to. This may change in the future once issue #2834 is resolved; please watch http://projects.puppetlabs.com/issues/2834 for up-to-date information. If you would like to manage the environment from the Puppet master, we recommend having Puppet manage the node's puppet.conf file and specify the environment parameter in the managed configuration file. After the bug is resolved, it will be possible to set environments using an external node classifier (more on those later) or a Puppet master.

Running the Puppet agent on mailtest.example.com in the testing environment should produce the same results as running the agent in the production environment.

▓ **Tip**   We recommend developing a habit of testing changes to Puppet using the --noop command-line option. As mentioned in Chapter 1, the --noop option tells Puppet to check the current state of the system against the configuration catalog, but does it not manage the resources on the node. This provides a safe way to determine if Puppet is going to make a change. It's also a unique feature of Puppet, unavailable in other tools.

You can switch between the production and testing environments by simply removing the environment command-line option. The default environment is production (defined in the main stanza in the puppet.conf file); therefore, you need only leave the environment unspecified to switch back to the production environment:

```
# puppet agent --noop --test
```

Notice that no resources are changing when switching between the two environments. This is because the testing environment is a clone of the production environment, and you have not made any changes to either of these two environments. In the last section, however, you made a change to the postfix module in the development environment, and we expect the Puppet agent to update the main.cf configuration file for postfix with this change.

Let's check the development environment in Listing 3-34.

Listing 3-34. Testing changes in the development environment

```
# puppet agent --noop --test --environment=development
err: Could not retrieve catalog from remote server: Error 400 on SERVER:
Error: Syntax error at 'is' at /etc/puppet/environments/development/modules/postfix/manifests/init.pp:1 on
 node mailtest.example.com/config.pp:17

warning: Not using cache on failed catalog
err: Could not retrieve catalog; skipping run
```

Unlike the testing and production environments we ran the Puppet agent in, this run in the development environment resulted in an error. Such a bad error, in fact, that we didn't even receive a valid configuration catalog from the Puppet master. What happened?

Notice that the error message returned by the Puppet master provides the exact line number in the manifest where the error occurred. The Puppet parser is choking on the nonsense we wrote into the beginning of the postfix init.pp class. If we run the Puppet agent against the production environment, we can see in Listing 3-35 that everything is still OK.

Listing 3-35. Verifying that the production environment is stable

```
# puppet agent --test --noop
...
notice: Finished catalog run in 0.68 seconds
```

Let's go back and fix the problem with the postfix class by removing the nonsense at the top. As you can see in Listing 3-36, we've fixed the problem in the first line of the file.

Listing 3-36. Git diff of the fix

```
diff --git a/postfix/manifests/init.pp b/postfix/manifests/init.pp
index 3331237..241b4bb 100644
--- a/postfix/manifests/init.pp
+++ b/postfix/manifests/init.pp
@@ -1,3 +1,4 @@
+#The main postfix class

class postfix {
  include postfix::install
  include postfix::config
  include postfix::service
```

This `git` output shows that we changed the top line to be a documentation comment.

Now, when we run Puppet agent in the development environment, we're no longer getting the error:

```
# puppet agent --test --noop --environment=development
```

This verification step allowed us to make changes and test them in an isolated environment without impacting Puppet nodes that have their agent running against the production environment. Now that you're confident our change will not break production, you can commit the changes as shown in Listing 3-37.

Listing 3-37. Commiting changes to git

```
$ git add
/etc/puppet/environments/development/modules/postfix/manifests/init.pp
$ git commit -m 'Addeddocs comment to postfix class..'
Created commit d69bc30: Added docs comment to postfix class.
 1 files changed, 2 insertions(+), 1 deletions(-)
```

In the next section, we examine the workflow of merging changes like this into the testing and production environments. This workflow helps teams of developers and system administrators work together while making changes to the system, without impacting production systems, through the use of Puppet environments.

Environment Branching and Merging

As you saw in the previous section, configuring multiple environments in Puppet requires three things:

- Modifying the Puppet configuration file on the Puppet master

- Populating the directories specified in the modulepath

- Maintaining a set of version control working copies in each of those directories

One of the key benefits of version control systems is the ability to manage and organize the contributions from a group of people. In this section, we'll explore how a group of people may use Puppet environments, version control, and the concept of a *branch* to effectively coordinate and manage their changes to the configuration system. Branches are lines of independent development in a repository that share a common history. A branch could be a copy of our development environment with changes made to it; it shares a common history with the development environment but has a history of its own, too. Branches allow multiple people to maintain copies of an environment, work on them independently, and potentially combine changes between branches or back into the main line of development.

Expanding on our hypothetical company, imagine we have a small team of people working together: a system administrator, a developer, and an operator. In this exercise, we'll explore how this team effectively makes changes that do not impact one another, can be merged into the main development and testing branch, and ultimately make their way to the production infrastructure.

Setting Up a Central Repository

Before the small group is able to work together in harmony, you'll need to make a few slight changes to the version control system. Git is unique compared to other version control systems, such as Subversion, in that each repository stands apart and is complete without the need to perform a checkout from a central repository. When working with a team, however, it is convenient to have a central place to store and track changes over time.

In this section, you'll clone a copy of the /etc/puppet/modules repository into /var/lib/puppet/git/modules.git and use this location as the "central" repository. It is central by convention only; there is technically nothing different about the repository that makes it any different from the other Git repositories we've been working with in this chapter.

Once you have a repository designated as the central location, everyone will clone this repository and submit their changes back to it for review and testing. Let's go through this process now. Using a bare Git repository on the Puppet master is less than ideal for production use. It is recommended that you use a Git server such as Gitolite. However, a bare Git repository provides all the essential ingredients for our demonstration of the iterative development process using Puppet.

Creating a Bare Repository for the Modules

First, you need to create a "bare" repository containing your Puppet modules (Listing 3-38). A bare repository in Git is a repository with a history of commits, but no working copy. We want to create a bare repository to help make sure files aren't accidentally directly modified in the central location. Modifications should only happen through commits pushed to this location. We're going to perform these steps as the Puppet user, who is usually running as puppet, in order to help ensure that file permissions and ownership remain consistent when different users are modifying the repository.

Listing 3-38. Creating a central repository for Git

```
$ cd /var/lib/puppet
$ mkdir git
$ chown puppet:puppet git
$ sudo -H -u puppet -s
$ cd /var/lib/puppet/git
$ git clone --bare /etc/puppet/modules modules.git
Initialized empty Git repository in /var/lib/puppet/git/modules.git/
```

■ **Note** We recommend storing the central version control repository in the home directory of the Puppet user to start. This may vary from system to system, and it may not be /var/lib/puppet on your platform.

Making Individual Changes

Once you have a central repository, it's time for everyone in the group to check out their own personal copies to work on. We recommend they do this in their home directories. Changes will be made there and submitted to the central repository for review.

In small environments with few administrators, especially test environments where people are still getting used to Puppet and Git, the workflow just outlined can be performed. The workflow is essentially this:

1. Clone the Puppet repository from the central repository.

2. Make changes and then push a testing branch to the central repository.

3. Change directory to the development environment and check out the branch from the central repository.

4. Run puppet --test --environment=development on a test machine.

5. Repeat steps 2-4 until good code is produced.

6. Merge branch into master with local clone, push to central repository.

7. Change directory to the production environment and checks out the master branch.

■ **Tip** To help prevent typographical errors from being accepted into the repository, it is a good idea to execute `puppet parser validate` as a precommit hook in your version control system. Most version control systems support hook scripts to accept or deny a commit. If you use Subversion or Git, example precommit hooks are available online at `http://projects.puppetlabs.com/projects/1/wiki/Puppet_Version_Control`. The `puppet-lint` command can also be run at this time.

Dynamic Puppet Environments with Git Branches

Puppet environments are a powerful tool for rapidly testing changes to Puppet code. There is a way to dynamically create them via post-receive hook in your version control system. A post-receive hook is a simple program or shell script that runs on the Git server after a successful push has been performed. A new workflow is created from this:

1. Clone the puppet repository from a central repository.

2. Make changes, and then push a testing branch named `feature1`.

3. The Git server fires off a post-receive hook that takes the following action:

   a. Create a new folder `/etc/puppet/environments/feature1`.

   b. Perform a Git clone of the central repository in the folder `feature1`.

   c. Check out the branch `feature1`.

4. Go to a test machine and issue `puppet --test --environment=feature1`.

5. Repeat steps 2–4 until good code is produced.

6. Merge the branch `feature1` into the master, and push it to the Git server.

7. The Git server fires off the same post-receive hook, which now detects it is updating an environment and performs only an update.

This workflow looks very similar to the previous one, but with the creation of environments being done by a script. The key optimization is that all Git branches that aren't master/production are testing branches. There is no time spent moving a code base into a testing environment; it's automatically put into one whenever you push. The Git hook is clever enough to know when to create a new environment, when to update one, and when to delete one once it's no longer needed. This means that the full power of the branch, develop, test, and merge model of modern coding can be brought to bear on your Puppet code repository. The manual testing environment workflow is tedious and error-prone, whereas dynamic Git environments are all created automatically and by experimentally vetted procedural code.

The first step in configuring this is to further modify the Puppet master's `puppet.conf` file to look like Listing 3-39. You can safely remove the `[production]` stanza now.

Listing 3-39. Setting up dynamic environments in puppet.conf

```
[main]
modulepath=/etc/puppet/environments/$environment/modules/
manifest=/etc/puppet/environments/$environment/manifests/site.pp
```

Here we have used the $environment variable, which expands out to the name of the environment. Because we have a clone of our Puppet repository in a directory under environments, this will work perfectly. The environment production is the default environment and will be the environment that minimally configured nodes will check-in under. This means that you should run the master branch of your Git repository under the name production. To accomplish this, navigate to the top of the bare repo on your Git server and make the changes specified in Listing 3-40.

Listing 3-40. Setting default branch to production on the central repository

```
root@pro-puppet:puppet.git# ls
HEAD            config          hooks           info            objects         packed-refs     refs

root@pro-puppet4:~# cat HEAD
ref: refs/heads/master

root@pro-puppet4:~# echo "ref: refs/heads/production" > HEAD

root@pro-puppet4:~# cat HEAD
ref: refs/heads/production
```

This change will make fresh clones and pulls use the production branch by default.

If you are using Hiera and the YAML back-end, whose configuration and use will be covered in Chapter 12, you will have to make a choice. In some cases you may want one Hiera directory for all environments; in others you may want to have per-environment Hiera directories. In the latter case, it is common to have a data directory within your Puppet manifest Git repository. There are a number of approaches to implementing that strategy. The most direct is to put your Hiera YAML files under Git in a directory called data. Other popular (but more complex) methods include using a second Git repository only for Hiera files and using either git subtree or git submodule to attach it to the Puppet manifest Git repository. In this example we will assume that you are using Hiera files that are directly available in the Puppet manifests Git repository. The hiera.yaml configuration looks very similar to the puppet.conf configuration and is shown in Listing 3-41.

Listing 3-41. Hiera configuration for dynamic environments

```
---
:backends:
  - yaml
  - file

:hierarchy:
  - environments/%{::environment}/data/fqdn/%{::fqdn}
  - environments/%{::environment}/data/osfamily/%{::osfamily}/common
  - environments/%{::environment}/data/common

:yaml:
  :datadir: /etc/puppet/

:file:
  :datadir: /etc/puppet/
```

Hiera configuration will be covered in more detail in Chapter 12.

The Git Hook

We will need to create a post-receive hook. The Computer Action Team (CAT) at Portland State University is where the original implementation of Git dynamic environments was developed. They have a two-component hook on GitHub for anyone to use. A small shell script serves as the post-receive hook and uses SSH to log into the Puppet master to run the second component of the hook. We will need to set up ssh-key auth in two directions. The Git user on the Git server will need to be able to ssh to the Puppet master as the Puppet user, and the Puppet user on the Puppet master will need read access to all branches of the Puppet manifests Git repository. Having accomplished this, let's install the two component hook in Listing 3-42.

Listing 3-42. Installing a Puppet hook

```
root@pro-puppet:~# cd /tmp/
root@pro-puppet:/tmp# git clone https://github.com/pdxcat/puppet-sync.git
root@pro-puppet:/tmp# ls
puppet-sync
root@pro-puppet:/tmp# cd puppet-sync/
root@pro-puppet:/tmp/puppet-sync# ls
README.textile  extra  post-receive  puppet-sync
root@pro-puppet:/tmp/puppet-sync# cd ~git/repositories/puppet.git
root@pro-puppet:~git/repositories/puppet.git# ls
HEAD        config       hooks       info       objects      packed-refs      refs
root@pro-puppet:~git/repositories/puppet.git# cp /tmp/puppet-sync/post-receive hooks/post-receive
root@pro-puppet:~git/repositories/puppet.git# scp puppet-sync puppet@puppemaster:/usr/local/bin/
puppet-sync
```

With all the files in place, bounce the Puppet master to reread puppet.conf and make an attempt to push a testing branch in Listing 3-43.

Listing 3-43. Testing the Puppet hook

```
dev@machine:~/puppet$ ls
data            extras         manifests       modules
dev@machine:~/puppet$ git co -b testing_environment
Switched to a new branch 'testing_environment'
dev@machine:~/puppet$ git push origin testing_environment
Total 0 (delta 0), reused 0 (delta 0)
remote: Trying puppet@puppetmaster
remote: .------------------------------------------------ PuppetSync ---
remote: | Host        : promaster.example.com
remote: | Branch      : testing_environment
remote: | Deploy To   : /etc/puppet/environments/testing_environment
remote: | Repository  : git@gitserver.example.com:puppet.git
remote: `-----------------------------------------------------------
```

If everything went well, you can run Puppet against this new environment, as shown in Listing 3-44.

Listing 3-44. Testing the dynamic environment using a Puppet client

```
root@pro-puppet-client# puppet agent --test --environment=testing_environment
Info: Retrieving plugin
Info: Loading facts in ...
....
```

```
Info: Caching catalog for pro-puppet-client.example.com
Info: Applying configuration version '1367388457'
Notice: Finished catalog run in 19.36 seconds
```

One common error is that displayed when you test against an environment that doesn't exist, as shown in Listing 3-45.

Listing 3-45. The error Puppet gives when a client connects to an environment that doesn't exist

```
root@pro-puppet-client# puppet agent --test --environment=testing_environ
Info: Retrieving plugin
Error: /File[/var/lib/puppet/lib]: Could not evaluate: Could not retrieve information from
environment testing_environ source(s) puppet://puppetmaster.example.com/plugins
Notice: /File[/var/lib/puppet/lib/puppet]: Dependency File[/var/lib/puppet/lib] has failures: true
Warning: /File[/var/lib/puppet/lib/puppet]: Skipping because of failed dependencies
Notice: /File[/var/lib/puppet/lib/puppet/provider]: Dependency File[/var/lib/puppet/lib] has
failures: true
Warning: /File[/var/lib/puppet/lib/puppet/provider]: Skipping because of failed dependencies
Notice: /File[/var/lib/puppet/lib/puppet/provider/database_user]: Dependency
File[/var/lib/puppet/lib] has failures: true
Warning: /File[/var/lib/puppet/lib/puppet/provider/database_user]: Skipping because of failed dependencies
Notice: /File[/var/lib/puppet/lib/puppet/provider/database_user/mysql.rb]: Dependency
File[/var/lib/puppet/lib] has failures: true
```

You should learn to recognize this error, because it is both common and nonobvious.

Once the Git dynamic environment methodology is in place, you and your team can branch and merge as well. Getting tested code into production is as easy as merging a test branch into production and pushing up to the Git server. PuppetSync is even smart enough to handle forced pushes and rebases!

Summary

You've seen how Puppet environments enable a team of contributors to work effectively and efficiently. Puppet environments, combined with a modern version control system, enable teams to make changes simultaneously and in parallel without obstructing each other's work. The process a single team member may follow in order to make changes is summarized here:

1. Develop changes in a local topic branch.

2. Rebase against the master branch to remove any unnecessary commits.

3. Publish the topic branch to the central repository, creating a dynamic environment.

4. Try the changes using puppet agent --test --environment.

5. Merge to production and push; the code is now live!

Resources

- Debian stable, testing, unstable releases and distributions:
  http://www.debian.org/doc/FAQ/ch-ftparchives.en.html

- Puppet Labs environments curated documentation:
  http://docs.puppetlabs.com/guides/environment.html

CHAPTER 4

■ ■ ■

Scaling Puppet

You've seen that the Puppet agent and master require very little work to get up and running on a handful of nodes using the default configuration. It is, however, a significantly more involved undertaking to scale Puppet to handle hundreds of nodes. Yet many installations are successfully using Puppet to manage hundreds, thousands, and tens of thousands of nodes. In this chapter, we cover a number of proven strategies that are employed to scale Puppet.

- You'll see how to enable a single Puppet master system to handle hundreds of nodes using the Apache web server.

- We also demonstrate how to configure more than one Puppet master system to handle thousands of nodes using a load balancer.

- Throughout, we make a number of recommendations to help you avoid the common pitfalls related to performance and scalability.

- We will demonstrate a masterless Puppet configuration, in which each node has a full checkout of the puppet code and runs puppet apply locally, usually via cron. This approach enables infinite scalability and redundancy; the nodes no longer share any single bottleneck.

- Finally, you'll learn how to measure the performance of the Puppet master infrastructure in order to determine when it's time to add more capacity. We also provide two small scripts to avoid the "thundering-herd effect" and to measure catalog compilation time.

First, though, we to need review some of the challenges you'll be facing along the way.

Identifying the Challenges

Earlier in the book, you learned a bit about Puppet's client-server configuration and the use of SSL to secure connections between the agent and the master. Puppet uses SSL, specifically the HTTPS protocol, to communicate. As a result, when we're scaling Puppet we are in fact scaling a web service, and many of the problems (and the solutions) overlap with those of traditional web scaling. Consequently, the two challenges we're going to need to address when scaling Puppet are these:

- Scaling the transport

- Scaling SSL

The first challenge requires that we increase the performance and potential number of possible master and agent connections. The second requires that we implement good management of the SSL certificates that secure the connection between the master and the agent. Both challenges require changes to Puppet's out-of-the-box configuration.

In Chapter 1 we started the Puppet Master using the puppet master command. The default Puppet Master configuration makes use of the Webrick Ruby-based HTTP server. Puppet ships Webrick to eliminate the need to set up a web server like Apache to handle HTTPS requests immediately. While the Webrick server provides quick and easy testing, it does not provide a scalable solution and should not be used except to evaluate, test, and develop Puppet installations. In production situations, a more robust web server such as Apache or Nginx is necessary to handle the number of client requests. Therefore, the first order of business when scaling Puppet is to replace the default Webrick HTTP server. In the following section, we first replace Webrick with the Apache web server on a single Puppet master system and then show how this strategy can be extended to multiple Puppet master systems working behind a load balancer.

The second change to Puppet's out-of-the-box configuration is the management of the SSL certificates that Puppet uses to secure the connection between agent and master. The Puppet master stores a copy of every certificate issued, along with a revocation list. This information needs to be kept in sync across the Puppet worker nodes. So, together with the transport mechanism between the agent and master, we'll explore the two main options of handling SSL certificates in a scalable Puppet deployment:

- Using a single Certificate Authority (CA) Puppet master
- Distributing the same CA across multiple Puppet masters

Running the Puppet Master with Apache and Passenger

The first scaling example we're going to demonstrate is the combination of the Apache web server with a module called Phusion Passenger, which is also known as mod_rails, mod_passenger, or just Passenger. Passenger is an Apache module that allows the embedding of Ruby applications, much as mod_php or mod_perl allow the embedding of PHP and Perl applications. The Passenger module is not a standard module that ships with Apache web server and, as a result, must be installed separately. Passenger is available as a RubyGem package, or it may be downloaded and installed from http://www.modrails.com/. In some distributions, Passenger may be available from packages. We will discuss installing Passenger in depth.

For networks of one to two thousand Puppet-managed nodes, a single Puppet master system running inside Apache with Passenger is often sufficient. Later in this chapter, we will examine how to run multiple Puppet master systems to provide high availability or support for an even larger number of Puppet-managed nodes. These more complex configurations will all build on the basic Apache and Passenger configuration we introduce to you here. We will also build upon the Puppet master configuration we created in Chapter 2 and the environment structure we introduced in Chapter 3.

First, you need to install Apache and Passenger, and then configure Apache to handle the SSL authentication and verification of the Puppet agent, and finally connect Apache to the Puppet master and ensure that everything is working as expected.

As we scale Puppet up, it is important to draw the distinction between the idea of a front-end HTTP request handler and a back-end Puppet master worker process. The front-end request handler is responsible for accepting the TCP connection from the Puppet agent, selecting an appropriate back-end worker, routing the request to the worker, accepting the response, and finally serving it back to the Puppet agent. This distinction between a front-end request handler and a back-end worker process is a common concept when scaling web services.

Installing Apache and Passenger

To get started, you need to install Apache and Passenger. Both are relatively simple and easy to set up.

Installing Apache and Passenger on Debian/Ubuntu LTS

Installing a Puppet master on Debian/Ubuntu is trivial because Puppet Labs supplies a package from its apt.puppetlabs.com repository to do all the work.

First, set up the apt.puppetlabs.com repository as described in Chapter 1. Second, install the puppetlabs-passenger package:

```
root@pro-puppet-master:~# apt-get install puppetmaster-passenger
```

This will install all the dependencies and set up your Puppet master for use. You can copy your modules and manifests from earlier chapters into /etc/puppet. The package has created a certificate authority for you by detecting the machine's fully qualified domain name (FQDN) and has started the service. Somewhat confusingly, the Puppet master is controlled through the service apache2, so for instance restarting the Puppet master looks like this:

```
root@pro-puppet-master:~# service apache2 restart
```

■ **Note** When you revoke a certificate on the Puppet master, it won't take effect until Apache is restarted. This is because Apache only reads the CRL (Certificate Revocation List) file on startup. When debugging certificate and SSL errors anywhere in the Puppet toolchain, it is a good idea to restart Apache frequently, because it does a lot of certificate caching.

If appropriate, disable the Webrick server:

```
root@pro-puppet-master-ubuntu:~# update-rc.d -f puppetmaster remove
```

Installing Apache and Passenger on Enterprise Linux

Precompiled Passenger packages may not be available for your platform, however, making configuration a little more complex. This section covers the installation of Apache and Passenger on the Enterprise Linux family of systems such as CentOS, RedHat Enterprise Linux, and Oracle Enterprise Linux.

Begin by installing the Puppet Labs yum repository, as explained in Chapter 1. Then install the puppet-server package. Also run puppet-master once to generate all necessary certificates. Finally disable the Puppet Webrick server. Listing 4-1 summarizes the setup sequence.

Listing 4-1. Initial Puppet master setup on Enterprise Linux

```
[root@pro-puppet-master-centos ~]# yum install puppet-server
[root@pro-puppet-master-centos ~]# puppet master
[root@pro-puppet-master-centos ~]# pgrep -lf puppet
725 /usr/bin/ruby /usr/bin/puppet master
[root@pro-puppet-master-centos ~]# ls /etc/init.d/puppet*
puppet           puppetmaster  puppetqueue
[root@pro-puppet-master-centos ~]# /etc/init.d/puppet stop
Stopping puppet agent:                                     [FAILED]
[root@pro-puppet-master-centos ~]# /etc/init.d/puppetmaster stop
Stopping puppetmaster:                                     [  OK  ]
[root@pro-puppet-master-centos ~]# /etc/init.d/puppetqueue stop
Stopping puppet queue:                                     [FAILED]
[root@pro-puppet-master-centos ~]# chkconfig puppetmaster off
```

■ **Note** The `failed` messages in the output simply mean those services were off to begin with. Turning them off here is just for clarity to the reader. Puppet Queue is legacy and should always be off.

In Listing 4-1, we've used the yum command to ensure that Apache and the Apache SSL libraries are installed. We've also ensured that the Apache service is not currently running. The next step is to obtain Passenger, which is implemented as an Apache-loadable module, similar to mod_ssl or mod_perl. Listing 4-2 shows the steps.

Listing 4-2. Installing Apache on Enterprise Linux

```
[root@pro-puppet-master-centos ~]# puppet resource package httpd ensure=present
Notice: /Package[httpd]/ensure: created
package { 'httpd':
  ensure => '2.2.15-28.el6.centos',
}

[root@pro-puppet-master-centos ~]# puppet resource package mod_ssl ensure=present
Notice: /Package[mod_ssl]/ensure: created
package { 'mod_ssl':
  ensure => '2.2.15-28.el6.centos',
}

[root@pro-puppet-master-centos ~]# puppet resource service httpd ensure=stopped
service { 'httpd':
  ensure => 'stopped',
}
```

In order to install Passenger on our Enterprise Linux system, we need to install it from RubyGems. This is not the only way to install Passenger, but it is the recommended way at this time. First install RubyRems from packages, as shown in Listing 4-3.

Listing 4-3. Install the rubygems, rack, and passenger packages

```
[root@pro-puppet-master-centos ~]# puppet resource package rubygems ensure=present
package { 'rubygems':
  ensure => '1.3.7-1.el6',
}

[root@pro-puppet-master-centos ~]# puppet resource package rack ensure=present provider=gem
Notice: /Package[rack]/ensure: created
package { 'rack':
  ensure => ['1.5.2'],
}

[root@pro-puppet-master-centos ~]# puppet resource package passenger ensure=present provider=gem
Notice: /Package[passenger]/ensure: created
package { 'passenger':
  ensure => ['4.0.5'],
}
```

■ **Note** In Listing 4-3 we've added another parameter to the `puppet resource` commands: we're using the `gem` provider to install a package from RubyGems. This selection of which provider to use is one of the very powerful features of Puppet and one of the features that distinguishes it from other tools. Provider selection is automatic on most systems; that is, Puppet will default to using the `yum` provider on RedHat systems, but if you want to install a gem from RubyGems, you must manually specify which provider you want to use. There are package providers for all the major dynamic languages' package archives: pip for Python and CPAN for Perl, for example. There are a couple of modules on the Puppet Forge that bring support for an NPM provider into Puppet. Provider selection comes into play for other types as well; for example, the user type can be managed either by `useradd`, which is the default, or by hitting LDAP. There are some caveats to using the `gem` provider, namely that the provider is nonfunctional until the `rubygems` package is installed from system packages (or a functional `gem` binary is placed in the path by some other method, such as RVM or source).

Installing from Gems requires that we compile and install the actual Apache module. The RubyGem includes a script to make this very easy:

```
[root@pro-puppet-master-centos ~]# passenger-install-apache2-module
```

The output of the `passenger-install-apache2-module` script is quite long and has been omitted. The script is mostly friendly and is happy to suggest additional packages to install in order to enable correct compilation. For additional information and troubleshooting tips related to installing Passenger using RubyGems, please see:

```
http://www.modrails.com/documentation/Users%20guide%20Apache.html
```

Often installing Passenger dependencies essentially boils down to the following:

```
 [root@pro-puppet-master-centos ~]# yum install curl-devel ruby-devel httpd-devel
apr-devel apr-util-devel
```

■ **Tip** Up-to-date information about Passenger versions known to work with Puppet (and updated installation documentation) is available online at `http://docs.puppetlabs.com/guides/passenger.html`.

Configuring Apache and Passenger

Again, if you haven't already done so, make sure you've started the Puppet master at least once to create the SSL certificates you're going to configure Apache to use. Apache will then verify that the Puppet agent certificate is signed with the generated Puppet CA and present a certificate that the Puppet agent uses to verify the authenticity of the server. Once you have your SSL certificates in place, configure Apache by enabling the Passenger module and creating an Apache virtual host for the Puppet master service. The virtual host configures Apache to listen on TCP port 8140 and to encrypt all traffic using SSL and the certificates generated for use with the Puppet master. The virtual host also configures Passenger to use the system's Ruby interpreter, and it provides the path to the Rack configuration file named `config.ru` (Listing 4-4).

Listing 4-4. The Apache Passenger and Puppet master vhost example configuration file

```
[root@pro-puppet-master-centos ~]# cat /etc/httpd/conf.d/passenger.conf
LoadModule passenger_module /usr/lib/ruby/gems/1.8/gems/passenger-4.0.10/buildout/apache2/mod_passenger.so
PassengerRoot /usr/lib/ruby/gems/1.8/gems/passenger-4.0.10
PassengerRuby /usr/bin/ruby

# And the passenger performance tuning settings:
PassengerHighPerformance On
# Set this to about 1.5 times the number of CPU cores in your master:
PassengerMaxPoolSize 6
# Recycle master processes after they service 1000 requests
PassengerMaxRequests 1000
# Stop processes if they sit idle for 10 minutes
PassengerPoolIdleTime 600

Listen 8140
<VirtualHost *:8140>
    SSLEngine On

    # Only allow high security cryptography. Alter if needed for compatibility.
    SSLProtocol             All -SSLv2
    SSLCipherSuite          HIGH:!ADH:RC4+RSA:-MEDIUM:-LOW:-EXP
    SSLCertificateFile      /var/lib/puppet/ssl/certs/pro-puppet-master-centos.pem
    SSLCertificateKeyFile   /var/lib/puppet/ssl/private_keys/pro-puppet-master-centos.pem
    SSLCertificateChainFile /var/lib/puppet/ssl/ca/ca_crt.pem
    SSLCACertificateFile    /var/lib/puppet/ssl/ca/ca_crt.pem
    SSLCARevocationFile     /var/lib/puppet/ssl/ca/ca_crl.pem
    SSLVerifyClient         optional
    SSLVerifyDepth          1
    SSLOptions              +StdEnvVars +ExportCertData

    # These request headers are used to pass the client certificate
    # authentication information on to the puppet master process
    RequestHeader set X-SSL-Subject %{SSL_CLIENT_S_DN}e
    RequestHeader set X-Client-DN %{SSL_CLIENT_S_DN}e
    RequestHeader set X-Client-Verify %{SSL_CLIENT_VERIFY}e

    PassengerEnabled On
    DocumentRoot /usr/share/puppet/rack/puppetmasterd/public/
    <Directory /usr/share/puppet/rack/puppetmasterd/>
        Options None
        AllowOverride None
        Order Allow,Deny
        Allow from All
    </Directory>
</VirtualHost>
```

▨ **Tip**   For more information about tuning Passenger, please see http://www.modrails.com/documentation/
Users%20guide%20Apache.html.

This configuration file may appear a little overwhelming, but we're going to go over it and make sure it is correctly configured for your environment.

This file configures two things: mod_passenger and the Puppet virtual host. The configuration here is dependent on using Passenger 4.0.10. You may need to change the LoadModule line to the actual location of mod_passenger.so, and you may need to change the PassengerRoot line as well. Listing 4-5 shows one trick for finding where mod_passenger.so is located, though it will consume some time is to run.

Listing 4-5. Finding mod_passenger.so

```
[root@pro-puppet-master-centos-II ~]# find /usr -name 'mod_passenger.so'
/usr/lib/ruby/gems/1.8/gems/passenger-4.0.10/buildout/apache2/mod_passenger.so
```

If that doesn't work, try the version in Listing 4-6.

Listing 4-6. Finding mod_passenger.so with a larger scope

```
[root@pro-puppet-master-centos-II ~]# find / -name 'mod_passenger.so'
/usr/lib/ruby/gems/1.8/gems/passenger-4.0.10/buildout/apache2/mod_passenger.so
```

Set the PassengerMaxPoolSize to 1.5 times the number of CPU cores on your Puppet master. You can find the number of cores in your computer by running this command:

```
[root@pro-puppet-master-centos-II ~]# facter processorcount
4
```

In particular, the RequestHeader statements are the source of much confusion among Puppet newcomers and veterans alike. When using this configuration file example, make sure to replace pro-puppet-master-centos with the FQDN of your own Puppet master system. The FQDN is easily found with the command shown in Listing 4-7.

Listing 4-7. Find the fully qualified domain name

```
[root@pro-puppet-master-centos-II ~]# facter fqdn.
Pro-puppet-master-centos-II
```

You can also find what the certs are named simply by looking in the /var/lib/puppet/ssl/certs and /var/lib/puppet/ssl/private directories. These certs are created by Puppet the first time it runs in master mode.

The line before the VirtualHost stanza, Listen 8140, makes sure Apache is binding and listening on TCP port 8140, the standard port for a Puppet master server.

Next, the virtual host stanza begins with <VirtualHost *:8140>. Please refer to the Apache version 2.2 configuration reference (http://httpd.apache.org/docs/2.2/) for more information about configuring Apache virtual hosts.

SSL is enabled for the Puppet master–specific virtual host, turning SSLEngine on and setting the SSLCipherSuite parameters. In addition to enabling SSL encryption of the traffic, certificates are provided to prove the identity of the Puppet master service. Next, revocation is enabled using the SSLCARevocationFile parameter. The puppet cert command will automatically keep the ca_crl.pem file updated as we issue and revoke new Puppet agent certificates.

Finally, Apache is configured to verify the authenticity of the Puppet agent certificate. The results of this verification are stored in the environment as a standard environment variable. The Puppet master process running inside Passenger will check the environment variables set by the SSLOptions and StdEnvVars configuration in order to authorize the Puppet agent. In the section immediately following the SSL configuration, the results of verifying the Puppet agent's certificate are stored as client request headers as well as in standard environment variables. Later in this chapter, you'll see how client request headers may be consulted by downstream workers to provide authentication using standard environment variables.

The last section of the Puppet master virtual host is the Rack configuration. Rack provides a common API for web servers to exchange requests and responses with a Ruby HTTP service like Puppet. Rack is commonly used as middleware between a Ruby application like Puppet and a web server like Apache or Nginx. This stanza looks for a special file called config.ru in /usr/share/puppet/rack/puppetmaster (see Listing 4-8).

To install the Rack configuration file, we must first build out the directory structure needed by the Rack application interface:

```
[root@pro-puppet-master-centos-II ~]# mkdir -p /usr/share/puppet/rack/puppetmasterd/{public,tmp}
```

Then create the Rack configuration file config.ru shown in Listing 4-8.

Listing 4-8. Puppet master Rack configuration file

```
[root@pro-puppet-master-centos-II ~]# cat /usr/share/puppet/rack/puppetmasterd/config.ru
# a config.ru, for use with every rack-compatible webserver.
# SSL needs to be handled outside this, though.

# if puppet is not in your RUBYLIB:
# $LOAD_PATH.unshift('/opt/puppet/lib')

$0 = "master"

# if you want debugging:
# ARGV << "--debug"

ARGV << "--rack"

# Rack applications typically don't start as root. Set --confdir and --vardir
# to prevent reading configuration from ~puppet/.puppet/puppet.conf and writing
# to ~puppet/.puppet
ARGV << "--confdir" << "/etc/puppet"
ARGV << "--vardir" << "/var/lib/puppet"

# NOTE: it's unfortunate that we have to use the "CommandLine" class
# here to launch the app, but it contains some initialization logic
# (such as triggering the parsing of the config file) that is very
# important. We should do something less nasty here when we've
# gotten our API and settings initialization logic cleaned up.
#
# Also note that the "$0 = master" line up near the top here is
# the magic that allows the CommandLine class to know that it's
# supposed to be running master.
#
# --cprice 2012-05-22

require 'puppet/util/command_line'
# we're usually running inside a Rack::Builder.new {} block,
# therefore we need to call run *here*.
run Puppet::Util::CommandLine.new.execute
```

Finally, chown the config.ru file to the puppet user:

```
[root@pro-puppet-master-centos-II ~]# chown puppet /usr/share/puppet/rack/puppetmasterd/config.ru
```

▨ **Tip** If you installed Puppet from packages, check your share directory structure for a config.ru example provided by the package maintainer, often located at /usr/share/puppet/ext/rack/files/config.ru. For up-to-date Rack configuration files, check the ext directory in the most recently released version of Puppet. This may be found online at https://github.com/puppetlabs/puppet/tree/master/ext/rack/files.

The config.ru Rack configuration file should be owned by the puppet user and group. Passenger will inspect the owner of this file and switch from the root system account to this less privileged Puppet service account when Apache is started.

APACHE SERVER NAME

In some cases when you are setting up a Puppet master without an FQDN, in Vagrant for testing purposes, for example, it is sometimes necessary to modify the ServerName attribute of /etc/httpd/conf/httpd.conf to be the same as your cert name. If this is the case you will see errors such as this:

```
Starting httpd: httpd: Could not reliably determine the server's fully qualified domain name,
using 127.0.0.1 for ServerName
```

The cert name is the name of the Issuer CA. All x509 certificates have an Issuer. The Common Name (CN) of your CA certificate (as well as lots of other information about your certificate) can be found by running the following openssl command:

```
[root@puppet-master-centos ~]# openssl x509 -in /var/lib/puppet/ssl/certs/puppet-master-1.
pdx.edu.pem -noout -text

...
 Issuer: CN=Puppet CA: puppet-master-1.example.com
...
```

The cert name is the string following CA:

Testing the Puppet Master in Apache

We've covered the steps required to install and configure Apache and Passenger. You're now ready to test your changes by starting the Apache service. Before doing so, make sure to double-check the ownership of the config.ru file. If there is a certificate problem, make sure the existing SSL certificates are configured in the Puppet master Apache virtual host configuration file, as shown in Listing 4-3 earlier in the chapter. You also want to make sure the Puppet master is not already running. To start Apache and the new Puppet master service, you can again use the puppet resource command, as shown in Listing 4-9.

Listing 4-9. Starting Apache

```
# puppet resource service httpd ensure=running enable=true hasstatus=true
service { 'httpd':
    ensure => 'running',
    enable => 'true'
}
```

Running the Puppet agent against the Apache Puppet master virtual host (Listing 4-10) will allow you to test the system:

Listing 4-10. Running Puppet

```
root@pro-puppet4:~# puppet agent --test
Info: Retrieving plugin
Info: Caching catalog for pro-puppet4
Info: Applying configuration version '1373245539'
Notice: /Stage[main]//Node[pro-puppet]/Package[emacs]/ensure: ensure changed 'purged' to 'latest'
Notice: Finished catalog run in 79.57 seconds
```

The Puppet agent does not provide any indication that the Puppet master service has switched from Webrick to Apache. The best way to tell if everything is working is to use to Apache access logs (see Listing 4-11). The Puppet master virtual host will use the combined access logs to record incoming requests from the Puppet agent.

Listing 4-11. Puppet requests in the Apache access logs

```
 [root@pro-puppet-master-centos-II ~]# tail -f /var/log/httpd/access_log
10.0.3.124 - - [07/Jul/2013:21:58:16 -0400] "GET /production/node/pro-puppet4?
HTTP/1.1" 200 3689 "-" "Ruby"
10.0.3.124 - - [07/Jul/2013:21:58:18 -0400] "GET /production/file_metadatas/plugins?
links=manage&recurse=true&&ignore=---+%0A++-+%22.svn%22%0A++-+%22CVS%0A++-+%22.git%22&checksum_type=md5
HTTP/1.1" 200 283 "-" "Ruby"
10.0.3.124 - - [07/Jul/2013:21:58:19 -0400] "POST /production/catalog/pro-puppet4 HTTP/1.1" 200
1239 "-" "Ruby"
10.0.3.124 - - [07/Jul/2013:21:58:20 -0400] "PUT /production/report/pro-puppet4
HTTP/1.1" 200 14 "-" "Ruby"
```

In the access_log file we can see that the Puppet agent issues an HTTP GET request using the URI /production/node/pro-puppet4. We can also see that the Puppet agent sends the list of facts about itself in the request URI. The Puppet master compiles the modules and manifests into a configuration catalog and provides this catalog in the HTTP. The 200 status code indicates that this operation was successful. Following the catalog run, the Puppet agent submits a report using the PUT request to the URI /production/catalog/pro-puppet4. You'll find more information about reports and reporting features in Puppet in Chapter 10.

In addition to the Apache access_log, the Puppet master process itself continues to log information about itself to the system log. This information is available in /var/log/messages on Enterprise Linux based systems and in /var/log/daemon on Ubuntu/Debian systems.

And that's it! You've added an Apache and Passenger front-end to your Puppet master that will allow you to scale to a much larger number of hosts.

Load-Balancing Multiple Puppet Masters

You've replaced the Webrick HTTP server with the Apache web server. Sometimes, though, you need more capacity than a single machine can provide. In this case, you can scale the Puppet master horizontally rather than vertically. Horizontal scaling uses the resources of multiple Puppet masters in a cluster to get more capacity than any one system can provide. This configuration can accommodate environments with tens of thousands of managed nodes.

There are many options and strategies available to provide a front-end request handler. We're going to use HTTP load balancing to direct client requests to available back-end services. Each Puppet master worker is configured independently, using different Apache virtual host configurations bound to different ports on the loopback interface 127.0.0.1. This allows multiple Puppet master workers to be configured and tested on the same operating system instance and easily redistributed to multiple hosts; all you have to do is change the listening IP address and port numbers in the load balancer and worker configuration files.

LOAD BALANCING

For an introduction to the general problem of load balancing and scalable web architectures, we recommend the Wikipedia article titled "Load balancing (computing)" at `http://en.wikipedia.org/wiki/Load_balancing_ (computing)`. In particular, the idea of horizontal and vertical scaling is an important one to consider. The Puppet master scales well both horizontally and vertically, either by adding more systems working in parallel or by increasing the amount of memory and processor resources.

HTTP Load Balancing

The problem of scaling HTTP-based web services to tens of thousands of clients has been around for quite some time. There are many technical solutions provided by commercial products like Citrix NetScaler, Cisco IOS, and F5 BIG-IP. Many open-source software projects also exist, including Apache itself, HAProxy, Nginx, and Pound.

We're going to build upon the single Puppet master configuration we just created and then split the work across two Puppet master systems. We'll use the Apache Web server to handle the incoming Puppet agent requests and route them to an available back-end Puppet master. If we require additional capacity, we can add additional Puppet master processes. This configuration has the added benefit of high availability. If a particular Puppet master system has trouble or needs to be taken out of service, the front-end load balancer will stop routing Puppet agent requests to that master process.

We're going to configure two Puppet master Apache virtual hosts, much like the virtual host we created in the previous section. However, there is one important difference: we will disable SSL for the Apache virtual hosts. Instead, we'll configure a new front-end Apache virtual host to authorize incoming Puppet agent requests and handle the SSL encryption and decryption of the traffic. This front-end load balancer will terminate the SSL connection, authenticate (or not) the Puppet agent request, and then present this authentication information to the back-end Puppet master workers for authorization.

You'll see how Apache is able to pass the authentication information along through the use of client request headers, and how the back-end virtual hosts are able to set environment variables for the Puppet master based on the values of these client request headers.

■ **Caution**   It is important to keep in mind that the load-balancing configuration discussed in this section authorizes and terminates SSL connections at the load balancer. All traffic between the front-end load balancer and the back-end Puppet master system is unencrypted. Requests directly to the worker virtual hosts may easily be forged and should only be allowed from the load balancer. If this is an unacceptable configuration for your environment, consider using a TCP load balancer in order to preserve the SSL encryption and pass it through to the back-end Puppet master virtual hosts. Use of a TCP load balancer will be introduced at the end of the chapter.

Puppet Master Worker Configuration

When the Puppet master is running behind a load balancer, multiple Puppet master processes will be running on different hosts behind the load balancer. The load balancer will listen on the Puppet port of 8140. Incoming requests will be dispatched to available back-end worker processes, as illustrated in Figure 4-1. The example configuration presented in this chapter configures the Puppet CA and workers all on the same host using unique TCP ports bound to the loopback interface.

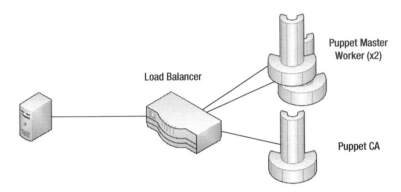

Figure 4-1. *Puppet master workers*

To get started with our load-balancing configuration, you'll copy the existing Puppet master virtual host we configured in the previous section into two additional virtual host configurations. Each of these two virtual hosts will have SSL disabled. You'll then create a third virtual host, listening on the standard Puppet master port of 8140 with SSL enabled. This virtual host will forward a request to any available back-end virtual host. This won't actually provide any performance gains, but it will enable us to separate the concerns of building a functional HTTP proxy for Puppet and building a multi-node Puppet configuration.

■ **Note** Running two Puppet master virtual hosts on the same server is not a recommended configuration. This is meant to simulate running two servers both running Puppet behind a load balancer. Later on in this chapter we'll build that configuration; this is simply a stop-over to build the system in small steps.

First, move aside the existing Puppet master config, /etc/httpd/conf.d/passenger.conf, if you followed the earlier example, so that it does not interfere with our new setup:

```
[root@pupept-master-1 ~]#mv /etc/httpd/conf.d/passenger.conf
/etc/httpd/conf.d/passenger_moved_aside
```

Then, with a clean starting point, we will create the following four files in /etc/httpd/conf.d needed to get a load-balancing Apache setup working:

- passenger.conf, which contains the Passenger configuration.
- puppetmaster_proxy.conf, which will terminate the SSL, rewrite some headers, and proxy/load balance to workers.

- puppetmaster_worker_1.conf, which will contain a virtual host and points to a Rack directory from which to serve Puppet requests.

- puppetmaster_worker_2.conf, which will also contain a virtual host but points to a different Rack configuration directory; this worker also serves Puppet requests.

First, create the file /etc/httpd/conf.d/passenger.conf, where Passenger configuration will be stored. As shown in Listing 4-12, this is a direct copy of what was in the top of our old configuration file.

Listing 4-12. Contents of the new passenger.conf

```
[root@pupept-master-1 ~]#cat /etc/httpd/conf.d/passenger.conf
LoadModule passenger_module /usr/lib/ruby/gems/1.8/gems/passenger-4.0.10/buildout/apache2/mod_
passenger.so
PassengerRoot /usr/lib/ruby/gems/1.8/gems/passenger-4.0.10
PassengerRuby /usr/bin/ruby

# And the passenger performance tuning settings:
PassengerHighPerformance On
# Set this to about 1.5 times the number of CPU cores in your master:
PassengerMaxPoolSize 2
# Recycle master processes after they service 1000 requests
PassengerMaxRequests 1000
# Stop processes if they sit idle for 10 minutes
PassengerPoolIdleTime 600
```

Second, create the file /etc/httpd/conf.d/puppetmaster_proxy.conf where SSL will be terminated and load balancing will be configured. As shown in Listing 4-13, this file again has some of the same configuration as the earlier config, especially relating to the SSL Certificate file paths. Look over it carefully to make sure you have tweaked it for your environment.

Listing 4-13. The puppetmaster_proxy.conf file

```
[root@pupept-master-1 ~]#cat /etc/httpd/conf.d/puppetmaster_proxy.conf
# Available back-end worker virtual hosts
# NOTE the use of cleartext unencrypted HTTP.
<Proxy balancer://puppetmaster>
  BalancerMember http://127.0.0.1:18140
  BalancerMember http://127.0.0.1:18141
</Proxy>

Listen 8140
<VirtualHost *:8140>
    SSLEngine on
    # SSLCipherSuite SSLv2:-LOW:-EXPORT:RC4+RSA
    SSLProtocol -ALL +SSLv3 +TLSv1
    SSLCipherSuite ALL:!ADH:RC4+RSA:+HIGH:+MEDIUM:-LOW:-SSLv2:-EXP
    SSLProtocol          All -SSLv2
    SSLCipherSuite       HIGH:!ADH:RC4+RSA:-MEDIUM:-LOW:-EXP
    # Puppet master should generate initial CA certificate.
    # ensure certs are located in /var/lib/puppet/ssl
    SSLCertificateFile   /var/lib/puppet/ssl/certs/puppet-master-1.pem
    SSLCertificateKeyFile  /var/lib/puppet/ssl/private_keys/puppet-master-1.pem
```

```
SSLCertificateChainFile /var/lib/puppet/ssl/ca/ca_crt.pem
SSLCACertificateFile    /var/lib/puppet/ssl/ca/ca_crt.pem
SSLCARevocationFile     /var/lib/puppet/ssl/ca/ca_crl.pem
# optional to allow CSR request, required if certificates distributed to client during provisioning.
SSLVerifyClient optional
SSLVerifyDepth 1
SSLOptions +StdEnvVars

# The following client headers record authentication information for downstream workers.
RequestHeader set X-SSL-Subject %{SSL_CLIENT_S_DN}e
RequestHeader set X-Client-DN %{SSL_CLIENT_S_DN}e
RequestHeader set X-Client-Verify %{SSL_CLIENT_VERIFY}e

<Location />
  SetHandler balancer-manager
  Order allow,deny
  Allow from all
</Location>

ProxyPass / balancer://puppetmaster/
ProxyPassReverse / balancer://puppetmaster/
ProxyPreserveHost On

</VirtualHost>
```

Third, create the file /etc/httpd/conf.d/puppetmaster_worker_1.conf shown in Listing 4-14, where we will create a worker process.

Listing 4-14. The puppetmaster_worker_1.conf file

```
[root@pupept-master-1 ~]#cat /etc/httpd/conf.d/puppetmaster_worker_1.conf
Listen 18140
<VirtualHost 127.0.0.1:18140>
SSLEngine off

# Obtain Authentication Information from Client Request Headers
SetEnvIf X-Client-Verify "(.*)" SSL_CLIENT_VERIFY=$1
SetEnvIf X-SSL-Client-DN "(.*)" SSL_CLIENT_S_DN=$1

PassengerEnabled On
DocumentRoot /usr/share/puppet/rack/puppetmasterd_18140/public
<Directory  /usr/share/puppet/rack/puppetmasterd_18140>
   Options None
   AllowOverride None
   Order allow,deny
   allow from all
</Directory>
</VirtualHost>
```

Notice that the DocumentRoot has changed. Each Rack application needs a separate Rack directory structure to run in. Since we are putting two Puppet master applications on the same host, to demonstrate load balancing, we need to create directories for each (Listing 4-15).

Listing 4-15. Create directories for two Rack environments

```
[root@pupept-master-1 ~]# mkdir -p /usr/share/puppet/rack/puppetmasterd_18140/{public,tmp}
[root@pupept-master-1 ~]# cp /usr/share/puppet/rack/puppetmasterd/config.ru
/usr/share/puppet/rack/puppetmasterd_18140/config.ru
[root@pupept-master-1 ~]# chown puppet /usr/share/puppet/rack/puppetmasterd_18140/config.ru
```

Here we depend on having a `config.ru` left over from when we initially set up Puppet to run under Passenger. If you did not do that step, create the file as shown in Listing 4-8, earlier in this chapter.

Again it is critical that the `config.ru` file be owned by the puppet user, as this parameter decides which user the Puppet master process runs under.

■ **Caution**   The back-end worker process is listening on the local interface of 127.0.0.1. This prevents network systems from reaching the unencrypted, plain-text back-end worker virtual host. In a production deployment, the back-end virtual host is often on a different machine than the front-end load balancer. Care must be taken to ensure that the unencrypted traffic is secure and protected. In general, the back-end virtual host should not accept connections from any machine other than the front-end load balancer.

Fourth, repeat the steps for step 3, being sure to modify the number 18140 with 18141 everywhere. The file you will create is `/etc/httpd/conf.d/puppetmaster_worker_2.conf`, and you will need to modify four lines inside it, the Listen, Virtualhost, DocumentRoot, and Directory directives.

Front End Load Balancer Configuration Details

After we configure the first back-end Puppet master worker, we need to configure the front-end virtual host. This front-end virtual host is going to perform the following tasks:

1.   Terminate the SSL connection.

2.   Authenticate the client request.

3.   Set the authentication information in client request headers.

4.   Pass the request along to one of the available back-end worker processes.

The configuration file for the front-end load balancer (Listing 4-14) is very similar to the original Apache Passenger configuration file, with the addition of a reverse proxy stanza and the removal of the Passenger and Rack configuration stanzas.

There are three main differences between the front-end load balancer configuration file in Listing 4-14 and the stand-alone Apache Puppet master configuration in Listing 4-4. At the top of the load-balancer virtual host configuration, a pool of back-end virtual hosts is defined in the Proxy stanza. Notice that two virtual hosts are listed, port 18140 and port 18141, even though we have only configured the one listening on port 18140 so far.

Part of the responsibility of the front-end load balancer is to determine if each back-end worker is online and available to handle requests. Since no worker virtual host is available on port 18141 yet, the front-end virtual host will automatically take `http://127.0.0.1:18141` out of rotation until it becomes available. The Puppet agent nodes will not see an error message unless all back-end worker virtual hosts are marked as offline.

In addition to defining the list of back-end worker virtual hosts, the Proxy stanza gives the name `balancer://puppetmaster` to the collection. When additional back-end virtual hosts are added to the system, they should be listed using the `BalancerMember` keyword in the Proxy stanza. Once listed, they'll automatically be added to the rotation of back-end workers used by the front-end virtual host listening on port 8140.

The second important section of the front-end virtual host configuration file is the three RequestHeader lines. These three configuration statements configure the front-end load balancer to set three client request headers containing authentication information. When a back-end Puppet master virtual host receives a client request from the load balancer, it will inspect these client request headers and set environment variables based on their contents. The Puppet master process will look to these environment variables while authorizing the Puppet agent request.

For the Puppet agent running on `mail.pro-puppet.com`, the client request headers used for authentication look as shown in Listing 4-16.

Listing 4-16. Puppet agent authentication and authorization request headers

```
X-SSL-Subject: /CN=mail.pro-puppet..com
X-Client-DN: /CN=mail.pro-puppet.com
X-Client-Verify: SUCCESS
```

The `X-SSL-Subject` and `X-Client-DN` headers contain the same information, the common name from the verified SSL certificate presented by the Puppet agent. This information is provided in two headers to support back-end HTTP servers other than Apache. The `X-Client-Verify` header indicates to the back-end worker whether or not the load balancer was able to verify the authenticity of the client SSL certificate. This value will be SUCCESS in Apache if the client certificate is signed by a trusted CA, is not listed in the Certificate Revocation List, and has not expired.

The information set in the client request headers directly matches the `SetEnvIf` configuration lines configured in the back-end Puppet master virtual host. We can see these lines in `/etc/httpd/conf.d/puppetmaster_worker_1.conf` as we configured them in Listing 4-17.

Listing 4-17. Setting the Apache environment variables

```
# Obtain Authentication Information from Client Request Headers
SetEnvIf X-Client-Verify "(.*)" SSL_CLIENT_VERIFY=$1
SetEnvIf X-SSL-Client-DN "(.*)" SSL_CLIENT_S_DN=$1
```

The authentication information in a load-balanced Puppet master configuration is passed from the load balancer to the back-end workers using client request headers. This design allows heterogeneous front-end and back-end HTTP systems to work together as long as the back-end HTTP server is able to read the Puppet agent certificate common name and determine whether the certificate is currently valid. Once read from the headers, the back-end HTTP server sets this information in two environment variables for Puppet to reference.

The third important section in the front-end load balancer configuration in Listing 4-14 tells Apache to route all requests to the pool of Puppet master virtual hosts. This section is composed of the three lines `ProxyPass`, `ProxyPassReverse`, and `ProxyPreserveHost`. These three statements tell Apache the virtual host listening on port 8140 should forward all Puppet agent requests to the pool of Puppet master workers named `balancer://puppetmaster`.

▓ **Tip** You can find detailed information about `mod_proxy` and additional configuration options online at `http://httpd.apache.org/docs/2.0/mod/mod_proxy.html`.

Testing the Load Balancer Configuration

We're now almost ready to test the new Puppet master configuration using the Puppet agent. Before doing so, you need to make sure each virtual host is logging information in a clearly defined location. This will allow you to trace the Puppet agent request as it passes through the front-end load balancer to the back-end worker virtual host.

To make it easier, let's separate out the logging events for each virtual host by adding ErrorLog and CustomLog configuration options to each configuration file, as shown in Listing 4-18.

Listing 4-18. Configuring front-end logging

```
ErrorLog /var/log/httpd/balancer_error.log
CustomLog /var/log/httpd/balancer_access.log combined
CustomLog /var/log/httpd/balancer_ssl_requests.log "%t %h %{SSL_PROTOCOL}x %{SSL_CIPHER}x \"%r\" %b"
```

Only three lines need to be inserted into the VirtualHost stanza to enable logging on the front end. Every request coming into the Puppet master infrastructure will pass through the front-end virtual host and will be logged to the balancer_access.log file.

Worker virtual hosts do not handle SSL encrypted traffic and require only two configuration lines to be inserted into the VirtualHost stanza. Every request routed to a specific worker will be logged into that worker's access log file. In Listing 4-19, we've included the TCP port number of the worker to uniquely identify the log file and the associated worker.

Listing 4-19. Configuring worker logging

```
ErrorLog /var/log/httpd/puppetmaster_worker_error_1.log
CustomLog /var/log/httpd/puppetmaster_worker_access_1.log combined
.
.
.
ErrorLog /var/log/httpd/puppetmaster_worker_error_2.log
CustomLog /var/log/httpd/puppetmaster_worker_access_2.log combined
```

Once the front-end load balancer and back-end worker virtual hosts have been configured to log to their own log files, you need to restart Apache and makes sure the log files were created properly, as shown in Listing 4-20.

Listing 4-20. Restart Apache and check the /var/log/httpd directory

```
 [root@pupept-master-1 /etc/httpd/conf.d]# service httpd restart
Stopping httpd:                                    [  OK  ]
Starting httpd:                                    [  OK  ]
[root@pupept-master-1 /var/log/httpd]# ls -l {balancer,puppetmaster}*.log
-rw-r--r-- 1 root root 0 July 14 15:36 balancer_access.log
-rw-r--r-- 1 root root 0 July 14 15:36 balancer_error.log
-rw-r--r-- 1 root root 0 July 14 15:36 balancer_ssl_requests.log
-rw-r--r-- 1 root root 0 July 14 15:36 puppetmaster_worker_access_1.log
-rw-r--r-- 1 root root 0 July 14 15:36 puppetmaster_worker_access_2.log
-rw-r--r-- 1 root root 0 July 14 15:36 puppetmaster_worker_error_1.log
-rw-r--r-- 1 root root 0 July 14 15:36 puppetmaster_worker_error_2.log
```

With the appropriate log files in place, you can now test the load balancer with a single back-end worker using puppet agent, turning off one worker beforehand. Listing 4-21 shows the test.

Listing 4-21. Disable a worker and test Puppet

```
[root@pupept-master-1 /etc/httpd/conf.d]# mv puppetmaster_worker_1.conf puppetmaster_worker_1.disabled
root@localhost: ~ > puppet agent --test
Info: Retrieving plugin
Info: Caching catalog for puppet-client-1
```

```
Info: Applying configuration version '1373830011'
Notice: puppet is runnning
Notice: /Stage[main]//Node[default]/Notify[puppet is runnning]/message: defined 'message' as
'puppet is runnning'
Notice: Finished catalog run in 0.06 seconds
```

Here we've run the puppet agent command and obtained a catalog from the Puppet master. The Apache load-balancing virtual host listened on puppet.example.com port 8140 and received the Puppet agent request, forwarded it along to the backend Puppet master virtual host listening on port 18140, and then provided the response back to the Puppet agent.

We can check the Apache logs to verify that this is what actually happened, as shown in Listings 4-22 and 4-23.

Listing 4-22. Load balancer request log

```
[root@pupept-master-1 /etc/httpd/conf.d]# less /var/log/httpd/balancer_access.log
192.168.1.12 - - [14/Jul/2013:19:26:47 +0000] "GET /production/node/puppet-client-1?
HTTP/1.1" 200 3851 "-" "-"
192.168.1.12 - - [14/Jul/2013:19:26:49 +0000] "GET /production/file_metadatas/
plugins?links=manage&checksum_type=md5&recurse=true&&ignore=----+%0A++-+%22.svn%22%0A++-
+CVS%0A++-+%22.git%22 HTTP/1.1" 200 283 "-" "-"
192.168.1.12 - - [14/Jul/2013:19:26:51 +0000] "POST /production/catalog/puppet-client-1
HTTP/1.1" 200 978 "-" "-"
192.168.1.12 - - [14/Jul/2013:19:26:51 +0000] "PUT /production/report/puppet-client-1
HTTP/1.1" 200 14 "-" "-"
```

Listing 4-23. First Puppet master worker request log

```
[root@pupept-master-1 /etc/httpd/conf.d]# tail -f /var/log/httpd/balancer_error.log
[Sun Jul 14 19:26:47 2013] [error] (111)Connection refused: proxy: HTTP: attempt to connect to
127.0.0.1:18140 (127.0.0.1) failed
[Sun Jul 14 19:26:47 2013] [error] ap_proxy_connect_backend disabling worker for (127.0.0.1)

[root@pupept-master-1 /etc/httpd/conf.d]# less /var/log/httpd/puppetmaster_worker_access_1.log
127.0.0.1 - - [14/Jul/2013:19:26:47 +0000] "GET /production/node/puppet-client-1?
HTTP/1.1" 200 3851 "-" "-"
127.0.0.1 - - [14/Jul/2013:19:26:51 +0000] "POST /production/catalog/puppet-client-1
HTTP/1.1" 200 978 "-" "-"
```

In Listing 4-22, you can see the incoming Puppet agent catalog request at 7:26 PM. The front-end load balancer receives the request and, according to the balancer_error.log shown in Listing 4-23, disables the worker virtual host on Port 18140. This leaves one additional worker in the balancer://puppetmaster pool, which receives the request, as indicated in the puppetmaster_worker_access_1.log shown in the second part of the listing. Finally, the Puppet agent uploads the catalog run report a few seconds later.

What happens, however, if all the back-end workers are disabled? Well, let's see. To do this, disable the Puppet master virtual host by renaming the configuration file, as shown in Listing 4-24.

Listing 4-24. Disable worker_2 and restart Puppet

```
[root@pupept-master-1 /etc/httpd/conf.d]# mv puppetmaster_worker_2.conf puppetmaster_worker_2.disabled
[root@pupept-master-1 /etc/httpd/conf.d]# service httpd restart
Stopping httpd:                                          [  OK  ]
Starting httpd:                                          [  OK  ]
```

And then run puppet agent again (Listing 4-25).

Listing 4-25. Test the puppet agent command

```
root@localhost: ~ > puppet agent --test
Warning: Unable to fetch my node definition, but the agent run will continue:
Warning: Error 503 on SERVER: <!DOCTYPE HTML PUBLIC "-//IETF//DTD HTML 2.0//EN">
<html><head>
<title>503 Service Temporarily Unavailable</title>
</head><body>
...
```

We've discovered that the Puppet agent receives error 503 when no back-end Puppet master worker virtual hosts are available. The front-end load balancer runs through its list of back-end workers defined in the Proxy balancer://puppetmaster section of the puppetmaster_proxy.conf file. Finding no available back-end workers, the front-end returns HTTP error code 503, "Service Temporarily Unavailable," to the client. This HTTP error code is also available in the front-end load balancer's error log file (Listing 4-26).

Listing 4-26. Apache front end load balancer error log

```
root@pupept-master-1 /etc/httpd/conf.d]# tail -f /var/log/httpd/balancer_error.log
[Sun Jul 14 19:39:02 2013] [error] (111)Connection refused: proxy: HTTP: attempt to connect to
127.0.0.1:18141 (127.0.0.1) failed
[Sun Jul 14 19:39:02 2013] [error] ap_proxy_connect_backend disabling worker for (127.0.0.1)
[Sun Jul 14 19:39:03 2013] [error] (111)Connection refused: proxy: HTTP: attempt to connect to
127.0.0.1:18141 (127.0.0.1) failed
[Sun Jul 14 19:39:03 2013] [error] ap_proxy_connect_backend disabling worker for (127.0.0.1)
[Sun Jul 14 19:39:03 2013] [error] (111)Connection refused: proxy: HTTP: attempt to connect to
127.0.0.1:18140 (127.0.0.1) failed
[Sun Jul 14 19:39:03 2013] [error] ap_proxy_connect_backend disabling worker for (127.0.0.1)
```

Now that you've seen one and no back-end masters working, let's bring back both workers back online (Listing 4-27).

Listing 4-27. Enable both workers

```
[root@pupept-master-1 /etc/httpd/conf.d]# mv puppetmaster_worker_1.disabled puppetmaster_worker_1.conf
[root@pupept-master-1 /etc/httpd/conf.d]# mv puppetmaster_worker_2.disabled puppetmaster_worker_2.conf

[root@pupept-master-1 /etc/httpd/conf.d]# service httpd restart
Stopping httpd:                                            [  OK  ]
Starting httpd:                                            [  OK  ]
```

Both back-end Puppet master virtual hosts are now online and responding to requests. You can check the status of the Ruby processes Passenger has started using the passenger-status command. It shows that the Puppet master process IDs started by Passenger when Puppet agent requests are routed to the back-end worker virtual hosts (see Listing 4-28).

Listing 4-28. The passenger-status command

```
[root@puppet-master-1 ~]# passenger-status
Version : 4.0.10
Date    : Mon Jul 15 17:47:42 +0000 2013
Instance: 3153
----------- General information -----------
Max pool size : 2
Processes     : 2
Requests in top-level queue : 0

----------- Application groups -----------
/usr/share/puppet/rack/puppetmasterd_18141#default:
  App root: /usr/share/puppet/rack/puppetmasterd_18141
  Requests in queue: 0
  * PID: 3249    Sessions: 0        Processed: 9       Uptime: 12h 26m 55s
    CPU: 0%      Memory  : 57M      Last used: 3m 53s

/usr/share/puppet/rack/puppetmasterd_18140#default:
  App root: /usr/share/puppet/rack/puppetmasterd_18140
  Requests in queue: 0
  * PID: 3221    Sessions: 0        Processed: 10      Uptime: 12h 26m 57s
    CPU: 0%      Memory  : 57M      Last used: 3m 52s
```

You can see the two Passenger processes servicing the front-end. With that, we've configured a simple and very scalable Puppet master implementation. To scale it further, all you now need to do is follow a subset of these steps to add additional back-end workers to the configuration and into the pool.

We also chose to configure the front-end and back-end virtual hosts all on the same system, as we can see through the use of 127.0.0.1 in each of the back-end configuration files and the Proxy section of the front-end virtual host. The choice to run all of the worker processes on the same host has greatly simplified the signing of SSL certificates when connecting new Puppet agent nodes. As mentioned previously in this chapter, the serial number and certificate revocation lists must be kept in sync across Puppet master systems that issue new client certificates. In the next section, you'll see how to manage back-end worker processes on separate systems.

To complete the example, let's start a Puppet master worker on a completely different host. This host and the load balancer host, puppet-master-2 and puppet-master-1, respectively, will have unencrypted communication so you should architect your network accordingly. If that is impossible, building a secure point-to-point tunnel with IPsec or stunnel is a good option. Configure puppet-master-2 much as you did at the beginning of this chapter; as a single-host Puppet master running under Rack/Passenger/Apache. The script build-puppetmaster-centos.sh, available where other supplementary materials are, will streamline this procedure. On puppet-master-2 change the configuration of /etc/httpd/conf.d/puppetmaster.conf to that shown in Listing 4-29.

Listing 4-29 The puppetmaster.conf file for Puppet master 2

```
[root@puppet-master-2 /etc/httpd/conf.d]# cat /etc/httpd/conf.d/puppetmaster.conf
LoadModule passenger_module /usr/lib/ruby/gems/1.8/gems/passenger-4.0.10/buildout/apache2/mod_passenger.so
PassengerRoot /usr/lib/ruby/gems/1.8/gems/passenger-4.0.10
PassengerRuby /usr/bin/ruby

# And the passenger performance tuning settings:
PassengerHighPerformance On
# Set this to about 1.5 times the number of CPU cores in your master:
PassengerMaxPoolSize 6
```

```
# Recycle master processes after they service 1000 requests
PassengerMaxRequests 1000
# Stop processes if they sit idle for 10 minutes
PassengerPoolIdleTime 600


Listen 8140
<VirtualHost *:8140>

SSLEngine off

# Obtain Authentication Information from Client Request Headers
SetEnvIf X-Client-Verify "(.*)" SSL_CLIENT_VERIFY=$1
SetEnvIf X-SSL-Client-DN "(.*)" SSL_CLIENT_S_DN=$1

    PassengerEnabled On
    DocumentRoot /usr/share/puppet/rack/puppetmasterd/public/
    <Directory /usr/share/puppet/rack/puppetmasterd/>
        Options None
        AllowOverride None
        Order Allow,Deny
        Allow from All
    </Directory>

ErrorLog /var/log/httpd/puppetmaster_worker_error.log
CustomLog /var/log/httpd/puppetmaster_worker_access.log combined

</VirtualHost>
```

As you can see, this host is configured to run only one Passenger, and it is configured to run on port 8140, the standard Puppet port.

Next we need to add the external worker to the load balancer's configuration. Modify /etc/httpd/conf.d/puppetmaster_proxy.conf to have another member of the Puppet proxy group, as shown in Listing 4-30.

Listing 4-30. Snippet of /etc/httpd/conf.d/puppetmaster_proxy.conf

```
# Available back-end worker virtual hosts
# NOTE the use of cleartext unencrypted HTTP
<Proxy balancer://puppetmaster>
  BalancerMember http://127.0.0.1:18140
  BalancerMember http://127.0.0.1:18141
  BalancerMember http://192.168.1.11:8140
</Proxy>
...  ,
```

Here puppet-master-2 has the IP address 192.168.1.11, and it has been added alongside the other balance members.

Finally, we can restart the Apache daemons on both servers and attempt to connect with a client (Listing 4-31).

Listing 4-31. Restart httpd

```
[root@puppet-master-2 ~]# service httpd restart
Stopping httpd:                                        [  OK  ]
Starting httpd:                                        [  OK  ]

[root@puppet-master-1 ~]# service httpd restart
Stopping httpd:                                        [  OK  ]
Starting httpd:                                        [  OK  ]

root@puppet-client-1: ~ > puppet agent --test
Info: Retrieving plugin
Info: Caching catalog for puppet-client-1
Info: Applying configuration version '1373865649'
Notice: puppet is runnning
Notice: /Stage[main]//Node[default]/Notify[puppet is runnning]/message: defined 'message' as
'puppet is runnning'
Notice: Finished catalog run in 0.05 seconds
```

And we can view the log on the load balancer to confirm that the external worker is participating in the cluster (Listing 4-32).

Listing 4-32. Puppet logs

```
[root@puppet-master-1 ~]# tail -f /var/log/httpd/balancer_
balancer_access.log          balancer_error.log           balancer_ssl_requests.log
[root@puppet-master-1 ~]# tail -f /var/log/httpd/balancer_access.log
192.168.1.12 - - [15/Jul/2013:04:49:54 +0000]
"POST /production/catalog/puppet-client-1.hsd1.or.comcast.net HTTP/1.1" 200 978 "-" "-"
192.168.1.12 - - [15/Jul/2013:04:49:54 +0000]
"PUT /production/report/puppet-client-1.hsd1.or.comcast.net HTTP/1.1" 200 14 "-" "-"
192.168.1.12 - - [15/Jul/2013:05:18:46 +0000]
"GET /production/node/puppet-client-1.hsd1.or.comcast.net? HTTP/1.1" 200 3851 "-" "-"
192.168.1.12 - - [15/Jul/2013:05:18:47 +0000]
"GET /production/file_metadatas/plugins?links=manage&checksum_type=md5&recurse=true&&ignore=---
+%0A++-+%22.svn%22%0A++-+CVS%0A++-+%22.git%22 HTTP/1.1" 200 283 "-" "-"
```

■ **Caution**   Each Puppet master has its own /etc/puppet/modules and /etc/puppet/manifests. It is critical that these directories contain the same files on both hosts. The dynamic environments workflow and scripts described in Chapter 3 can be adapted to do this automatically. Other solutions include using an NFS mount on both hosts or running an rsync triggered by inotify running on one Puppet master.

Scaling Further

So far in this chapter, you've configured the Puppet master service in a stand-alone Apache virtual host. Scaling the Puppet master system horizontally, you configured a number of Apache virtual hosts working together behind a reverse proxy load balancer. Then you added an external Puppet master behind the proxy to increase your capacity even further. Because the second Puppet master was only handling requests behind the first Puppet master, it provided additional performance, but not additional availability. To get to the point where we have highly available Puppet workers, we need to build out some more infrastructure. We will need to balance the Puppet master workers so that they are equal and redundant. This means putting them behind the same proxy and externalizing the Puppet CA service to another host. Eventually we will build redundancy into the Puppet CA service.

Puppet Certificate Authority Service Externalization

With a single Puppet master acting as an endpoint for all Puppet requests, both CA traffic and regular traffic, the configuration of the CA service is straightforward. To remove that single point of failure, complexity must increase. We will push the Puppet CA service onto a new host, actually a pair of hosts providing high availability.

We're going to show you how to use a hot (active) standby CA model to keep your certificate data synchronized. This architecture allows you to keep all Puppet CA data in one place, thereby minimizing the effort needed to maintain the Puppet master infrastructure (see Figure 4-2).

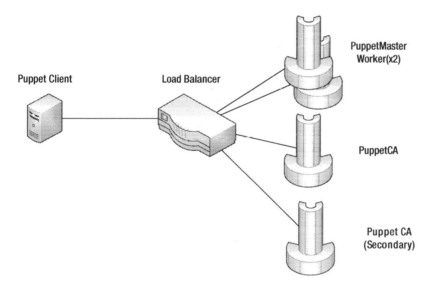

Figure 4-2. Puppet agent HTTPS load balancing

To do this, you will configure a second system to periodically synchronize the Puppet CA files. If the active Puppet CA system falls offline, the front-end load balancer will automatically redirect certificate requests to the hot standby. With the CA kept in sync, the hot standby will be ready to serve certificate-signing requests for new hosts.

The hot standby model requires the front-end Apache load balancer to redirect all certificate requests from all Puppet agent nodes to a specific set of Puppet master workers. We'll demonstrate how to do this and see how to test the new configuration. Finally, we'll show how to take the primary Puppet CA offline for maintenance and back online again, including handling whether Puppet agents have submitted certificate requests to the hot standby.

Puppet CA Worker Configuration

The first step in building our HA Puppet Certificate Authority system is to build out two more hosts with the Puppet/Rack/Passenger/Apache stack. We will call these two new hosts puppet-ca-1 and puppet-ca-2. You can again follow the instructions from earlier in this chapter or run the script included with the supplemental materials. After that, we can configure them to be CA servers for our existing Puppet infrastructure. First purge the existing SSL files to ensure a clean starting point, as shown in Listing 4-33.

Listing 4-33. Purging the Puppet SSL files

```
[root@puppet-ca-1 ~]# rm -fr /var/lib/puppet/ssl
[root@puppet-ca-2 ~]# rm -fr /var/lib/puppet/ssl
```

We do this to ensure that nothing leaks from initial setup into the new configuration we are setting up.

Create Endpoint Certificates for CA Hosts

Use the puppet agent command to generate a certificate (Listing 4-34) and have it signed by the current CA server. This is the cert that the Puppet CA server will use as its SSL endpoint.

Listing 4-34. Creating and signing a certificate for puppet-ca-2

```
[root@puppet-ca-2 ~]# rm -fr /var/lib/puppet/ssl/
[root@puppet-ca-2 ~]# puppet agent --test
Info: Creating a new SSL key for puppet-ca-2.pro-puppet.com
Info: Caching certificate for ca
Info: Creating a new SSL certificate request for puppet-ca-2.pro-puppet.com
Info: Certificate Request fingerprint (SHA256):
23:89:D3:02:D5:09:C4:DD:AF:CC:18:E3:EF:39:8E:2C:BC:
FB:48:47:63:84:2A:3B:C7:8D:2D:EE:41:A1:A8:D8
Exiting; no certificate found and waitforcert is disabled
[root@puppet-ca-2 ~]#

[root@puppet-master-1 ~]# puppet cert list
  "puppet-ca-2.pro-puppet.com" (SHA256)
23:89:D3:02:D5:09:C4:DD:AF:CC:18:E3:EF:39:8E:2C:BC:FB:48:47:63:84:2A:3B:C7:8D:2D:EE:41:A1:A8:D8
[root@puppet-master-1 ~]# puppet cert sign puppet-ca-2.pro-puppet.com
Notice: Signed certificate request for puppet-ca-2.pro-puppet.com
Notice: Removing file Puppet::SSL::CertificateRequest puppet-ca-2.pro-puppet.com at
'/var/lib/puppet/ssl/ca/requests/puppet-ca-2.pro-puppet.com.pem'

[root@puppet-ca-2 ~]# service httpd restart
Stopping httpd:                                            [FAILED]
Starting httpd:                                            [  OK  ]
```

Do the same for puppet-ca-1.

Sync CA Data to CA Hosts

Copy the SSL directory from puppet-master-1 to puppet-ca-1 and puppet-ca-2, as shown in Listing 4-35.

Listing 4-35. Copying the SSL directory

```
[root@puppet-master-1 ~]# rsync -PHaze ssh /var/lib/puppet/ssl/ca puppet-ca-1:/var/lib/puppet/ssl/
sending incremental file list
ca/
ca/ca_crl.pem
        1023 100%    0.00kB/s    0:00:00 (xfer#1, to-check=14/16)
ca/ca_crt.pem
        1903 100%    1.81MB/s    0:00:00 (xfer#2, to-check=13/16)
ca/ca_key.pem
```

```
        3243 100%    1.03MB/s     0:00:00 (xfer#3, to-check=12/16)
ca/ca_pub.pem
         775 100%  151.37kB/s     0:00:00 (xfer#4, to-check=11/16)
ca/inventory.txt
         768 100%  125.00kB/s     0:00:00 (xfer#5, to-check=10/16)
ca/serial
           4 100%    0.49kB/s     0:00:00 (xfer#6, to-check=9/16)
ca/private/
ca/private/ca.pass
          20 100%    1.95kB/s     0:00:00 (xfer#7, to-check=5/16)
ca/requests/
ca/signed/
ca/signed/puppet-client-1.pro-puppet.com.pem
        1931 100%  125.72kB/s     0:00:00 (xfer#10, to-check=2/16)
ca/signed/puppet-master-1.pro-puppet.com.pem
        2061 100%  125.79kB/s     0:00:00 (xfer#11, to-check=1/16)

sent 14064 bytes  received 256 bytes  3182.22 bytes/sec
total size is 17734  speedup is 1.24
[root@puppet-master-2 ~]# rsync -PHaze ssh /var/lib/puppet/ssl/ca puppet-ca-1:/var/lib/puppet/ssl/

[root@puppet-ca-1 ~]# ls /var/lib/puppet/ssl/ca/
total 44
drwxrwx--- 5 puppet 4096 Jul 15 04:49 .
drwxr-xr-x 3 root   4096 Jul 17 05:38 ..
-rw-rw-r-- 1 puppet 1023 Jul 14 18:35 ca_crl.pem
-rw-rw---- 1 puppet 1903 Jul 13 06:25 ca_crt.pem
-rw-rw---- 1 puppet 3243 Jul 13 06:25 ca_key.pem
-rw-r----- 1 puppet  775 Jul 13 06:25 ca_pub.pem
-rw-r--r-- 1 puppet  768 Jul 15 04:49 inventory.txt
drwxrwx--- 2 puppet 4096 Jul 13 06:25 private
drwxr-xr-x 2 puppet 4096 Jul 15 04:49 requests
-rw-r--r-- 1 puppet    4 Jul 15 04:49 serial
drwxrwx--- 2 puppet 4096 Jul 15 04:49 signed
[root@puppet-ca-2 ~]# ls /var/lib/puppet/ssl/ca/
```

Again, it is critical to understand the meaning of the trailing slashes when using the rsync command. What we've done here is put the /var/lib/puppet/ssl/ca folder from puppet-master-1 into the /var/lib/puppet/ssl folder of puppet-ca-1 and puppet-ca-2, and then used the ls utility to verify that we've done so correctly.

Configure Apache on CA Hosts

We next need to modify the /etc/httpd/conf.d/puppetmaster.conf file to point to the correct SSLCertificateFile and SSLCertificateKeyFile; again, these files were generated when we ran puppet master and are located in /var/lib/puppet/ssl/. We also need to set the SSLProxyEngine variable and comment out or remove the lines that set the certificate verification headers before passing the request on to Rack, as shown in Listing 4-36.

Listing 4-36. The /etc/httpd/conf.d/puppetmaster.conf file for puppet-ca-2

```
LoadModule passenger_module /usr/lib/ruby/gems/1.8/gems/passenger-4.0.8/buildout/apache2/mod_passenger.so
PassengerRoot /usr/lib/ruby/gems/1.8/gems/passenger-4.0.8
PassengerRuby /usr/bin/ruby


# And the passenger performance tuning settings:
PassengerHighPerformance On
# Set this to about 1.5 times the number of CPU cores in your master:
PassengerMaxPoolSize 6
# Recycle master processes after they service 1000 requests
PassengerMaxRequests 1000
# Stop processes if they sit idle for 10 minutes
PassengerPoolIdleTime 600


Listen 8140
<VirtualHost *:8140>
    SSLEngine On

    # Only allow high security cryptography. Alter if needed for compatibility.
    SSLProtocol             All -SSLv2
    SSLCipherSuite          HIGH:!ADH:RC4+RSA:-MEDIUM:-LOW:-EXP
    SSLCertificateFile      /var/lib/puppet/ssl/certs/puppet-ca-1.pro-puppet.com.pem
    SSLCertificateKeyFile   /var/lib/puppet/ssl/private_keys/puppet-ca-1.pro-puppet.com.pem
    SSLCertificateChainFile /var/lib/puppet/ssl/ca/ca_crt.pem
    SSLCACertificateFile    /var/lib/puppet/ssl/ca/ca_crt.pem
    SSLCARevocationFile     /var/lib/puppet/ssl/ca/ca_crl.pem
    SSLVerifyClient         optional
    SSLVerifyDepth          1
    SSLOptions              +StdEnvVars +ExportCertData

    # These request headers are used to pass the client certificate
    # authentication information on to the puppet master process
    #RequestHeader set X-SSL-Subject %{SSL_CLIENT_S_DN}e
    #RequestHeader set X-Client-DN %{SSL_CLIENT_S_DN}e
    #RequestHeader set X-Client-Verify %{SSL_CLIENT_VERIFY}e

    PassengerEnabled On
    DocumentRoot /usr/share/puppet/rack/puppetmasterd/public/
    <Directory /usr/share/puppet/rack/puppetmasterd/>
        Options None
        AllowOverride None
        Order Allow,Deny
        Allow from All
    </Directory>
</VirtualHost>
```

Again, your Passenger version will undoubtedly be different from the one in this example configuration. The Puppet certificate service is very lightweight compared to the Puppet master service, so tweaking Passenger isn't necessary, but you might as well set pool size according to the power of the machine hosting the service. The Puppet CA service can easily run on a modern machine with a single thread.

■ **Tip** Both hosts have the same files in the /var/lib/puppet/ssl/ca directory, but each has its own unique cert and key as well.

We should now restart the Apache service to make sure the changes are valid, but at this point the HTTPS reverse proxy running on puppet-master-1 has not yet been configured to route any requests to either of these two Puppet CA workers.

Configure Load Balancer to use external CA in HA Configuration

We now need to configure the front-end load balancer to redirect all certificate related requests to the new CA Servers. We configure puppet-ca-1 to be the default CA and puppet-ca-2 to be the hot-standby CA. Put the configuration shown in Listing 4-37 into /etc/httpd/conf.d/puppetmaster_proxy.conf.

Listing 4-37. Standby Puppet CA Load Balancer configuration snippet from /etc/httpd/conf.d/puppetmaster_proxy.conf

```
...
<Proxy balancer://puppetmasterca>
  # Puppet CA Active Worker
  BalancerMember https://puppet-ca-1:8140
  # Puppet CA Hot Standby
  BalancerMember https://puppet-ca-2:8140 status=+H
</Proxy>
...
```

As you can see in Listing 4-37, a new Proxy section configures the load balancer to first connect to https://puppet-ca-1:8140, and then connect to https://puppet-ca-2:8140 when a request is sent to the balancer named puppetmasterca. The option status=+H tells the front end that the second member is a hot standby.

With the back-end Puppet CA workers configured, the load balancer must now be configured to route certificate requests, and only certificate requests, to the two member workers. This configuration listing goes in the main Apache front-end virtual host block, as shown in Listing 4-38.

Listing 4-38. Load Balancer certificate request routing configuration

```
# Ordering of ProxyPass directives is important
# Direct all Puppet agent CA requests to a specific set of workers.
ProxyPassMatch ^(/.*?)/(certificate.*?)/(.*)$ balancer://puppetmasterca
ProxyPassReverse ^(/.*?)/(certificate.*?)/(.*)$ balancer://puppetmasterca
# Direct all other Puppet agent requests to the default set of workers.
 ProxyPass / balancer://puppetmaster/
 ProxyPassReverse / balancer://puppetmaster/
 ProxyPreserveHost On
```

Here, we configured the load balancer to handle requests matching a pattern indicating they are certificate-related. We configured the load balancer to direct these requests to the group of workers named balancer://puppetmasterca, which were defined in Listing 4-38. Using this group of workers guarantees that the load balancer will send the request to the worker on puppet-ca-1 if it is online, and puppet-ca-2 if puppet-ca-1 is down, and return HTTP status 503, "Temporarily Unavailable," if neither is available.

The ProxyPassMatch directive configures a regular expression to match against the request URI of the Puppet agent. In this case, we have configured the URI-containing certificate in the second path element as a match. This ensures that certificate requests are directed appropriately, regardless of the environment or the Puppet agent name.

After configuring the two back-end Puppet CA worker virtual hosts on puppet-ca-1 and puppet-ca-2, you need to restart Apache on puppet-master-1, as shown in Listing 4-39.

Listing 4-39. Restarting Apache

```
# service httpd restart
Stopping httpd:                                        [  OK  ]
Starting httpd:                                        [  OK  ]
```

Test the HA CA Configuration

Let's test the new configuration, with a new system named puppet-client-2.pro-puppet.com, as shown in Listing 4-40.

Listing 4-40. Running puppet agent to generate a new client cert

```
root@puppet-client-2: ~ > puppet agent --test
Info: Creating a new SSL key for puppet-client-2.pro-puppet.com
Info: Caching certificate for ca
Info: Creating a new SSL certificate request for puppet-client-2.pro-puppet.com
Info: Certificate Request fingerprint (SHA256):
16:61:3D:A6:06:24:59:F4:15:06:B2:57:52:59:6A:33:85:23:C4:24:D8:B3:E3:E5:C0:90:96:5A:20:FA:C5:5D
Exiting; no certificate found and waitforcert is disabled
```

Once the new Puppet agent creates a certificate-signing request and submits it to the load balancer, we can check the Apache logs to make sure that CA requests are being routed properly to the worker listening on port 18142.

In Listing 4-41, you can see a number of HTTP 404 status results on the second and third line of the logs. Apache is returning status 404 "Not Found" because the Puppet node puppet-client-2.pro-puppet.com is a new node and no signed certificates or certificate requests exist for this system. Until we sign the new certificate request using the puppet cert --sign command, the Puppet CA worker will continue to return 404 "Not Found" status codes to the Puppet agent on puppet-client-2.pro-puppet.com.

Listing 4-41. HTTP 404 status results due to certificate errors

```
 [root@puppet-ca-1 ~]# tail -f /var/log/httpd/access_log
192.168.8.10 - - [07/Aug/2013:11:04:18 +0000]
"GET /production/certificate/puppet-client-2.pro-puppet.com? HTTP/1.1" 200 1944 "-" "-"
192.168.8.10 - - [07/Aug/2013:11:04:18 +0000]
"GET /production/certificate_revocation_list/ca? HTTP/1.1" 200 1259 "-" "-"
192.168.8.10 - - [07/Aug/2013:11:54:41 +0000]
"GET /production/certificate/ca? HTTP/1.1" 200 1903 "-" "-"
192.168.8.10 - - [07/Aug/2013:11:54:41 +0000]
"GET /production/certificate/puppet-client-2.pro-puppet.com? HTTP/1.1" 200 1944 "-" "-"
192.168.8.10 - - [07/Aug/2013:11:55:07 +0000]
"GET /production/certificate/ca? HTTP/1.1" 200 1903 "-" "-"
192.168.8.10 - - [07/Aug/2013:11:55:08 +0000]
"GET /production/certificate/puppet-client-2.pro-puppet.com? HTTP/1.1" 404 57 "-" "-"
192.168.8.10 - - [07/Aug/2013:11:55:08 +0000]
"GET /production/certificate_request/puppet-client-2.pro-puppet.com? HTTP/1.1" 404 65 "-" "-"
```

```
192.168.8.10 - - [07/Aug/2013:11:55:08 +0000]
"PUT /production/certificate request/puppet-client-2.pro-puppet.com HTTP/1.1" 200 4 "-" "-"
192.168.8.10 - - [07/Aug/2013:11:55:08 +0000]
"GET /production/certificate/puppet-client-2.pro-puppet.com? HTTP/1.1" 404 57 "-" "-"
192.168.8.10 - - [07/Aug/2013:11:55:08 +0000]
"GET /production/certificate/puppet-client-2.pro-puppet.com? HTTP/1.1" 404 57 "-" "-"
```

To make sure the Puppet agent is routed to the correct worker system, you need to sign the new certificate request (Listing 4-42).

Listing 4-42. Sign the client's certificate request.

```
[root@puppet-ca-1 ~]# puppet cert list
  "puppet-client-2.pro-puppet.com" (SHA256)
16:61:3D:A6:06:24:59:F4:15:06:B2:57:52:59:6A:33:85:23:C4:24:D8:B3:E3:E5:C0:90:96:5A:20:FA:C5:5D
[root@puppet-ca-1 ~]# puppet cert sign puppet-client-2.pro-puppet.com
Notice: Signed certificate request for puppet-client-2.pro-puppet.com
Notice: Removing file Puppet::SSL::CertificateRequest puppet-client-2.pro-puppet.com at
'/var/lib/puppet/ssl/ca/requests/puppet-client-2.pro-puppet.com.pem'
```

Once the certificate has been signed, you can run the Puppet agent on the new node again to make sure the agent is able to download its catalog from the master. Since the client is using its cert for client-cert authentication, this proves that the certificate chain from the certificate authority through the Puppet master to the clients is functioning. Listing 4-43).

Listing 4-43. Sign the client's certificate request

```
root@puppet-client-2: ~ > puppet agent --test
Info: Retrieving plugin
Info: Caching catalog for puppet-client-2.pro-puppet.com
Info: Applying configuration version '1375876603'
Notice: puppet is runnning
Notice: /Stage[main]//Node[default]/Notify[puppet is runnning]/message: defined 'message' as
'puppet is runnning'
Notice: Finished catalog run in 0.04 seconds
```

You can also check the logs again (Listing 4-44) to make sure HTTP Status 200 is present, now that the Puppet agent has the signed certificate:

Listing 4-44. Tailing Apache Access logs

```
[root@puppet-ca-1 ~]# tail -2 /var/log/httpd/access_log
192.168.8.10 - - [07/Aug/2013:11:59:58 +0000]
"GET /production/certificate/puppet-client-2.pro-puppet.com? HTTP/1.1" 200 1944 "-" "-"
192.168.8.10 - - [07/Aug/2013:11:59:58 +0000]
"GET /production/certificate_revocation_list/ca? HTTP/1.1" 200 1397 "-" "-"
```

You can see two log entries, matching the Puppet agent downloading its signed certificate and the certificate revocation list maintained by the Puppet CA worker. Both entries contain HTTP Status 200 "OK" codes, indicating that the Puppet agent successfully transferred the certificate and revocation list from the Puppet CA.

You can also see that the access log for the active Puppet CA worker does not contain any catalog requests. Check the access logs of the two load-balanced Puppet master workers to make sure catalog requests are being routed correctly to only those two systems (Listing 4-45).

Listing 4-45. Tailing Apache Puppet Master Worker logs

```
[root@puppet-master-1 ~]# tail -f /var/log/httpd/puppetmaster_worker_access_1.log
127.0.0.1 - - [07/Aug/2013:12:01:51 +0000] "GET /production/node/puppet-client-2.pro-puppet.com?
HTTP/1.1" 200 2917 "-" "-"
127.0.0.1 - - [07/Aug/2013:12:01:51 +0000] "GET /production/file_metadatas/plugins?checksum_type=md
5&links=manage&recurse=true&ignore=---+%0A++-+%22.svn%22%0A++-+CVS%0A++-+%22.git%22& HTTP/1.1" 200
283 "-" "-"
127.0.0.1 - - [07/Aug/2013:12:01:51 +0000] "POST /production/catalog/puppet-client-2.pro-puppet.com
HTTP/1.1" 200 973 "-" "-"
127.0.0.1 - - [07/Aug/2013:12:01:52 +0000] "PUT /production/report/puppet-client-2.pro-puppet.com
HTTP/1.1" 200 14 "-" "-"
```

Note that the catalog requests are still being directed by the front-end load balancer to the workers running locally on puppet-master-1 and remotely on puppet-master-2, while certificate requests are being directed to the active Puppet CA server on puppet-ca-1.

With this, you've configured the front-end HTTPS load balancer to direct all certificate-related requests to a single Puppet CA worker. This redirection ensures that the certificate revocation list and serial.txt files are maintained properly.

Synchronizing the Hot Standby Puppet CA Directory

Now that the certificate requests are being handled properly, the next step is to configure the hot standby Puppet CA worker. If the primary Puppet CA worker fails, another worker should quickly take over responsibility for responding to certificate requests. We will take advantage of the load balancer's ability to redirect requests in order to quickly fail over to the backup Puppet CA worker.

You've already configured the load balancer to use the secondary worker as a hot standby, automatically activated in the event the primary worker goes offline. You next need to configure a periodic task to synchronize the CA directory automatically across the primary and secondary workers. Finally, you will test the new configuration and work through the exercise of testing the failover and failback to the primary Puppet CA worker.

Copy the certificate authority directory on puppet-ca-1 to the hot standby (puppet-ca-2) using rsync. This command could also be configured as a cron task or inotify hook, to keep the hot standby directory contents up to date:

First, remove the ssl/ca directory on the secondary CA server, puppet-ca-2:

```
[root@puppet-ca-2 ~]# rm -fr /var/lib/puppet/ssl/ca/
```

Then copy over the ca files from puppet-ca-1, as shown in Listing 4-46.

Listing 4-46. Running rsync over ca files

```
 [root@puppet-ca-1 ~]# rsync -delete -PHaze ssh
/var/lib/puppet/ssl/ca puppet-ca-2:/var/lib/puppet/ssl/
sending incremental file list
ca/
ca/ca_crl.pem
        1442 100%    0.00kB/s    0:00:00 (xfer#1, to-check=23/25)
ca/ca_crt.pem
        1903 100%    1.81MB/s    0:00:00 (xfer#2, to-check=22/25)
```

```
ca/ca_key.pem
        3243 100%    3.09MB/s    0:00:00 (xfer#3, to-check=21/25)
ca/ca_pub.pem
         775 100%  252.28kB/s    0:00:00 (xfer#4, to-check=20/25)
ca/inventory.txt
        1970 100%  480.96kB/s    0:00:00 (xfer#5, to-check=19/25)
ca/serial
           4 100%    0.78kB/s    0:00:00 (xfer#6, to-check=18/25)
ca/private/
ca/private/ca.pass
          20 100%    3.91kB/s    0:00:00 (xfer#7, to-check=14/25)
ca/requests/
ca/signed/
ca/signed/puppet-ca-1.pro-puppet.com.pem
        1935 100%  269.95kB/s    0:00:00 (xfer#10, to-check=11/25)
ca/signed/puppet-ca-2.pro-puppet.com.pem
        1935 100%  209.96kB/s    0:00:00 (xfer#12, to-check=9/25)
...
```

This rsync command synchronizes the primary CA directory into the standby CA directory, deleting any files existing in the destination and not in the source.

Now let's create a one-minute cron job to synchronize the files from puppet-ca-1 to puppet-ca-2. This requires host-based trust or passwordless SSH key-based trust to work. Use whatever synchronization system your security model allows.

```
[root@puppet-ca-1 ~]# crontab -l
* * * * *  rsync -delete -PHaze ssh /var/lib/puppet/ssl/ca puppet-ca-2:/var/lib/puppet/ssl/ >/dev/null
```

This uses the rsync utility to synchronize the contents of the two directories. The -delete flag makes sure that files that exist on the target but not on the source are removed.

Puppet CA Hot Standby

Once the certificate data has been synchronized, you can test failover between the Puppet CA servers. We're going to stop Apache on the primary CA server. We expect the load balancer configuration to automatically redirect certificate requests to the hot standby (Listing 4-47).

Listing 4-47. Stopping Apache

```
[root@puppet-ca-1 ~]# service httpd stop
Stopping httpd:                                      [  OK  ]
```

Once the primary Puppet CA worker is inaccessible, you can test that certificate requests are automatically redirected to the secondary worker using the curl command, shown in Listing 4-48.

Listing 4-48. Using curl at the Puppet master to test redirection

```
[root@puppet-master-1 ~]# curl --silent -o /dev/null -D /dev/stdout -q -k -H "Accept: s"
https://localhost:8140/production/certificate/ca
HTTP/1.1 200 OK
Date: Wed, 14 Aug 2013 08:57:14 GMT
```

```
Server: Apache/2.2.15 (CentOS)
X-Powered-By: Phusion Passenger 4.0.10
Content-Length: 1903
Status: 200 OK
Content-Type: text/plain; charset=UTF-8
Connection: close
```

You can see the results of this curl in the logs (Listings 4-49 and 4-50).

Listing 4-49. Reading the Apache Balancer log

```
[root@puppet-master-1 ~]# tail -f /var/log/httpd/balancer_error.log
[Wed Aug 14 08:57:14 2013] [error] (111)Connection refused: proxy: HTTPS: attempt to connect to
192.168.8.13:8140 (puppet-ca-1) failed
[Wed Aug 14 08:57:14 2013] [error] ap_proxy_connect_backend disabling worker for (puppet-ca-1)
```

Listing 4-50. Reading the Apache Puppet Master Worker Access log

```
$ tail -n1 /var/log/httpd/puppetmaster_worker_access_18143.log
127.0.0.1 - - [04/Dec/2010:15:42:36 -0800] "GET /production/certificate/ca
HTTP/1.1" 200 839 "-" "curl/7.15.5 (x86_64-redhat-linux-gnu) libcurl/7.15.5
OpenSSL/0.9.8b zlib/1.2.3 libidn/0.6.5"

[root@puppet-ca-2 ~]# tail -f /var/log/httpd/access_log
192.168.8.10 - - [14/Aug/2013:08:57:14 +0000] "GET /production/certificate/ca HTTP/1.1" 200 1903
"-" "curl/7.19.7 (x86_64-redhat-linux-gnu) libcurl/7.19.7 NSS/3.14.0.0 zlib/1.2.3 libidn/1.18
libssh2/1.4.2"
```

The first command we've executed is a standard curl HTTP request. Rather than display the contents of the request body, we display the HTTP Response headers on standard output. The HTTP header output provides an indication of the status of the response, with anything other than status 200 indicating an error.

After requesting the Puppet CA certificate, you can look at the error log file of the front-end load balancer to see how the request was handled. As expected, the load balancer could not forward the request to the primary Puppet CA worker. The load balancer properly failed over to the hot standby Puppet CA worker and forwarded the request to it.

Looking at the access logs in /var/log/httpd/access.log of puppet-ca-2, we can see the incoming request and resulting HTTP 200 "OK" status code for the response.

Now we want to make sure we can still provision new Puppet managed nodes while the hot standby certificate authority is currently active. Going to a new host, we get a test run as shown in Listing 4-51.

Listing 4-51. Test a new agent

```
 [root@puppet-client-3 ~]# puppet agent --test
Info: Creating a new SSL key for puppet-client-3.pro-puppet.com
Info: Caching certificate for ca
Info: Creating a new SSL certificate request for puppet-client-3.pro-puppet.com
Info: Certificate Request fingerprint (SHA256): EA:F7:C1:6A:C8:91:3F:85:8D:1E:33:AA:AD:D7:9E:DC:CF:C
3:70:1E:D5:01:94:2B:38:E7:11:19:FB:D6:27:EA
Exiting; no certificate found and waitforcert is disabled
```

The first time a Puppet agent is run, a new certificate request is generated and submitted to the Puppet master (Listing 4-52).

Listing 4-52. Listing the pending certificate queue

```
[root@puppet-ca-2 ~]# puppet cert list
  "puppet-client-3.pro-puppet.com" (SHA256)
EA:F7:C1:6A:C8:91:3F:85:8D:1E:33:AA:AD:D7:9E:DC:CF:C3:70:1E:D5:01:94:2B:38:E7:11:19:FB:D6:27:EA
```

Because the primary Puppet CA worker is offline, we expect to see the pending certificate request in the standby directory (Listing 4-53).

Listing 4-53. Signing a CSR on the standby Puppet CA

```
[root@puppet-ca-2 ~]# puppet cert sign puppet-client-3.pro-puppet.com
Notice: Signed certificate request for puppet-client-3.pro-puppet.com
Notice: Removing file Puppet::SSL::CertificateRequest puppet-client-3.pro-puppet.com at
'/var/lib/puppet/ssl/ca/requests/puppet-client-3.pro-puppet.com.pem'
```

Finally, you can run the agent on `puppet-client-3` to verify that everything is working as expected (Listing 4-54).

Listing 4-54. Testing Puppet functionality

```
[root@puppet-client-3 ~]# puppet agent --test
Info: Caching certificate for puppet-client-3.pro-puppet.com
Info: Caching certificate_revocation_list for ca
Info: Retrieving plugin
Info: Caching catalog for puppet-client-3.pro-puppet.com
Info: Applying configuration version '1376471067'
Notice: puppet is runnning
Notice: /Stage[main]//Node[default]/Notify[puppet is runnning]/message: defined 'message' as
'puppet is runnning'
Notice: Finished catalog run in 0.08 seconds
```

Primary Puppet CA Fail Back

The failover to the secondary CA is now working properly, and new certificates can be signed. Let's test the process of reactivating the primary Puppet CA worker. The load balancer will automatically start using the primary worker when it comes online again, so the process becomes a matter of synchronizing the secondary certificate authority back to the primary CA directory. You need to synchronize changes before reactivating the Apache server to allow traffic back to the primary certificate authority.

Similar to the `rsync` command that synchronized the primary CA directory into the standby location, the `rsync` command shown in Listing 4-55 reverses the direction and synchronizes the standby CA directory into the primary location before re-enabling the primary CA using the host firewall.

Listing 4-55. How to `rsync` standby CA back to the primary CA

```
[root@puppet-ca-2 ~]# rsync -delete -PHaze ssh /var/lib/puppet/ssl/ca puppet-ca-1:/var/lib/puppet/ssl/
sending incremental file list
ca/
ca/inventory.txt
        2058 100%    1.30MB/s    0:00:00 (xfer#1, to-check=21/27)
ca/serial
           4 100%    3.91kB/s    0:00:00 (xfer#2, to-check=20/27)
```

```
ca/requests/
ca/signed/
ca/signed/puppet-client-3.pro-puppet.com.pem
         1944 100%    1.85MB/s     0:00:00 (xfer#3, to-check=6/27)

sent 2553 bytes  received 106 bytes  759.71 bytes/sec
total size is 40852  speedup is 15.36

[root@puppet-ca-1 ~]# service httpd start
Starting httpd:                                     [  OK  ]
```

You performed twosimple tasks to re-activate the primary Puppet CA worker. First, you synchronized the CA directory from the standby in Listing 4-55. Notice that three files have changed since the hot standby worker has become active. These three files changed when you signed the certificate request for puppet-client-3.pro-puppet.com. Immediately after synchronizing the CA directory, you started Apache on the primary Puppet CA worker.

■ **Caution**   When failing back to the primary Puppet CA worker, there will be a short delay while certificate requests are still directed to the hot standby. This delay is determined by how frequently the load balancer polls failed worker nodes to find out if they're back online. In situations where a large number of certificate requests are being handled while the Puppet CA is being switched online, it is recommended to make the CA directory on the standby CA read-only to the puppet user and group to prevent changes from occurring after synchronization.

Load Balancing Alternatives

Up until now, we've relied on an HTTP load balancer using Apache to scale Puppet. However, the following alternative technologies and implementations can be used to achieve the same results:

- DNS round robin
- DNS SRV records
- TCP load balancing
- IP anycast
- Masterless Puppet

Let's review them now.

Load Balancing with DNS Round Robin

We could also use DNS round robin to easily redirect and consolidate all certificate requests to a single Puppet CA worker.

DNS round robin is commonly used to cluster a group of worker processes providing the same service. In this configuration, redirection to different workers is performed at the name resolution stage instead of using a reverse HTTP proxy. As a result, the Puppet master infrastructure is no longer able to make decisions about the redirection based on the client request. Furthermore, if a specific Puppet master worker is offline, the DNS system is not checking the state of the worker and as a result, a portion of the Puppet agent systems will receive timeout errors when they are directed to connect to the failed worker system. We recommend deploying HTTP load balancing whenever possible to scale Puppet because of these shortcomings in DNS round robin.

As in our HTTP load balancing, all certificate-related requests should be consolidated onto one worker system to mitigate problems with certificate serial numbers and revocation lists diverging among the Puppet CA systems. To this end, the Puppet agent supports the configuration of a Puppet CA server other than the Puppet master server the configuration catalog is obtained from. When configuring Puppet using round robin DNS, it is recommended to maintain a single Puppet CA worker in addition to the number of Puppet master workers required. The Puppet agent configuration should set the --ca_server configuration option to bypass the round robin DNS configuration and contact the appropriate Puppet CA worker directly.

Load Balancing with DNS SRV records

Puppet currently supports, as an experimental feature, using DNS SRV records to allow clients to discover their Puppet masters and Puppet CA servers. This can be used to load-balance Puppet agents across an unlimited number of master workers, and it allows for neat separation of the CA service from the Puppet master services. There are currently some drawbacks; for instance, SRV records can only be used at the exclusion of hard-coded server names. There is no way to fall back on a server name written down in puppet.conf, and there is no way to set a timeout to bail early if the lookup is probably going to fail. If you are interested in deploying this solution, look at the current documentation on docs.puppetlabs.com.

Load Balancing with a TCP Load Balancer

The core of the example in this chapter is performed by using the Apache proxying load balancer. This means a server creates an SSL and HTTP endpoint, and then opens a new connection to another server or set of servers. There is another kind of load balancing, TCP load balancing, that occurs at a lower level of the TCP/IP stack.

In this model a load balancer running HA proxy will terminate all TCP sessions from the Puppet clients, and then open new TCP sessions to a set of Puppet master workers. SSL is terminated on the Puppet master workers, and the entire conversation is encrypted and impenetrable to the HA proxy. SSL Certificate signing is handled by creating a separate CA server and populating client configs to set the caserver configuration option.

The puppetmaster.conf of each worker in this configuration looks very much like that of the puppet-master-1 from earlier. Listing 4-56 is a puppetmaster configuration file from an Ubuntu 12.04 host running Passenger 3.x.

Listing 4-56. Puppet master worker vhost for use with HA-proxy and Passenger 3 on Ubuntu 12.04

```
# you probably want to tune these settings
PassengerHighPerformance on
PassengerMaxPoolSize 12
PassengerPoolIdleTime 1500
# PassengerMaxRequests 1000
PassengerStatThrottleRate 120
RackAutoDetect Off
RailsAutoDetect Off


Listen 8140

<VirtualHost *:8140>
        SSLEngine on
        SSLProtocol -ALL +SSLv3 +TLSv1
        SSLCipherSuite ALL:!ADH:RC4+RSA:+HIGH:+MEDIUM:-LOW:-SSLv2:-EXP

        SSLCertificateFile      /var/lib/puppet/ssl/certs/puppet-master-4.pro-puppet.com.pem
        SSLCertificateKeyFile   /var/lib/puppet/ssl/private_keys/puppet-master-4.pro-puppet.com.pem
        SSLCertificateChainFile /var/lib/puppet/ssl/certs/ca.pem
```

```
        SSLCACertificateFile     /var/lib/puppet/ssl/certs/ca.pem
        # If Apache complains about invalid signatures on the CRL, you can try disabling
        # CRL checking by commenting the next line, but this is not recommended.
        SSLCARevocationFile      /var/lib/puppet/ssl/ca/ca_crl.pem
        SSLVerifyClient optional
        SSLVerifyDepth  1
        # The `ExportCertData` option is needed for agent certificate expiration warnings
        SSLOptions +StdEnvVars +ExportCertData

        # This header needs to be set if using a loadbalancer or proxy
        RequestHeader unset X-Forwarded-For

        RequestHeader set X-SSL-Subject %{SSL_CLIENT_S_DN}e
        RequestHeader set X-Client-DN %{SSL_CLIENT_S_DN}e
        RequestHeader set X-Client-Verify %{SSL_CLIENT_VERIFY}e

        DocumentRoot /usr/share/puppet/rack/puppetmasterd/public/
        RackBaseURI /
        <Directory /usr/share/puppet/rack/puppetmasterd/>
                Options None
                AllowOverride None
                Order allow,deny
                allow from all
        </Directory>
</VirtualHost>
```

Then include the HA proxy configuration that allows load balancing across many of these workers (Listing 4-57).

Listing 4-57. HA Proxy configuration

```
global
  chroot  /var/lib/haproxy
  daemon
  group  haproxy
  log  10.0.2.1 local0
  maxconn  4000
  pidfile  /var/run/haproxy.pid
  stats  socket /var/lib/haproxy/stats
  user  haproxy

defaults
  log  global
  maxconn  8000
  option  redispatch
  retries  3
  stats  enable
  timeout  http-request 10s
  timeout  queue 1m
  timeout  connect 10s
  timeout  client 1m
  timeout  server 1m
  timeout  check 10s
```

```
listen puppet
  bind 10.0.2.10:8140
  mode  tcp
  balance  source
  option  ssl-hello-chk
  timeout client  1000000
  timeout server  1000000
  server puppet-master-4.pro-puppet.com puppet-master-4.pro-puppet.com:8140   check
  server puppet-master-5.pro-puppet.com puppet-master-5.pro-puppet.com:8140   check
```

In this example, two puppet master workers, puppet-master-4 and puppet-master-5, are both running Apache and Passenger. They have had their certs signed with a DNS-alternate name of puppet.pro-puppet.com. This means they can listen both as themselves and on the puppet.pro-puppet.com IP address. That IP address is assigned in DNS to 10.0.2.10 and is held by the HA proxy. Because the traffic is being tunneled at a lower level, the certificate verification is transparent to the proxy. This means both Puppet masters need to be able to identify as puppet.pro-puppet.com. The way to accomplish that is to sign their certificates with additional DNS names, called dns_alt_names.

First create a certificate (through puppet agent --test) using the --dns_alt_names flag, as shown in Listing 4-58.

Listing 4-58. Creating a certificate request with a dns_alt_name on puppet-master-5

```
root@puppet-master-5:~# puppet agent --test --dns_alt_names=puppet,puppet.pro-puppet.com,
puppet-master-5,puppet-master-5.pro-puppet.com
Info: Creating a new SSL key for puppet-master-5.testcorpn.lan
Info: Caching certificate for ca
Info: Creating a new SSL certificate request for puppet-master-5.testcorp.lan
Info: Certificate Request fingerprint (SHA256):
FF:65:C9:F0:FF:4A:3B:2D:BA:6D:01:21:8E:6E:86:30:92:8F:BC:7B:B9:93:C5:0E:C3:20:66:06:D8:F6:AA:A7
Exiting; no certificate found and waitforcert is disabled
```

Second, list the certificates pending in the queue on the CA server (Listing 4-59).

Listing 4-59. Listing pending certificate requests on the Puppet CA server

```
[root@puppet-ca-1 ~]# puppet cert list
  "puppet-master-5.testcorp.lan" (SHA256)
FF:65:C9:F0:FF:4A:3B:2D:BA:6D:01:21:8E:6E:86:30:92:8F:BC:7B:B9:93:C5:0E:C3:20:66:06:D8:F6:AA:A7
(alt names: "DNS:puppet", "DNS:puppet-master-5", "DNS:puppet-master-5.testcorp.lan",
"DNS:puppet-master-5.pro-puppet.com", "DNS:puppet.pro-puppet.com")
```

Finally, sign the certificate using the --allow-dns-alt-names flag (Listing 4-60).

Listing 4-60. Signing certificate requests with dns_alt_names

```
[root@puppet-ca-1 ~]# puppet cert sign puppet-master-5.testcorp.lan --allow-dns-alt-names
Notice: Signed certificate request for puppet-master-5.testcorp.lan
Notice: Removing file Puppet::SSL::CertificateRequest puppet-master-5.testcorp.lan at
'/var/lib/puppet/ssl/ca/requests/puppet-master-5.testcorp.lan.pem'
```

Anycast

In some cases, where you have multiple datacenters or sites, anycast is an option for scaling and segmenting your Puppet infrastructure. Anycasting a service is typically done with services that require the utmost uptime such as DNS. Anycasting means running a Puppet master, or load-balancing virtual IP, on a host that is also running a dynamic routing protocol such as BGP or OSPF. Quagga is a common daemon on Unix/Linux to speak these protocols. The Linux machine uses a BGP or OSPF or other routing protocol link to directly inject a route to the virtual IP Puppet is running on into the routing table of the core router for the datacenter. This can be done at multiple datacenters. All IP traffic to the Puppet IP will follow the shortest cost path, which will mean connecting to the local Puppet master. If that device experiences a failure, the BGP/OSPF session will end and the upstream router will use the second-shortest-cost path, which means finding another anycasted Puppet master. This is an advanced configuration and should only be done in close coordination with your networking team.

Masterless Puppet

A simple approach to massive scaling with Puppet infrastructure is to run the Puppet standalone client on each machine. Puppet can be run from cron on an hourly basis and local code used to configure the node. The challenge then becomes pushing code to each and every server. This can be accomplished via an NFS mount, or by running a git pull (or your version control system's equivalent) just before running puppet agent (Listing 4-61).

Listing 4-61. Creating an environments directory and cloning a production checkout of Puppet code

```
[root ~ ]# mkdir -p /etc/puppet/environments/
[root environments]# git clone git@git.pro-puppet.com:puppet production
Cloning into 'production'...
done.
[root@pdxudev01 environments]# ls
production
```

Listing 4-62 shows what we've created.

Listing 4-62. Inspecting the Puppet code we checked out

```
[root@box1 /etc/puppet/environments]# find . | grep -v '.git'
.
./production
./production/data
./production/data/dev.yaml
./production/data/defaults.yaml
./production/data/box1.yaml
./production/data/global.yaml
./production/data/production.yaml
./production/manifests
./production/manifests/site.pp
./production/modules
./production/modules/mysql
./production/modules/mysql/manifests
./production/modules/mysql/manifests/init.pp
./production/modules/mysql/Modulefile
./production/modules/mysql/README
./production/modules/workstation
./production/modules/workstation/manifests
```

```
./production/modules/workstation/manifests/init.pp
./production/modules/workstation/Modulefile
./production/modules/workstation/README
./production/modules/ldap
./production/modules/ldap/manifests
./production/modules/ldap/manifests/init.pp
./production/modules/ldap/Modulefile
./production/modules/ldap/README
./production/modules/sudo
./production/modules/sudo/manifests
./production/modules/sudo/manifests/init.pp
./production/modules/sudo/Modulefile
./production/modules/sudo/README
```

We have to grep -v the Git directories because they pollute the structure shown here. What you can see is that a set of manifests, a set of modules, and a set of Hiera data have all been copied into the production directory. Hiera will be covered in depth in Chapter 12; all you need to know right now is that there are Hiera data files that need to go in the data directory.

This is a good start, but we still need a corresponding puppet.conf file, as shown in Listing 4-63.

Listing 4-63. Puppet.conf for box1.pro-puppet.com for masterless Puppet

```
[main]
    # The Puppet log directory.
    # The default value is '$vardir/log'.
    logdir = /var/log/puppet

    # Where Puppet PID files are kept.
    # The default value is '$vardir/run'.
    rundir = /var/run/puppet

    # Where SSL certificates are kept.
    # The default value is '$confdir/ssl'.
    ssldir = $vardir/ssl
    certname = box1.pro-puppet.com
    modulepath = /etc/puppet/environments/$environment/modules
    manifests = /etc/puppet/environments/$environment/site.pp
```

Note that we are still setting certname here, and it should be set uniquely for every unique host. With that configuration file in place, we can make an initial run of puppet apply (Listing 4-64).

Listing 4-64. Running puppet apply manually

```
[root@box1 /e/p/environments]# puppet apply production/manifests/site.pp
Notice: /Stage[main]//Node[default]/Notify[puppet is runnning]/message: defined 'message' as
'puppet is runnning'
Notice: Finished catalog run in 0.09 seconds
```

But what does the site.pp look like? It looks exactly the same as it does for mastered Puppet (Listing 4-65).

Listing 4-65. The `site.pp` file for use in masterless Puppet

```
[root@box1 /etc/puppet]# cat environments/production/manifests/site.pp

node 'box1.pro-puppet.com' {

  class { 'mysql':
    databases => ['prod','staging','dev']
  }


  class { 'sudo': }
}

node 'box2.pro-puppet.com' {

  class { 'ldap':
    allow_connections => 'localonly',
  }


  class { 'sudo': }
}

node 'box3.pro-puppet.com' {

  class { 'workstation':
    roles => ['webdev', 'dba']
  }


  class { 'sudo': }
}
```

Puppet still looks up the node definition by `certname`.

Going further, if we want to use Hiera we need to create a `hiera.yaml` for each client (Listing 4-66).

Listing 4-66. The `/etc/puppet/hiera.yaml` needed for each client

```
[root@box1 /etc/puppet]# cat hiera.yaml
---
:backends:
  - yaml
:hierarchy:
  - %{environment}/data/defaults
  - %{environment}/data/%{clientcert}
  - %{environment}/data/%{environment}
  - %{environment}/data/global

:yaml:
  :datadir:
    - /etc/puppet/environments/
```

The environment settings here allow us to have environmentally aware data, as we showed in Chapter 3. Again, Hiera will be fully discussed in Chapter 12. You can skip there immediately after reading this chapter.

Going further still, you might want to connect masterless Puppet to PuppetDB or a Dashboard. That configuration is possible, but it is outside of the scope of this book. The last thing we need is a `cron` job to fire off the Puppet run:

```
0 * * * * (cd /etc/puppet/environments/production && git pull && puppet apply
/etc/puppet/environments/production/manifests/site.pp ) >/dev/null
```

In this example, an individual Puppet client acts as its own bottleneck in compiling Puppet catalogs and applying configuration. The only requirement is a Git clone from a Git server, and scaling read-only Git access is relatively simple.

Measuring Performance

Catalog retrieval time is the primary measure of how one or more Puppet masters are performing. Catalog compilation is a very I/O-, CPU-, and memory- intensive process. All of the imported manifests must be located and read from the file system, and CPU and memory are used to parse and compile the catalog. In order to measure this process, you can use a simple `curl` script to periodically obtain a compiled catalog. If the command takes longer than is normal for the environment, there is a strong indication that additional capacity should be added to the Puppet master infrastructure.

Using the unencrypted Puppet master back-end workers configured when setting up the Apache load balancer, you can write a small script to measure the catalog compilation time of the node `test.example.com`.

To do this, you need to know the four components of a catalog request:

- The URI containing the environment, catalog, and node to obtain a catalog from
- The SSL authentication headers
- A list of facts and their values
- A header telling the Puppet master what encoding formats the client accepts

All of this information is available in the Apache access logs (see Listing 4-67). The list of facts is easily obtained by running the Puppet agent normally, and then inspecting the HTTP access logs and copying the URL into a script.

Listing 4-67. Curl URL based on Apache access logs

```
[root@puppet-master-1 ~]# tail -f /var/log/httpd/balancer_access.log
192.168.8.12 - - [14/Aug/2013:10:14:50 +0000] "GET /production/node/puppet-client-4.pro-puppet.com?
HTTP/1.1" 200 3842 "-" "-"
```

The path following the GET verb contains `/production/node/puppet-client-4.pro-puppet.com`. This indicates a catalog request for the host `puppet-client-4.pro-puppet.com` from the production environment. The query portion of the URL contains two pieces of information: the format of the facts listing, and the listing of facts itself. These pieces of information are encoded in the `facts_format` and `facts_query` parameters of the URL. Since Puppet 3, these parameters have been optional, as they are by default sent via a header, but you can still append them to the end of the request to perform testing. To construct the full URL, prefix the URL from Listing 4-67 with `http://127.0.0.1:8141`, the address of the Apache worker virtual host. Listing 4-68 shows the command the operator uses to measure catalog compilation time.

Listing 4-68. A curl catalog request command

```
[root@puppet-master-1 ~]# time curl -v -H "Accept: pson, yaml" \
   -H "X-Client-DN: /CN=puppet-client-test.pro-puppet.com" \
   -H "X-Client-Verify: SUCCESS"  \
'http://127.0.0.1:18140/production/node/puppet-client-test.pro-puppet.com'

* About to connect() to 127.0.0.1 port 18140 (#0)
*   Trying 127.0.0.1... connected
* Connected to 127.0.0.1 (127.0.0.1) port 18140 (#0)
> GET /production/node/puppet-client-test.pro-puppet.com HTTP/1.1
> User-Agent: curl/7.19.7 (x86_64-redhat-linux-gnu) libcurl/7.19.7 NSS/3.14.0.0 zlib/1.2.3
libidn/1.18 libssh2/1.4.2
> Host: 127.0.0.1:18140
> Accept: pson, yaml
> X-Client-DN: /CN=puppet-client-test.pro-puppet.com
> X-Client-Verify: SUCCESS
>
< HTTP/1.1 200 OK
< Date: Thu, 15 Aug 2013 04:59:46 GMT
< Server: Apache/2.2.15 (CentOS)
< X-Powered-By: Phusion Passenger 4.0.8
< Content-Length: 103
< Status: 200 OK
< Connection: close
< Content-Type: text/pson
<
* Closing connection #0
{"document_type":"Node","data":{"environment":"production","name":"puppet-client-test.pro-puppet.com"}}
real    0m0.320s
user    0m0.002s
sys     0m0.005s
```

Placing this command in a script and executing it on the Puppet master worker nodes allows us to know when catalog compilation time grows beyond normal thresholds.

Splay Time

Related to catalog compilation time, Puppet agent processes sometimes present a "thundering herd" problem when all systems have their clocks synchronized and are configured to run from the cron daemon at a specific time. The catalog compilation process is quite processor-intensive, and if the Puppet master receives too many requests in a short time, the systems may start to thrash and degrade in performance.

We recommend that when running a Puppet agent out of cron, you introduce a small random splay time to ensure that all of the Puppet agent nodes do not request their configuration catalog at exactly the same moment. The Example.com operator follows this recommendation and uses the Puppet agent wrapper script shown in Listing 4-69 when executing the Puppet agent out of cron.

Listing 4-69. Bash script to splay Puppet agents

```
#! /bin/bash
set -e
set -u
sleep $((RANDOM % 300))
exec puppet agent --no-daemonize --onetime
```

The `sleep` command in this shell script causes a delay of between zero and five minutes. With hundreds of Puppet agent–managed nodes, this random delay will ensure that incoming requests to the Puppet Master workers are spread out over a short time. The `splay` option in `puppet.conf` also works to avoid the thundering herd problem when running the `puppet agent` daemon.

Summary

In this chapter, you've configured the Puppet master infrastructure in a number of ways. Specifically, you configured the Apache web server as a reverse HTTPS proxy to handle the SSL verification and authentication of incoming Puppet agent–managed nodes. Once authenticated, the Apache system behaves as a HTTP load balancer, distributing requests automatically to some number of back-end Puppet master worker virtual hosts.

In addition, we showed you how to handle incoming certificate requests in a special manner, forwarding all certificate requests to a single Puppet CA worker process with a hot standby ready and waiting for redundancy. The consolidation of certificate requests to a single Puppet CA worker mitigates the overhead and problems associated with keeping the Puppet CA certificate revocation list, serial numbers, and index synchronized across workers.

In addition to HTTP load balancing, several alternative technologies and implementations were introduced.

Finally, you learned how to measure the catalog compilation time of the Puppet master workers and use splay time to avoid overwhelming the Puppet masters.

Going Further

It is possible to configure your Puppet infrastructure using an external CA such as your site's root CA instead of a self-contained and self-signed root. For information on this, consult the following resources. In Chapter 8 you will learn how to use PuppetDB to scale the `storeconfigs` service.

Resources

- Using Passenger: `http://docs.puppetlabs.com/guides/passenger.html`

- Using multiple masters: `http://docs.puppetlabs.com/guides/scaling_multiple_masters.html`

- Using an external CA: `http://docs.puppetlabs.com/puppet/3/reference/config_ssl_external_ca.html`

- Apache Configuration Reference: `http://httpd.apache.org/docs/2.2/`

- Apache Mod Proxy Balancer: `http://httpd.apache.org/docs/2.2/mod/mod_proxy_balancer.html`

- DNS Round Robin: `http://en.wikipedia.org/wiki/Round_robin_DNS`

- Masterless Puppet with Jordan Sissel (formerly of Loggly, now of Dreamhost): `http://semicomplete.com/presentations/puppet-at-loggly/puppet-at-loggly.pdf.html`

- Masterless Puppet with Capistrano: `https://www.braintreepayments.com/braintrust/decentralize-your-devops-with-masterless-puppet-and-supply-drop`

- Puppet Splay: `http://docs.puppetlabs.com/references/latest/configuration.html#splay`

- HA Proxy Load Balancer: `http://haproxy.1wt.eu/`

- Anycast: `http://en.wikipedia.org/wiki/Anycast`

- DNS SRV Records: `http://en.wikipedia.org/wiki/SRV_record`

- Puppet DNS SRV Records: `http://docs.puppetlabs.com/guides/scaling_multiple_masters.html#option-4-dns-srv-records`

- Puppet REST API: `http://docs.puppetlabs.com/guides/rest_api.html`

- Rsync: `http://en.wikipedia.org/wiki/Rsync`

- Certificate Authority: `http://en.wikipedia.org/wiki/Certificate_authority`

- X.509 Certificates: `http://en.wikipedia.org/wiki/X.509`

- Basics of a Puppet Run: `http://docs.puppetlabs.com/learning/agent_master_basic.html`

CHAPTER 5

Externalizing Puppet Configuration

In Chapter 2 we talked about the ways you can define your hosts or nodes to Puppet. We talked about specifying them in a variety of forms as node statements in your Puppet manifest files. We also mentioned that Puppet has the capability to store node information in external sources. This avoids the need to specify large numbers of nodes manually in your manifest files, a solution that is time-consuming and not scalable.

Puppet has two ways to store node information externally:

- External Node Classification
- LDAP server classification

The first capability, called External Node Classification (ENC), is a script-based integration system that Puppet queries for node data. The script returns classes, inheritance, variables and environment configuration that Puppet can then use to define a node and configure your hosts.

■ **Tip**   External node classifiers are also one of the means by which tools like the Puppet Enterprise and Foreman can be integrated into Puppet and provide node information, as you will see in Chapter 7.

The second capability allows you to query Lightweight Directory Access Protocol (LDAP) directories for node information. This integration is used less often than ENCs, but it is especially useful because you can specify an existing LDAP directory, such as your asset management database or an LDAP DNS backend, for your node data.

Using external node classification, either via an ENC or via LDAP, is the recommended way to scale your Puppet implementation for large volumes of hosts. Some sites have begun using hiera, as discussed in chapter 12.Most of the sites using Puppet that have thousands of nodes, for example Google and Zynga, make use of external node classification systems to deal with the large number of nodes. Rather than managing files containing hundreds, thousands, or even tens of thousands of node statements, you can use this syntax:

```
node mail.example.com { ... }
node web.example.com { ... }
node db.examplc.com { ... }
...
```

This capability allows you to specify a single source of node information and make quick and easy changes to that information without needing to edit files.

In this chapter, we discuss both approaches to storing node information in external sources. First we look at creating an external node classifier, and we provide some simple examples of these for you to model your own on; then we demonstrate the use of the LDAP node classifier.

External Node Classification

Writing an ENC is very simple. An ENC is merely a script that takes a node name, for example mail.example.com, and then returns the node's configuration in the form of YAML data. YAML, or Yet Ain't Markup Language (http://www.yaml.org/), is a serialization language used in a variety of programming languages. YAML is human-friendly, meaning that it's structured and is designed to be easy to read. It is often used as a configuration file format; for example, the database configuration file used in Ruby on Rails applications, database.yml, is a YAML file.

Some simple YAML examples will give you an idea of how it works. YAML is expressed in a hash, where structure is important. Let's start by specifying a list of items:

```
---
- foo
- bar
- baz
- qux
```

The start of a YAML document is identified with three dashes, ---. Every ENC needs to return these three dashes as the start of its output. You've then got a list of items, each preceded by a dash.

You can also express the concept of assigning a value to an item, for example:

```
---
foo: bar
```

Here you've added our three dashes and then expressed that the value of item foo is bar. You can also express grouped collections of items (a feature we're going to use extensively in our ENCs):

```
---
foo:
 - bar
baz:
 - qux
```

You've again started with three dashes and then specified the names of the lists you're creating: foo and baz. Inside each list are the list items, each one again preceded with a dash, but this time indented one space to indicate its membership in the list.

This indentation is very important. For the YAML to be valid, it must be structured correctly. This can sometimes be a real challenge, but there are tools you can use to structure suitable YAML. For example, VIM syntax highlighting will recognize YAML (if the file you're editing has a .yml or .yaml extension), or you can use the excellent Online YAML Parser to confirm that the YAML you're generating is valid: http://yaml-online-parser.appspot.com/.

But before generating your first YAML node, you need to configure Puppet to use an external node classifier; in addition, you need to do file-based node configuration.

■ **Note**   You can see a more complete example of structured YAML at http://www.yaml.org/start.html.

Configuring Nodes Using an External Node Classifier

To use external nodes, you first need to tell Puppet to use a classifier to configure the nodes rather than use node definitions. Do this by specifying the node_terminus option and the name and location of the classifier in the [master] section of the puppet.conf configuration file on your Puppet master. You can see this in Listing 5-1, where you've specified a classifier called puppet_node_classifier located in the /usr/bin directory.

Listing 5-1. The external_nodes configuration option

```
[master]
node_terminus = exec
external_nodes = /usr/bin/puppet_node_classifier
```

The node_terminus configuration option is used to configure Puppet for node sources other than the default flat file manifests. Available options are plain, exec, and ldap. The exec option tells Puppet to use an external node classifier script.

A classifier can be written in any language, including shell script, Ruby, Perl, Python, and a variety of other languages. The only requirement is that the language can output the appropriate YAML data. For example, you could also easily add a database backend to a classifier that queries a database for the relevant hostname and returns the associated classes and any variables. If the ENC script returns a nonzero status, Puppet will ignore the results of the execution and treat the node as not found.

Following are some example node classifiers written in different languages.

■ **Note**   You can have nodes specified in both Puppet manifests and external node classifiers. For this to work correctly, though, your ENC must return an empty YAML hash.

An External Node Classifier in a Shell Script

In Listing 5-2, you can see a very simple node classifier, the puppet_node_classifier script specified in Listing 5-1. This classifier is written in shell script.

Listing 5-2. A simple node classifier

```
#!/bin/sh
cat <<"END"
---
classes:
  - base
parameters:
  puppetserver: puppet.example.com
environment: production
END
exit 0
```

The script in Listing 5-2 will return the same classes and variables each time it is called, irrespective of the hostname passed to the script. For example, calling

```
$ /usr/bin/puppet_node_classifier web.example.com
```

returns this:

```
---
classes:
  - base
parameters:
  puppetserver: puppet.example.com
```

The classes block holds a list of the classes that belong to this node, and the parameters block contains a list of the variables this node specifies. In this case, the node includes the base class and has a variable called $puppetserver with a value of puppet.example.com.

Puppet will use this data to construct a node definition as if you'd defined a node statement. That node statement would look like Listing 5-3.

Listing 5-3. Node definition from Listing 5-2's classifier

```
node web.example.com {
        $puppetserver = 'puppet.example.com'
        include base
}
```

This is the simplest ENC we can devise. More complex variations of this script can return different results depending on the particular node name being passed to the classifier, in the same way different nodes would be configured with different classes, definitions, and variables in your manifest files.

■ **Tip**   Any parameters specified in your ENC will be available as top-scope variables.

Parameterized Classes in YAML

It is possible to pass parameters to classes in YAML. Using ENCs to populate parameters passed to classes means that information in your external data store can produce logic in Puppet modules. This capability is very powerful, and the syntax looks like this:

```
classes:
  -base
ntp:
  servers:
0.pool.ntp.org
1.pool.ntp.org
manageservice: "false"
parameters:
  puppetserver: puppet.example.com
```

A Ruby External Node Classifier

Let's look at another example of an ENC, this time specifying a list of hosts or returning an empty YAML hash if the host is not found. This ENC is written in Ruby, and you can see it in Listing 5-4.

Listing 5-4. Ruby node classifier

```ruby
#!/usr/bin/env ruby

require 'yaml'

node = ARGV[0]
default = { 'classes' => []}

# Hostname must match: 'hostname.example.com'
unless node =~ /(^\S+)\.(\S+\.\S+)$/
  print default.to_yaml
  exit 0
end

hostname = $1

base = { 'environment' => 'production',
         'parameters' => {
                     'puppetserver' => 'puppet.example.com'
         },
         'classes' => [ 'base' ],
       }

case hostname
  when /^web?\w+$/
     web = { 'classes' => 'apache'  }
     base['classes'] << web['classes']
     puts YAML.dump(base)
  when /^db?\w+$/
     db = { 'classes' => 'mysql'  }
     base['classes'] << db['classes']
     puts YAML.dump(base)
  when /^mail?\w+$/
     mail = { 'classes' => 'postfix'  }
     base['classes'] << mail['classes']
     puts YAML.dump(base)
  else
    print default.to_yaml
end

exit 0
```

The simple ENC here captures the incoming node name and rejects it by returning an empty hash (defined in the default variable) if it is not an appropriately formed fully-qualified domain name (FQDN).

The code then sets up some basic defaults, including the puppetserver variable, the environment, and a base class. The ENC then takes the host name portion of the FQDN and checks it against a list of host names, for example matching it against web, web1, web123 and so on for database and mail hosts.

For example, if you passed the ENC a node name of web.example.com, it would return the following YAML hash:

```
---
parameters:
  puppetserver: puppet.example.com
classes:
 - base
 - apache
environment: production
```

That would result in this node definition:

```
node web.example.com {
  $puppetserver = puppet.example.com
  include base
  include apache
}
```

This would specify that the node belonged to the production environment.

If the ENC doesn't match any host names, it will return an empty YAML hash, which looks like this:

```
---
classes: []
```

A Perl External Node Classifier

In Listing 5-5, you can see another node classifier, this one written in Perl.

Listing 5-5. Perl-based node classifier

```perl
#!/usr/bin/perl -w
use strict;
use YAML qw( Dump );

my $hostname = shift || die "No hostname passed";

$hostname =~ /^(\w+)\.(\w+)\.(\w{3})$/
    or die "Invalid hostname: $hostname";

my ( $host, $domain, $net ) = ( $1, $2, $3 );

my @classes = ( 'base', $domain );
my %parameters = (
    puppetserver    => "puppet.$domain.$net"
    );
my $environment = "production";

print Dump( {
    classes     => \@classes,
    parameters  => \%parameters,
  environment => \$environment,
} );
```

In Listing 5-5, we've created a Perl node classifier that makes use of the Perl YAML module. The YAML module can be installed via CPAN or your distribution's package management system. For example, on Debian it is the libyaml-perl package, and on Fedora it is the perl-YAML package.

The classifier slices our hostname into sections; it assumes the input will be a fully qualified domain name and will fail if no hostname or an inappropriately structured hostname is passed. The classifier then uses those sections to classify the nodes and set parameters. If you called this node classifier with the hostname web.example.com, it would return this node classification:

```
---
classes:
  - base
  - example
parameters:
  puppetserver: puppet.example.com
```

That would result in a node definition in Puppet structured like this:

```
node 'web.example.com' {
        include base
        include example

        $puppetserver = "puppet.example.com"
}
```

Back-Ending a Node Classification

Finally, as mentioned, you could also back-end the node classification script with a database, as demonstrated in Listing 5-6.

Listing 5-6. A database back-end node classifier

```perl
#!/usr/bin/perl -w
use strict;
use YAML qw( Dump );
use DBI;

my $hostname = shift || die "No hostname passed";

$hostname =~ /^(\w+)\.(\w+)\.(\w{3})$/
    or die "Invalid hostname: $hostname";

my ( $host, $domain, $net ) = ( $1, $2, $3 );

# MySQL Configuration
my $data_source = "dbi:mysql:database=puppet;host=localhost";
my $username = "puppet";
my $password = "password";

# Connect to the server
my $dbh = DBI->connect($data_source, $username, $password)
    or die $DBI::errstr;
```

147

```
# Build the query
my $sth = $dbh->prepare( qq{SELECT class FROM nodes WHERE node = '$hostname'})
    or die "Can't prepare statement: $DBI::errstr";

# Execute the query
my $rc = $sth->execute
    or die "Can't execute statement: $DBI::errstr";

# Set parameters
my %parameters = (
    puppet_server   => "puppet.$domain.$net"
    );

# Set classes
my @class;
while (my @row=$sth->fetchrow_array)
 { push(@class,@row) }

# Check for problems
die $sth->errstr if $sth->err;

# Disconnect from database
$dbh->disconnect;

# Print the YAML
print Dump( {
    classes     => \@class,
    parameters  => \%parameters,
} );
```

This node classifier would connect to a MySQL database called puppet running on the local host. Using the hostname, the script receiving it would query the database and return a list of classes to assign to the node. The nodes and classes would be stored in a table. The next lines form a SQL statement to create a very simple table to do this:

```
CREATE TABLE 'nodes' (
'node' varchar(80) NOT NULL,
'class' varchar(80) NOT NULL ) TYPE=MyISAM;
```

The classes, and whatever parameters you set (which you could also place in the database in another table), are then returned and output as the required YAML data.

▓ **Tip** You can also access fact values in your node classifier scripts. Before the classifier is called, the $vardir/yaml/ facts/ directory is populated with a YAML file named for the node containing fact values, for example /var/lib/puppet/yaml/facts/web.example.com.yaml. This file can be queried for fact values.

All of these external node classifiers are very simple and could easily be expanded to provide more sophisticated functionality. It is important to remember that external nodes override node configuration in your manifest files. If you enable an external node classifier, any duplicate node definitions in your manifest files will not be processed; they will be ignored by Puppet.

Storing Node Configuration in LDAP

In addition to external node classifiers, Puppet also allows the storage of node information in LDAP directories. Many organizations already have a wide variety of information about their environments, such as DNS, user and group data, stored in LDAP directories. This allows organizations to leverage these already-existing assets stored in LDAP directories or to decouple their configuration from Puppet and centralize it. Additionally, it also allows LDAP-enabled applications to have access to your configuration data.

■ **Note**   The use of LDAP nodes overrides node definitions in your manifest files and your ENC. If you use LDAP node definitions, you cannot define nodes in your manifest files or in an ENC.

Installing Ruby LDAP Libraries

The first step in using LDAP for your node configuration is to ensure that the Ruby LDAP libraries are installed. First, check for the presence of the LDAP libraries:

```
# ruby -rldap -e "puts :installed"
```

If this command does not return installed, the libraries are not installed. You can either install them via your distribution's package management system or download them from the Ruby/LDAP site. For Red hat and derivatives, and for Ubuntu/Debian, this is the ruby-ldap package.

If there isn't a package for your distribution, you can download the required libraries in the form of either an RPM or a source package from the Ruby/LDAP site. The Ruby/LDAP site is located at http://ruby-ldap.sourceforge.net/.

Check out the current Ruby LDAP source code:

```
$ svn checkout http://ruby-activeldap.googlecode.com/svn/ldap/trunk/ ruby-ldap-ro
```

Then, change into the resulting directory and make and install the code:

```
$ cd ruby-ldap-ro
$ ruby extconf.rb
$ sudo make && make install
```

Setting Up the LDAP Server

Next, you need to set up your LDAP server. We're going to assume you've either already got one running or can set one up yourself. For an LDAP server, you can use OpenLDAP, Red Hat Directory Server (or Fedora Directory Server), Sun's Directory Server, or one of a variety of other servers. We're going to use OpenLDAP for the purpose of demonstrating how to use LDAP node definitions.

■ **Tip**   For some quick-start instructions on setting up OpenLDAP, you can refer to http://www.openldap.org/doc/admin23/quickstart.html.

Adding the Puppet Schema

Now we need to add the Puppet schema to our LDAP directory's configuration.

■ **Caution**   You may need to tweak or translate the default LDAP schema for some directory servers, but it is suitable for OpenLDAP.

The Puppet schema document is available in the Puppet source package in the ext/ldap/puppet.schema file, or you can take it from the project's Git repository at https://github.com/puppetlabs/puppet/blob/master/ext/ldap/puppet.schema.

We need to add it to our schema directory and slapd.conf configuration file. For example, on an Ubuntu or Debian host, the schema directory is /etc/ldap/schema, and the slapd.conf configuration is located in the /etc/ldap directory. On Red Hat, the configuration file is located in /etc/openldap, and the schemas are located in /etc/openldap/schema. Copy the puppet.schema file into the appropriate directory, for example on Ubuntu:

```
$ cp puppet/ext/ldap/puppet.schema /etc/ldap/schema
```

Now you can add an include statement to your slapd.conf configuration file; there should be a number of existing statements you can model:

```
include          /etc/ldap/schema/puppet.schema
```

Or you can add a schema to a running OpenLDAP server, like so:

```
$ ldapadd -x -H ldap://ldap.example.com/ -D "cn=config" -W -f puppet.ldif
```

To update OpenLDAP with the new schema, you may also now need to restart your server.

```
# /etc/init.d/slapd restart
```

Now that you've added the schema and configured the LDAP server, you need to tell Puppet to use an LDAP server as the source of its node configuration.

■ **Note**   Your LDAP server may be able to accept new schema without a restart. We recommend it here in case your LDAP server can't.

Configuring LDAP in Puppet

LDAP configuration is very simple. Let's look at the required configuration options from the [master] section of the puppet.conf configuration file in Listing 5-7.

Listing 5-7. LDAP configuration in Puppet

```
[master]
node_terminus = ldap
ldapserver = ldap.example.com
ldapbase = ou=Hosts,dc=example,dc=com
```

First, we set the node_terminus option to ldap to tell Puppet to look to an LDAP server as our node source. Next, we specify the hostname of our LDAP server, in this case ldap.example.com, in the ldapserver option. Finally, in the ldapbase option, we specify the base search path. Puppet recommends that hosts be stored in an OU called Hosts under our main directory structure, but you can configure this to suit your environment.

If required, you can specify a user and password using the ldapuser and ldappassword options and override the default LDAP port of 389 with the ldapport option. There is some limited support for TLS or SSL, but only if your LDAP server does not require client-side certificates.

■ **Tip** You can see a full list of the potential LDAP options at
http://docs.puppetlabs.com/references/stable/configuration.html.

After configuring Puppet to use LDAP nodes, you should restart your Puppet master daemon to ensure that the new configuration is updated.

Now you need to add your node configuration to the LDAP server. Let's take a quick look at the Puppet LDAP schema in Listing 5-8.

Listing 5-8. The LDAP schema

```
attributetype ( 1.3.6.1.4.1.34380.1.1.3.10 NAME 'puppetClass'
        DESC 'Puppet Node Class'
        EQUALITY caseIgnoreIA5Match
        SYNTAX 1.3.6.1.4.1.1466.115.121.1.26 )

attributetype ( 1.3.6.1.4.1.34380.1.1.3.9 NAME 'parentNode'
        DESC 'Puppet Parent Node'
        EQUALITY caseIgnoreIA5Match
        SYNTAX 1.3.6.1.4.1.1466.115.121.1.26
        SINGLE-VALUE )

attributetype ( 1.3.6.1.4.1.34380.1.1.3.11 NAME 'environment'
        DESC 'Puppet Node Environment'
        EQUALITY caseIgnoreIA5Match
        SYNTAX 1.3.6.1.4.1.1466.115.121.1.26 )

attributetype ( 1.3.6.1.4.1.34380.1.1.3.12 NAME 'puppetVar'
        DESC 'A variable setting for puppet'
        EQUALITY caseIgnoreIA5Match
        SYNTAX 1.3.6.1.4.1.1466.115.121.1.26 )
objectclass ( 1.3.6.1.4.1.34380.1.1.1.2 NAME 'puppetClient' SUP top AUXILIARY
        DESC 'Puppet Client objectclass'
        MAY ( puppetclass $ parentnode $ environment $ puppetvar ))
```

The Puppet schema is made up of an object class, puppetClient, and four attributes: puppetclass, parentnode, environment, and puppetvar. The object class puppetClient is assigned to each host that is a Puppet node. The puppetclass attribute contains all the classes defined for that node. At this stage, you cannot add definitions, just classes. The parentnode attribute allows you to specify node inheritance, environment specifies the environment of the node, and puppetvar specifies any variables assigned to the node.

In addition, any attributes defined in your LDAP node entries are available as variables to Puppet. This compatibility works in much the same way as Facter facts (see Chapter 1); for example, if the host entry has the ipHost class, the ipHostNumber attribute of the class is available as the variable $ipHostNumber. You can also specify attributes with multiple values; these are created as arrays.

You can also define default nodes in the same manner as doing so in your manifest node definitions: creating a host in your directory called default. The classes assigned to this host will be applied to any node that does not match a node in the directory. If no default node exists and no matching node definition is found, Puppet will return an error.

You can now add your hosts, or the relevant object class and attributes to existing definitions for your hosts, in the LDAP directory. You can import your host definitions using LDIF files or manipulate your directory using your choice of tools, such as phpLDAPadmin (http://phpldapadmin.sourceforge.net/wiki/index.php/Main_Page).

Listing 5-9 is an LDIF file containing examples of node definitions.

Listing 5-9. LDIF nodes

```
# LDIF Export for: ou=Hosts,dc=example,dc=com
dn: ou=Hosts,dc=example,dc=com
objectClass: organizationalUnit
objectClass: top
ou: Hosts

dn: cn=default,ou=Hosts,dc=example,dc=com
cn: default
description: Default
objectClass: device
objectClass: top
objectClass: puppetClient
puppetclass: base

dn: cn=basenode,ou=Hosts,dc=example,dc=com
cn: basenode
description: Basenode
objectClass: device
objectClass: top
objectClass: puppetClient
puppetclass: base

dn: cn=web,ou=Hosts,dc=example,dc=com
cn: web
description: Webserver
objectClass: device
objectClass: top
objectClass: puppetClient
parentnode: basenode
puppetclass: apache

dn: cn=web1.example.com, ou=Hosts,dc=example,dc=com
cn: web1
description: webserving host
objectclass: device
objectclass: top
objectclass: puppetClient
objectclass: ipHost
parentnode: web
ipHostNumber: 192.168.1.100
```

This listing includes a default node, a node called basenode, and a template node called web. Each node has particular classes assigned to it, and the web node has the basenode defined as its parent node and thus inherits its classes also. Last, we define a client node, called web1, which inherits the web node as a parent.

Summary

In this chapter we've explored how you can use both external node classification and the LDAP node terminus. Both of these allow you to scale to larger numbers of nodes without needing to maintain large numbers of nodes in your manifest files. In Chapter 7, we'll also look at how you can use Puppet Dashboard or the Foreman dashboard as an external node classifier.

Resources

The following links will take you to Puppet documentation related to external nodes:

- External nodes: http://docs.puppetlabs.com/guides/external_nodes.html

- LDAP nodes: http://projects.puppetlabs.com/projects/puppet/wiki/Ldap_Nodes

- Puppet configuration reference:
  http://docs.puppetlabs.com/references/stable/configuration.html

CHAPTER 6

■ ■ ■

Exporting and Storing Configuration

So far in the book, you've seen how Puppet models configuration on a single host. In many cases, however, you have configuration on multiple hosts that have a relationship; for example, your monitoring system needs to know about configuration on hosts being monitored. In this chapter we look at three Puppet features that help you model resources on multiple hosts: virtual resources, exported resources, and stored configuration using PuppetDB.

- Virtual resources are a method of managing resources that may be required by multiple configurations. For example, a user may be required on some hosts but not others. Virtual resources allow you to define a resource and select where you instantiate that resource.

- Exported resources allow you to take resources defined on one host and use them on other hosts; for example, you can tell a Puppet-managed load balancer about each of the workers available to it. Puppet collects and stores each of these resources when configuration runs occur, and then it provides these resources and their information to other hosts if they ask.

- Stored configuration provides a mechanism to store these resources. This feature allows Puppet to write resources into a SQL database. This database will then be queried by Puppet, and required resources will be collected and included in the configuration catalog.

In this chapter you will learn how to use virtual and exported resources, including how to use the exported resource feature to collect specific resources from stored configuration. We cover a number of use cases, including the automatic management of SSH host keys, automated load balancer reconfiguration, and automated monitoring with Nagios.

We demonstrate how to configure Puppet with PuppetDB for stored configurations and how to prune old configuration data from the SQL database in order to prevent other systems from collecting stale resources.

Virtual Resources

Virtual resources are closely related to the topic of exported resources. Because of the similarity, it's important to cover virtual resources first to provide a foundation for learning about exported resources.

Virtual resources are designed to address the situation where multiple classes require a single resource to be managed. This single resource doesn't clearly "belong" to any one class, and it is cumbersome to break each of these resources out into a unique class. Virtual resources also help solve the problem of duplicate resource declaration errors in Puppet.

To illustrate the problem, suppose you were the Example.com operator. You would like the ability to declare user resources to manage the accounts for your colleagues, but each person should have their account managed on only some systems. For example, all developer accounts need to be managed on all development and testing systems, while being absent from the production systems. Conversely, the system administrator accounts need to be present on every system. Finally, there are service accounts, for example, the apache and mysql users and groups required by multiple Puppet classes, such as the apache, mysql, and webapp classes. The webapp class requires the mysql and apache service accounts, but it should not declare the resource itself, because the mysql class is likely to have a conflicting resource declaration.

Virtual resources enable you, in managing a site like Example.com, to define a large set of user resources in once place and selectively add a smaller subset of those users to the configuration catalog. You don't need to worry about duplicate resource declarations, because the resources are only declared once and then instantiated, or "realized," one or more times.

Declaring a virtual resource is easy; just add the @ character to the beginning of the resource declaration to make the resource virtual. You can then use one of two methods to realize your virtual resources:

- The "spaceship" syntax <| |>[1]

- The realize function

Declaring and Realizing a Virtual Resource

Let's see how you might declare and realize the Example.com user and service accounts in Listing 6-1.

Listing 6-1. Virtual user resources <modulepath>/accounts/virtual.pp

```
class accounts::virtual {
  @user { 'mysql':
    ensure    => present,
    uid       => '27',
    gid       => '27',
    home      => '/var/lib/mysql',
    shell     => '/bin/bash',
  }
  @user { 'apache':
    ensure    => present,
    uid       => '48',
    gid       => 'apache',
    home      => '/var/www',
    shell     => '/sbin/nologin',
  }
}
```

Resources declared virtually will not be managed until they're-realized. Simply declaring the accounts::virtual class makes these virtual resources available, but that is not enough to manage the mysql and apache user accounts. Listing 6-2 shoes how you make sure the mysql user account is present on the system.

Listing 6-2. Realizing a virtual resource using the spaceship operator

```
class webapp {
  include accounts::virtual
  package { 'webapp': ensure => present }
  User <| title == 'mysql'|>
}
```

---

[1]So named because the syntax looks like a spaceship.

The last line of this webapp class uses the spaceship operator to find the user resource with the title of mysql. This syntax specifies a very specific resource to realize; Puppet will not throw an error, however, if there is no virtual user resource with the title mysql. The spaceship operator is analogous to a search function, where returning no results is perfectly valid. In situations where a specific resource is required, the realize() function may be used to generate an error if the virtual resource is not found.

Applying the realize Function

The realize() function provides another method of making a virtual resource real. A specific resource identified by its type and title must be passed as an argument to the realize() function. This requirement of a specific resource makes realize()much less flexible than the collection syntax and spaceship operator. The realize() function is more appropriate to use when an error should be thrown if the virtual resource has not been declared in the catalog. For example, you may want catalog compilation to fail if there is no mysql user resource, as illustrated in Listing 6-3.

Listing 6-3. The realize() function

```
class webapp {
  realize(User['mysql]')
  package { 'webapp':
    ensure => present,
  }
}
```

The configuration catalog resulting from the webapp class defined in Listing 6-3 is the same as the configuration catalog generated from the webapp class shown in Listing 6-2. You've seen how to realize a specific resource, the mysql user, but how to handle the situation where you need to make a number of virtual resources real? Puppet provides a convenient way to solve this problem without forcing you to specify each and every resource by name.

Making Virtual Resources Real

When using the spaceship operator, you can use any parameter to collect resources. This feature allows a large number of relationships to be managed in a concise and clear style. For example, if there are multiple user accounts with a primary group of apache, you can realize all of them using a single statement:

```
User <| gid == 'apache' |>
```

So far you've seen how to realize collections of virtual resources using the spaceship operator and specific resources using the realize() function. A key aspect of the Puppet model is specifying relationships between resources, and we haven't yet discussed how to establish a relationship to a realized virtual resource. Resource collections may also have a block associated with them to add additional parameters. When realizing virtual resources, you can specify the relationship metaparameters to ensure that the resource is managed in the correct order. Listing 6-4 shows how to ensure that the mysql user account in Example.com is always managed before the webapp package.

Listing 6-4. Specifying parameters in a collection

```
class webapp {
  User <| title == mysql |> { before => Package['webapp'] }
  package { 'webapp':
    ensure => present,
  }
}
```

As you can see, appending a block containing parameters after the collection will add the parameter to all of the realized resources. This also works for collections that contain many resources, as in this example:

```
User <| gid == 'apache' |> { before => Package['apache'] }
```

In addition to a block associated with a collection, Puppet also supports a relationship-chaining syntax. This syntax allows relationships to be declared without using the metaparameters before, require, subscribe, and notify as we'll see in the next section.

Relationship-Chaining Syntax

The relationship-chaining syntax allows you to replace the before, require, subscribe, and notify parameters with arrow operators. These new operators allow relationships to be declared outside the blocks where the resources are declared.

For example, two resources may be declared without any relation to each other, and their relationship established at a later time (Listing 6-5).

Listing 6-5. Example of arrow relationship syntax

```
define apache::account($ensure=present) {
  user { 'apache':
    ensure => $ensure,
    gid    => 48,
  }
  group { "apache":
    ensure => $ensure,
    gid    => 48,
  }
  if ($ensure == present) {
    Group['apache'] -> User['apache']
  } else {
    User['apache'] -> Group['apache']
  }
}
```

In this code example, Puppet will manage the group before the user if the apache account is present. However, if the apache account is absent, then the user is managed before the group to prevent the operating system from complaining that a group cannot be removed when a user exists with the same gid number.

The syntax arrows are ->, and ~> . The tilde arrows add notifications to the relationship, just as the subscribe and notify parameters do.

```
Group['apache'] -> User['apache']
```

The apache group is before the apache user.

```
File['httpd.conf'] ~> Service['httpd']
```

The httpd.conf file notifies the httpd service.

■ **Note**   You may also see use of the <- and <~ syntax arrows. They are discouraged by the Puppet Style Guide, however.

Additional information about the relationship-chaining syntax is available online at http://docs.puppetlabs.com/guides/language_tutorial.html.

In the next section, we extend the concept of virtual resources and make resources available across nodes and configuration catalogs. Resources available for collection across nodes are called *exported* resources, although it's important to think of them in terms of the virtual resource feature they aredesigned to resemble.

Getting Started with Exported and Stored Configurations

Now that you're ready to look at exported resources and stored configuration using the groundwork we've introduced with virtual resources, let's start with a database server.

The easiest way to install PuppetDB is through the puppetlabs puppetdb module on the Puppet Forge. Make sure the puppetlabs repositories are enabled for your distribution as described in Chapter 1.

You can install the puppetlabs/puppetdb module via the puppet module tool or you can download it from https://forge.puppetlabs.com/puppetlabs/puppetdb. Your installation dialog should look like Listing 6-6.

Listing 6-6. Bringing down the puppetdb module from the forge

```
$ puppet module install puppetlabs/puppetdb
Notice: Preparing to install into /etc/puppet/modules ...
Notice: Created target directory /etc/puppet/modules
Notice: Downloading from https://forge.puppetlabs.com ...
Notice: Installing -- do not interrupt ...
/etc/puppet/modules
└─┬ puppetlabs-puppetdb (v1.6.0)
  ├── cprice404-inifile (v0.10.4)
  ├── puppetlabs-firewall (v0.4.2)
  ├─┬ puppetlabs-postgresql (v2.5.0)
  │ ├── puppetlabs-apt (v1.2.0)
  │ └── ripienaar-concat (v0.2.0)
  └── puppetlabs-stdlib (v4.1.0)
```

Next add the following to your node definition for your puppetmaster:

```
node 'puppetmaster' {
  include puppetdb
  include puppetdb::master::config
}
```

If you don't have your Puppet master currently configured to be a node, you can use puppet apply instead:

```
$ puppet apply -e 'include puppetdb'
$ puppet apply -e 'incldue puppetdb::master::config'
```

The puppetdb class will install the puppetdb package, configure the service, and install PostgreSQL as its database backend. The puppetdb::master::config class will configure your puppetmaster to use puppetdb and will enable stored configurations.

You should now be able to see puppet agents connecting to puppetdb in the logs (Listing 6-7).

Listing 6-7. The PuppetDB log

```
$ tail -f /var/log/puppetdb/puppetdb.log
2013-05-19 01:29:22,483 INFO  [pool-2-thread-1] [cli.services] Starting sweep of stale reports
(threshold: 7 days)
2013-05-19 01:29:22,486 INFO  [pool-2-thread-1] [cli.services] Finished sweep of stale reports
(threshold: 7 days)
2013-05-19 01:35:12,577 INFO  [command-proc-56] [puppetdb.command] [dce6599f-d10d-4a01-87dc-
6b9d8aea6357] [replace facts] pro-master.lan
2013-05-19 01:35:17,896 INFO  [command-proc-58] [puppetdb.command] [6bbc81f0-793c-469a-b408-
55b28f662408] [replace catalog] pro-master.lan
2013-05-19 01:38:12,306 INFO  [command-proc-55] [puppetdb.command] [a3873da2-ffe4-4306-b3de-
5b72989dd0ae] [replace facts] pro-client.lan
2013-05-19 01:38:15,590 INFO  [command-proc-57] [puppetdb.command] [34785404-8508-450b-9374-
d48ce3f650ea] [replace catalog] pro-client.lan
```

You can also choose to run PuppetDB or PostgreSQL on a separate machine:

```
http://docs.puppetlabs.com/puppetdb/latest/install_via_module.html
```

If you would like to install PuppetDB from packages, refer to the official documentation.

```
http://docs.puppetlabs.com/puppetdb/latest/install_from_packages.html
```

In addition to allowing exported resources to work, Puppetdb will collect the facts and catalogs for all of your nodes and offers an API to query this metadata. The official documentation has more information about how to query the API.

```
http://docs.puppetlabs.com/puppetdb/latest/api/index.html
```

Using Exported Resources

With stored configurations enabled in the Puppet master, youcan now export resources from a node's catalog. These exported resources may then be collected on another node, allowing nodes to exchange configuration information dynamically and automatically. In this section we'll examine a number of common use cases for exported resources.

The first example will export the public SSH host identification key from each Puppet-managed node and store the resources centrally in PuppetDB. Every node may then collect all of the public host keys from all other nodes. This configuration increases security and eliminates the "unknown host" warning commonly encountered when logging in via SSH for the first time.

The second example uses exported resources to reconfigure a load balancer dynamically when additional Puppet master worker processes come online.

Finally, you'll see how to dynamically and automatically reconfigure the Nagios monitoring system to check the availability to new Puppet-managed systems.

Automated SSH Public Host Key Management

When new systems are brought online in a large network, the known_hosts files of all other systems become stale and out of date, causing "unknown host" warnings when users log in using SSH. Puppet provides a simple and elegant solution to this problem using stored configurations and exported resources. When new systems are brought online, Puppet updates the known_hosts file on all other systems by adding the public host key of the new system. This automated management of the known_hosts file also improves security, by reducing the likelihood of a "man-in-the-middle" attack remaining unnoticed.

You've learned in this chapter that any resource may be declared virtually using the @ symbol before the resource declaration. A similar syntax, @@, is used when resources should be declared virtually and exported to all other nodes using stored configurations. The use of @@ allows any node's catalog to collect the resource. Listing 6-8 shows how this looks for SSH public keys.

Listing 6-8. Exporting sshkey resources

```
class ssh::hostkeys {

  @@sshkey { "${::fqdn}_dsa":
    host_aliases => [ $::fqdn, $::hostname, $::ipaddress ],
    type         => dsa,
    key          => $::sshdsakey,
  }

  @@sshkey { "${::fqdn}_rsa":
    host_aliases -> [ $::fqdn, $::hostname, $::ipaddress ],
    type         => rsa,
    key          => $::sshrsakey,
  }

}
```

This Puppet code snippet looks a little strange compared to what we've worked with so far.

The class ssh::hostkeys should be included in the catalog of all nodes in the network for their SSH public host keys to be exported and collectible. All of the resources and parameters are set to variables coming from Facter fact values. In Listing 6-8, two sshkey resources have been declared as virtual resources and exported to the central stored configuration database, as indicated by the @@ symbols. The titles of each resource contain the suffixes _dsa or _rsa, preventing these two resources from conflicting with each other. To make sure each resource has a unique title for the entire network, the title also contains the fully qualified domain name of the node exporting the public host keys.

The host_aliases parameter provides additional names and addresses the node may be reached by. This information is important to prevent the "unknown host" warnings when connecting to the node from another system. In this example, we're providing the fully qualified domain name, short hostname, and IP address of the system. Each of these values comes from Facter and is automatically provided.

They type and key parameters provide the public key information itself. The values of $::sshdsakey and $::sshrsakey also come from Facter and are automatically available on each host.

Exporting these two sshkey resources is not sufficient to configure the known_hosts file on each node. You must also collect all exported sshkey resources for Puppet to fully manage and keep updated the known_hosts file shown in Listing 6-9.

Listing 6-9. Collecting exported sshkey resources

```
class ssh::knownhosts {
  Sshkey <<| |>> { ensure => present }
}
```

The ssh::knownhosts class should be included in the catalog for all nodes where Puppet should manage the SSH known_hosts file. Notice that we've used double angle braces to collect resources from PuppetDB. The syntax is similar to that for collecting virtual resources; however, virtual resources use only a *single* pair of angle braces. We're also specifying that the ensure parameter should take on the value "present" when collecting the exported sshkey resources.

With the two classes configured and added to the node classification for every host in the network, you can verify that host keys are collected on every node in the network.

First, run the Puppet agent on the mail.cxample.com host. Since this is the first host to run the Puppet agent, you expect only two SSH keys to be collected: the keys exported by the mail host itself, as you can see in Listing 6-10.

Listing 6-10. The first Puppet agent on mail.example.com

```
# puppet agent --test
info: Caching catalog for mail.example.com
info: Applying configuration version '1293584061'
notice: /Stage[main]//Node[default]/Sshkey[mail.example.com_dsa]/ensure: created
notice: /Stage[main]//Node[default]/Sshkey[mail.example.com _rsa]/ensure: created
notice: Finished catalog run in 0.02 seconds
```

Notice the two sshkey resources being collected from the stored configuration database, the SSH dsa and rsa public key exported from the mail.example.com host.

In Listing 6-11, you run Puppet on the web server, expecting the public keys for both the web host and the mail host to be collected.

Listing 6-11. The second Puppet agent run on web.example.com

```
# puppet agent --test
info: Caching catalog for web.example.com
info: Applying configuration version '1293584061'
notice: /Stage[main]//Node[default]/Sshkey[mail.example.com_rsa]/ensure: created
notice: /Stage[main]//Node[default]/Sshkey[mail.example.com_dsa]/ensure: created
notice: /Stage[main]//Node[default]/Sshkey[web.example.com_rsa]/ensure: created
notice: /Stage[main]//Node[default]/Sshkey[web.example.com_dsa]/ensure: created
notice: Finished catalog run in 0.43 seconds
```

Here, the Puppet agent on web.example.com collects a total of four SSH host key resources. The rsa and dsa keys from the mail host and the web host are pulled down from PuppetDB and created on the web host.

Finally, running the Puppet agent once more on the mail.example.com host should result in the two public keys exported by the web host being collected and managed. Listing 6-12 shows how to verify this.

Listing 6-12. The third Puppet agent run on mail.example.com

```
# puppet agent --test
info: Caching catalog for mail.example.com
info: Applying configuration version '1293584061'
notice: /Stage[main]//Node[default]/Sshkey[web.example.com_rsa]/ensure: created
notice: /Stage[main]//Node[default]/Sshkey[web.example.com_dsa]/ensure: created
info: FileBucket adding /etc/ssh/ssh_known_hosts as {md5}815e87b6880446e4eb20a8d0e7298658
notice: /Stage[main]//Node[default]/Notify[hello]/message: defined 'message' as 'Hello World!'
notice: Finished catalog run in 0.04 seconds
```

As expected, the two SSH public key resources exported by the web host are correctly being collected on the mail host. By exporting and collecting two sshkey resources, you can rely on all Example.com hosts automatically knowing the identity of all other hosts, even as new hosts are added to the network. So long as Puppet runs frequently, every system will have a known_hosts file containing the public key of every other system in the network.

In the next example, you'll see how this feature also allows the automatic addition of worker nodes to a load balancer pool.

Exporting Load Balancer Worker Resources

In the previous example, you exported SSH public key resources and stored them in the configuration database so that every host in the network is able to collect the public identification keys of every other host in the network. Along the same lines, but on a much smaller scale, you can also export resources to a single node on the network, such as a load balancer.

In this example, HTTP worker nodes will export configuration resources that only the load balancer will collect. This combination eliminates the need to manually reconfigure the load balancer every time a new worker node is added to the network.

Each load balancer worker will export a defined resource type representing the load balancer configuration. Let's see how you configure the Example.com system now. The load balancer software being used in this example is Apache. As Example.com operator, you model the configuration of an HTTP worker using a file fragment placed into the directory /etc/httpd/conf.d.members/. Let's first take a look at the defined resource type, shown in Listing 6-13.

Listing 6-13. Load balancer worker-defined resource type

```
define balancermember($url) {
  file { '/etc/httpd/conf.d.members/worker_${name}.conf':
    ensure  => file,
    owner   => 'root',
    group   => 'root',
    mode    => '0644',
    content => "BalancerMember $url \n",
  }
}
```

This configuration file fragment contains a single line, the URL to a member of the load balancer pool. Puppet recommends using a defined resource type because all resources declared within the type will be exported when the defined type itself is exported.

The load balancer configuration is similar to the Apache configuration presented in the Chapter 4 discussion of scaling Puppet. Without using exported resources, you might define your load balancer configuration statically, as shown in Listing 6-14.

Listing 6-14. Load balancer front-end configuration

```
<Proxy balancer://puppetmaster>
  BalancerMember http://puppetmaster1.example.com:18140
  BalancerMember http://puppetmaster2.example.com:18140
  BalancerMember http://puppetmaster3.example.com:18140
</Proxy>
```

In this example, three Puppet master workers have been statically defined. To add additional capacity, you would have to add a fourth line to this Apache configuration block. Exported resources allow you to save this manual step and automatically add the configuration once a new worker node comes online and is configured by Puppet. To accomplish this, you replace all of the BalancerMember statements with an Include statement to read in all of the file fragments. In the Puppet manifest, these configuration statements are modeled using the balancermember defined type, shown in Listing 6-15.

Listing 6-15. Including exported file fragments in the load balancer configuration

```
<Proxy balancer://puppetmaster>
  Include /etc/httpd/conf.d.members/*.conf
</Proxy>
```

You no longer need to add each line manually once you configure Apache to include all files in the conf.d.members directory. Instead, you configure Puppet to manage the individual file fragments using exported resources.

The Puppet configuration to export each load balancer member is very similar to what we saw with the SSH host key example. The Puppet configuration is very simple. Each worker node needs to export a single balancermember resource for itself:

```
class worker {
  @@balancermember { $::fqdn:
    url => "http://${::fqdn}:18140",
  }
}
```

Notice that you use the fully qualified domain name as the title of the resource. In doing so, you are guaranteed that there will be no duplicate resource declarations, because each worker node should have a unique value for its fqdn fact. Declaring the defined resource in this manner exports two resources into the stored configuration database, the balancermember resource and the contained file resource shown in Listing 6-14. Neither of these resources will be collected on the worker nodes themselves.

The last step in automating the configuration is to collect all of the exported resources on the load balancer node itself, as you can see in Listing 6-16.

Listing 6-16. Collecting exported load balancer workers

```
class loadbalancer_members {
  Balancermember <<| |>> { notify => Service['apache'] }
}
```

This code uses the double angle brace syntax to collect all balancermember resources from the stored configuration database. In addition, it uses a parameter block to notify the Apache service of any changes Puppet makes to the balancermember resources. Just as with virtual resources, a parameter block may be specified to add further parameters to collected resources. In this example, you've seen a simplified version of the file fragment pattern using Apache's Include configuration statement. Web server worker nodes can easily model their configuration in Puppet using a defined resource type. Using that technique, you have exported load balancer resources to automatically reconfigure the front-end load balancer as new members come online.

In the next section, you'll see how exported resources are ideal for automatically reconfiguring a central Nagios monitoring system as new hosts are added to the network.

Automating Nagios Service Checks

So far, you've seen how exported resources enable Puppet to automatically reconfigure the Example.com systems as new machines are brought online. You've seen how to automate the management of SSH known hosts keys to improve security, and how to automatically reconfigure Apache as additional capacity is added into a load balancer pool.

In this final example of exported resources, you'll again be the Example.com operator, configuring Puppet to automatically monitor new systems as they're brought online. The problem of monitoring service availability is something all sites share. Puppet helps solve this problem quickly and easily, and reduces the amount of time and effort required to manage the monitoring system.

This example specifically focuses on Nagios. Puppet has native types and providers for Nagios built into the software. The concepts in this section, however, apply to any software requiring a central system to be reconfigured when new hosts come online and need to be monitored.

In Nagios, the system performing the service checks is called the monitor system. The Nagios service running on the monitor system looks to the configuration files in /etc/nagios to sort out which target systems need to be monitored. For Example.com, we want Puppet to automatically reconfigure the monitor system when a new target system comes online.

To accomplish this goal, you first configure two classes in Puppet. The first class, named nagios::monitor, manages the Nagios service and collects the service check resources exported by the nagios::target class. Let's take a look at these two classes now (see Listing 6-17).

Listing 6-17. Collecting Nagios resources

```
# Manage the Nagios monitoring service
class nagios::monitor {

  # Manage the packages
  package { [ 'nagios', 'nagios-plugins' ]:
    ensure => installed,
  }

  # Manage the Nagios monitoring service
  service { 'nagios':
    ensure    => running,
    hasstatus => true,
    enable    => true,
    subscribe => [ Package['nagios'], Package['nagios-plugins'] ],
  }

  # collect resources and populate /etc/nagios/nagios_*.cfg
  Nagios_host    <<||>> { notify => Service['nagios'] }
  Nagios_service <<||>> { notify => Service['nagios'] }
}
```

As you can see, this code has configured Puppet to manage the Nagios packages and service. The class nagios::monitor should be included in the catalog for the monitor node. In addition to the packages and the service, the code collects two additional resource types from the stored configuration database, all nagios_host and nagios_service resources. When collecting these host and service resources, you add the notify metaparameter to ensure that the Nagios monitoring service automatically reloads its configuration if any new nodes have exported their information to the stored configuration database.

■ **Note** Additional information about the nagios_host and nagios_service Puppet types is available online. There are a number of additional resource types related to Nagios management in addition to these two basic service checks. If you need to make Nagios aware of the interdependencies between hosts to reduce the number of notifications generated during a service outage, or manage custom Nagios service checks and commands, please see the comprehensive and up-to-date Puppet type reference at http://docs.puppetlabs.com/references/stable/type.html.

Let's see how to implement the nagios::monitor class in the Example.com Puppet configuration. With the nagios::monitor class added to the monitor node's classification in site.pp, run the Puppet agent on node monitor1, as shown in Listing 6-18.

Listing 6-18. The first Puppet agent run to configure Nagios

```
# puppet agent --test
info: Caching catalog for monitor1
info: Applying configuration version '1294374100'
notice: /Stage[main]/Nagios::Monitor/Package[nagios]/ensure: created
info: /Stage[main]/Nagios::Monitor/Package[nagios]: Scheduling refresh of Service[nagios]
notice: /Stage[main]/Nagios::Monitor/Package[nagios-plugins]/ensure: created
info: /Stage[main]/Nagios::Monitor/Package[nagios-plugins]: Scheduling refresh of Service[nagios]
notice: /Stage[main]/Nagios::Monitor/Service[nagios]/ensure: ensure changed 'stopped' to 'running'
notice: /Stage[main]/Nagios::Monitor/Service[nagios]: Triggered 'refresh' from 2 events
notice: Finished catalog run in 14.96 seconds
```

Notice that the first Puppet agent configuration run on monitor1 does not mention anything about managing Nagios_host or Nagios_service resources. This is because no nodes have yet been classified with the nagios::target class, and as a result there are no exported host or service resources in the stored configuration database.

The Example.com operator configures Puppet to export Nagios service and host resources using the class nagios::target. As you can see in Listing 6-16, the class contains only exported resources. The resources will not be managed on any nodes until they are collected as in Listing 6-19.

Listing 6-19. Exporting Nagios host and service resources

```
# This class exports nagios host and service check resources
class nagios::export::target {

  @@nagios_host { $::fqdn:
    ensure  => present,
    alias   => $::hostname,
    address => $::ipaddress,
    use     => 'generic-host',
  }

  @@nagios_service { "check_ping_${::hostname}":
    check_command       => 'check_ping!100.0,20%!500.0,60%',
    use                 => 'generic-service',
    host_name           => $::fqdn,
    notification_period => '24x7',
    service_description => "${::hostname}_check_ping"
  }

}
```

In Listing 6-19, you have configured two exported resources, one of which provides the monitor node with information about the target host itself. This resource defines a Nagios host in /etc/nagios/*.cfg on the nodes collecting these resources. The title of the nagios_host resource is set to the value of the $::fqdn fact. Using the fully qualified domain name as the resource title ensures that there will be no duplicate resources in the stored configuration database. In addition, you have added an alias for the target host using the short hostname in the $hostname fact. Finally, the address of the target node is set to the $ipaddress variable coming from Facter.

Once a resource describing the target host is exported, the code also exports a basic service check for the host. As you can see, this service check is performing a basic ICMP ping command to the target node. The host_name parameter of the resource is also provided from Facter via the $fqdn fact. The check_command parameter looks a bit confusing, and rightly so, as it is directly using the Nagios configuration file syntax. Reading the check_ping line left to right, we interpret it to mean that Nagios will issue a warning when the ping takes longer than 100 milliseconds or experiences 20% packet loss. Nagios will also issue a critical alert if the ping command takes longer than 500 milliseconds to complete or experiences more than 60% packet loss. The notification period is also set to 24 hours a day, 7 days a week, the notification period provided by the default Nagios configuration. Finally, you have configured a descriptive label for the service using the short name of the host set by Facter.

Let's see how the monitor1 node is configured automatically when a target node is classified with this nagios::target class. First, run the Puppet agent on a new system named target1 (Listing 6-20).

Listing 6-20. Puppet agent on target1 exporting Nagios checks

```
# puppet agent --test
info: Caching catalog for target1
info: Applying configuration version '1294374100'
notice: Finished catalog run in 0.02 seconds
```

It appears the Puppet agent run on target1 didn't actually manage any resources. This is true; the resources exported in the nagios::target class are actually being exported to the stored configuration database rather than being managed on the node. They are not being collected on the node target1, which is why the output of Listing 6-20 does not mention them.

We expect the Puppet agent on the node monitor1 to collect the resources exported by node target1. Let's see the results in Listing 6-21.

Listing 6-21. Puppet agent collecting resources in monitor1

```
# puppet agent --test
info: Caching catalog for monitor1
info: Applying configuration version '1294374100'
notice: /Stage[main]/Nagios::Monitor/Nagios_service[check_ping_puppet]/ensure: created
info: /Stage[main]/Nagios::Monitor/Nagios_service[check_ping_puppet]: Scheduling refresh of
Service[nagios]
notice: /Stage[main]/Nagios::Monitor/Nagios_host[target1.example.com]/ensure: created
info: /Stage[main]/Nagios::Monitor/Nagios_host[target1.example.com]: Scheduling refresh of
Service[nagios]
notice: /Stage[main]/Nagios::Monitor/Service[nagios]: Triggered 'refresh' from 2 events
notice: monitor
notice: /Stage[main]//Node[monitord]/Notify[monitor]/message: defined 'message' as 'monitor'
notice: Finished catalog run in 0.87 seconds
```

As we expect, running the Puppet agent on monitor1 after target1 has checked in causes the resources to be collected from the stored configuration database. Looking back to the nagios::monitor class in Listing 6-18, you can also see the notify parameter, added to ensure that the Nagios service automatically reloads the new configuration information after all of the resources are collected.

When bringing new systems online at Example.com, you would only need to ensure they have the nagios::target class included in their catalog, and Puppet will automatically take care of reconfiguring the central Nagios monitoring system. In addition, if you would like more than one system to monitor all of these nodes, you only need to include the nagios::monitor class in the catalog of additional monitors and they'll automatically collect all of the host and service resources from the stored configuration database.

In the next section, we'll cover methods to scale stored configuration to support a large number of nodes and reduce the amount of time each Puppet agent requires to submit a copy of its configuration to the Puppet master.

Expiring Stale Resources

A potential pitfall of using stored configurations is the situation where nodes retired from service still have configuration resources stored in PuppetDB. Unless you periodically prune the configuration database, these stale resources will linger indefinitely, tainting the configurations of remaining nodes. The puppet node command can be used to deactivate nodes from PuppetDB (Listing 6-22).

Listing 6-22. Removing retired nodes from PuppetDB

```
$ puppet node deactivate mail.example.com
Submitted 'deactivate node' for mail.example.com with UUID aa3d34df-b84b-4fd1-a449-711ac06c9f3c
```

After you've run this on the puppet master, any resources exported by this node will no longer be collected on your Puppet clients.

▓ **Note** Deactivated node resources will not be removed from the systems that collected them. You will need to clean up those configurations manually; or some resources can be purged using the `resource` metatype.

PuppetDB will automatically deactivate nodes if you enable the `node-ttl` setting. The syntax and config file are described here:

```
http://docs.puppetlabs.com/puppetdb/latest/configure.html#node-ttl
```

Summary

Exported resources and stored configuration are two very powerful features in Puppet. Using the central stored configuration database, each Puppet master system is capable of exporting and collecting resources as new hosts are brought online.

In this chapter, you've learned about the basics of virtual resources and how to export resources from one catalog and collect them in another. You saw three examples of how we might use exported resources:

- SSH public host keys that are easily stored centrally and distributed

- Adding load balancer members to an Apache configuration

- Exported resources to allow Nagios to automatically add new systems

Resources

- Virtual Resources http://docs.puppetlabs.com/guides/virtual_resources.html

- Exported Resources http://docs.puppetlabs.com/guides/exported_resources.html

- PuppetDB http://docs.puppetlabs.com/puppetdb/latest

CHAPTER 7

■ ■ ■

Puppet Consoles

Puppet has three console products: the Foreman, Puppet Enterprise Console, and Puppetboard. The Foreman is a provisioning tool with Puppet integration that can act as an external node carrier (ENC) and has reporting features, Puppet Enterprise Console (PE Console) is Puppet Labs' commercial product, and Puppetboard is a reporting dashboard for PuppetDB.

■ **Note** Puppet Dashboard, which was covered in the first edition of this book, is now a community project. It is unclear how much longer it will be maintained; therefore, we felt it was better not to recommend it to our readers for new installations.

The Foreman

The Foreman, or simply Foreman (http://theforeman.org/) is an integrated data center lifecycle management tool that provides provisioning, configuration management, and reporting. Foreman has a focus on provisioning and managing data center capabilities, such as integration with bootstrapping tools, PXE boot servers, DHCP servers, and provisioning tools.

To get started with Foreman, you will learn how to do the following:

- Install Foreman.
- Configure Foreman.
- Integrate Foreman with Puppet.
- Connect your first client.
- Use Foreman as an ENC.
- Display reports in Foreman.
- Search for facts in Foreman.

Installing Foreman

Foreman can be installed using either its own installer or via system packages. We will use the installer, as it's the easiest way to get started using Foreman. The Foreman installer currently supports RedHat packages (RPM) and Debian packages (DEB). Choose the instructions in Listings 7-1 or 7-2 for your operating system.

■ **Note**   Make sure you have the `Puppetlabs` repositories enabled as described in Chapter 1 before proceeding.

Listing 7-1. The Foreman rpm installer

```
$ yum -y install http://yum.theforeman.org/releases/1.2/el6/x86_64/foreman-release.rpm
$ yum -y install foreman-installer
```

Listing 7-2. The Foreman deb installer

```
$ echo "deb http://deb.theforeman.org/ precise stable" > /etc/apt/sources.list.d/foreman.list
$ wget -q http://deb.theforeman.org/foreman.asc -O- | apt-key add -
$ apt-get update && apt-get install foreman-installer
```

Running the Foreman Installer

The Foreman installer is a packaged collection of Puppet modules that can set up a complete Foreman installation with a running Puppet master. To start, run the command in Listing 7-3.

■ **Note**   The Foreman installer currently does not support MCollective or PuppetDB installation. You will need to do that manually if you wish to enable those features.

Listing 7-3. Starting the Foreman installer

```
$ ruby /usr/share/foreman-installer/generate_answers.rb
Welcome to the Foreman Installer!
---------------------------------

This installer will help you set up Foreman and the associated extra
configuration necessary to get you up and running. There is an interactive shell
which will ask you questions, but if you just want to get up and running as fast
as possible, answer 'yes' to the all-in-one install at the beginning

Ready to start? (y/n)
y
```

We are going to modify the default configuration because we want to focus on the Puppet integration. Choose menu item 2, Configure Foreman_proxy Settings, and disable TFTP in the Foreman proxy settings as shown in Listing 7-4.

Listing 7-4. Disabling TFTP in the Foreman installer

```
Do you want to use the default all-in-one setup?
This will configure Foreman, Foreman-Proxy, Puppet (including a puppetmaster),
several puppet environments, TFTP (for provisioning) and sudo (for puppet
certificate management) (y/n)
n
```

```
Main Config Menu
1. Configure Foreman settings
2. Configure Foreman_proxy settings
3. Configure Puppet settings
4. Configure Puppetmaster settings
5. Display current config
6. Save and Exit
7. Exit without Saving
Choose an option from the menu... 2

Current config is:
Foreman_proxy is enabled with defaults

Foreman_proxy Config Menu
1. Enable foreman_proxy with all defaults
2. Disable foreman_proxy completely
3. Should Foreman_proxy manage Puppet (needed for puppet classes)? (default:
true)
4. Should Foreman_proxy manage DNS? (default: false)
5. Should Foreman_proxy be installed from the stable,rc, or nightly repo?
(default: stable)
6. Should Foreman_proxy manage DHCP? (default: false)
7. Should Foreman_proxy manage TFTP? (default: true)
8. Should Foreman_proxy manage PuppetCA (needed for certificates)? (default:
true)
9. Add other key/value pair to the config
10. Go up to main menu
Choose an option from the menu... 7
y/n?
n

Current config is:
Foreman_proxy is enabled with overrides:
---
tftp: false
```

■ **Note** If you would like to use dynamic environments, as described in Chapter 3, go to the Puppet master menu and enable the feature there.

Once you're satisfied with the configuration, type "y" to have the Foreman installer run, as shown in Listing 7-5, and Foreman will be installed.

Listing 7-5. Foreman installer save and exit

```
Do you want to run Puppet now with these settings? (y/n)
Y
```

> **Note** To install Foreman from packages or source, refer to the documentation provided at the following site: http://theforeman.org/manuals/latest/index.html#3.InstallingForeman.

The installer will generate an answer file (Listing 7-6), which you can use for future upgrades or installs.

Listing 7-6. A Foreman answer file

```
# cat /usr/share/foreman-installer/foreman_installer/answers.yaml
---
foreman_proxy:
  tftp: false
puppet: true
foreman: true
puppetmaster: true
```

If your installer output has any errors, try running it a second time:

```
$ echo include foreman_installer | puppet apply --modulepath /usr/share/foreman-installer -v
```

After the Foreman installer runs, Foreman will be accessible at https://fqdn/ with a default username/password of admin and changeme. Figure 7-1 shows the opening screen.

Welcome

Before you can use Foreman for the first time there are a few tasks that must be performed. You must decide how you wish to use the software, and update the primary settings file **config/settings.yaml** and the settings to indicate your selections.

Operating Mode

You may operate Foreman in basic mode, in which it acts as a reporting and external node classifier or you may also turn on unattended mode operation in which Foreman creates and manages the configuration files necessary to completely configure a new host. When operating in unattended mode Foreman will require more information, so expect more questions, but it will be able to automate host installations for redhat, debian, suse and solaris operating systems (and their clones), see here for more details.

Create a Smart Proxy

If you're planning to do anything more than just handle reports, you'll be in need of a smart proxy - either on this machine or elsewhere on your network. You can find details of how to set up the proxy at Smart-Proxy Installation.

Important Once installed you should head over to Smart Proxies to point Foreman at it.

User Authentication

Foreman, by default, operates in anonymous mode where all operations are performed without reference to the user who is performing the task. If you wish to track the actions of a particular user then it is possible to use an additional authentication stage and provide a user account. At present, authentication is performed against the internal Database or a LDAP service provided by one or more LDAP servers.

Additionally, you may restrict user permissions based on many criteria, make sure you check the roles settings tab.

- For internal Users, simply create a new user at the Users page
- If you chose to use LDAP authentication then you must provide connection details for your authentication provider on LDAP page
- For Roles and permissions, see the Roles page

Figure 7-1. *The Foreman welcome page*

Configuring Foreman

To complete the installation, choose More ➤ Configuration ➤ Smart Proxies and add a new proxy with the URL `https://fqdn:8443/`, where `fqdn` is the fully qualified domain name of the Foreman server as shown in Figure 7-2.

Figure 7-2. *Adding a Puppet master smart proxy*

MULTIPLE PUPPET MASTER ENVIRONMENT

In an environment with multiple Puppet masters, you will need to add the Foreman repository on each master as just described and then install the `foreman-proxy` package:

```
$ puppet resource package foreman-proxy ensure=present
```

Then modify `/etc/foreman-proxy/settings.yml` and add your foreman server under `trusted_hosts`.

Your Foreman server must use the same CA server as your Puppet masters; so when you install it, either make it the Puppet CA server or make sure to disable its CA functionality. Finally, add each master as a proxy in the Foreman configuration menu as described earlier.

Our next step is to disable provisioning. Set `unattended` to `false` in `/etc/foreman/settings.yaml` as shown in Listing 7-7 and then restart Apache on your Foreman host.

Listing 7-7. Disable the unattended setting

```
root@pro-puppet-foreman:/etc/puppet# cat /etc/foreman/settings.yaml | grep unattended
:unattended: false
```

After you've restarted Apache, the provisioning tabs on the Add Host page should disappear. Our next step is to import our Puppet modules.

Importing Data from Puppet

To import our Puppet modules, select More ➤ Configuration ➤ Environments in the navigation menu and click Import From *Puppetmaster*, where *Puppetmaster* is the name of your Puppet master; in Figure 7-3 it is `pro-master`.

Puppet classes

Figure 7-3. Importing Puppet environments from your Puppet master

Then follow the instructions to import your environments. If you're just starting off, click the New Environment button and create a production environment.

After the import is complete, all of your Puppet classes should be available for use, as shown in Figure 7-4. Each time you add a new class or module you will need to come back to this page to import it.

Puppet classes

Class name	Environments and documentation	Host group	Hosts	Keys	
accounts::virtual	development production		0	0	Delete
apache	development production		0	5	Delete
apache::dev	development production		0	0	Delete
apache::mod::auth_basic	development production		0	0	Delete
apache::mod::auth_kerb	development production		0	0	Delete
apache::mod::cache	development production		0	0	Delete
apache::mod::cgi	development production		0	0	Delete
apache::mod::dav	development production		0	0	Delete
apache::mod::dav_fs	development production		0	0	Delete
apache::mod::default	development production		0	0	Delete
apache::mod::dev	development production		0	0	Delete

Figure 7-4. Imported Puppet classes

Connecting Your First Client

After your environments are imported, you can begin connecting clients to the Puppet master running on the Foreman server. First configure your Puppet client to use the Foreman server as its Puppet master, using the general configuration instructions in Chapter 1. Then request a certificate as shown in Listing 7-8.

Listing 7-8. First Puppet run

```
root@pro-puppet-foreman-client1:~# puppet agent -t
info: Creating a new SSL key for pro-puppet-foreman-client1.lan
info: Caching certificate for ca
info: Creating a new SSL certificate request for pro-puppet-foreman-client1.lan
```

```
info: Certificate Request fingerprint (md5): 5E:C6:A7:2C:27:5D:57:2A:AE:25:5E:18:C8:40:B8:A4
Exiting; no certificate found and waitforcert is disabled
```

After the Puppet client has requested a certificate, you can sign it in Foreman. Go to More ➤ Configuration ➤ Smart Proxies ➤ Certificates. The Certificates button will take you to a menu like Figure 7-5, where you can sign, view, and revoke certificates.

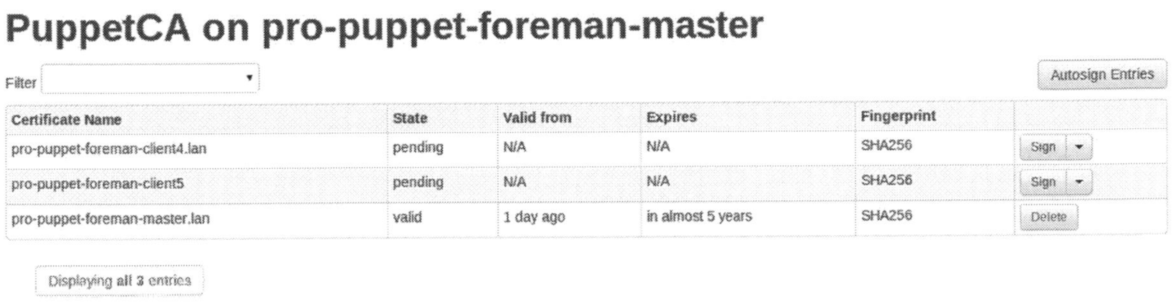

PuppetCA on pro-puppet-foreman-master

Filter [▼]   [Autosign Entries]

Certificate Name	State	Valid from	Expires	Fingerprint	
pro-puppet-foreman-client4.lan	pending	N/A	N/A	SHA256	[Sign ▼]
pro-puppet-foreman-client5	pending	N/A	N/A	SHA256	[Sign ▼]
pro-puppet-foreman-master.lan	valid	1 day ago	in almost 5 years	SHA256	[Delete]

[Displaying all 3 entries]

Figure 7-5. *The Foreman PuppetCA*

After your agent connects the second time, as shown in Listing 7-9, you should see it appear under the Hosts tab (Figure 7-6).

Listing 7-9. Second Puppet run

```
root@pro-puppet-foreman-client1:~# puppet agent -t
info: Caching certificate for pro-puppet-foreman-client1.lan
info: Caching certificate_revocation_list for ca
info: Caching catalog for pro-puppet-foreman-client1.lan
info: Applying configuration version '1379704950'
info: Creating state file /var/lib/puppet/state/state.yaml
notice: Finished catalog run in 0.02 seconds
```

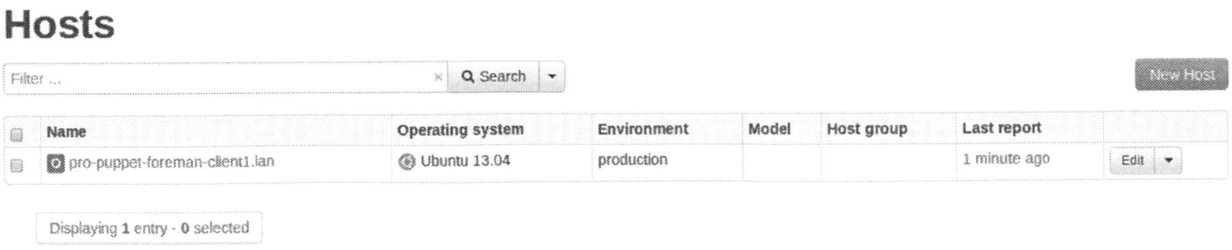

Hosts

Filter ...   [×] [🔍 Search ▼]   [New Host]

	Name	Operating system	Environment	Model	Host group	Last report	
☐	⊙ pro-puppet-foreman-client1.lan	⊛ Ubuntu 13.04	production			1 minute ago	[Edit ▼]

[Displaying 1 entry - 0 selected]

Figure 7-6. *The Foreman host page*

If you click the hostname, it will drill down to a detail view of the host's information (Figure 7-7). From this page you can access reports about the host, along with facts, auditing, and metrics about recent Puppet runs.

pro-puppet-foreman-client1.lan

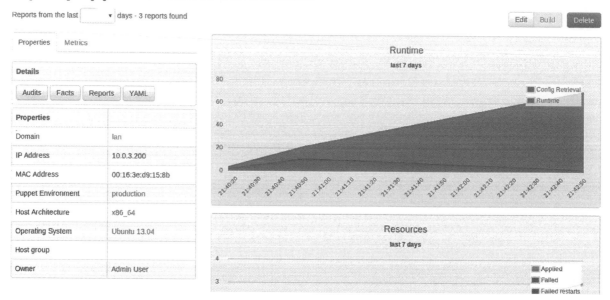

Figure 7-7. Foreman drilldown for a client

Using Foreman as an ENC

Now that you have an agent connected to Foreman, we want to apply some configuration to that node. The Foreman behaves as an ENC (ENCs were first introduced in Chapter 5). We can use the web interface on the Foreman to apply classes and configuration to our nodes. This can be used in tandem with version controlled site.pp files to manage your infrastructure. Foreman has this functionality out of the box.

Adding Classes to Nodes

To add a class to a node, click the Edit button on the host page and choose the Puppet classes tab. All the classes that you added when you imported your Puppet code are now available via a filter box and drop-down menus (Figure 7-8).

Edit pro-puppet-foreman-client1.lan

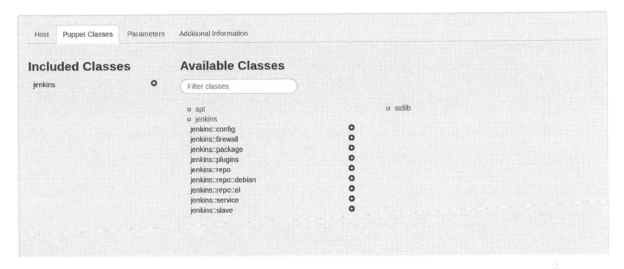

Figure 7-8. Adding a class to the Foreman client

■ **Note**   To exclude specific classes, such as internal module classes, refer to the official docs, at
`http://theforeman.org/manuals/1.2/index.html#4.2.2Classes`.

You can see that we included the `jenkins` class on our client. The jenkins class handles the installation and configuration of the Jenkins service. After we hit submit, the client will install `Jenkins` on its next Puppet run. Once it completes we can access Jenkins at `http://pro-puppet-foreman-client1.lan:8080/`.

Parameterized Classes

If you are using parameterized classes and want to change the defaults, you can do that in the Parameters tab (Figure 7-9). Check the Override box for the parameter you want to change and give it a new default value. Once you save the change, a flag will appear next to the list of parameters to indicate that it has been changed from the default. Foreman supports a variety of parameter types and supports the major Puppet attribute types like arrays and hashes.

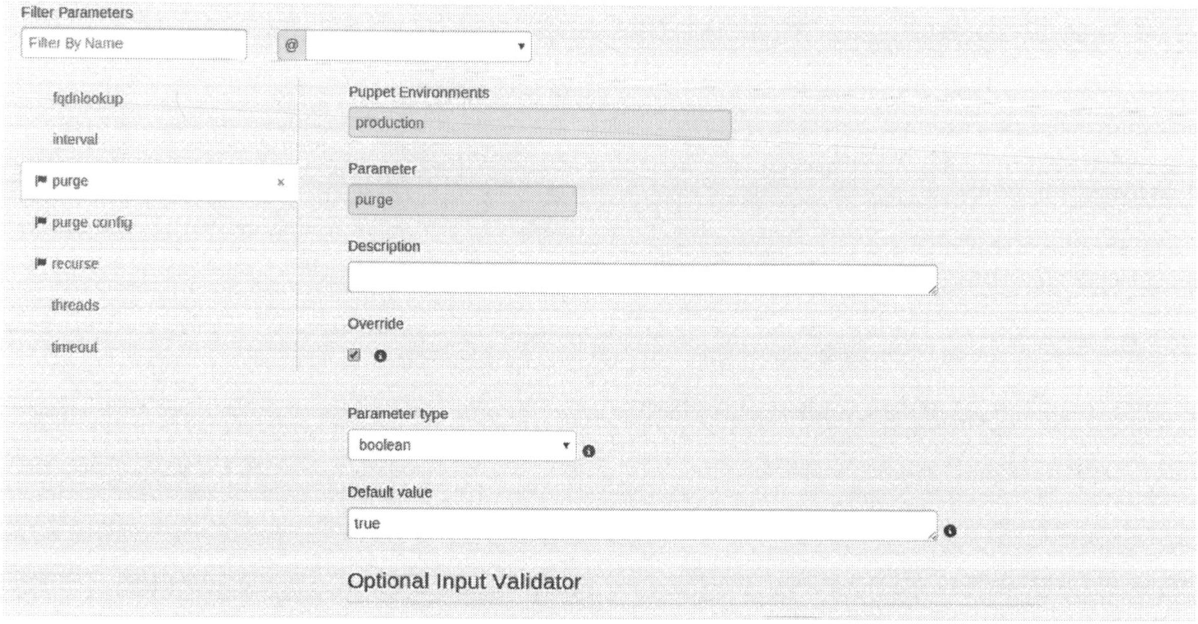

Figure 7-9. *Changing defaults on parameterized classes*

Now that you know how to apply configuration to nodes from Foreman, let's take a look at its reporting features.

Displaying Reports in Foreman

Foreman has the capability to import and display your Puppet reports. If you used the Foreman installer or are using Foreman as an ENC, reporting is already set up for you. You can access reports from the Reports tab. Clients that have eventful reports will be displayed by default, as shown in Figure 7-10.

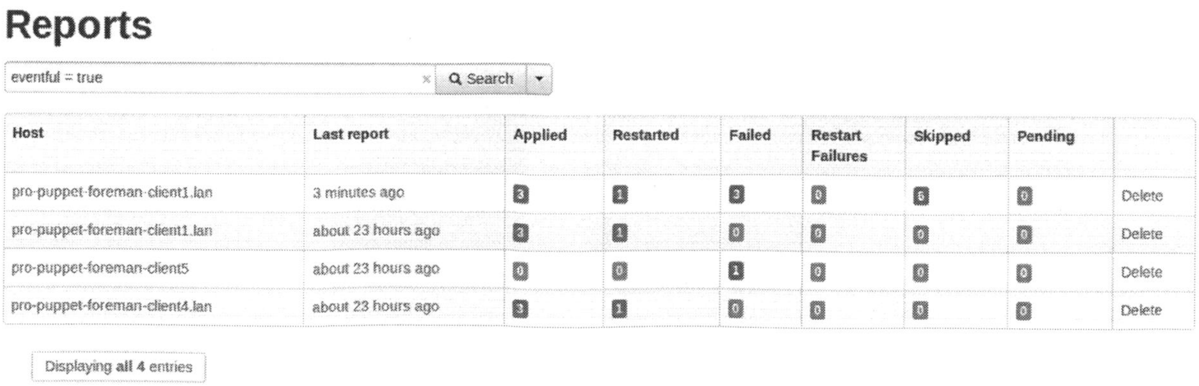

Reports

Host	Last report	Applied	Restarted	Failed	Restart Failures	Skipped	Pending	
pro-puppet-foreman-client1.lan	3 minutes ago	3	1	3	0	6	0	Delete
pro-puppet-foreman-client1.lan	about 23 hours ago	3	1	0	0	0	0	Delete
pro-puppet-foreman-client5	about 23 hours ago	0	0	1	0	0	0	Delete
pro-puppet-foreman-client4.lan	about 23 hours ago	3	1	0	0	0	0	Delete

Displaying **all 4** entries

Figure 7-10. *Foreman eventful reports*

From the Reports tab you can drill down into the different reports to see the logs from the node. Figure 7-11 shows a node with errors and warning.

pro-puppet-foreman-client1.lan

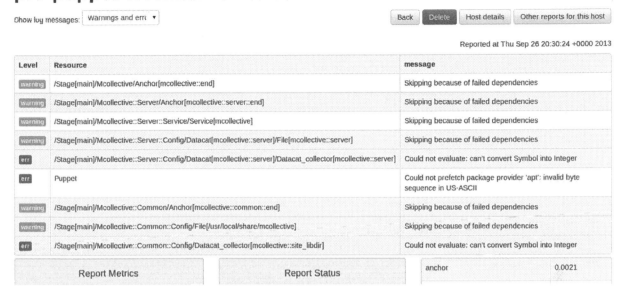

Figure 7-11. *Foreman report for an eventful node*

Searching for Facts in Foreman

Foreman collects facts for each node, and they can be queried via the Fact page. In Figure 7-12 you can see that we can query for all of the nodes by entering **osfamily = Debian**. You can write much more complicated queries using the operators available, and you can also save them with a bookmark via the drop-down button in the Search box.

Fact Values

Figure 7-12. *Searching for facts*

■ **Note**   Foreman also has a REST API that you can interact with. It uses JSON and provides access to most of its capabilities via a Web Services interface. You can see full details on the API and how to interact with it at http://theforeman.org/api.html.

Foreman is a large project and is being actively developed. Unfortunately, we don't have enough space in this chapter to cover all the features available, but the official documentation is a great place to learn about the new features. In the next section we will cover Puppet Enterprise Console, which like Foreman, has ENC support and advancing reporting tools.

▨ **Note** Foreman also has integration with MCollective, which was not covered in this chapter. If you install it manually, you can enable support to start Puppet runs from the Foreman dashboard. You can find information at `http://theforeman.org/manuals/1.2/index.html#4.3.2SmartProxySettings`.

Puppet Enterprise Console

Puppet Enterprise Console (`http://puppetlabs.com/puppet/puppet-enterprise`) is developed by Puppet Labs as part of their enterprise product line and support. Like Foreman, PE Console is a dashboard for your Puppet infrastructure. It has similar reporting, inventory, and ENC functionality to access all of the data Puppet collects. One of the key differences from Foreman is that PE Console focuses on Puppet and its related products; for example, it includes Live Management, which is built upon MCollective (introduced in Chapter 11). In this section we will cover all of these features and how to connect your first PE agent to the PE console.

Installing Puppet Enterprise

Begin by downloading Puppet Enterprise for your platform from `http://info.puppetlabs.com/download-pe.html`. Puppet Enterprise is free for up to 10 nodes; if you have a larger deployment you can contact the Puppet Labs sales team for a license.

For this section will be running the installation on Ubuntu 12.04 LTS, but the instructions should be the same for all of the operating systems that PE Puppet supports. After downloading, extract the tar file and execute the installer as shown in Listing 7-11.

Listing 7-11. Installing Puppet Enterprise

```
$ wget --no-check-certificate  https://pm.puppetlabs.com/puppet-enterprise/3.0.1/puppet-
enterprise-3.0.1-ubuntu-12.04-amd64.tar.gz
$ tar -xvf puppet-enterprise-3.0.1-ubuntu-12.04-amd64.tar.gz
$ cd puppet-enterprise-3.0.1-ubuntu-12.04-amd64
$ ./puppet-enterprise-installer
```

The installer will guide you through setting up a Puppet master, PuppetDB, and PE Console. We went with the defaults. After following the instructions in the installer, you should be able to access the console at the link it provides (Figure 7-13).

▨ **Note** Puppet Labs has a Deployment Strategy Guide, available at `http://docs.puppetlabs.com/guides/deploy-ment_guide/index.html`

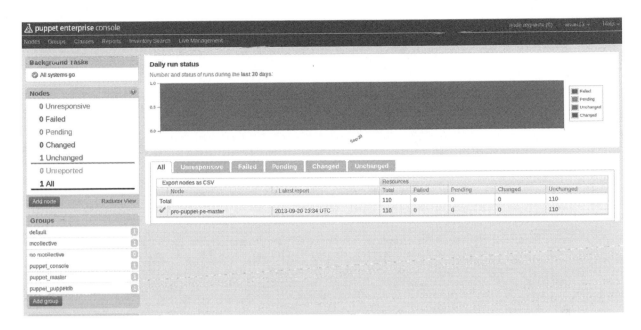

Figure 7-13. *PE Console*

Next run the installer on each Puppet node, but this time enable only the Puppet Agent role. Then connect your PE Puppet client to your PE master by running puppet agent --test.

Connecting PE Agents to PE Console

In the PE Console the node request link should have the number of PE clients that want to connect to the PE master. You can sign their certificates by clicking the Accept button, as shown in Figure 7-14.

Figure 7-14. *Accepting node requests in PE*

Once our nodes have checked in, we can begin applying configuration to them.

Adding Classes to Nodes

Next we will add the mysql class to our node using the Puppet Console. This will bring the mysql class onto the node and that will cause mysql to be installed and configured. First click the Add Class button and choose the name of a class in one of your modules. Then click the Add Group button and add your class to that group. If you're using parameterized classes, you can add default parameters via the Group page, as seen in Figure 7-15.

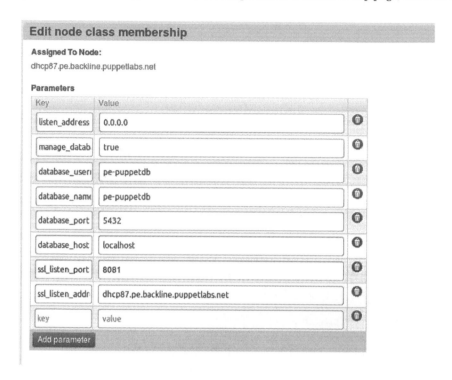

Figure 7-15. *Editing parameterized classes*

■ **Note** Currently default parameters work only with string-based values. Hashes and arrays are not supported. As a workaround, you can put those data types in Hiera and then include the class in PE Console.

Inventory Service

Under the Inventory tab (Figure 7-16), PE Console provides the ability to query facts in your infrastructure. This can be useful if you want to query the list of all hosts that are running a certain OS family. Here we are searching for all the Debian machines that have registered with PE Console.

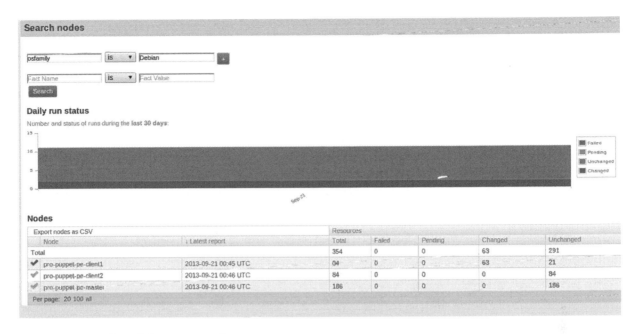

Figure 7-16. PE Console Inventory service

■ **Note**   The Inventory service is case-sensitive. So you must use the case of the value as returned by Facter.

Live Management

Live Management gives you direct access to your nodes, allowing you to query them, run commands on them, and even kick off Puppet runs. Under the hood, it uses MCollective, which is in the subject of Chapter 11.

From the Live Management tab, choose Control Puppet ➤ Run Once. On the right you can select the group of nodes you want to change and on the left you can input parameters for the Puppet run. Once your click Run, a notification will be sent to all of the nodes selected to run Puppet (Figure 7-17).

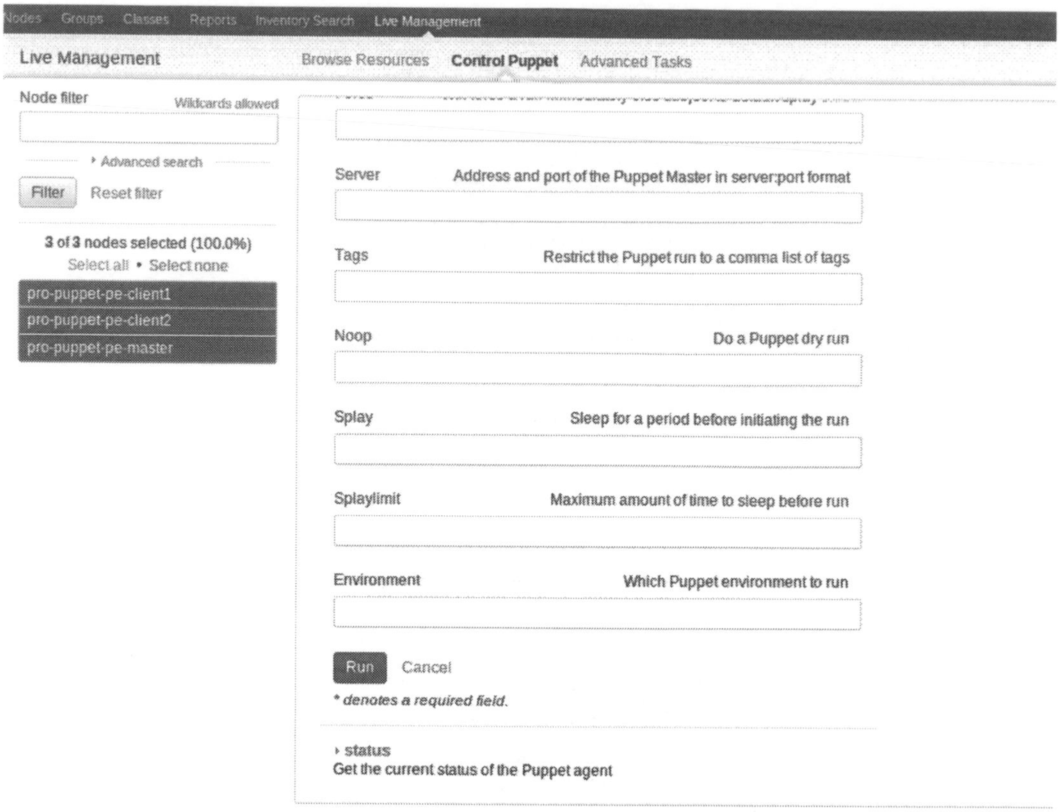

Figure 7-17. PE Console Live Management

Under the Advanced Tasks tab you can choose from a variety of actions, such as installing packages, starting and stopping services, and even updating machines.

Puppetboard

Puppetboard was created to provide an alternative to Puppet Dashboard. Its aim is to replace the reporting functionality of Puppet Dashboard and give you access to the data PuppetDB stores on your behalf.

Puppetboard differs from Puppet Dashboard on a few key points:

- It's written in Python, not Ruby, with the help of the Flask microframework and the requests HTTP library.

- It doesn't store any data itself; everything is queried live from PuppetDB.

- It cannot function without PuppetDB.

- It does not provide External Node Classifier facilities.

PuppetDB manages to store, very efficiently, an enormous amount of information about your infrastructure. Every node that runs is known to PuppetDB, along with its facts. If the capability is enabled, it can also give you access to events that occurred on a node and a complete report. Prior to PuppetDB 1.5, reports and event storage were considered experimental. This is no longer the case, and we can advise you to turn these features on as they will greatly increase the utility of PuppetDB and Puppetboard.

Installation

Because Puppetboard is a very young project, the installation procedure and documentation aren't the most user-friendly. Unfortunately, you will have to run Puppetboard from source for now.

You can choose to either clone the repository from GitHub or download the 0.0.1 release tarball. You will additionally need either Apache with `mod_wsgi` or another httpd, like Nginx, that proxies your requests to Puppetboard running in `uwsgi` (or any other application server that supports WSGI, like Passenger). You can even use something like Python FastCGI and proxy to that instead.

Because Puppetboard is still evolving and we expect things to change, including the installation instructions, we decided not to include those here. Instead, please look at the Readme that ships with Puppetboard, which contains instructions about getting started. If you can't make it work, feel free to contact the author or file an issue on GitHub; he'll gladly help you out.

Reviewing the Dashboard Tabs

Puppetboard is meant to be self-explanatory. When you access Puppetboard, you will be presented with the dashboard shown in Figure 7-18, displaying some statistics about PuppetDB and your environment in the Overview tab. Also shown are nodes who changed, failed, and haven't reported in recently.

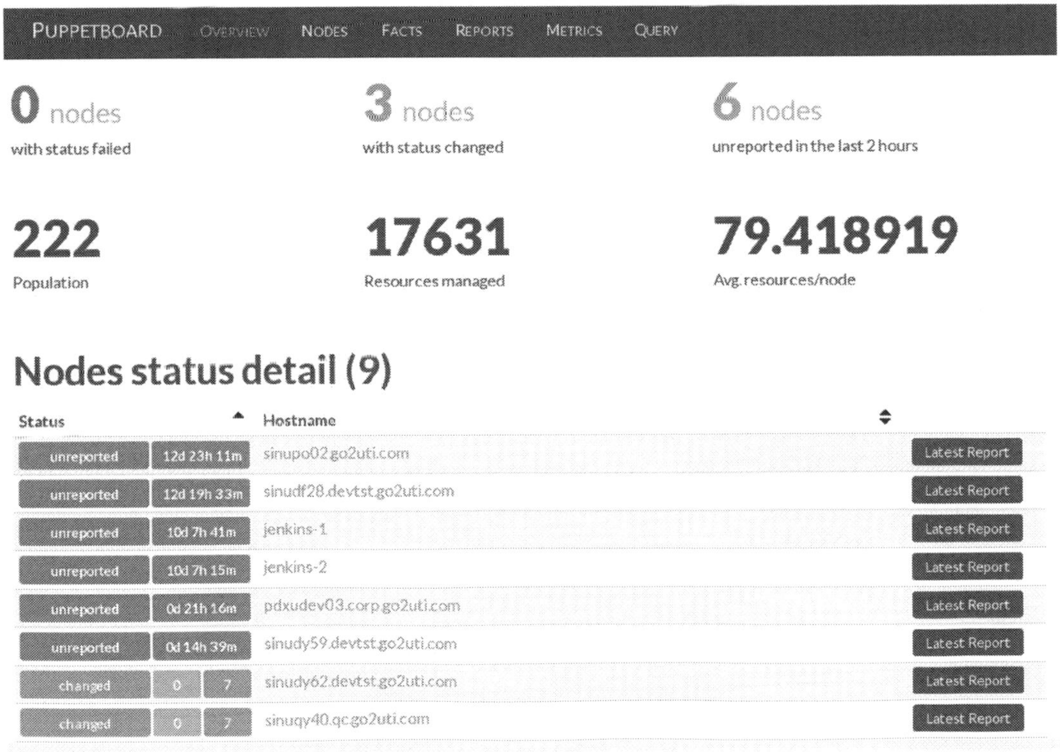

Figure 7-18. *The Puppetboard Overview tab*

Nodes

Next up is the Nodes tab, which should give you a list of all the (active) nodes known to PuppetDB and a search box that will filter the table for you (Figure 7-19). Depending on how many nodes you have, this page might take a few seconds to load. If you run into timeout errors, you should increase the PUPPETDB_TIMEOUT value in your settings (see the Readme).

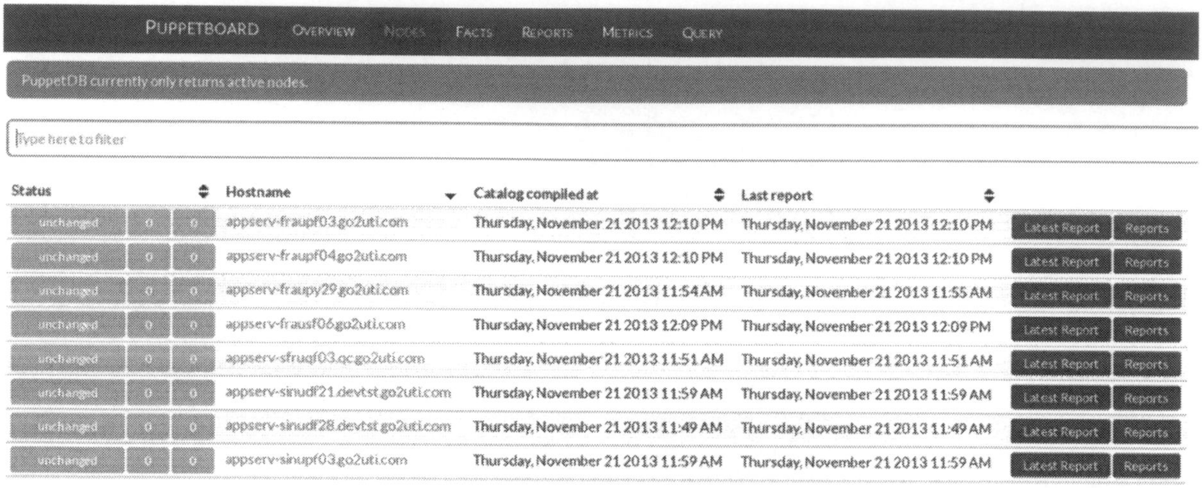

Figure 7-19. *The Nodes tab*

From the Nodes tab, you can access an individual node's basic information, along with all the facts that are known about this host. If you have reporting enabled, as shown in Figure 7-20 it will give you access to the last ten reports.

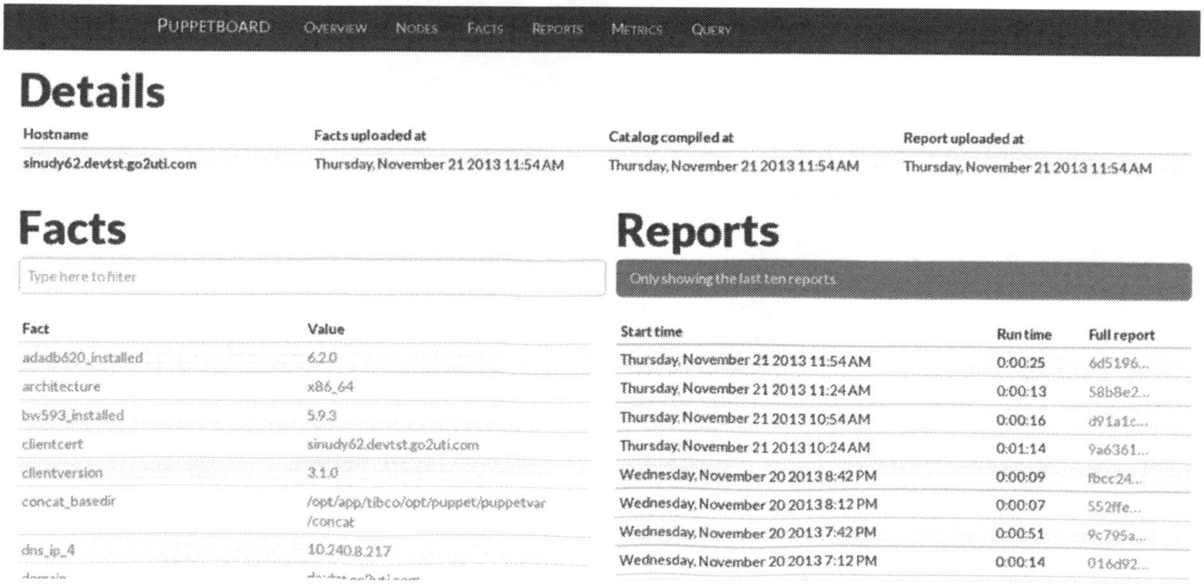

Figure 7-20. *A node overview*

Facts

The Facts tab serves a similar purpose, listing all facts that are currently known to PuppetDB. Clicking on a fact will take you to a page showing for which nodes this fact is known and what their values are.

Reports

The Reports tab (Figure 7-21) allows you to view the reports of Puppet runs. All runs that are on file for the current host are listed. You can drill down into a report by clicking its unique ID (Figure 7-22).

Figure 7-21. The Reports tab

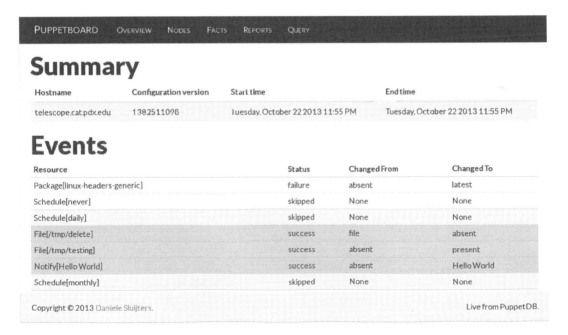

Figure 7-22. A single report. Resources that have been changed show before and after states

Query

The Query tab (Figure 7-23) is to be used with caution. It allows you to execute freeform, user-submitted queries against any of the API endpoints of PuppetDB. Your query must adhere to the API syntax and will be passed, as is, to PuppetDB. This will return either a result or an error page, depending on whether PuppetDB understood the query. It's a very powerful feature, giving you full access to all the data in PuppetDB and allows you to test out queries against PuppetDB that you wish to use in other scripts.

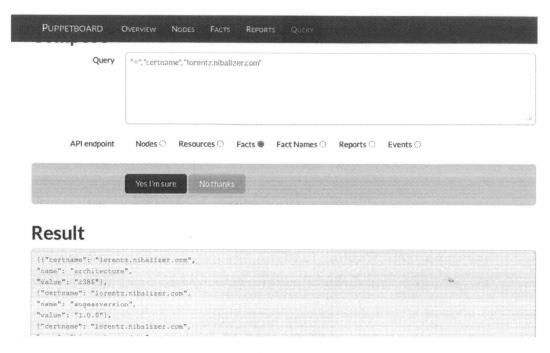

Figure 7-23. *The Query tab is a place to test puppetdb queries, as the syntax is somewhat obtuse*

The Future of Puppetboard

Puppetboard is still undergoing a lot of changes (along with its underlying library, pypuppetdb) as we try to keep up with PuppetDB releases and the new features.

At the time of writing, PuppetDB 1.5 has just been released, introducing a new version of the PuppetDB API. This new API version introduces pagination to most endpoints and many other features, making it significantly easier to build a good user interface. It also includes major improvements to the reports and events endpoints, which Puppetboard will greatly benefit from.

As such, Puppetboard and pypuppetdb are going to change quite a bit in the coming months to take advantage of all those great new capabilities and will continue to do so as PuppetDB's capabilities are expanded along the way.

Summary

In this chapter, we've explored how you can use the Foreman, the Puppet Console, and Puppetboard as web-based front-ends to your Puppet environment. We examined how to install, configure, use, and manage each tool, and we looked at their respective capabilities. Each offers powerful additional visualization and management capabilities that you'll find useful in managing your environment, and that enable you to provide graphing to your team.

Resources

The following links will take you to documentation related to the Puppet consoles that we have covered and related topics:

- Foreman: http://theforeman.org/projects/foreman
- The Foreman mailing list: http://groups.google.com/group/foreman-users
- The Foreman IRC channel: #theforeman on Freenode
- The Foreman Forums: http://theforeman.org/projects/foreman/boards
- External nodes: http://docs.puppetlabs.com/guides/external_nodes.html
- Puppet configuration reference: http://docs.puppetlabs.com/references/stable/configuration.html
- Puppet Enterprise overview: http://puppetlabs.com/puppet/puppet-enterprise
- Installing Puppet Enterprise: http://docs.puppetlabs.com/pe/latest/install_basic.html
- Puppetboard: https://github.com/nedap/puppetboard

CHAPTER 8

■ ■ ■

Tools and Integration

The Puppet community has written many tools for Puppet. In this chapter, we will cover a variety of these tools to help you write better modules and increase productivity. We will cover the Puppet Forge, which is a central place for members of the Puppet community to publish and download reusable modules. Next we will cover module deployment tools like librarian puppet and r10k which help manage Puppet module dependences. Afterwards, we will explore testing tools such as rspec-puppet, rspec-system and integrating the tests with TravisCI, a continuous integration tool. Finally, we will learn how to use Geppetto, an IDE for Puppet module development.

Puppet Forge and the Module Tool

The Puppet Forge, located at http://forge.puppetlabs.com/ (Figure 8-1), provides an online repository of Puppet modules. This service provides the means to publish and locate modules for commonly managed services like iptables, Apache, and NTP. In addition, there are modules targeted for specific use cases, such as Hadoop and OpenStack.

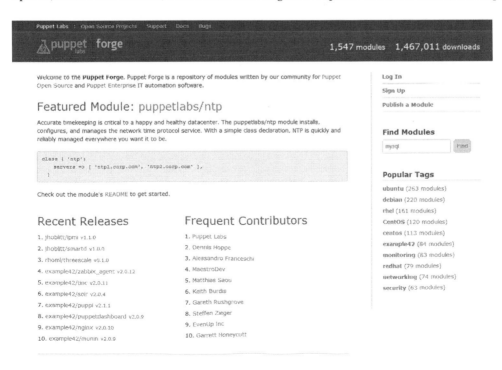

Figure 8-1. *Puppet Forge*

If you find yourself needing quick deployment of a complex infrastructure like Hadoop, the Puppet Forge will save you much time and effort. Modules on the Forge provide a reference configuration that may be easily modified if necessary. Puppet modules may be manually downloaded from the Forge using a standard web browser, but the process is made much easier through the use of the Puppet Module tool.

Puppet's module command provides an interface to the Forge API. This command-line interface allows you to create skeleton Puppet modules for your own work, search the Forge for existing modules, and install them into your configuration. In this section, we cover the processes of downloading an existing module and publishing a new module to the Forge. The Puppet Module tool is bundled with Puppet and can be accessed via the module subcommand (Listing 8-1).

Listing 8-1. Puppet Module help

```
$ puppet help module
ACTIONS:
    build       Build a module release package.
    changes     Show modified files of an installed module.
    generate    Generate boilerplate for a new module.
    install     Install a module from the Puppet Forge or a release archive.
    list        List installed modules
    search      Search the Puppet Forge for a module.
    uninstall   Uninstall a puppet module.
    upgrade     Upgrade a puppet module.
```

Searching and Installing a Module from the Forge

The first step to downloading and installing a Puppet module is to search for the name of a module providing the configuration you're looking for. For example, a service managed in many application stacks is MySQL. Before setting out to write your own Puppet module to manage MySQL, you can search on the Puppet Forge (Figure 8-2), or you can use the puppet module search command in Listing 8-2 to see if one has been published to the Forge already.

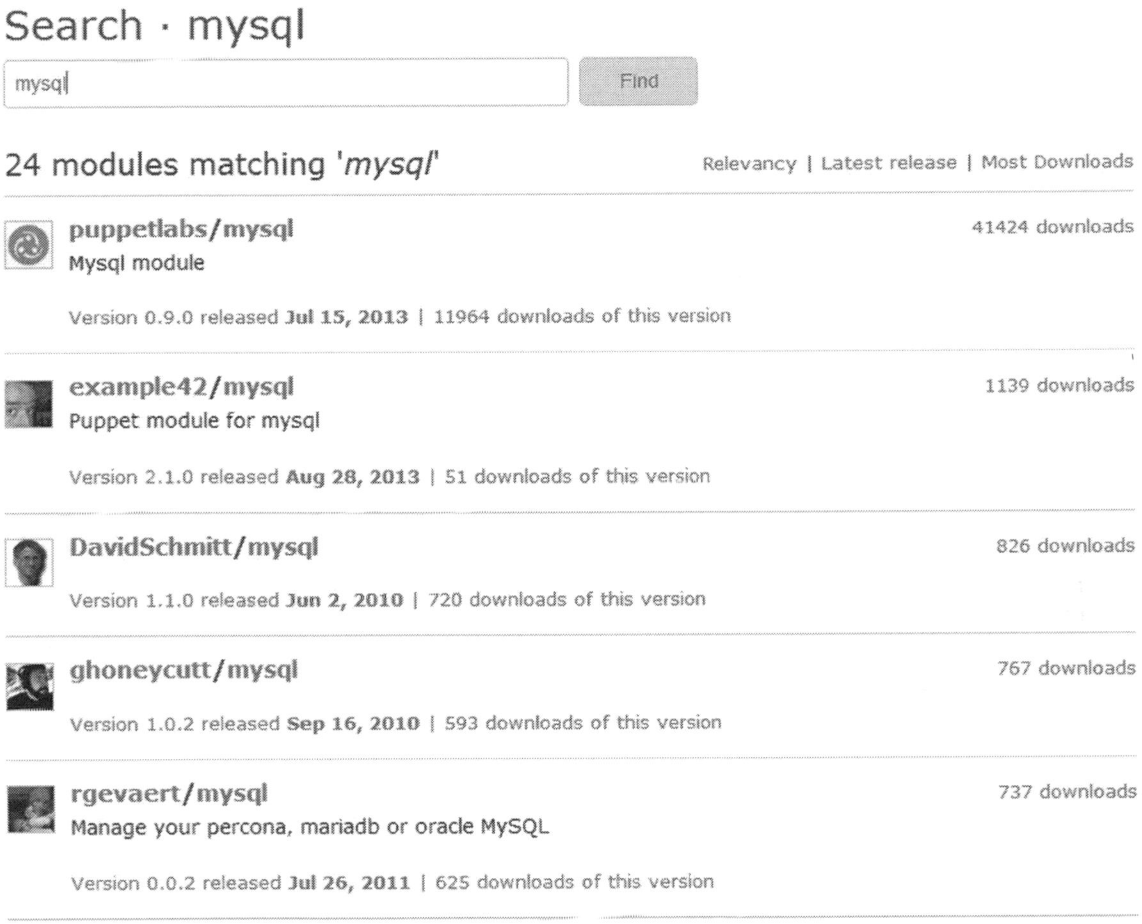

Search · mysql

```
mysql
```
Find

24 modules matching 'mysql'

Relevancy | Latest release | Most Downloads

puppetlabs/mysql
Mysql module

41424 downloads

Version 0.9.0 released **Jul 15, 2013** | 11964 downloads of this version

example42/mysql
Puppet module for mysql

1139 downloads

Version 2.1.0 released **Aug 28, 2013** | 51 downloads of this version

DavidSchmitt/mysql

826 downloads

Version 1.1.0 released **Jun 2, 2010** | 720 downloads of this version

ghoneycutt/mysql

767 downloads

Version 1.0.2 released **Sep 16, 2010** | 593 downloads of this version

rgevaert/mysql
Manage your percona, mariadb or oracle MySQL

737 downloads

Version 0.0.2 released **Jul 26, 2011** | 625 downloads of this version

Figure 8-2. *Searching for MySQL modules using the Forge*

Listing 8-2. Searching for MySQL modules using puppet-module

```
$ puppet module search mysql
NAME                     DESCRIPTION        AUTHOR         KEYWORDS
puppetlabs-mysql         Mysql module       @puppetlabs    database mysql
DavidSchmitt-mysql                          @DavidSchmitt  resources database mysql
bjoernalbers-mysql_osx   Manage MySQL       @bjoernalbers  osx apple mac db database mysql
brucem-ezpublish         eZ Publish Module  @brucem        apache mysql php cms ezpublish
```

There are many modules to manage MySQL on the Forge, and currently there is no rating system; so finding good modules is a bit of a challenge. Recommendations on the mailing lists and IRC channels are a good place to start, but you should select modules by examining each one for quality and whether it solves your needs. A good indicator of a module's quality is the number of downloads it has and the number of contributors on the module's GitHub page. You can search for a module by the number of downloads using the Forge web page, and filter-based search is planned for a future release of the Forge.

We're going to install the module authored by Puppetlabs because it supports a variety of operating systems and is actively maintained by the Puppet module team and the Puppet community. To automatically download and install the module, use the `install` action in Listing 8-3 or download a tar file from the Forge via the web page. The module will be installed into `/etc/puppet/modules` if you are the root user; otherwise, it will be installed into your home directory under `.puppet/modules`.

Listing 8-3. Installing a module using puppet module

```
$ puppet module install puppetlabs/mysql
Notice: Preparing to install into /etc/puppet/modules ...
Notice: Downloading from https://forge.puppetlabs.com ...
Notice: Installing -- do not interrupt ...
/etc/puppet/modules
••┬ puppetlabs-mysql (v0.9.0)
  ••• puppetlabs-stdlib (v4.1.0)

$ tree -L 1 mysql/
mysql/
├── CHANGELOG
├── files
├── Gemfile
├── Gemfile.lock
├── lib
├── LICENSE
├── manifests
├── metadata.json
├── Modulefile
├── Rakefile
├── README.md
├── spec
├── templates
├── tests
••• TODO
```

As you can see, the Puppet Module tool downloaded and unpacked the MySQL module, as well as handling any dependencies on other modules (in this case `puppetlabs/stdlib`). Once installed, the module contents indicate that the documentation is in the `README.md` file.

Examples are also located in the `tests/` directory. These examples provide a quick way to get started using the new `mysql::server` class and `mysql::db` provider provided by the module.

Now that you have a module installed from the Forge, you can begin using it immediately. If you've installed it on your puppet master, you can begin using MySQL classes in your manifests; if you've installed it locally, you can create a MySQL server as shown in Listing 8-4.

Listing 8-4. Using the MySQL module

```
$ puppet apply -e 'class { 'mysql::server': config_hash => { 'root_password' => 'changeme' } }'
notice: /Stage[main]/Mysql::Server/Package[mysql-server]/ensure: ensure changed 'purged' to 'present'
notice: /Stage[main]/Mysql/Package[mysql_client]/ensure: ensure changed 'purged' to 'present'
notice: /Stage[main]/Mysql::Config/File[/etc/mysql/my.cnf]/content: content changed '{md5}77f15d6c87
f9c136c4efcda072017f71' to '{md5}471b6c669c3b45a4d490c3dd60c0788e'
notice: /Stage[main]/Mysql::Config/Exec[set_mysql_rootpw]/returns: executed successfully
```

```
notice: /Stage[main]/Mysql::Config/File[/root/.my.cnf]/ensure: defined content as '{md5}103cbbe23ade
bafb38d7e074b3951e0d'
notice: /Stage[main]/Mysql::Config/Exec[mysqld-restart]: Triggered 'refresh' from 2 events
notice: Finished catalog run in 24.23 seconds
```

Generating a Module

Now that you know how to use modules from the Forge, let's create our own module. We are going to use the Puppet Module tool to generate the default structure for us:

```
$ puppet module generate propuppet-demoapp
Generating module at /root/propuppet-demoapp
propuppet-demoapp
propuppet-demoapp/Modulefile
propuppet-demoapp/tests
propuppet-demoapp/tests/init.pp
propuppet-demoapp/manifests
propuppet-demoapp/manifests/init.pp
propuppet-demoapp/spec
propuppet-demoapp/spec/spec_helper.rb
propuppet-demoapp/README
```

You can also use your own skeletons to add organization-specific boilerplate. In Listing 8-5 you can see we have cloned a skeleton by Puppet community member Gareth Rushgrove.

Listing 8-5. A Puppet module skeleton

```
$ git clone https://github.com/garethr/puppet-module-skeleton
$ cd puppet-module-skeleton
$ find skeleton -type f | git checkout-index --stdin --force --prefix="$HOME/.puppet/var/puppet-module/" --
```

Now when we generate a module, we will get a lot more boilerplate and files to assist in our Puppet development, as shown in Listing 8-6. You will learn more about some of these files later in the chapter.

Listing 8-6. A Puppet module generated with a skeleton

```
$ puppet module generate propuppet/demoapp
Notice: Generating module at /home/vagrant/propuppet-demoapp
propuppet-demoapp
propuppet-demoapp/templates
propuppet-demoapp/templates/.gitkeep
propuppet-demoapp/CONTRIBUTORS
propuppet-demoapp/Modulefile
propuppet-demoapp/.nodeset.yml
propuppet-demoapp/Rakefile
propuppet-demoapp/LICENSE
propuppet-demoapp/tests
propuppet-demoapp/tests/init.pp
propuppet-demoapp/files
propuppet-demoapp/files/.gitkeep
propuppet-demoapp/Gemfile
```

```
propuppet-demoapp/manifests
propuppet-demoapp/manifests/install.pp
propuppet-demoapp/manifests/params.pp
propuppet-demoapp/manifests/config.pp
propuppet-demoapp/manifests/service.pp
propuppet-demoapp/manifests/init.pp
propuppet-demoapp/CHANGELOG
propuppet-demoapp/spec
propuppet-demoapp/spec/spec_helper_system.rb
propuppet-demoapp/spec/spec_helper.rb
propuppet-demoapp/spec/system
propuppet-demoapp/spec/system/basic_spec.rb
propuppet-demoapp/spec/classes
propuppet-demoapp/spec/classes/example_spec.rb
propuppet-demoapp/.travis.yml
propuppet-demoapp/.fixtures.yml
propuppet-demoapp/README.markdown
propuppet-demoapp/lib
propuppet-demoapp/lib/puppet
propuppet-demoapp/lib/puppet/provider
propuppet-demoapp/lib/puppet/provider/.gitkeep
propuppet-demoapp/lib/puppet/type
propuppet-demoapp/lib/puppet/type/.gitkeep
propuppet-demoapp/.gitignore
```

You can see in Listing 8-6 that the generate action creates quite a bit of boilerplate for us to fill in and use as a guide. The puppet-module tool prefixes each module with the author of the class, so the module is actually named demoapp.

At this point you will want to modify the boilerplate to install and configure the application you want managed. Afterward, we can build the module with the command shown in Listing 8-7.

Listing 8-7: Building a Puppet module

```
$ puppet module build
Notice: Building /home/vagrant/propuppet-demoapp for release
Module built: /home/vagrant/propuppet-demoapp/pkg/propuppet-demoapp-0.0.1.tar.gz
```

Now that our module is built, let's move it to /etc/puppet/modules/demoapp:

```
$ sudo mv pkg/propuppet-demoapp-0.0.1 /etc/puppet/modules/demoapp
```

And finally, we apply our new module:

```
$ sudo puppet apply -e 'include demoapp'
```

■ **Note** Puppet apply will fail if you did not modify the params.pp file in the demoapp module and replace the package and service names with valid names for your platform.

At this point you will want to verify that your module is working correctly and add it to a version control system if you have not already done so. If this is a public module, you can now upload the pkg file in pkg/propuppet-demoapp-0.0.1.tar.gz to the Forge via the web interface.

Managing Module Dependencies

In the next few sections we will explore some ways to manage all of the public modules you are using from the Puppet Forge.

Puppet Librarian

Puppet librarian (http://librarian-puppet.com/) is a tool written by Puppet community member Tim Sharpe (rodjek) to manage puppet module dependencies. It can pull dependencies off the Puppet Forge or directly from GitHub.

To get started you can install it via RubyGems:

```
$ gem install librarian-puppet
```

Puppet librarian will insist on managing /etc/puppet/modules, so if you currently have the folder in your version control, you will need to remove the contents. To get started, run librarian-puppet init as shown in Listing 8-8.

Listing 8-8. Running librarian-puppet init

```
$ librarian-puppet init
     create  Puppetfile
```

Let's examine the newly created Puppetfile. The first line tells librarian-puppet to use the Puppet Forge.

```
forge "http://forge.puppetlabs.com"
```

The next line instructs librarian-puppet to install the latest version of puppetlabs/stdlib from the Puppet Forge.

```
mod 'puppetlabs/stdlib'
```

You can specify the version by adding the version number after the module name:

```
mod 'puppetlabs/stdlib', '4.1.0'
```

To grab it from Git instead, we would use this syntax:

```
mod 'puppetlabs/stdlib', :git => 'git://github.com/puppetlabs/puppetlabs-stdlib'
```

Let's add the Apache module to our Puppetfile:

```
$ cat Puppetfile
forge "http://forge.puppetlabs.com"

mod 'puppetlabs/apache'
```

Then run librarian-puppet install and watch as the module and its dependencies are installed into our module folder (Listing 8-9).

Listing 8-9. Running librarian puppet install

```
$ librarian-puppet install
$ ls modules/
apache  concat  stdlib
```

We can display the module names and versions by running librarian-puppet show (Listing 8-10).

Listing 8-10. Running librarian-puppet show

```
$ librarian-puppet show
puppetlabs/apache (0.8.1)
puppetlabs/stdlib (4.1.0)
ripienaar/concat (0.2.0)
```

As you can, see librarian-puppet has eliminated the need to add modules from the Forge to version control as long as you keep Puppetfile and Puppetfile.lock in version control. This will help you keep track of the versions of a module you are using and let you easily experiment with newer versions in development. Next we will look at similar tool called r10k.

R10K

R10k (https://github.com/adrienthebo/r10k) was written by Puppetlabs employee Adrien Thebo as a drop-in replacement for librarian-puppet. Like librarian-puppet, it supports the same Puppetfile syntax. R10K was designed to support dynamic environments with functionality similar to librarian-puppet. Adrien's blog goes into the details about why he built r10k (http://somethingsinistral.net/blog/rethinking-puppet-deployment/) and is a good starting point for learning about it.

r10k can be installed via RubyGems:

```
$ gem install r10k
```

Next you need to modify your Git repository to a slightly different layout. Like librarian-puppet, r10k wants to manage the module directory, so you need to remove all modules from the module directory and add /modules to your .gitignore. Next place your custom modules in a different directory, which we will call site. Finally, place a Puppetfile in the root of your repository. The Puppetfile should include the list of public modules you are using from the Puppet Forge, GitHub, or internal Git repositories. Your repository layout should look similar to Listing 8-11.

Listing 8-11. r10k layout

```
$ tree -L 1
.
|-- manifests
|-- modules
|-- Puppetfile
|-- README.md
`-- site
```

Next we need to configure r10k to use our repository, which we can do by updating the myrepo remote in Listing 8-12.

Listing 8-12. Configuring r10k

```
$ cat /etc/r10k.yaml
# The location to use for storing cached Git repos
:cachedir: '/var/cache/r10k'

# A list of git repositories to create
:sources:
  # This will clone the git repository and instantiate an environment per
  # branch in /etc/puppet/environments
  :myorg:
    remote: 'git@github.com:my-org/puppet-repo'
    basedir: '/etc/puppet/environments'

# This directory will be purged of any directory that doesn't map to a
# git branch
:purgedirs:
  - '/etc/puppet/environments'
```

Assuming we've configured Puppet for dynamic environments as described in Chapter 3, we can now run the r10k deploy command (Listing 8-13).

Listing 8-13. Running the r10k deploy command

```
$ r10k deploy environment

$ ls -l /etc/puppet/environments/
total 8
drwxr-xr-x 6 root root 4096 Aug 24 21:18 master
drwxr-xr-x 6 root root 4096 Aug 24 21:19 refactor_for_r10k
```

As you can see from listing 8-13, /ctc/puppet/environments/ now contains each branch in your Git repository, and the modules directory in each environment contains the modules specified in the Puppetfile for that branch. Now that we have explored options for easier Puppet deployment, let's examine tools that help us write better Puppet modules. First up is puppet lint.

Puppet-lint

Puppet-lint (http://puppet-lint.com/) is another tool written by Tim Sharpe, to help developers keep Puppet code consistent with the Puppet style guide (http://docs.puppetlabs.com/guides/style_guide.html). It can easily be installed via RubyGems:

```
$ gem install puppet-lint
```

Once it is installed, all you have to do is run puppet-lint. In Listing 8-14 we have cloned the puppetlabs/rsync module and have run puppet-lint. You can see it has quite a few style guide violations, which we can now easily fix.

Listing 8-14. Running puppet-lint

```
$ puppet-lint --with-filename manifests
manifests/server.pp - WARNING: line has more than 80 characters on line 55
manifests/server/module.pp - WARNING: line has more than 80 characters on line 15
manifests/server/module.pp - WARNING: line has more than 80 characters on line 16
manifests/server/module.pp - WARNING: line has more than 80 characters on line 18
manifests/server/module.pp - WARNING: line has more than 80 characters on line 19
manifests/server/module.pp - WARNING: line has more than 80 characters on line 20
manifests/server/module.pp - WARNING: line has more than 80 characters on line 21
manifests/get.pp - WARNING: line has more than 80 characters on line 11
manifests/get.pp - WARNING: line has more than 80 characters on line 69
manifests/get.pp - WARNING: line has more than 80 characters on line 72
manifests/get.pp - WARNING: line has more than 80 characters on line 74
manifests/get.pp - WARNING: indentation of => is not properly aligned on line 67
```

For a full of list of checks refer to http://puppet-lint.com/checks/. To disable certain checks, you can add them to ~/.puppet-lint.rc. The most common check to add to the .rc file is --no-80chars-check.

■ **Note**　It's a good idea to add a puppet-lint check to your deployment process. If you're using Git, you can add it as a precommit hook, or, if you have your Puppet code in continuous integration, you can add a lint check.

Testing the Modules

Now that our code is following the Puppet Style guide, we want to make sure it is working as expected. As your modules get more complex and support a large variety of configuration options, you will need testing to make sure code changes don't introduce regressions. The testing tools we'll explore in this section include rspec-puppet, TravisCI, and rspec-system.

rspec-puppet

Rspec-puppet (http://rspec-puppet.com/), another tool by Tim Sharpe, was written to assist in testing Puppet manifests. Rspec-puppet can be installed via RubyGems.

```
$ gem install rspec-puppet
```

As an example, we will be adding tests to the pdxcat/collectd module (Listing 8-15).

Listing 8-15. Cloning the collectd module

```
$ git clone git://github.com/pdxcat/puppet-module-collectd.git
$ cd puppet-module-collectd
```

The first thing we need to do is some setup. To bootstrap our development environment, we are going to copy a Gemfile from a module that already has tests to manage (Listing 8-16).

Listing 8-16. Adding a Gemfile

```
$ wget https://raw.github.com/puppetlabs/puppetlabs-mysql/master/Gemfile
$ gem install bundler
$ bundle install
```

Bundler will install all the test tools defined in the Gemfile (Listing 8-17).

Listing 8-17. The contents of the Gemfile

```
$ cat Gemfile
source 'https://rubygems.org'

group :development, :test do
  gem 'rake',                     :require => false
  gem 'rspec-puppet',             :require => false
  gem 'puppetlabs_spec_helper',   :require => false
  gem 'rspec-system',             :require => false
  gem 'rspec-system-puppet',      :require => false
  gem 'rspec-system-serverspec',  :require => false
  gem 'serverspec',               :require => false
  gem 'puppet-lint',              :require => false
end

if puppetversion = ENV['PUPPET_GEM_VERSION']
  gem 'puppet', puppetversion, :require => false
else
  gem 'puppet', :require => false
end

# vim:ft=ruby
```

We will also want a Rakefile (Listing 8-18).

Listing 8-18. Adding a Rakefile

```
$ wget https://raw.github.com/puppetlabs/puppetlabs-mysql/master/Rakefile
$ cat Rakefile
require 'puppetlabs_spec_helper/rake_tasks'
require 'rspec-system/rake_task'
```

Once the Rakefile is in place, the puppetlabs_spec_helper gem will provide some tasks to assist in module development, as shown in Listing 8-19.

Listing 8-19. Listing available rake tasks

```
$ rake -T
rake build          # Build puppet module package
rake clean          # Clean a built module package
rake coverage       # Generate code coverage information
rake help           # Display the list of available rake tasks
rake lint           # Check puppet manifests with puppet-lint
rake spec           # Run spec tests in a clean fixtures directory
```

```
rake spec:system      # Run system tests
rake spec_clean       # Clean up the fixtures directory
rake spec_prep        # Create the fixtures directory
rake spec_standalone  # Run spec tests on an existing fixtures directory
rake spec_system      # Run RSpec code examples
```

Next we want to create a folder structure for rspec-puppet in the spec directory (Listing 8-20).

Listing 8-20. Creating the spec directory layout

```
$ mkdir spec
$ mkdir spec/classes
$ mdkir spec/defines
$ mkdir spec/unit
$ cd spec
$ wget https://raw.github.com/puppetlabs/puppetlabs-mysql/master/spec/spec.opts
$ wget https://raw.github.com/puppetlabs/puppetlabs-mysql/master/spec/spec_helper.rb
```

If you have dependencies on other modules, you will also want a fixtures file (Listing 8-21). You will need to modify it for your module.

Listing 8-21. Adding a .fixtures.yml file

```
$ cd ..
$ wget https://raw.github.com/puppetlabs/puppetlabs-mysql/master/.fixtures.yml
```

For the collectd module, we have modified fixtures.yml to look like Listing 8-22:

Listing 8-22. The .fixtures.yml file

```
$ cat .fixtures.yml
fixtures:
  repositories:
    'stdlib': 'git://github.com/puppetlabs/puppetlabs-stdlib'
  symlinks:
    'collectd': "#{source_dir}"
```

Now we are ready to start writing tests. We are testing the collectd class first. We create a file called spec/classes/collectd_init_spec.rb and add the code shown in Listing 8-23.

Listing 8-23. The spec/classes/collectd_init_spec.rb file

```
# spec/classes/collectd_init_spec.rb
require 'spec_helper'

describe 'collectd' do

end
```

■ **Note** The filename must end in _spec.rb or the rake task will not run the test.

The first line includes our spec_helper library, and the describe block establishes what we want to test; this block is the outline of our initial test. At this point you should be able to run your test suite without any errors, as in Listing 8-24. You should also see that any dependencies in your .fixtures.yml file should be pulled in before the test suite runs.

Listing 8-24. Running spec tests

```
$ rake spec
Cloning into 'spec/fixtures/modules/stdlib'...
remote: Counting objects: 4097, done.
remote: Compressing objects: 100% (2316/2316), done.
remote: Total 4097 (delta 1600), reused 3730 (delta 1279)
Receiving objects: 100% (4097/4097), 716.80 KiB | 530 KiB/s, done.
Resolving deltas: 100% (1600/1600), done.
HEAD is now at 2a78cbf Merge pull request #170 from ptomulik/fix_delete_values
/usr/bin/ruby1.9.1 -S rspec spec/classes/collectd_init_spec.rb --color
/usr/lib/ruby/1.9.1/rubygems/custom_require.rb:55:in `require': iconv will be deprecated in the
future, use String#encode instead.
No examples found.

Finished in 0.00006 seconds
0 examples, 0 failures
```

Now let's add tests. Inside the describe block we can test whether the collectd package is being installed with the contain_package function. We will also need to specify osfamily as one of the OS families the module supports; otherwise, it will throw an error. Listing 8-25 shows the code:

Listing 8-25. A simple spec test

```
let :facts do
 {:osfamily => 'RedHat'}
end

it { should contain_package('collectd').with(
 :ensure => 'installed'
)}
```

We should also verify that it throws errors for unsupported OS families. By adding a context block, we can change the facts and add a raise_error check (Listing 8-26).

Listing 8-26. A spec test for an unsupported operating system

```
context 'on non supported operating systems' do
  let :facts do
    {:osfamily => 'foo'}
  end

  it 'should fail' do
    expect { subject }.to  raise_error(/foo is not supported/)
  end
end
```

Now if we run our test suite, we should see two tests passing (Listing 8-27).

Listing 8-27. Running the spec tests a second time

```
$ rake spec
..

Finished in 1.15 seconds
2 examples, 0 failures
```

We've added a few more contain functions for files and the service, so our example now looks like Listing 8-28.

Listing 8-28. The spec/classes/collectd_init_spec.rb file

```
require 'spec_helper'

describe 'collectd' do

  let :facts do
    {:osfamily => 'RedHat'}
  end

  it { should contain_package('collectd').with(
    :ensure => 'installed'
  )}

  it { should contain_service('collectd').with(
    :ensure => 'running'
  )}

  it { should contain_file('collectd.conf') }

  it { should contain_file('collectd.d').with(
   :ensure => 'directory'
  )}

  context 'on non supported operating systems' do
    let :facts do
      {:osfamily => 'foo'}
    end

    it 'should fail' do
      expect { subject }.to  raise_error(/foo is not supported/)
    end
  end

end
```

So far we've only tested for the existence of several named resources with some parameters specified. What we're really interested in is testing the conditional logic that the collectd class uses. The collectd class changes its behavior based on whether the user sets $purge_config equal to true. If it is set, Puppet will purge the distribution-supplied config file and manage all plug-ins through Puppet resources. To test this, we need to add another test case. Let's add a context block and set the purge_config parameter to true. Then we can use .with_content on the file resource to see if the first line is # Generated by Puppet, which means that it is using our template. We will also use should_not to make sure that the file_line resource isn't being included. Listing 8-29 shows the code.

Listing 8-29. A spec test for conditional logic

```
context 'when purge_config is enabled' do
  let :params do
    { :purge_config => true }
  end
  it { should contain_file('collectd.conf').with_content(
   /^# Generated by Puppet$/
  )}
  it { should_not contain_file_line('include_conf_d') }
end
```

Let's also modify the default test to ensure both that the content is nil when purge_config is false and that the file_line resource is included (Listing 8-30).

Listing 8-30. A spec test for file_line

```
it { should contain_file('collectd.conf').with(
 :content => nil
)}

it { should contain_file_line('include_conf_d') }
```

Now that we have some tests, we can start integrating them with TravisCI and GitHub.

TravisCI

TravisCI (https://travis-ci.org/) is a continuous-integration-as-a-service platform that provides free testing for public repositories and can run rspec-puppet tests.

Create a .travis.yml file .with the code shown in Listing 8-31.

Listing 8-31. A .travis.yml file

```
# .travis.yml
branches:
  only:
    - master
language: ruby
bundler_args: --without development
script: "bundle exec rake spec SPEC_OPTS='--format documentation'"
rvm:
  - 1.8.7
  - 1.9.3
  - 2.0.0
```

```
env:
  matrix:
    - PUPPET_GEM_VERSION="~> 2.7.0"
    - PUPPET_GEM_VERSION="~> 3.0.0"
    - PUPPET_GEM_VERSION="~> 3.1.0"
    - PUPPET_GEM_VERSION="~> 3.2.0"
matrix:
  exclude:
    - rvm: 1.9.3
      env: PUPPET_GEM_VERSION="~> 2.7.0"
    - rvm: 2.0.0
      env: PUPPET_GEM_VERSION="~> 2.7.0"
    - rvm: 2.0.0
      env: PUPPET_GEM_VERSION="~> 3.0.0"
    - rvm: 2.0.0
      env: PUPPET_GEM_VERSION="~> 3.1.0"
    - rvm: 1.8.7
      env: PUPPET_GEM_VERSION="~> 3.2.0"
notifications:
  email: false
```

Go to your repository on GitHub and activate the Travis hook under Settings ➤ Service Hooks ➤ Travis. Follow the instructions to activate the hook and run your first test.

Once the hook is activated, you will want to let the consumers of your module know that it is being tested and is currently passing the builds. You can add the text in Listing 8-32 to your README.md to display the current status. It also provides a handy link to the build page (Figure 8-3).

Collectd module for Puppet

Figure 8-3. *README.md rendered on GitHub*

Listing 8-32. TravisCI build image text for Markdown

```
[![Build Status](https://travis-ci.org/pdxcat/puppet-module-collectd.png?branch=master)]
(https://travis-ci.org/pdxcat/puppet-module-collectd)
```

After a few minutes your tests should finish. If they are all green, then your tests successfully ran against multiple versions of Ruby and Puppet (Figure 8-4).

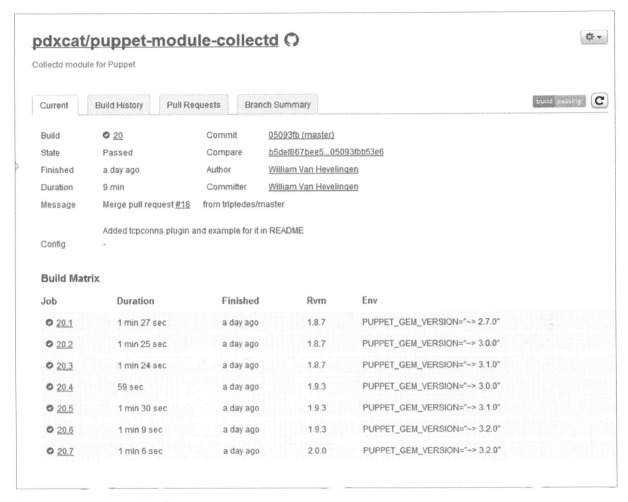

Figure 8-4. *The TravisCI build page*

So now you have some simple rspec-puppet tests, but this barely scratches the surface of testing Puppet modules. You can check out other well-tested modules like (`puppetlabs/mysql` and `puppetlabs/apache`) for more advanced examples. Next we are going to cover rspec-system.

rspec-system

Rspec-system (`https://github.com/puppetlabs/rspec-system`) is a framework for running tests on different operating systems. It spins up test systems, applies Puppet code, and tests that the services are configured as described by the Puppet code. Rspec-system uses Vagrant (`http://www.vagrantup.com/`) to provision the virtual machines and currently supports VirtualBox and VSphere, but support for more providers is planned in the future.

To get started, you will need to download and install VirtualBox (`https://www.virtualbox.org/`) and Vagrant. Then install rspec-system, as shown here:

```
$ gem install rspec-system
```

As we did earlier with rspec-puppet, we will add rspec-system tests to the collectd module. First we want to create a system directory in our spec folder, and since the collectd module is in Git we will want to add .rspec_system to the .gitignore file (Listing 8-33).

Listing 8-33. creating the rspec system directory layout

```
$ cd collectd
$ mkdir spec/system
```

Next we need to create spec/spec_helper_system.rb to be our hook that will run during the initial provisioning. We're going to start with an existing one and modify it for our needs:

```
$ wget https://raw.github.com/puppetlabs/puppetlabs-apache/master/spec/spec_helper_system.rb
```

After some minor tweaks our file now looks like Listing 8-34.

Listing 8-34. The spec/spec_helper_system.rb file

```
# spec/spec_helper_system.rb
require 'rspec-system/spec_helper'
require 'rspec-system-puppet/helpers'
require 'rspec-system-serverspec/helpers'
include Serverspec::Helper::RSpecSystem
include Serverspec::Helper::DetectOS
include RSpecSystemPuppet::Helpers

RSpec.configure do |c|
  # Project root
  proj_root = File.expand_path(File.join(File.dirname(__FILE__), '..'))

  # Enable colour
  c.tty = true

  c.include RSpecSystemPuppet::Helpers

  # This is where we 'setup' the nodes before running our tests
  c.before :suite do
    # Install puppet
    puppet_install

    # Install modules and dependencies
    puppet_module_install(:source => proj_root, :module_name => 'collectd')
    shell('puppet module install puppetlabs-stdlib')
  end
end
```

This hook will install puppet and any dependencies our module might need. Now let's create our first test. In our test we are going to apply the collectd class and then verify that the package is installed and that the service is running (Listing 8-35).

Listing 8-35. The spec/system/basic_spec.rb file

```
# spec/system/basic_spec.rb
require 'spec_helper_system'

describe 'collectd class' do

  package_name = 'collectd'
  service_name = 'collectd'

  context 'default parameters' do
    # Using puppet_apply as a helper
    it 'should work with no errors' do
      pp = <<-EOS
      class { 'collectd': }
      EOS

      # Run it twice and test for idempotency
      puppet_apply(pp) do |r|
        r.exit_code.should_not == 1
        r.refresh
        r.exit_code.should be_zero
      end
    end

    describe package(package_name) do
      it { should be_installed }
    end

    describe service(service_name) do
      it { should be_enabled }
      it { should be_running }
    end
  end
end
```

Next we create a .nodeset.yml file (Listing 8-36) and create some nodes we want to test. Further examples are documented at https://github.com/puppetlabs/rspec-system#creating-a-nodeset-file. We will create an Ubuntu and Centos virtual machine to work with.

Listing 8-36. A .nodeset.yml file

```
# .nodeset.yml

---
default_set: 'centos-64-x64'
sets:
  'centos-64-x64':
    nodes:
      "main.foo.vm":
        prefab: 'centos-64-x64'
```

```
'ubuntu-server-12042-x64':
  nodes:
    "main.foo.vm":
      prefab: 'ubuntu-server-12042-x64'
```

If you are using the puppetlabs_spec_helper gem, spec:system is available in your Rakefile. Otherwise, add require 'rspec-system/rake_task' to your Rakefile. Then run the rake task, as shown in Listing 8-37. The virtual machine image will be downloaded and provisioned, and then the tests will run.

Listing 8-37. Running rspec-system

```
$ rake spec:system
================================================================

Running test: 4 of 4
Description:
  collectd class default parameters Service "collectd"

-----------------
main.foo.vm$ service collectd status | grep 'running'
collectd (6941) is running.
Exit code: 0
-----------------

Result: passed

================================================================
```

For debugging you may want to preserve the virtual machines after the tests run. To do that, you can use the RSPEC_DESTROY variable and then CD to the Vagrant folder to use vagrant ssh (Listing 8-38).

Listing 8-38. Accessing rspec system Vagrant machines

```
$ RSPEC_DESTROY=no rake spec:system
$ cd .rspec_system/vagrant_projects/ubuntu-server-12042-x64/
$ vagrant ssh
```

To specify a nodeset, you can use the RSPEC_SET variable:

```
$ RSPEC_SET=ubuntu-server-12042-x64 rake spec:system
```

Developing Puppet modules With Geppetto

Geppetto (http://puppetlabs.github.io/geppetto/) is an IDE for writing Puppet manifests and modules. It was written and open sourced by DevOps startup Cloudsmith (acquired by Puppetlabs in 2013). It's based on Eclipse and can be run as a standalone application or installed as a plug-in in Eclipse. To install Geppetto, you can download the version for your platform at (http://puppetlabs.github.io/geppetto/download.html). Then you just need to extract it and double-click the Geppetto file to start it. To create a new project, go to File ➤ New ➤ Project, at which point you can select whether to import a module from the Puppet Forge, create a new one, or import from version control. In Figure 8-5 you can see that the module has been imported, and you can immediately start working on it.

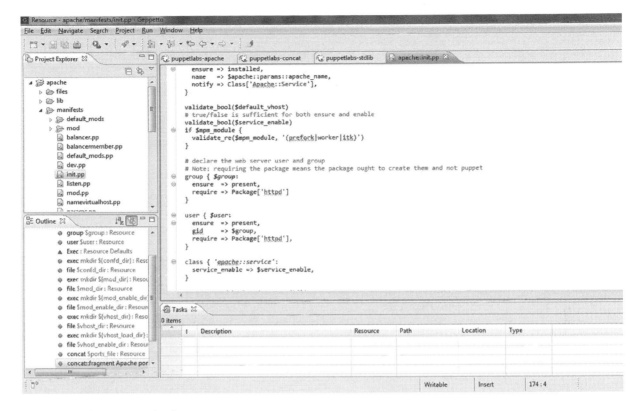

Figure 8-5. *Geppetto project import*

> ■ **Note** The apache module in Listing 8-17 will have errors until you add the concat and stdlib modules to your workspace and then right click on the Project ➤ Properties ➤ Project References and check the boxes next to concat and stdlib. Once checked the stdlib and concat resources will be recognized.

For demonstration purposes, we've created some examples in Figures 8-6 and 8-7 that contain common errors. Geppetto automatically marks the Puppet syntax errors and provides helpful error messages to help debug the problem.

```
    # duplicate attribute
    user { 'dawn':
      shell => '/bin/zsh',
      home  => '/home/dawn',
      shell => '/bin/bash',
    }
        Duplicate attribute: 'shell'
                    Press 'F2' for focus

    }
```

Figure 8-6. *Geppetto display for a duplicate attribute*

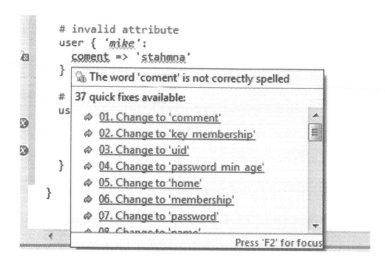

Figure 8-7. *Geppetto display for an invalid attribute*

If you hover over function names such as validate_bool from stdlib, Geppetto displays a tool tip (Figure 8-8) describing the function and documentation the authors have added.

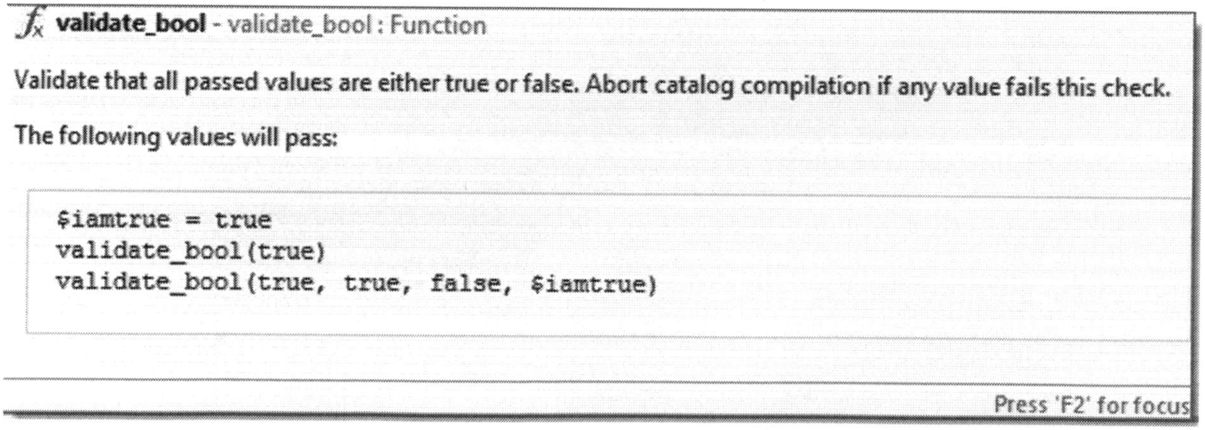

f_x **validate_bool** - validate_bool : Function

Validate that all passed values are either true or false. Abort catalog compilation if any value fails this check.

The following values will pass:

```
$iamtrue = true
validate_bool(true)
validate_bool(true, true, false, $iamtrue)
```

Press 'F2' for focus

Figure 8-8. *Geppetto tool tips*

After Geppetto has helped you write a module, you can use it to push your module directly to the Forge (Figure 8-9). First increment the version number in your modulefile and then go to File ➤ Export to begin the process.

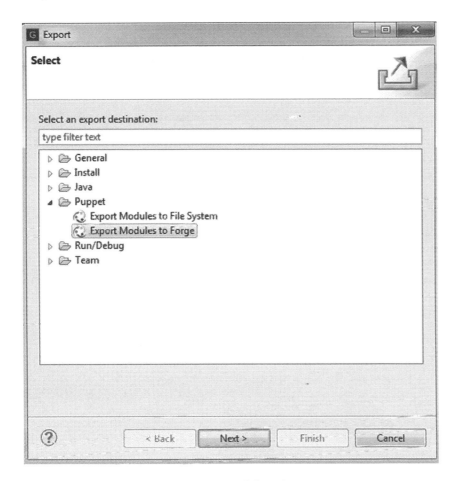

Figure 8-9. *Using Geppetto to export a module to the Forge, step 1*

Then select the module you want to export to the Forge and click Finish to upload it, as shown in Figure 8-10.

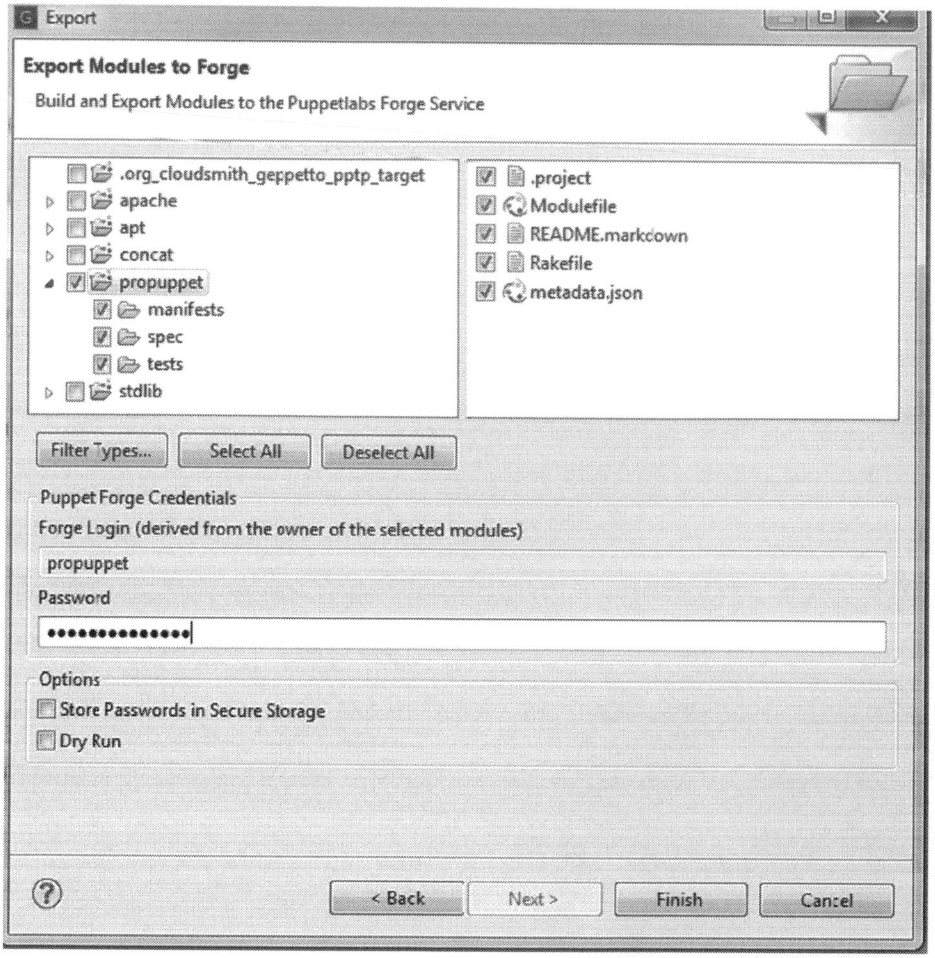

Figure 8-10. *Geppetto export module to the Forge, step II*

Summary

In this chapter, you've seen a number of tools, some that are related to Puppet, and some that are part of it. First, the Puppet Module tool provides a command line interface to working with Puppet modules and the Puppet Forge. Tools like librarian-puppet and r10k allow us to manage module dependencies from the Puppet Forge or Git. You have learned how to test your modules with rspec-puppet and rspec-system and use TravisCI to run your rspec-puppet tests automatically. Finally, we explored Geppetto as an IDE solution for developing Puppet modules.

Puppet is a fast-moving project with a very active community. Tools designed to work with Puppet will continue to be written. Looks for posts on the `puppet-users` and `puppet-dev` sites for the newest tools and updates.

Resources

The following resources are a great place to keep track of the tools and work being done by members of the Puppet community.

- Puppet projects on Github: `https://github.com/search?q=puppet`

- Puppet Users Mailing List: `mailto:puppet-users+subscribe@googlegroups.com`

- Puppet Developer Mailing List: `mailto:puppet-dev+subscribe@googlegroups.com`

- Puppet Labs blog: `http://blog.puppetlabs.com/`

- rspec-puppet tutorial: `http://rspec-puppet.com/tutorial`

- Geppetto: `http://puppetlabs.com/blog/geppetto-a-puppet-ide`

- Geppetto FAQ: `http://puppetlabs.github.io/geppetto/faq.html`

## CHAPTER 9

Reporting with Puppet

One of the most important aspects of any configuration management system is reporting. Reporting is critical for providing information on accuracy, performance, and compliance to policy and standards, and it can provide graphical representations of the overall state of your configuration. Indeed, we've already seen some examples of how to display Puppet reports (via a management console) in Chapter 7, when we looked at Puppet Dashboard and Foreman.

In this chapter, you'll learn what command-line and data-based reports are available, how to configure reporting and reports, and how to work with them; then you'll see how to graph reporting data and build custom reports.

Getting Started

Puppet agents can be configured to return data at the end of each configuration run. Puppet calls this data a *transaction report*. The transaction reports are sent to the master server, which contains a number of report processors that can utilize this data and present it in a variety of forms. You can also develop your own report processors to customize the reporting output.

The default transaction report comes in the form of a YAML file. As mentioned in earlier chapters, YAML is a recursive acronym for "YAML Ain't Markup Language." YAML is a human-readable data serialization format that draws heavily from concepts in XML and the Python and C programming languages.

The transaction reports contain all events and log messages generated by the transaction and some additional metrics. The metrics fall into three general types: time, resource, and change metrics. Within each of these types there are one or more values. They include the time taken for the transaction, the number of resources and changes in the transaction, and the success or failure of those resources.

In Listing 9-1 you can see an example of a portion of a YAML Puppet transaction report.

Listing 9-1. A partial Puppet transaction report

```
--- !ruby/object:Puppet::Transaction::Report
  external_times:
    !ruby/sym config_retrieval: 0.280263900756836
  host: mail.example.com
  logs:
    - !ruby/object:Puppet::Util::Log
      level: !ruby/sym info
      message: Caching catalog for mail.example.com
      source: //mail.example.com/Puppet
      tags:
        - info
      time: 2010-12-18 08:41:19.252599 -08:00
      version: &id001 2.6.4
```

```
      - !ruby/object:Puppet::Util::Log
        level: !ruby/sym info
        message: Applying configuration version '1292690479'
        source: //mail.example.com/Puppet
        tags:
          - info
        time: 2010-12-18 08:41:19.330582 -08:00
        version: *id001
      - !ruby/object:Puppet::Util::Log
        level: !ruby/sym info
        message: "FileBucket adding /etc/sudoers as {md5}49085c571a7ec7ff54270c7a53a79146"
        source: //mail.example.com/Puppet
        tags:
          - info
        time: 2010-12-18 08:41:19.429069 -08:00
        version: *id001
...
    resources: !ruby/object:Puppet::Util::Metric
      label: Resources
      name: resources
      values:
        - - !ruby/sym out_of_sync
          - Out of sync
          - 1
        - - !ruby/sym changed
          - Changed
          - 1
        - - !ruby/sym total
          - Total
          - 8
    changes: !ruby/object:Puppet::Util::Metric
      label: Changes
      name: changes
      values:
        - - !ruby/sym total
          - Total
          - 2
    events: !ruby/object:Puppet::Util::Metric
      label: Events
      name: events
      values:
        - - success
          - Success
          - 2
        - - !ruby/sym total
          - Total
          - 2
  time: 2010-12-18 08:41:15.515624 -08:00
```

Here you can see that the YAML file is divided into sections. The first section contains any log messages. The log messages are any events generated during the Puppet run; for example, the messages that would typically go to standard out or syslog. The second section contains events related to resources, and it tracks each resource managed by Puppet and the changes made to that resource during the Puppet run. The remaining sections detail the value of each metric that Puppet collects. Each metric has a label, a name, and values that make it easy to parse the data, if you wish to use it for reporting or manipulation. Metrics include the number of changes Puppet made, the number of resources managed, and the number and type of events during the run.

The YAML format of the reporting output is very well supported by Ruby, and it can be easily consumed in Ruby and other languages to make use of Puppet reporting data.

Configuring Reporting

On the agent nodes, report should be set to true in /etc/puppet/puppet.conf:

```
[agent]
report = true
```

▓ **Tip** By default, the agent will send the reports back to the Puppet master configuring it. You can set up a separate Puppet master for reports only, if you like. Direct all reports to this server by using the report_server option on the agent (see http://docs.puppetlabs.com/references/latest/configuration.html#reportserver).

By default, the reports generated by the agent will be sent to the master and stored as YAML-formatted files in the report directory. These files are the output of the default report processor, store. Reports are written into subdirectories under the report directory and a directory created for each agent that is reporting. A report file name consists of the datestamp when the report was generated, suffixed with .yaml, for example: 201010130604.yaml.

The report directory is $vardir/reports (usually /var/lib/puppet/reports on most distributions), but you can override this by configuring the reportdir option on the Puppet master puppet.conf configuration file, as shown here:

```
[master]
reportdir = /mnt/nfs/puppet/reports
```

Here, we've set the new report directory to /mnt/nfs/puppet/reports. You can specify whichever directory suits your environment.

Report Processors

There are a number of report processors available. Report processors are stored on the Puppet master. We've already seen one in Chapter 7, when we used the http report processor to send reports from the master to the Puppet Dashboard.

The default report, store, simply stores the report file on the disk. There are also the log processor, which sends logs to the local log destination, to syslog for example, and the tagmail report processor, which sends email messages based on particular tags in transaction reports. Next we'll discuss the rrdgraph report processor, which converts transaction reports into RRD-based graphs. Finally, the puppetdb report processor is the newest addition and at the time of writing offers experimental API endpoints to access reports.

To select which report processors will run, use the `reports` configuration option in the `puppet.conf` configuration file:

```
[master]
reports = store,log,tagmail,rrdgraph
```

Each report processor you want to enable should be listed in the `reports` option, with multiple processors separated by commas. By default, only `store` is enabled. You can also enable report processors on the command line, as shown here:

```
$ sudo puppet master --reports log,tagmail
```

Now let's look at each individual report processor, starting with the `log` processor.

log

The `log` report processor sends the log entries from transaction reports to syslog. It is the simplest of the report processors. The syslog destination facility is controlled by the `syslogfacility` configuration option, which defaults to the daemon facility.

```
[master]
syslogfacility = user
```

In this example, we've directed all syslog output to the user facility.

■ **Note** The log report processor logs entries only if the Puppet master is running in daemon mode. If you keep it running in the foreground, no syslog messages will be generated.

---

tagmail

The `tagmail` report sends log messages via email based on the tags that are present in each log message. Tags allow you to set context for your resources; for example, you can tag all resources that belong to a particular operating system, location, or any other characteristic. Tags can also be specified in your `puppet.conf` configuration file to tell your agents to apply only configurations tagged with the specified tags.

The `tagmail` report uses the same tags to generate email reports. The tags assigned to your resources are added to the log results, and then Puppet generates email based on matching particular tags with particular email addresses. This matching occurs in a configuration file called `tagmail.conf`. By default, the `tagmail.conf` file is located in the `$confdir` directory, usually /etc/puppet. This is controlled by the `tagmap` configuration option in the `puppet.conf` file:

```
[master]
tagmap = $confdir/tagmail.conf
```

The `tagmail.conf` file contains a list of tags and email addresses separated by colons. You can specify multiple tags and email addresses by separating them with commas. Listing 9-2 shows an example of this file.

Listing 9-2. A sample `tagmail.conf` file

```
all: configuration@example.com
mail, www: operations@example.com
db, !mail: dba@example.com,apps@example.com
```

The first tag in Listing 9-2, `all`, is a special tag that tells Puppet to send all reports to the specified email address.

■ **Tip** There is also a special tag called `err`. Specifying this tag will make the report return all error messages generated during a configuration run.

The second set of tags specifies that Puppet should send all reports with the tags `mail` and `www` to the email address `operations@example.com`. The last tags tell Puppet to send reports for all log entries with the `db` tag but not the `mail` tag to both the `dba@example.com` and `apps@example.com` email addresses. You can see that the `mail` tag has been negated using the `!` symbol.

rrdgraph

One of the most useful built-in report processors is the `rrdgraph` type, which takes advantage of Tobias Oetiker's RRD (round-robin database) graphing libraries. The `rrdgraph` report processor generates RRD files, graphs, and some HTML files to display those graphs. It is a very quick and easy way of implementing graphs of your Puppet configuration activities.

In order to make use of this report processor we'll first need to install RRDTools and the Ruby bindings for RRD. We can install RRDTools via package on most platforms and distributions. The Ruby bindings, unfortunately, are less well supported on a lot of platforms. They can be installed from source; alternatively, some distributions do have packages available. Dag Wieer's repository at `http://dag.wieers.com/rpm/packages/rrdtool/` also offers suitable `rrdtool-ruby` RPMs that should work on most RPM-based distributions, including Red Hat, CentOS, and Mandriva versions. There is also a development package for Gentoo called `ruby-rrd` that provides the required bindings; you should be able to install it via `emerge`.

You can see a list of the required packages for Debian/Ubuntu, Fedora, and Red Hat platforms in Table 9-1.

Table 9-1. *Package names for rrdtools*

OS	Required Packages		
Debian/Ubuntu	rrdtool	librrd2	librrd2-dev
Fedora	rrdtool	rrdtool-ruby	
Red Hat	rrdtool	rrdtool-ruby	

■ **Note** Your package manager may prompt you to install additional packages when installing RRDTool.

You can also install the RRD Ruby bindings via one of two gems, `RubyRRDtool` or `librrd`:

```
$ sudo gem install RubyRRDtool
$ sudo gem install librrd
```

Both gems should work to produce the appropriate RRD graphs.

To customize RRD support, you can also change some configuration options in the puppet.conf configuration file:

```
[master]
rrddir = $vardir/rrd
rrdinternval = $runinterval
```

The rrddir directory specifies the default location for the generated RRD files. It defaults to $vardir/rrd, which is usually /var/lib/puppet/rrd. The rrdinterval specifies how often RRD should expect to receive data. This defaults to $runinterval, to match how often agents report back to the master.

Under the $vardir/rrd directory, Puppet will create a directory for each agent that reports to the master. Graphs (and the associated HTML files to display them) will be generated in that directory. A graph will be generated for each metric that Puppet collects. You can then serve from this directory using your webserver and display the graphs.

http

The http report processor sends Puppet reports to an HTTP URL and port. The Puppet reports are sent as a YAML dump in the form of an HTTP Post. You can control the destination with the reporturl configuration option in the puppet.conf configuration file on the master:

```
[master]
reporturl = http://localhost:3000/reports
```

Here the report destination is set to its default, which assumes that you are sending reports to Puppet Dashboard.

puppetdb

As of version 1.5, PuppetDB has support for sending reports to itself. You can send reports to PuppetDB by appending puppetdb to the reports option in the Puppet master's puppet.conf file.

```
reports = store,puppetdb
```

You can access the reports via puppetdb's API:

```
http://docs.puppetlabs.com/puppetdb/latest/api/query/v3/events.html
http://docs.puppetlabs.com/puppetdb/latest/api/query/v3/reports.html
```

Custom Reporting

You are not limited to the provided report processors; Puppet also allows you to create your own report processors. There are two methods for doing this. The first is to use the existing store reports, which are YAML files, and write an external report processor to make use of this information, for example graphing it or storing it in an external database. These external report processors can easily be written in Ruby to take advantage of Ruby's ability to deserialize the YAML files and make use of the resulting objects. You can use any tool that supports the importation of third-party YAML data.

The second method involves writing your own report processor and adding it to Puppet. Although it has plug-ins for facts, functions, types, and providers, Puppet doesn't have an automatic way to distribute custom reports.

■ **Note**   We show how to distribute other forms of custom code, like facts, in Chapter 10.

Instead, the report processors are stored in the `lib/puppet/reports` directory. For example, on an Ubuntu Puppet master we'd add our custom report processor to the `/usr/lib/ruby/vendor_ruby/puppet/reports` directory with the existing report processors. We would then specify the new report in the `reports` configuration option.

The existing report processors make excellent templates for new processors. In Listing 9-3 you can see the Ruby code for the HTTP report processor.

Listing 9-3. The HTTP report processor

```
require 'puppet'
require 'puppet/network/http_pool'require 'uri'

Puppet::Reports.register_report(:http) do

  desc <<-DESC
  Send report information via HTTP to the `reporturl`. Each host sends
  its report as a YAML dump and this sends this YAML to a client via HTTP POST.
  The YAML is the `report` parameter of the request."
  DESC

  def process
    url = URI.parse(Puppet[:reporturl])
    req = Net::HTTP::Post.new(url.path)
    req.body = self.to_yaml
    req.content_type = "application/x-yaml"
    Net::HTTP.new(url.host, url.port).start {|http|
      http.request(req)
    }
  end
end
```

As you can see from this example, it is very easy to create your own report processor.

■ **Tip**   Other ideas for Puppet report processors include RSS feeds for new reports, IRC, XMPP or instant messaging, and SMS notifications of new reports. You could also parse particular events in reports or collate metrics for use in other kinds of performance-management systems.

First, you need to require Puppet itself: `require 'puppet'`. Then you simply specify the `Puppet::Reports.register_report` method and the name of the new report processor you are creating. You can see a simple example of a report processor in Listing 9-4.

Listing 9-4. A custom summary report

```
require 'puppet'
require 'puppet/network/http_pool'
require 'uri'

Puppet::Reports.register_report(:http) do

  desc <<-DESC
    Send reports via HTTP or HTTPS. This report processor submits reports as
    POST requests to the address in the `reporturl` setting. The body of each POST
    request is the YAML dump of a Puppet::Transaction::Report object, and the
    Content-Type is set as `application/x-yaml`.
  DESC

  def process
    url = URI.parse(Puppet[:reporturl])
    body = self.to_yaml
    headers = { "Content-Type" => "application/x-yaml" }
    use_ssl = url.scheme == 'https'
    conn = Puppet::Network::HttpPool.http_instance(url.host, url.port, use_ssl)
    response = conn.post(url.path, body, headers)
    unless response.kind_of?(Net::HTTPSuccess)
      Puppet.err "Unable to submit report to #{Puppet[:reporturl].to_s} [#{response.code}]
#{response.msg}"
    end
  end
end
```

In this report processor, we've defined a method called process to hold our report's core logic. We've extracted some information from our report: the host, using the self.host method, and a summary of the changes, using the summary method. You also have access to the report's logs and metrics using the self.logs and self.metrics methods.

We also wrote our summary report out to a directory named after the Puppet agent host located under the reports directory, which we specified using the value of the reportdir configuration option.

We can then add our report name to Puppet in the puppet.conf configuration file:

```
reports=store,log,summary
```

After we restart the Puppet master and perform a Puppet run, the new report will be generated. In our case, the final report is contained in a file called summary.txt and looks something like this:

```
Changes:
            Total: 1
Events:
          Success: 1
            Total: 1
Resources:
          Changed: 1
      Out of sync: 1
            Total: 8
```

```
Time:
   Config retrieval: 0.19
              File: 0.05
        Filebucket: 0.00
          Schedule: 0.00
```

▓ **Tip** You can see other examples of how to use and extract reporting data from thecode of the existing reports, at https://github.com/puppetlabs/puppet/tree/master/lib/puppet/reports.

Other Puppet Reporters

James Turnbull, one of the original authors of this book, has written the following report processors and many more, which are available on his GitHub page.

- IRC: https://github.com/jamtur01/puppet-irc

- PagerDuty: https://github.com/jamtur01/puppet-pagerduty

- HipChat: https://github.com/jamtur01/puppet-hipchat

- Campfire: https://github.com/jamtur01/puppet-campfire

Summary

This chapter has demonstrated the basics of Puppet reporting, including how to configure reporting and some details on each report type and its configuration.

We've also shown you how to create custom reports of your own, making use of the report data in its YAML form or via processing with a custom report processor.

Resources

- Report Reference: http://docs.puppetlabs.com/references/latest/report.html

- Reports and Reporting: http://docs.puppetlabs.com/guides/reporting.html

- Existing reports: https://github.com/puppetlabs/puppet/tree/master/lib/puppet/reports

- PuppetDB Reporting API :
  http://docs.puppetlabs.com/puppetdb/latest/api/query/v3/reports.html

CHAPTER 10

■ ■ ■

Extending Facter and Puppet

Among the most powerful features of Puppet are its flexibility and extensibility. In addition to the existing facts, resource types, providers, and functions, you can quickly and easily add custom code specific to your environment or to meet a particular need.

In the first part of this chapter we're going to examine how to add your own custom facts. Adding custom facts is highly useful for gathering and making use of information specific to your environment. Indeed, we've used Facter extensively in this book to provide information about our hosts, applications, and services, and you've seen the array of facts available across many platforms. You may have noted, though, that Facter isn't comprehensive; many facts about your hosts and environments are not available as Facter facts.

In the second part of the chapter, we're going to examine how to add your own custom types, providers, and functions to Puppet and how to have Puppet distribute these items, and we'll discuss how to make use of them. Customizations are among Puppet's most powerful features and are at the heart of its flexibility and extensibility. The ability to add your own enhancements in addition to the existing resources types, providers and functions means that you can quickly and easily add custom code specific to your environment or to meet a particular need.

Writing and Distributing Custom Facts

Creating your own custom facts for Puppet is a simple process. Indeed, it requires only a basic understanding of Ruby. Luckily , Ruby is incredibly easy to pick up and there are many resources available to help (refer to the "Resources" section at the end of the chapter for some helpful links).

In the following sections, you'll see how to successfully extend Facter. We'll first configure Puppet so we can write custom facts, and then test our new facts to confirm that they are working properly.

■ **Note**   If the idea of learning any Ruby is at all daunting, a fast alternative way to add a fact without writing any Ruby code is via Facter's support for environmental variables. Any environmental variables set by the user Facter is running as (usually the `root` user) that are prefixed with `FACTER_` will be added to Facter as facts. So, if you were to set an environmental variable of `FACTER_datacenter` with a value of `Chicago`, it would become a fact called `datacenter` with the value of `Chicago`.

Configuring Puppet for Custom Facts

The best way to distribute custom facts is to include them in modules, using a Puppet concept called *plug-ins in modules*. This concept allows you to place your custom code in an existing or new Puppet module and then use that module in your Puppet environment. Custom facts, custom types, providers, and functions are then distributed to any host that includes a particular module.

Modules that distribute facts are no different from other modules, and there are two popular approaches to the task. Some people distribute facts related to a particular function in the module that they use to configure that function. For example, a fact with some Bind data in it might be distributed with the module you use to configure Bind. This clusters together facts specific to a function and allows a greater portability. Other sites include all custom facts (and other items) in a single, central module, such as a module called facts or plugins. This centralizes facts in one location for ease of management and maintenance.

Each approach has pros and cons, and you should select one that suits your organization and its workflow. We prefer the former approach because it limits custom facts and other items to only those clients that require them, rather than all hosts. For some environments, this may be a neater approach, and we'll use it in this section when demonstrating managing custom facts.

So where in our modules do facts go? Let's create a simple module called bind as an example:

```
bind/
bind/manifests
bind/manifests/init.pp
bind/files
bind/templates
bind/lib/facter
```

Here we've created our standard module directory structure, but we've added another directory, lib. The lib directory contains any *plug-ins* or additional facts, types, or functions we want to add to Puppet. We're going to focus on adding facts; these are stored in the lib/facter directory.

In addition to adding the lib/facter directory to modules that will distribute facts, you need to enable *plug-ins in modules* in your Puppet configuration. To do this, enable the pluginsync option in the [main] section of the Puppet master's puppet.conf configuration file, as you can see on the next line:

```
[main]
pluginsync = true
```

When set to true, the pluginsync setting turns on the plug-ins in modules capability. Now, when clients connect to the master, each client will check its modules for facts and other custom items. Puppet will take these facts and other custom items and sync them to the relevant clients, so they can then be used on these clients.

Writing Custom Facts

Now that you've configured Puppet to deliver custom facts, you should create some new facts! Each fact is a snippet of Ruby code wrapped in a Facter method to add the result of our Ruby code as a fact. Let's look at a simple example in Listing 10-1.

Listing 10-1. Our first custom fact

```
Facter.add("home") do
      setcode do
           ENV['HOME']
      end
end
```

In this example, our custom fact returns the value of the HOME environment value as a fact called home, which in turn would be available in our manifests as the variable $::home.

The Facter.add method allows us to specify the name of our new fact. We then use the setcode block to specify the contents of our new fact, in our case using Ruby's built-in ENV variable to access an environmental variable. Facter will set the value of our new fact using the result of the code executed inside this block.

In Listing 10-2, you can see a custom fact that reads a file to return the value of the fact.

Listing 10-2. Another custom fact

```
Facter.add("tzname") do
        confine :osfamily => :debian
        setcode do
            File.readlines("/etc/timezone").to_a.last
        end
end
```

Here, we're returning the time zone of a Debian host. We've also done two interesting things. First, we've specified a confine statement. This statement restricts the execution of the fact if a particular criterion is not met. This restriction is commonly implemented by taking advantage of the values of other facts. In this case, we've specified that the value of the osfamily fact should be Debian for the fact to be executed. Notice that unlike in the Puppet language, where we refer to osfamily with $ osfamily in manifests and @osfamily in templates, in custom facts we need to use a Ruby symbol, which we do by prepending a colon to the front of the value. We can also use the values of other facts, for example:

```
confine :kernel => :linux
```

As illustrated here, the confine statement is commonly used to limit the use of a particular fact to nodes with Linux-based kernels.

Second, we've used the readlines File method to read in the contents of the /etc/timezone file. The contents are returned as the fact timezone, which in turn would be available as the variable $::tzname.

```
tzname => Australia/Melbourne
```

We've established how to confine the execution of a fact, but we can also use other fact values to influence our fact determination, for example:

```
Facter.add("tzname") do
        setcode do
          if Facter.value(:osfamily) =='Debian'
              File.readlines("/etc/timezone").to_a.last
          else
              tz = Time.new.zone
          end
        end
end
```

Here, if osfamily is Debian, it will return a time zone value by returning the value from the /etc/timezone file. Otherwise, the fact will use Ruby's in-built time handling to return a time zone.

You could also use a case statement to select different fact values, for example as used in the operatingsystemrelease fact shown in Listing 10-3.

Listing 10-3. Using a case statement to select fact values

```
Facter.add(:operatingsystemrelease) do
    confine :operatingsystem => %w{CentOS Fedora oel ovs RedHat MeeGo}
    setcode do
        case Facter.value(:operatingsystem)
```

```
        when "CentOS", "RedHat"
            releasefile = "/etc/redhat-release"
        when "Fedora"
            releasefile = "/etc/fedora-release"
        when "MeeGo"
            releasefile = "/etc/meego-release"
        when "OEL", "oel"
            releasefile = "/etc/enterprise-release"
        when "OVS", "ovs"
            releasefile = "/etc/ovs-release"
        end
        File::open(releasefile, "r") do |f|
            line = f.readline.chomp
            if line =~ /\(Rawhide\)$/
                "Rawhide"
            elsif line =~ /release (\d[\d.]*)/
                $1
            end
        end
    end
  end
end
```

You can use other fact values for any purpose you like, not just for determining how to retrieve a fact. Some facts return another fact value if they cannot find a way to determine the correct value. For example, the operatingsystem fact returns the current kernel, Facter.value(:kernel), as the value of operatingsystem if Facter cannot determine the operating system it is being run on.

You can create more complex facts and even return more than one fact in your Ruby snippets, as demonstrated in Listing 10-4.

Listing 10-4. A more complex fact

```
netname = nil
 netaddr = nil
 test = {}
 File.open("/etc/networks").each do |line|
      netname = $1 and netaddr = $2 if line ↵
=~ /^(\w+.?\w+)\s+([0-9]+\.[0-9]+\.[0-9]+\.[0-9]+)/
      if netname != nil && netaddr != nil
            test["network_" + netname] = netaddr
            netname = nil
            netaddr = nil
            end
    end
    test.each{|name,fact|
            Facter.add(name) do
                setcode do
                    fact
                end
            end
    }
```

This fact creates a series of facts, each fact taken from information collected from the /etc/networks file. This file associates network names with networks. Our snippet parses this file and adds a series of facts, one per network in the file. So, if our file looked like this:

```
default     0.0.0.0
loopback    127.0.0.0
link-local  169.254.0.0
```

then three facts would be returned:

```
network_default => 0.0.0.0
network_loopback => 127.0.0.0
network_link-local => 169.254.0.0
```

You can take a similar approach to commands, or files, or a variety of other sources.

Testing the Facts

There is a simple process for testing your facts: Import them into Facter and use it to test them before using them in Puppet. To do this, you need to set up a testing environment. Create a directory structure to hold our test facts—we'll call ours lib/ruby/facter. Situate this structure beneath the root user's home directory. Then create an environmental variable, $RUBYLIB, that references this directory and will allow Facter to find our test facts:

```
# mkdir -p ~/lib/ruby/facter
# export RUBYLIB=~/lib/ruby
```

Next copy your fact snippets into this new directory:

```
# cp /var/puppet/facts/home.rb $RUBYLIB/facter
```

After this, you can call Facter with the name of the fact you've just created. If the required output appears, your fact is working correctly. On the following lines, we've tested our home fact and discovered it has returned the correct value:

```
# facter home
/root
```

If your fact is not working correctly, an error message you can debug will be generated. You can build automated testing using the Rspec framework. Refer to the spec folder in Facter (https://github.com/puppetlabs/facter/tree/master/spec) for examples.

External Facts

Starting with Facter 1.7.3 you can now write external facts, which come in two flavors, executable or structured.

Executable facts allow you to run scripts or executables to create new facts. You will need to put them in the following directory.

```
/etc/facter/facts.d/      # Puppet Open Source
/etc/puppetlabs/facter/facts.d/ # Puppet Enterprise
```

The scripts must be executable and output to stdout in key=value format. The following is a simple bash script that uses echo, but you can also create more complex scripts, as long as they return key/value pairs.

```
$ cat /etc/facter/facts.d/test.sh
#!/bin/bash
echo "food=pizza"
echo "drink=tea"
echo "starship=true"

$ facter food drink starship
drink => tea
food => pizza
starship => true
```

Structured facts are facts straight from YAML, JSON, or txt files. Adding files that end in .yaml, .json or .txt to the facts.d directory will add them as Puppet facts.

```
$ cat /etc/facter/facts.d/test.yaml
---
icecream: chocolate
pie: cherry
cake: carrot

$ facter icecream pie cake
cake => carrot
icecream => chocolate
pie => cherry
```

Facts just scratch the surface of Puppet's extensibility. As you'll see in the next section, adding to types, providers, and functions adds even more capability.

Developing Custom Types, Providers and Functions

When developing custom types, providers, and functions, it is important to remember that Puppet and Facter are open source tools developed by both Puppet Labs and a wide community of contributors. Sharing custom facts and resource types helps everyone in the community, and it means you can also get input from the community on your work. Extending Puppet or Facter is also an excellent way to give back to that community. You can share your custom code by uploading it as a module to the Puppet Forge (http://forge.puppetlabs.com).

Finally, don't underestimate the usefulness of code that people before you have already developed, and that you can use and adapt for your environment. Explore existing Puppet modules, plug-ins, facts, and other code via Google and on resources like GitHub. Like all systems administrators, we know that imitation is the ultimate form of flattery.

The following sections demonstrate how to configure Puppet to distribute your own custom code. You'll also see how to write a variety of custom types and providers, and finally how to write your own Puppet functions.

Configuring Puppet for Types, Providers and Functions

The best way to distribute custom types, providers, and functions is to include them in modules, using plug-ins in modules, the same concept introduced earlier this chapter to distribute custom facts. Just as with custom facts, you place your custom code into a Puppet module and use that module in your configuration. Puppet will take care of distributing your code to your Puppet masters and agents.

And just as you can with custom facts, you can take either of two approaches to managing custom code: placing it in function-specific modules or centralizing it into a single module. We're going to demonstrate adding custom code in a single, function-specific module.

So, where in our modules does custom code go? Let's create a simple module called apache as an example:

```
apache/
apache/manifests
apache/manifests/init.pp
apache/files
apache/templates
apache/lib/facter
apache/lib/puppet/type
apache/lib/puppet/provider
apache/lib/puppet/parser/functions
```

Here we've created our standard module directory structure, but we've added another directory, lib. We saw the lib directory earlier in the chapter when we placed custom facts into its Facter subdirectory. The lib directory also contains other plug-ins, like types, providers, and functions, which we want to add to Puppet. The lib/puppet/type and lib/puppet/provider directories hold custom types and providers, respectively. The last directory, lib/puppet/parser/functions, holds custom functions.

As we did when we configured Puppet for custom facts, you need to enable the plug-ins in modules feature in your Puppet configuration. To do this, enable the pluginsync option in the [main] section of the Puppet master's puppet.conf configuration file, as follows:

```
[main]
pluginsync = true
```

The pluginsync setting, when set to true, turns on the plug-ins in modules capability. Now, when agents connect to the master, each agent will check its modules for custom code. Puppet will take this custom code and sync it to the relevant agents. It can then be used on these agents. The only exception to this is with custom functions. Functions run on the Puppet master rather than the Puppet agents, so they won't be synced down to an agent. They will only be synced if the Puppet agent is run on the Puppet master; that is, if you are managing Puppet with Puppet.

Writing a Puppet Type and Provider

Puppet types are used to manage individual configuration items. Puppet has a package type, a service type, a user type, and all the other types available. Each type has one or more providers. Each provider handles the management of that configuration on a different platform or tool: for example, the package type has aptitude, yum, RPM, and DMG providers (among 22 others).

We're going to show you a simple example of how to create an additional type and provider, one that manages version control systems (VCS), which we're going to call repo. In this case we're going to create the type and two providers, one for Git and one for Subversion. Our type is going to allow you to create, manage, and delete VCS repositories.

A Puppet type contains the characteristics of the configuration item we're describing; for example, the VCS management type has these characteristics:

- The name of the repository being managed
- The source of the repository

Correspondingly, the Puppet providers specify the actions required to manage the state of the configuration item. Obviously, each provider has a set of similar actions that tell it how to

- Create the resource

- Delete the resource

- Check for the resource's existence or state

- Make changes to the resource's content

Creating Our Type

Let's start by creating our type. First we create a module called custom to store it in:

```
custom/
custom/manifests/init.pp
custom/lib/puppet/type
custom/lib/puppet/provider
```

Inside the lib/puppet/type directory, we create a file called repo.rb to store our type definition:

```
custom/lib/puppet/type/repo.rb
```

You can see that file in Listing 10-5.

Listing 10-5. The repo type

```
Puppet::Type.newtype(:repo) do
    @doc = "Manage repos"
    ensurable

    newparam(:source) do
        desc "The repo source"

        validate do |value|
            if value =~ /^git/
                resource[:provider] = :git
            else
                resource[:provider] = :svn
            end
        end

        isnamevar
    end

    newparam(:path) do
        desc "Destination path"

        validate do |value|
            path = Pathname.new(value)
```

```
            unless path.absolute?
                raise ArgumentError, "Path must be absolute: #{path}"
            end
        end
    end
end
```

In this example, we start our type with the Puppet::Type.newtype block and specify the name of the type to be created, repo. You can also see a @doc string, which is where we specify the documentation for the new type. We recommend you provide clear documentation, including examples of how to use the type; for a good example see the documentation provided for the cron type at https://github.com/puppetlabs/puppet/blob/master/lib/puppet/type/cron.rb.

The next statement, ensurable, is a useful shortcut that tells Puppet to create an ensure property for this type. The ensure property determines the state of the configuration item, for example:

```
service { 'sshd':
    ensure => present,
}
```

The ensurable statement tells Puppet to expect three methods: create, destroy and exists? in our provider (you'll see the code for this in Listing 10-6). These methods are, respectively:

- A command to create the resource

- A command to delete the resource

- A command to check for the existence of the resource

All we then need to do is specify these methods and their contents, and Puppet creates the supporting infrastructure around them. Types have two kinds of values—properties and parameters. Properties "do things." They tell us how the provider works. We've only defined one property, ensure, by using the ensurable statement. Puppet expects that properties will generally have corresponding methods in the provider; we'll see those later in this chapter. Parameters are variables and contain information relevant to configuring the resource the type manages, rather than "doing things."

Next, we've defined a parameter, called source:

```
newparam(:source) do
  desc "The repo source"

  validate do |value|
    if value =~ /^git/
      resource[:provider] = :git
    else
      resource[:provider] = :svn
  end
 end
   isnamevar
end
```

The source parameter will tell the repo type where to go to retrieve, clone, or check out our source repository.

In the source parameter we're also using a hook called validate. It's normally used to check the parameter value for appropriateness; here, we're using it to take a guess at what provider to use.

> ■ **Note** In addition to the `validate` hook, Puppet also has the `munge` hook, which you can use to adjust the value of the parameter rather than validating it before passing it to the provider.

Our `validate` code specifies that if the `source` parameter starts with `git`, Puppet should use the Git provider; if not, it should default to the Subversion provider. This is fairly crude as a default, and you can override it by defining the `provider` attribute in your resource, as follows:

```
repo { 'puppet':
  ensure   => present,
  source   => 'git://github.com/puppetlabs/puppet.git',
  path     => '/home/puppet',
  provider => git,
}
```

We've also used another piece of Puppet auto-magic, the `isnamevar` method, to make this parameter the "name" variable for this type so that its value is used as the name of the resource.

Finally, we've defined another parameter, `path`:

```
newparam(:path) do
  desc "Destination path"

  validate do |value|
    unless value =~ /^\/[a-z0-9]+/
      raise ArgumentError, "%s is not a valid file path" % value
    end
  end
end
```

This is a parameter value that specifies where the repo type should put the cloned/checked-out repository. In this parameter we've again used the `validate` hook to create a block that checks the value for appropriateness. In this case we're just checking, very crudely, to make sure it looks like the destination path is a valid, fully-qualified file path. We could also use this validation for the `source` parameter to confirm that a valid source URL/location is being provided.

Creating the Subversion Provider

Next, we need to create a Subversion provider for our type. We create the provider and put it in this location:

```
custom/lib/puppet/provider/repo/svn.rb
```

You can see the Subversion provider in Listing 10-6.

Listing 10-6. The Subversion provider

```
require 'fileutils'

Puppet::Type.type(:repo).provide(:svn) do
  desc "Provides Subversion support for the repo type"

  commands :svncmd => "svn"
  commands :svnadmin => "svnadmin"
```

```
  def create
    svncmd "checkout", resource[:name], resource[:path]
  end

  def destroy
    FileUtils.rm_rf resource[:path]
  end

  def exists?
    File.directory? resource[:path]
  end
end
```

In the provider code, we first required the fileutils library, from which we're going to use some methods. Next, we defined the provider block itself:

```
Puppet::Type.type(:repo).provide(:svn) do
```

We specified that the provider is called svn and is a provider for the type called repo.

Then we used the desc method, which allows us to add some documentation to our provider.

Next, we defined the commands that this provider will use, the svn and svnadmin binaries, to manipulate our resource's configuration:

```
commands :svncmd => "svn"
commands :svnadmin => "svnadmin"
```

Puppet uses these commands to determine whether the provider is appropriate to use on an agent. If Puppet can't find these commands in the local path, it will disable the provider. Any resources that use this provider will fail, and Puppet will report an error.

Next, we defined the three methods, create, destroy and exists?, that the ensurable statement expects to find in the provider.

The create method ensures that our resource is created. It uses the svn command to check out a repository specified by resource[:name]. This references the value of the name parameter of the type. In our case, the source parameter in our type is also the name variable of the type, so we could also specify resource[:source]. We also specified the destination for the checkout using the resource[:path] hash.

The delete method ensures the deletion of the resource. In this case, it deletes the directory and files specified by the resource[:path] parameter.

Finally, the exists? method checks to see if the resource exists. Its operation is pretty simple and closely linked with the value of the ensure attribute in the resource:

- If exists? is false and ensure is set to present, then the create method will be called.

- If exists? is true and ensure is set to absent, then the destroy method will be called.

In the case of our method, exists? works by checking to see if there is already a directory at the location specified in the resource[:path] parameter.

We can also add another provider, this one for Git, here:

```
custom/lib/puppet/provider/repo/git.rb
```

We can see this provider in Listing 10-7.

Listing 10-7. The Git provider

```
require 'fileutils'
Puppet::Type.type(:repo).provide(:git) do

  desc "Provides Git support for the repo provider"

  commands :gitcmd => "git"

  def create
    gitcmd "clone", resource[:name], resource[:path]
  end

  def destroy
    FileUtils.rm_rf resource[:path]
  end

  def exists?
    File.directory? resource[:path]
  end

end
```

You can see that this provider is nearly identical to the Subversion provider in Listing 10-3. We used the git command and its clone function rather than the Subversion equivalents, but you can see that the destroy and exists? methods are identical.

Using Your New Type

Once you've got your type and providers in place, you can run Puppet and distribute them to the agents where you wish to use the repo type and create resources that use this type, as in this example:

```
repo { 'wordpress':
  ensure   => present,
  source   => 'http://core.svn.wordpress.org/trunk/',
  path     => '/var/www/wp',
  provider => svn,
}
```

■ **Note** You can find a far more sophisticated version of the repo type, with additional providers, at https://github.com/puppetlabs/puppetlabs-vcsrepo.

Writing a Parsed File Type and Provider

You've just seen a very simple type and provider that use commands to create, delete, and check for the status of a resource. In addition to these kinds of types and providers, Puppet also comes with a helper that allows you to parse and edit simple configuration files. This helper is called ParsedFile.

Unfortunately, you can only manage simple files with ParsedFile, generally files with single lines of configuration like the /etc/hosts file or the example we're going to examine. This is a type that manages the /etc/shells file rather than multi-line configuration files.

To use a ParsedFile type and provider, we need to include its capabilities. Let's start with our /etc/shells management type, which we're going to call shells. This file will be located in

custom/lib/puppet/type/shells.rb

The Shells Type

Let's start with our type in Listing 10-8.

Listing 10-8. The shells type

```
Puppet::Type.newtype(:shells) do
    @doc = "Manage the contents of /etc/shells
    shells { "/bin/newshell":
                ensure => present,
    }"

ensurable

newparam(:shell) do
  desc "The shell to manage"
  isnamevar
end

newproperty(:target) do
  desc "Location of the shells file"
  defaultto {
    if @resource.class.defaultprovider.ancestors.include? (Puppet::Provider::ParsedFile)
      @resource.class.defaultprovider.default_target
    else
      nil
  end
  }
 end
end
```

In our type, we've created a block, Puppet::Type.newtype(:shells), that creates a new type, which we've called shells. Inside the block we've got a @doc string. As we've already seen, this should contain the documentation for the type; in this case, we've included an example of the shells resource in action.

We've also used the ensurable statement to create the basic create, delete, and ensure-exists structure we saw in our previous type.

We then defined a new parameter, called shell, that will contain the name of the shell we want to manage:

```
newparam(:shell) do
  desc "The shell to manage"
  isnamevar
end
```

We also used another piece of Puppet auto-magic that we saw earlier, `isnamevar`, to make this parameter the name variable for this type.

Finally, in our type we specified an optional parameter, `target`, that allows us to override the default location of the `shells` file, usually `/etc/shells`.

The `target` parameter is optional and would only be specified if the `shells` file wasn't located in the `/etc/` directory. It uses the `defaultto` structure to specify that the default value for the parameter is the value of the `default_target` variable, which we will set in the provider.

The Shells Provider

Let's look at the `shells` provider now, in Listing 10-9.

Listing 10-9. The `shells` provider

```
require 'puppet/provider/parsedfile'

shells = "/etc/shells"

Puppet::Type.type(:shells).provide(:parsed, :parent => Puppet::Provider::ParsedFile,
:default_target => shells, :filetype => :flat) do

  desc "The shells provider that uses the ParsedFile class"

  text_line :comment, :match => /^#/;
  text_line :blank, :match => /^\s*$/;

  record_line :parsed, :fields => %w{name}
end
```

Unlike other providers, ParsedFile providers are stored in a file called `parsed.rb`, located in the provider's directory, here:

```
custom/lib/puppet/provider/shells/parsed.rb
```

The file needs to be named `parsed.rb` to allow Puppet to load the appropriate ParsedFile support (unlike other providers, which need to be named for the provider itself).

In our provider, we first need to include the ParsedFile provider code at the top of our provider, using a Ruby `require` statement:

```
require 'puppet/provider/parsedfile'
```

We then set a variable called `shells` to the location of the `/etc/shells` file. We're going to use this variable shortly.

Then we tell Puppet that this is a provider called `shells`. The `:parent` value we specify tells Puppet that this provider should inherit the ParsedFile provider and make its functions available. We then specify the `:default_target` variable to the `shells` variable we just created. This tells the provider that unless it is overridden by the `target` attribute in a resource, the file to act upon is `/etc/shells`.

We then use a `desc` method that allows us to add some documentation to our provider.

The next lines in the provider are the core of a ParsedFile provider. They tell the Puppet how to manipulate the target file to add or remove the required shell. The first two lines, both called `text_line`, tell Puppet how to match comments and blank lines, respectively, in the configuration file. You should specify these for any file that might have blank lines or comments:

```
text_line :comment, :match => /^#/;
text_line :blank, :match => /^\s*$/;
```

We specify these to tell Puppet to ignore these lines as unimportant. The text_line lines are constructed by specifying the type of line to match, a comment or a blank, followed by a regular expression that specifies the content to be matched.

The next line performs the parsing of the relevant line of configuration in the /etc/shells file:

```
record_line :parsed, :fields => %w{name}
```

The record_line parses each line and divides it into fields. In our case, we only have one field, name. The name in this case is the shell we want to manage. So if we specify this:

```
shells { '/bin/anothershell':
    ensure => present,
}
```

Puppet would then use the provider to add the /bin/anothershell by parsing each line of the /etc/shells file and checking whether the /bin/anothershell shell is present. If it is, then Puppet will do nothing. If not, Puppet will add anothershell to the file.

If we changed the ensure attribute to absent, Puppet would go through the file and remove the anothershell shell if it is present.

This is quite a simple example of a ParsedFile provider. Some others that ship with Puppet, for example the cron type, demonstrate the sophisticated things you can do with the ParsedFile provider helper.

A More Complex Type and Provider

This section demonstrates a slightly more complex type and provider, used to manage HTTP authentication password files. It's a similarly ensurable type and provider, but it includes more sophisticated components.

The httpauth Type

Let's start by looking at the httpauth type, shown in Listing 10-10.

Listing 10-10. The httpauth type

```
Puppet::Type.newtype(:httpauth) do
    @doc = "Manage HTTP Basic or Digest password files." +
        "    httpauth { 'user':                    " +
        "       ensure       => present,                    " +
        "       file             => '/path/to/password/file',     " +
        "       password    => 'password',                " +
        "       mechanism => basic,              " +
        "    }                          "

    ensurable do
      newvalue(:present) do
```

```
            provider.create
        end

        newvalue(:absent) do
            provider.destroy
        end

        defaultto :present
    end

    newparam(:name) do
        desc "The name of the user to be managed."

        isnamevar
    end

    newparam(:file) do
        desc "The HTTP password file to be managed. If it doesn't exist it is created."
    end

    newparam(:password) do
        desc "The password in plaintext."

    end

    newparam(:realm) do
        desc "The realm - defaults to nil and mainly used for Digest authentication."

        defaultto "nil"
    end

    newparam(:mechanism) do
        desc "The authentication mechanism to use - either basic or digest. Default to basic."

        newvalues(:basic, :digest)

        defaultto :basic
    end

    # Ensure a password is always specified
    validate do
        raise Puppet::Error, "You must specify a password for the user." unless @parameters.
include?(:password)
    end

end
```

In the httpauth type we're managing a number of attributes, principally the user, password, and password file. We also provide some associated information, like the realm (an HTTP Digest Authentication value) and the mechanism we're going to use, Basic or Digest Authentication.

First, notice that we've added some code to our ensurable method. In this case, we're telling Puppet some specifics about the operation of our ensure attribute. We're specifying for each state, present and absent, exactly which method in the provider should be called; in this case they are create and destroy, respectively. We're also specifying the default behavior of the ensure attribute. This means that if when using this method we omit the ensure attribute, the httpauth resource will assume present as the value. The resource will then check for the presence of the user we want to manage, and if that user doesn't exist, the resource will create it.

Listing 10-10 also demonstrates some other useful methods. The first is the defaultto method, which specifies a default value for a parameter or property. If the resource does not specify this attribute, Puppet will use this default value to populate it. The other method is newvalues, which allows you to specify the values that the parameter or property will accept. In Listing 10-10, you can see the mechanism parameter that the newvalues method specifies takes the values basic or digest.

Finally, you can see that we used the validate method to return an error if the httpauth resource is specified without the password attribute.

The httpauth Provider

Now let's look at the provider for the httpauth type, shown in Listing 10-11.

Listing 10-11. The httpauth provider

```
begin
    require 'webrick'
rescue
    Puppet.warning "You need WEBrick installed to manage HTTP Authentication files."
end

Puppet::Type.type(:httpauth).provide(:httpauth) do
    desc "Manage HTTP Basic and Digest authentication files"

    def create
        # Create a user in the file we opened in the mech method
        @htauth.set_passwd(resource[:realm], resource[:name], resource[:password])
        @htauth.flush
    end

    def destroy
        # Delete a user in the file we opened in the mech method
        @htauth.delete_passwd(resource[:realm], resource[:name])
        @htauth.flush
    end

    def exists?
        # Check if the file exists at all
        if File.exists?(resource[:file])
            # If it does exist open the file
            mech(resource[:file])

            # Check if the user exists in the file
            cp = @htauth.get_passwd(resource[:realm], resource[:name], false)

            # Check if the current password matches the proposed password
            return check_passwd(resource[:realm], resource[:name], resource[:password], cp)
```

```
        else
            # If the file doesn't exist then create it
            File.new(resource[:file], "w")
            mech(resource[:file])
            return false
        end
    end

    # Open the password file
    def mech(file)
        if resource[:mechanism] == :digest
            @htauth = WEBrick::HTTPAuth::Htdigest.new(file)
        elsif resource[:mechanism] == :basic
            @htauth = WEBrick::HTTPAuth::Htpasswd.new(file)
        end
    end

    # Check password matches
    def check_passwd(realm, user, password, cp)
        if resource[:mechanism] == :digest
            WEBrick::HTTPAuth::DigestAuth.make_passwd(realm, user, password) == cp
        elsif resource[:mechanism] == :basic
            # Can't ask webbrick as it uses a random seed
            password.crypt(cp[0,2]) == cp
        end
    end
end
end
```

This provider is more complex than we've seen before. We still have the methods that handle Puppet's ensurable capabilities, create, destroy, and exists?, but we've also got methods that manipulate our password files.

Our provider first checks for the existence of the Webrick library, which it needs to manipulate HTTP password files. The provider will fail to run if this library is not present. Fortunately, Webrick is commonly present in most Ruby distributions.

▒ **Tip** As an alternative to requiring the Webrick library, we could use Puppet's feature capability. You can see some examples of this in https://github.com/puppetlabs/puppet/blob/master/lib/puppet/feature/base.rb. This capability allows you to enable or disable features based on whether certain capabilities are present or not. The obvious limitation is that this approach requires adding a new feature to Puppet's core, rather than simply adding a new type or provider.

Our provider then has the three ensurable methods. The create and destroy methods are relatively simple. They use methods from the Webrick library to either set or delete a password specified in the HTTP password file managed by the resource. That file is referred to here using the resource[:file] value, which is controlled by setting the file attribute in the httpauth resource, as in this example:

```
httpauth { 'bob':
  file      => '/etc/apache2/htpasswd.basic',
  password  => 'password',
  mechanism => basic,
}
```

Finally, you'll also see in the create and destroy methods that we call the flush method. It flushes the buffer and writes out our changes.

The exists? method is more complex and calls several helper methods to check whether the user and password already exist, and if they do, whether the current and proposed passwords match.

Testing Types and Providers

Like facts, your types and providers can be tested. The best way to do this is add them to a module in your development or testing environment and enable pluginsync to test them there before using them in your production environment. As an example, let's add our HTTPAuth type to a module called httpauth, first adding the required directories:

```
$ mkdir -p /etc/puppet/modules/httpauth/{manifests,files,templates,lib}
$ mkdir -p /etc/puppet/modules/httpauth/lib/{type,provider}
$ mkdir -p /etc/puppet/modules/httpauth/lib/provider/httpauth
```

Then we copy in the type and provider to the requisite directories:

```
# cp type/httpauth.rb /etc/puppet/modules/lib/type/httpauth.rb
# cp provider/httpauth.rb /etc/puppet/modules/lib/provider/httpauth/httpauth.rb
```

When Puppet is run (and pluginsync enabled), it will find your types and providers in these directories, deploy them, and make them available to be used in your Puppet manifests. For automated testing, refer to the Rspec examples in core Puppet (https://github.com/puppetlabs/puppet/tree/master/spec).

Writing Custom Functions

The last type of custom Puppet code we're going to look at is the function. You've seen a number of functions in this book already; for example, include, notice, and template are all functions we've used. Many more functions can be found in the Puppetlabs stdlib module, http://forge.puppetlabs.com/puppetlabs/stdlib, which is the first place you should look before writing your own functions and is a good starting place to learn how to write functions. Using functions such as validate_bool, validate_hash, and validate_array from stdlib is an easy way to make your module more user-friendly.

There are two types of functions: statements and rvalues. Statements, such as the fail function, which stops the Puppet run with a parser error, perform some action, and with rvalues you pass in a value, and the function processes it to return a value. The split function, which parses a string and returns array elements, is an example of an rvalue function.

■ **Note** Remember that functions are executed on the Puppet master. They have access only to resources and data that are contained on the master.

As an example, we're going to write a simple function and distribute it to our agents. As we did with plug-ins, we can use pluginsync to distribute functions to agents; they are stored in

```
custom/lib/puppet/parser/functions
```

The file containing the function must be named after the function it contains; for example, the template function should be contained in the template.rb file.

Let's take a look at a simple function in Listing 10-12.

Listing 10-12. The SHA512 function

```
Puppet::Parser::Functions::newfunction(:sha512, :type => :rvalue, :doc => "Returns a SHA1 hash value
from a provided string.") do |args|

  require 'sha1'

  Digest::SHA512.hexdigest(args[0])

end
```

Puppet contains an existing function called sha1 that generates a SHA1 hash value from a provided string. In Listing 10-12, we've updated that function to support SHA512 instead. Let's break that function down. To create the function, we call the Puppet::Parser::Functions::newfunction method and pass it some values. First, we name the function, in our case sha512. We then specify the type of function it is, here rvalue, for a function that returns a value. If we don't specify the type at all then Puppet assumes the function is a statement. Lastly, we specify a :doc string to document the function.

The newfunction block takes the incoming argument and processes it, first adding support for working with SHA hashes by requiring the sha1 library, and then passing the argument to the hexdigest method. Because this is an rvalue function, it will return the created hash as the result of the function.

■ **Note**   The last value returned by the newfunction block will be returned to Puppet as the rvalue.

We mentioned earlier that functions run on the Puppet master. This means you have access only to the resources and data available on the master; but that includes some quite useful information, particularly fact data. You can look up and use the value of facts in your functions using the lookupvar function, like so:

```
lookupvar('fqdn')
```

Replace fqdn with the name of the fact whose value you wish to look up.

You can see how easy it is to create very powerful functions in only a few lines of code. We recommend looking at the existing functions (most of which are very succinct) as a way to get started on your first functions. Some of the common functions include tools to manipulate paths, regular expressions, and substitutions, and functions to retrieve data from external sources. There are numerous examples (many on GitHub or searchable via Google) of functions that you can copy or adapt for your environment.

After you've created your function, you should test that it works correctly. There are a couple of ways you can do this. First, you can perform some basic testing of the function by executing the function file with Ruby, as shown here:

```
$ ruby -rpuppet sha512.rb
```

This command loads the Puppet library (Puppet must be installed on the host) and then runs the file containing the function we created in Listing 10-12. The result allows us to determine whether the file parses without error. It does not tell us if the function performed correctly.

▨ **Tip** You can raise an error in your function using `raise Puppet::ParseError, "raise this error"`. Replace *"raise this error"* with the error text you'd like to raise.

We can also use the Ruby IRB (Interactive Ruby Shell) to confirm that our function is properly defined:

```
$ irb
irb> require 'puppet'
=> true
irb> require '/tmp/sha512.rb'
=> true
irb> Puppet::Parser::Functions.function(:sha512)
=> "function_sha512"
```

Here we've launched `irb` and then required Puppet and our new function. We then confirm that Puppet can see the new function and that it parses as a correct function.

The best way to test a function is to use it in a manifest, and the easiest way to do that is to add your functions to Puppet's `libdir` and run a stand-alone manifest. Assuming Puppet is installed, first find your `libdir`:

```
$ sudo puppet -configprint | grep 'libdir'
/var/lib/puppet/lib
```

Then create a directory to hold our functions:

```
$ sudo mkdir -p /var/lib/puppet/lib/puppet/parser/functions
```

Copy in our function:

```
$ sudo cp sha512.rb /var/lib/puppet/lib/puppet/parser/functions
```

Create a manifest to execute our new function:

```
$ cat /tmp/sha.pp
$hash = sha512("test")
notify { $hash: }
```

And finally run the function:

```
$ puppet /tmp/sha.pp
notice: ee26b0dd4af7e749aa1a8ee3c10ae9923f618980772e473f8819a5d4940e0db27ac185f8a0e1d5f84f88bc887
fd67b143732c304cc5fa9ad8e6f57f50028a8ff
notice: /Stage[main]//Notify[ee26b0dd4af7e749aa1a8ee3c10ae9923f618980772e473f8819a5d4940e0db27
ac185f8a0e1d5f84f88bc887fd67b143732c304cc5fa9ad8e6f57f50028a8ff]/message: defined 'message' as
'ee26b0dd4af7e749aa1a8ee3c10ae9923f618980772e473f8819a5d4940e0db27ac185f8a0e1d5f84f88bc887fd67
b143732c304cc5fa9ad8e6f57f50028a8ff'
```

You can see that our `notify` resource returned a 512-bit hash generated by our `sha512` function.

■ **Note**   You can call a function from another function by prefixing the function to be called with `function_`; for example, `function_notice`.

Summary

In this chapter, you learned how to extend Puppet and Facter with your own custom types, providers, functions and facts. We demonstrated how to:

- Configure Puppet to distribute your custom facts in your modules
- Write your own custom facts
- Test your new custom facts
- Use external facts
- Use two ensure-style types and providers
- Use a ParsedFile type and provider to edit simple configuration files
- Write Puppet functions
- Test Puppet functions

Many examples of extensions and additions to Puppet are also available to add to your Puppet installation or use as examples of how to develop particular extensions. A good place to start looking for these is on GitHub (http://www.github.com).

Resources

- Adding custom facts: http://docs.puppetlabs.com/guides/custom_facts.html
- Try Ruby online tutorial: http://tryruby.org/
- Learn to Program online tutorial: http://pine.fm/LearnToProgram/
- *Programming Ruby*: http://ruby-doc.org/docs/ProgrammingRuby/
- *Beginning Ruby*: http://beginningruby.org/
- Creating custom types: http://docs.puppetlabs.com/guides/custom_types.html
- A complete example of resource type creation: http://docs.puppetlabs.com/guides/complete_resource_example.html
- Documentation on detailed provider development: http://docs.puppetlabs.com/guides/provider_development.html
- *Puppet Types and Providers* by Dan Bode and Nan Liu: http://www.amazon.com/Puppet-Types-Providers-Dan-Bode/dp/1449339328
- Writing your own functions: http://docs.puppetlabs.com/guides/custom_functions.html
- Writing tests for Puppet: http://projects.puppetlabs.com/projects/puppet/wiki/Development_Writing_Tests

CHAPTER 11

■ ■ ■

MCollective

Marionette Collective (MCollective) is an orchestration framework closely related to Puppet. Puppet excels at managing the state of your systems; however, the default 30-minute run interval of the Puppet agent makes it unsuitable for real-time command and control. MCollective addresses the need to execute commands in real time on a large number of systems in a novel and unique manner. MCollective takes advantage of message-passing technologies to handle communication between the nodes collectively. With MCollective, nodes are easily divided into collections based on information about the node itself rather than hostnames. The use of metadata means you don't need to maintain long lists of hostnames or IP addresses. All systems in the collection can report information about themselves in real time on demand. Armed with this information, the overall population of machines can be divided into collectives. Procedures are carried out remotely against a collective rather than against a single machine.

In this chapter, you'll learn how to install MCollective. Once it's installed, you'll also learn how integrate MCollective with Facter to provide a large amount of metadata that's useful to divide the population into collectives and then command them. In addition, you'll learn how Puppet works well with MCollective to orchestrate and reconfigure your nodes on demand and in a controlled manner. Plug-ins for MCollective provide these integrations with Puppet, specifically the Puppet Agent plug-in. But first, let's look a little more closely at this framework.

More Background on MCollective . . .

MCollective was created to provide an API for the orchestration tasks that systems engineers and developers frequently need to perform. Command and control tools are numerous and effectively provide the same functionality as the Unix shell. Though powerful, the shell interface is not an ideal application-programming interface. In addition, commands dispatched to systems in this manner are difficult to manage using the same tools and processes that you manage code with. With a robust API, orchestration actions may be implemented as small agent plug-ins and treated like other pieces of code in a software development lifecycle. MCollective agents are testable, version-controlled, and consistently repeatable.

There are a number of problems and use cases that MCollective is particularly well-suited to address. Through the use of real-time messaging and metadata addressing, a number of tasks previously carried out with SSH or other deployment tools are more efficiently solved with MCollective. In particular, Mcollective addresses questions and actions like the following extremely well:

- How many systems have 32GB of memory?

- What systems are online right now?

- Deploy version 1.2.3 of my application to all systems.

- Deploy version 1.2.4 of my application to the quality assurance systems.

- Deploy version 1.2.5rc2 of my application to the development systems.

- Run Puppet on all systems, ensuring that at most 10 runs are happening at once.

- Restart the Apache service on all systems in North America.

In addition to the actions MCollective already handles, writing custom agents in Ruby to carry out your own actions on all of your systems is quite straightforward. The MCollective RPC framework alleviates much of the effort you would otherwise have to spend writing code to connect to your machines, issue commands to them, and handle logging and exceptions. If you need to take action on all your systems, MCollective agents distributed through Puppet are an excellent way to tackle the problem quickly.

MCollective makes use of publish/subscribe messaging techniques. These publications and subscriptions are often implemented using asynchronous messaging software such as Apache ActiveMQ and Pivotal's RabbitMQ. The broad category of messaging software is often referred to as *messaging middleware*. MCollective is developed and tested with the ActiveMQ middleware; however, the requirements of Java and XML configuration files have driven increased attention to and interest in the RabbitMQ middleware service.

MCollective sends and receives messages using STOMP (Simple Text-Oriented Messaging Protocol). Any messaging middleware implementing a robust STOMP listener should work with MCollective. However, ActiveMQ and RabbitMQ are the two most widely deployed and tested middleware services used with MCollective. It is important to keep in mind that only one messaging service on one system is required to get started with MCollective. A single RabbitMQ server will easily support hundreds of connected MCollective server processes. Advanced configurations with multiple security zones and tens of thousands of nodes may consider deploying multiple, federated messaging services to scale with demand. In a multiple-datacenter configuration, ActiveMQ is an excellent choice. ActiveMQ and MCollective have been deployed together across multiple data centers and geographic continents in redundant and reliable configurations.

MCOLLECTIVE MESSAGING ARCHITECTURE

MCollective employs asynchronous messaging middleware services to broadcast messages and collect responses from nodes. An overview of this messaging architecture is available online here:

http://docs.puppetlabs.com/mcollective/reference/basic/messageflow.html

If you have multiple security zones or data centers, you may be interested in running multiple middleware servers to federate and distribute messaging requests. Information on this configuration with ActiveMQ is available online here:

http://docs.puppetlabs.com/mcollective/reference/integration/activemq_clusters.html

In addition, general information about publish/subscribe middleware is available online here:

http://en.wikipedia.org/wiki/Publish/subscribe

Now, let's get started with the installation of MCollective.

Installing and Configuring MCollective

We will be using the puppetlabs/mcollective module to install and configure all of the necessary components for our MCollective installation. It can be downloaded from the Puppet Forge at http://forge.puppetlabs.com/puppetlabs/mcollective or installed via the puppet module tool as shown in Listing 11-1.

Listing 11-1. Installing mcollective via the puppet module

```
root@mco-master:~# puppet module install puppetlabs/mcollective
Notice: Preparing to install into /etc/puppet/modules ...
Notice: Downloading from https://forge.puppetlabs.com ...
Notice: Installing -- do not interrupt ...
/etc/puppet/modules
```

```
┬── puppetlabs-mcollective (v1.0.0)
├─┬─ garethr-erlang (v0.2.0)
│ ├── puppetlabs-apt (v1.3.0)
│ └── stahnma-epel (v0.0.5)
├─┬─puppetlabs-activemq (v0.2.0)
│ └─puppetlabs-java (v1.0.1)
├──puppetlabs-java_ks (v1.2.0)
├──puppetlabs-rabbitmq (v3.0.0)
├──puppetlabs-stdlib (v4.1.0)
└──richardc-datacat (v0.4.2)
```

At the time of writing, the mcollective module supports both Debian and Enterprise Linux-based OS families. The module provides support for three different roles. The broker role is the node that will run the middleware; this can be ActiveMQ, RabbitMQ, or Redis. The second role is that of the MCollective servers, which are the nodes in our infrastructure. These nodes will run the mcollective daemon. The last node is the MCollective client node; this is where your admin users will administer MCollective. We will be running ActiveMQ as our middleware, which is the default for the module. In Listing 11-2 you can see how we are using the mcollective module to configure our node named mco-master to be the broker. The mco-master node we are using has already been configured to be a Puppet master, but you can run the middleware on a separate node if you want.

Listing 11-2. Configuring the middleware node

```
node 'mco-master.lan' {
  class { '::mcollective':
    middleware         => true,
    middleware_hosts   => [ 'mco-master.lan' ],
    middleware_ssl     => true,
    securityprovider   => 'ssl',
    ssl_client_certs   => 'puppet:///modules/site_mcollective/client_certs',
    ssl_ca_cert        => 'puppet:///modules/site_mcollective/certs/ca.pem',
    ssl_server_public  => 'puppet:///modules/site_mcollective/certs/mco-master.lan.pem',
    ssl_server_private => 'puppet:///modules/site_mcollective/private_keys/mco-master.lan.pem',
  }
}
```

If you would like to use RabbitMQ instead, you can set the connector parameter as shown in Listing 11-3.

Listing 11-3. Configuring the middleware node with RabbitMQ

```
class { '::mcollective':
  middleware         => true,
  connector          => 'rabbitmq',
  middleware_hosts   => [ 'mco-master.lan' ],
  middleware_ssl     => true,
  securityprovider   => 'ssl',
  ssl_client_certs   => 'puppet:///modules/site_mcollective/client_certs',
  ssl_ca_cert        => 'puppet:///modules/site_mcollective/certs/ca.pem',
  ssl_server_public  => 'puppet:///modules/site_mcollective/certs/mco-master.lan.pem',
  ssl_server_private => 'puppet:///modules/site_mcollective/private_keys/mco-master.lan.pem',
}
```

Generating and Storing Certificates

We will be using SSL for our MCollective installation, so we will need to provide some certificates for the mcollective module. We will need to generate a cert for our admin user as well. We can do this on the Puppet CA server using the puppet cert command. Our admin's username is mike, so we create a cert named mike:

```
$ puppet cert generate mike
```

The public and private keys will be placed in /var/lib/puppet/ssl/certs and /var/lib/puppet/private_keys, respectively.

Let's create a module called site_mcollective to store our certs. In your environment you would probably put these files in your own site module or in Hiera (Listing 11-4).

Listing 11-4. Create a site_mcollective module.

```
$ mkdir -p /etc/puppet/modules/site_mcollective/files/certs
$ mkdir -p /etc/puppet/modules/site_mcollective/files/client_certs
$ mkdir -p /etc/puppet/modules/site_mcollective/files/private_keys
```

Next copy the certs from your Puppet master's ssl directory into your module. You will need the public/private keys of your admin user, the public/private keys of your broker, and the public CA cert (Listing 11-5).

Listing 11-5. Copy the SSL certs into your module.

```
cp /var/lib/puppet/ssl/certs/mike.pem /etc/puppet/modules/site_mcollective/files/certs
cp /var/lib/puppet/ssl/private_keys/mike.pem /etc/puppet/modules/site_mcollective/files/private_keys
cp /var/lib/puppet/ssl/private_keys/mco-master.lan.pem /etc/puppet/modules/site_mcollective/files/
private_keys
cp /var/lib/puppet/ssl/certs/mco-master.lan.pem /etc/puppet/modules/site_mcollective/files/certs
cp /var/lib/puppet/ssl/certs/ca.pem /etc/puppet/modules/site_mcollective/files/certs
```

Your site_mcollective module should then look like Listing 11-6 and match up with the SSL parameters in our node definition.

Listing 11-6. Layout of the site_mcollective module

```
root@mco-master:~# tree /etc/puppet/modules/site_mcollective/files
/etc/puppet/modules/site_mcollective/files
├── certs
│   ├── mike.pem
│   ├── ca.pem
│   └── mco-master.lan.pem
├── client_certs
│   ├── mike.pem
├── private_keys
│   ├── mike.pem
│   ├── mco-master.lan.pem
```

Verifying Permissions

Next we will ensure that the permissions are correct after copying them into our site_mcollective module:

```
$ chown -R puppet:puppet /etc/puppet/modules/site_mcollective
```

At this point we can run puppet on our mco-master node, and our mcollective middleware will be installed and configured.

Our next step is to connect our clients and MCollective servers to our middleware. Apply the Puppet code in Listing 11-7 on all the nodes where you wish to run MCollective.

Listing 11-7. MCollective servers' configuration

```
node /mco-client[0-9].lan/ {
  class { '::mcollective':
    middleware_hosts    => [ 'mco-master.lan' ],
    middleware_ssl      => true,
    securityprovider    => 'ssl',
    ssl_client_certs    => 'puppet:///modules/site_mcollective/client_certs',
    ssl_ca_cert         => 'puppet:///modules/site_mcollective/certs/ca.pem',
    ssl_server_public   => 'puppet:///modules/site_mcollective/certs/mco-master.lan.pem',
    ssl_server_private  => 'puppet:///modules/site_mcollective/private_keys/mco-master.lan.pem',
  }
}
```

These nodes will run the mcollective daemon and can be queried from one or more MCollective client nodes. Our clients are configured similarly to the servers, except that the client parameter is set to true. We will use the mcollective::user define to provision our admin users as well. The mcollective::user define does not provision the system user. In Listing 11-8 we will create a system user named mike before creating the mcollective::user for mike.

Listing 11-8. MCollective client configuration

```
node 'mco-commander.lan' {
  class { '::mcollective':
    client              => true,
    middleware_hosts    => [ 'mco-master.lan' ],
    middleware_ssl      => true,
    securityprovider    => 'ssl',
    ssl_client_certs    => 'puppet:///modules/site_mcollective/client_certs',
    ssl_ca_cert         => 'puppet:///modules/site_mcollective/certs/ca.pem',
    ssl_server_public   => 'puppet:///modules/site_mcollective/certs/mco-master.lan.pem',
    ssl_server_private  => 'puppet:///modules/site_mcollective/private_keys/mco-master.lan.pem',
  }

  user { 'mike':
    ensure      => present,
    managehome  => true,
    shell       => '/bin/bash',
  } ->
```

```
mcollective::user { 'mike':
  certificate => 'puppet:///modules/site_mcollective/client_certs/mike.pem',
  private_key => 'puppet:///modules/site_mcollective/private_keys/mike.pem',
  }
}
```

After you run Puppet, the client and server nodes should now be configured with MCollective and ready for use.

Testing

To test the installation, log in as our user mike on the MCollective client node and run the mco ping command. You should see results similar to Listing 11-9.

Listing 11-9. Verifying installation

```
mike@mco-commander:~$ mco ping
mco-client1                   time=122.27 ms
mco-master                    time=125.95 ms
mco-client2                   time=137.08 ms
mco-commander                 time=139.84 ms

---- ping statistics ----
4 replies max: 139.84 min: 122.27 avg: 131.29
```

The mco ping command informs us that the MCollective server is running and responding to messages on all of our servers. This command verifies that the configuration settings in the middleware and the MCollective servers and client configuration files are working. Another verification step is to run the mco inventory command on a node (Listing 11-10). It will return server statistics, the plug-ins installed, and the facts a node has.

Listing 11-10. Running mco inventory

```
mike@mco-commander:~$ mco inventory mco-client1
Inventory for mco-client1:

   Server Statistics:
                      Version: 2.2.4
                   Start Time: Fri Sep 27 17:52:50 +0000 2013
                  Config File: /etc/mcollective/server.cfg
                  Collectives: mcollective
              Main Collective: mcollective
                   Process ID: 1019
               Total Messages: 9
       Messages Passed Filters: 9
             Messages Filtered: 0
              Expired Messages: 0
                 Replies Sent: 8
          Total Processor Time: 0.44 seconds
                  System Time: 0.02 seconds
```

```
Agents:
    discovery      rpcutil

Data Plugins:
    agent          fstat
```

With the MCollective server and client processes configured, we can now begin installing plug-ins.

Installing MCollective Plug-ins

MCollective is extensible in a number of ways. The most common way to extend MCollective is to reuse already written agent plug-ins. These small Ruby libraries enable MCollective to execute custom commands on the entire collective.

An agent plug-in usually contains a Ruby library that must be distributed to all of the nodes running the MCollective agent. In addition, a data definition file provides a description of the input parameters the plug-in accepts. This DDL file should be installed on the MCollective client systems. Finally, a script to execute MCollective using the specified agent plug-in should also be installed on all MCollective client systems.

In this section, you'll learn about a number of MCollective agent plug-ins. Additional plug-ins are also available at https://github.com/puppetlabs/mcollective-plugins. These plug-ins provide a good example of how to write your own agent plug-ins for MCollective to execute additional commands specific to the tasks you need to manage.

Puppet Agent MCollective Plug-ins

MCollective does not contain an agent for Puppet out of the box. An agent plug-in is provided, however, at https://github.com/puppetlabs/mcollective-puppet-agent. This plug-in allows you to execute Puppet agent runs on-demand. You will not need to wait for the run interval of the Puppet agent, or kick off jobs using other tools.

The mcollective module includes a define resource to install plug-ins. The puppet plug-in has packages for both DEB and RPM, so we will want to set the package parameter to true. Include the Puppet code in Listing 11-11 on all of your MCollective nodes.

Listing 11-11. Installing a plug-in

```
mcollective::plugin { 'puppet':
  package => true,
}
```

The mcollective::plugin resource will install the agent package on the MCollective server nodes and will install both the agent and client packages on the MCollective client nodes. Once Puppet has finished installing the puppet plug-in, we can access the help pages with the help command followed by the plug-in name (Listing 11-12).

Listing 11-12. Running mco help

```
mike@mco-commander:~$ mco help puppet
Schedule runs, enable, disable and interrogate the Puppet Agent
Usage: mco puppet [OPTIONS] [FILTERS] <ACTION> [CONCURRENCY|MESSAGE]
Usage: mco puppet <count|enable|status|summary>
Usage: mco puppet disable [message]
Usage: mco puppet runonce [PUPPET OPTIONS]
Usage: mco puppet resource type name property1=value property2=value
Usage: mco puppet runall [--rerun SECONDS] [PUPPET OPTIONS]
```

The ACTION can be one of the following:

```
count     - return a total count of running, enabled, and disabled nodes
enable    - enable the Puppet Agent if it was previously disabled
disable   - disable the Puppet Agent preventing catalog from being applied
resource  - manage individual resources using the Puppet Type (RAL) system
runall    - invoke a puppet run on matching nodes, making sure to only run
            CONCURRENCY nodes at a time
runonce   - invoke a Puppet run on matching nodes
status    - shows a short summary about each Puppet Agent status
summary   - shows resource and run time summaries
```

The puppet plug-in has many useful options to help us manage Puppet in our environment. To run puppet on all of our nodes, we can use the mco puppet runonce command (Listing 11-13).

Listing 11-13. Running mco puppet runonce

```
mike@mco-commander:~$ mco puppet runonce

 * [ ============================================================> ] 4 / 4

mco-master                            Request Aborted
   Puppet is currently applying a catalog, cannot run now
   Summary: Puppet is currently applying a catalog, cannot run now
```

Mcollective will warn you when it cannot apply a task, as shown in Listing 11-13. In this case the Puppet agent was already applying a catalog on the mco-master node. After sending Puppet jobs, you can check on their status with the mco puppet status command (Listing 11-14).

Listing 11-14. Running mco puppet status

```
mike@mco-commander:~$ mco puppet status

 * [ ============================================================> ] 4 / 4

      mco-master: Currently applying a catalog; last completed run 37 seconds ago
     mco-client1: Currently idling; last completed run 2 minutes 51 seconds ago
     mco-client2: Currently applying a catalog; last completed run 2 minutes 57 seconds ago
   mco-commander: Currently stopped; last completed run 03 seconds ago

Summary of Applying:

   true = 2
   false = 2

Summary of Daemon Running:

   running = 3
   stopped = 1

Summary of Enabled:

   enabled = 4
```

```
Summary of Idling:

    false = 3
     true = 1

Summary of Status:

    applying a catalog = 2
                idling = 1
               stopped = 1
```

We can see that one of them has finished, one is idling, and two are applying catalogs. We can even ask MCollective for a summary of the Puppet agents and how long it took to apply resources (Listing 11-15).

Listing 11-15. Running mco puppet summary

```
mike@mco-commander:~$ mco puppet summary
Summary statistics for 4 nodes:

                Total resources: █▁▁▁▁▁▁▁▁■▁▁■▁▁▁▁▁   min: 72.0   max: 99.0
          Out Of Sync resources: █▁▁▁▁▁▁▁▁▁▁▁▁▁▁▁▁   min: 1.0    max: 2.0
               Failed resources: _____   min: 0.0        max: 0.0
              Changed resources: █▁▁▁▁▁▁▁▁▁▁▁▁▁▁▁▁   min: 1.0    max: 2.0
 Config Retrieval time (seconds): ██▁▁▁▁▁▁▁▁▁▁▁▁▁▁   min: 2.6    max: 4.0
        Total run-time (seconds): █▁■▁▁▁▁▁▁▁▁▁▁▁▁▁   min: 13.2   max: 17.4
   Time since last run (seconds): █▁■▁■▁▁▁▁▁▁▁▁▁▁▁   min: 268.0  max: 273.0
```

Next we will explore the Facter plug-in for gathering real-time information from our infrastructure.

The Facter Plug-in for MCollective

MCollective allows systems to be addressed by metadata about the each system in addition to the system host name. This provides much more flexibility because any relevant information about each node can be used to group systems into collectives. MCollective integrates with the Facter library to collect this metadata on each server and on demand. By default, the metadata MCollective uses is statically defined in the file /etc/mcollective/facts.yaml. In most situations, a library like Facter should be used to generate metadata for each system dynamically.

This metadata can be accessed via the facts command, which is shipped with the mcollective package (Listing 11-16).

Listing 11-16. Running mco facts

```
mike@mco-commander:~$ mco facts lsbdistcodename
Report for fact: lsbdistcodename

        lucid                           found 1 times
        precise                         found 4 times
```

You can search for hosts by their metadata with the find command (Listing 11-17). For example, if we wanted to locate the Precise boxes, we could pass in lsbdistcodename=precise as a key/value pair to the mco find command.

Listing 11-17. Running `mco find`

```
mike@mco-commander:~$ mco find -F lsbdistcodename=precise
mco-client2
mco-master
mco-client1
mco-commander
```

The `mco find` command can give you real-time insight into the current state of your infrastructure.

The NRPE Plug-in for MCollective

The Nagios Remote Plugin Executor (NRPE) plug-in is great a way to aggregate your Nagios checks after a deployment or infrastructure change. You may want a quick check of whether your nodes are back to normal after one of these events; NRPE lets you quickly check all of the nodes you are interested in. To get started, the plug-in is available via packages, and the source code is at `https://github.com/puppetlabs/mcollective-nrpe-agent`; but first we need to install the NRPE daemon on all of our nodes.

We are going to use the `pdxcat/nrpe` module to do this for us. First download it from the Forge as shown in Listing 11-18.

Listing 11-18 Installing the `nrpe` module

```
root@mco-master:~# puppet module install pdxcat/nrpe
Notice: Preparing to install into /etc/puppet/modules ...
Notice: Downloading from https://forge.puppetlabs.com ...
Notice: Installing -- do not interrupt ...
/etc/puppet/modules
    pdxcat-nrpe (v0.0.3)
```

Then add the code in Listing 11-19 to your Puppet manifests and replace 10.0.3.69 with the name or IP address of your MCollective client. The `mcollective::plugin` definition will take care of the mcollective agent, and the `nrpe` class will install and configure the nrpe daemon. Next add some `nrpe::command` resources for the checks you are interested in.

Listing 11-19 Configuring NRPE

```
  mcollective::plugin { 'nrpe':
    package => true,
  }

  class { 'nrpe':
    allowed_hosts => ['127.0.0.1', '10.0.3.69'],
    purge         => true,
    recurse       => true,
  }
```

```
nrpe::command {
    'check_users':
      command => 'check_users -w 5 -c 10';
    'check_load':
      command => 'check_load -w 55,55,55 -c 100,90,80';
    'check_root':
      command => 'check_disk -w 10% -c 3% -p /';
    'check_var':
      command => 'check_disk -w 10% -c 3% -p /var';
}
```

Once you have run Puppet on your nodes, the nrpe plug-in will be ready to use. In Listing 11-20 you can see how to check the load on all of your nodes.

Listing 11-20. Running mco nrpe check_load

```
mike@mco-commander:~$ mco nrpe check_load

 * [ ============================================================> ] 4 / 4

Summary of Exit Code:

        OK : 4
  CRITICAL : 0
   WARNING : 0
   UNKNOWN : 0

Finished processing 4 / 4 hosts in 147.02 ms
```

Furthermore, we can filter our Nagios checks on a subset of machines. In Listing 11-21 we are only checking nodes that have the webserver Puppet class included. This is an immensely powerful feature that we will explore in more depth in the next section as we explore the package and service plug-ins.

Listing 11-21. Running mco nrpe check_load filtered

```
mike@mco-commander:~$ mco nrpe check_load -C webserver

 * [ ============================================================> ] 2 / 2

Summary of Exit Code:

        OK : 2
   UNKNOWN : 0
  CRITICAL : 0
   WARNING : 0

Finished processing 2 / 2 hosts in 153.82 ms
```

Addressing Hosts with Metadata

In the previous sections, you learned how you can use MCollective with Facter to obtain metadata about each system, and you saw a glimpse of MCollective's filtering features while using the NRPE plug-in. This dynamic information provides a unique way to execute commands on a large number of systems. Specific systems matching exact criteria may also be selected to execute MCollective commands on. You no longer need to maintain cumbersome spreadsheets with all of the hostnames for your systems. If a command needs to be executed, MCollective provides a simple and straightforward way to do so rather than connecting to each machine in succession over SSH. When Facter is used with Puppet and MCollective, hosts may be addressed by any Facter value or any class the host has been assigned from Puppet. These classes are read from /var/lib/puppet/state/classes.txt. (This file may be in a different location on your system and can be found using the command puppet agent --configprint classfile.)

We will demonstrate this functionality with the package and service plug-ins. First let's refactor our plug-in code from earlier, as shown in Listing 11-22. Then run Puppet on your nodes to install the new plug-ins.

Listing 11-22. Installing the service and package plug-ins

```
$plugins = [ 'service', 'package', 'puppet', 'nrpe' ]

mcollective::plugin { $plugins:
  package => true,
}
```

We have two new nodes, named mco-web1 and mco-web2. For demonstration purposes, suppose we want to install Apache on both nodes but not the other clients. You can use a regular expression for the hostname to execute on a subset of systems. By using this regular expression, you can easily exclude systems and obtain information only from the systems you are interested in.

Host filters work nearly everywhere in MCollective. The pervasiveness of filters is a key distinction between MCollective and other command and control tools. Notice in Listing 11-23 how the mco package command is able to execute agent plug-ins using host filtering.

This regular expression matching, in real time, allows you to write scripts that will take into account additional systems. Perhaps mco-web3 and mco-web4 will come online in the future, in addition to the current servers. With the ability to filter by hostname, any Facter value, or included Puppet classes, and to combine multiple filters, you can carry out actions that take into account the number of systems automatically. Scripts no longer need to be updated as hosts are added and removed from the network.

Listing 11-23. Running mco package install

```
mike@mco-commander:~$ mco package install apache2 -W /web/

 * [ ============================================================> ] 2 / 2

Summary of Ensure:

   2.2.22-1ubuntu1.4 = 2

Finished processing 2 / 2 hosts in 48173.38 ms
```

The filter syntax remains the same across plug-ins. As an example, in Listing 11-24 you can restart the Apache service with similar command syntax.

Listing 11-24. Running mco service restart

```
mike@mco-commander:~$ mco service restart apache2 -W /web/

 * [ ============================================================> ] 2 / 2

Summary of Service Status:

   running = 2

Finished processing 2 / 2 hosts in 3204.57 ms
```

You can chain filters together, as demonstrated in Listing 11-25, where we restart Apache only on the nodes that contain web in their names and that are running Precise.

Listing 11-25. Running mco service restart with chained filters

```
mike@mco-commander:~$ mco service restart apache2 -W /web/ -F lsbdistcodename=precise

 * [ ============================================================> ] 2 / 2

Summary of Service Status:

   running = 2

Finished processing 2 / 2 hosts in 2905.33 ms
```

Additional Plug-ins

The MCollective plug-ins mentioned in this chapter contain a number of useful agent plug-ins for MCollective. However, you may find the need to write your own agents and actions to carry out deployment or administrative tasks on your systems. Please visit the latest MCollective documentation at http://docs.puppetlabs.com/ to learn more about writing agents for MCollective.

We also recommend you fork the mcollective-plugins on GitHub and use some of the small agent plug-ins as a reference to writing your own. The filemgr.rb plug-in is a great starting point to get started with MCollective. If you do write a new agent, please don't hesitate to submit a pull request to share your work with the rest of the MCollective community.

Summary

In this chapter, you learned how MCollective provides real-time, metadata-driven command and control of Puppet-managed systems. MCollective takes an innovative and unique approach to the problem of orchestrating a large number of systems. Instead of using hostnames to uniquely identify and access systems, MCollective integrates with Facter, allowing you to filter out machines you do not want to carry out actions on.

In addition to the unique approach of addressing machines through metadata, MCollective uses the STOMP messaging protocol to communicate. The MCollective client (accessed through the mco command) and the MCollective server take advantage of the proven scalability and performance of asynchronous messaging services.

MCollective gives you the ability to obtain information from your systems in real time, without the tedium of scripting SSH connections to each and every hostname on the network. Systems may be added and removed from the network quickly without the need to update scripts or other programs communicating with these systems. In addition, MCollective works extremely well with Facter and Puppet, enabling control of the Puppet agent and filtering of hosts through Facter with ease.

Resources

- The blog of R.I. Pienaar, the author of MCollective: `http://devco.net/`.

- MCollective documentation is located on the Puppet Labs curated documentation site: `http://docs.puppetlabs.com/`.

- An architectural overview of how messages travel from client to server processes in MCollective: `http://docs.puppetlabs.com/mcollective/reference/basic/messageflow.html`.

- Information about setting up multiple ActiveMQ middleware services for use with MCollective (may be useful for deployments among multiple data centers or geographic locations): `http://docs.puppetlabs.com/mcollective/reference/integration/activemq_clusters.html`.

- Overview of the publish-and-subscribe methodology used by MCollective: `http://en.wikipedia.org/wiki/Publish/subscribe`.

- The MCollective puppet module is available for installation using the `puppet-module` tool from the Puppet Forge: `http://forge.puppetlabs.com/`.

- MCollective packages and source may be downloaded from the Puppet Labs website: `http://puppetlabs.com/downloads/`.

- Many agent plug-ins for MCollective are located in the `mcollective-plugins` Git repository on GitHub: `https://github.com/puppetlabs/mcollective-plugins`.

## CHAPTER 12

Hiera: Separating Data from Code

With Puppet 3.0, Puppet has a tool called Hiera (short for Hierarchal data store), built into its core. Hiera was developed in 2011 to allow Puppeteers to separate configuration from code. Puppet is very good at describing state, but using Puppet code as a place to store configuration data eventually becomes inconvenient. Hiera solves this problem by performing external lookups for data, and then exposing that data to the Puppet compiler. Two good candidates for data that can be hoisted out of Puppet code and into Hiera are, generally, "arbitrary site-specific strings" and "lists of things."

In this chapter, we're going to install Hiera, introduce its configuration, get comfortable on the command line, and make some lookups. Then we're going to look at a number of Hiera backends, including the mysql and gpg backends, Puppet data bindings, advanced Puppet function usage, and a few Puppet examples using Hiera.

But before we get to installing Hiera and its advanced features, let's quickly review what using Hiera looks like and what the advantages are for you, the administrator.

The Power of Hiera . . .

The example in Listing 12-1 will create a MySQL database.

Listing 12-1. A mysql::db example

```
mysql::db { 'myapp':
  user     => 'appuser',
  password => 'hunter2',
  grant    => ['all'],
}
```

Here the site-specific string is the database password: hunter2. In previous chapters we've taught you to abstract these variables into a class or defined type and take them as parameters, changing the mysql::db stanza to look like Listing 12-2.

Listing 12-2. A mysql::db example with abstracted parameters

```
mysql::db { $database:
  user     => $db_user,
  password => $db_password,
  grant    => ['all'],
}
```

But all this does is move the $db_password variable into a superior class or node definition. It is still right next to your Puppet code, even though the string for $db_password is definitely configuration *data*.

Hiera gives a place for that configuration data to live. It can be pulled out using the `hiera()` function call. Thus our `mysql::db` stanza changes to look like Listing 12-3.

Listing 12-3 A `mysql::db` example with Hiera

```
mysql::db { $database:
  user     => $db_user,
  password => hiera('database_password'),
  grant    => ['all'],
}
```

In this way, Hiera becomes the source of record for things like passwords, and Puppet becomes the driver that ensures the state specified by Hiera.

You'll see how to configure Hiera and its backing data stores in the next section, but right now let's turn our attention to the second category of data: lists of things.

Lists

Eventually, many sites end up with Puppet manifests that look like Listing 12-4.

Listing 12-4. Installing a list of packages

```
$pkgs_list = [
  'yelp',
  'notify-osd-icons',
  'libpeas-1.0-0',
  'linux-image-3.5.0-26-generic',
  'python-cairo',
  'python-pygame',
  'ubuntu-sso-client-qt',
  'evolution-data-server',
  'libghc-xmonad-dev',
  'librasqal3',
  'libgnome2-bin',
  'gettext',
  'gpgsm',
  'kde-telepathy-auth-handler',
  'libv4l-0:i386',
  'libqt5v8-5:amd64',
  'libsepol1:amd64',
  'gstreamer0.10-alsa:amd64',
  'libwmf0.2-7-gtk',
  'ipsec-tools',
]

package { $pkgs_list:
  ensure => latest,
}
```

While most daemons will require an entire class to install and configure, most of the files installed through the package manager require only a simple package resource, and they end up in lists like the one just shown. The existence of this list is a good thing; it means that the site has committed to using Puppet for configuration management. But that list of packages, the list itself, is data. It doesn't belong in Puppet code; it belongs in an external data store, and Hiera is how we're going to get it out. We're going to shorten the code from Listing 12-4 to what you see in Listing 12-5.

Listing 12-5. Installing a list of packages with Hiera

```
$pkgs_list = hiera('packages')

package { $pkgs_list:
  ensure => latest,
}
```

A further problem with the "list of things" and the "site-specific strings" being in your Puppet manifests is that this data is often different based on which node is asking. A development server will have a `testpassword2` password on the database, but a production server will have a much more complex password. An Ubuntu Precise server will have one list of packages, and an Ubuntu Trusty server will have a similar list but a few package names will be different. Hiera is designed to search through a hierarchy of data sources, starting at the most specific and moving to the most general, returning the most specific piece of data it can. Hiera has access to, and can split on, any variable available to Puppet, and it can merge data from multiple hierarchies.

Installing Hiera on Earlier Versions of Puppet

If you are running Puppet 3.0, then you don't need to do anything to install Hiera; it is already available to you. All you need to do is create a `hiera.yaml` file in the correct place. We'll discuss `hiera.yaml` in the section on configuring Hiera. If you are running Puppet 2.7.x, there are some steps to follow to install Hiera.

For each Puppet master, install the Hiera package from either your system's package manager or Gems. Hiera does not need to be installed on clients. Hiera can be installed from system packages (Listing 12-6) or with RubyGems (Listing 12-7).

Listing 12-6. Installing Hiera with packages

```
$ puppet resource package hiera ensure=present
$ puppet resource package hiera-puppet ensure=present
```

Listing 12-7. Installing Hiera via RubyGems

```
$ gem install hiera
$ gem install hiera-puppet
```

Note that the `hiera-puppet` package places a new Puppet function into your Puppet master's Puppet auto-loading path. This is because of the way Hiera was an external tool to Puppet in the 2.7 era. With Puppet 3, `hiera-puppet` is now fully integrated into core. Hiera is a separate open source project, but Puppet has fully developed hooks into it. A consequence of this situation is that the `hiera-puppet` shim is no longer maintained. Only the most critical of bugs will be fixed in it. If you are on Puppet 2.7, you should consider moving to 3.0 if only for the Hiera benefits.

▓ **Note**   If you are on a Puppet Enterprise version earlier than 3.x, you will not be able to use Hiera. Beginning with version 3.x, Hiera is already installed and all you need to do is configure it.

Initial Hiera Configuration

As mentioned, Hiera is configured through hiera.yaml. There are two hiera.yaml files on your system:

- The system Hiera configuration file (generally found in /etc//hiera.yaml). This file is used when a user is requesting a Hiera lookup through the hiera command-line utility.

- The Puppet Hiera configuration file (generally found in /etc/puppet/hiera.yaml). The file /etc/puppet/hiera.yaml is used when Puppet is performing a Hiera lookup, usually in the context of a Puppet master catalog compilation. The location of this file can be configured in puppet.conf using the hiera_config directive. It defaults to $confdir/hiera.yaml.

The command-line utility is a great way to debug how your hierarchy and data directory are behaving. Its use will be covered in a later section. Since there are two hiera.yaml files, and they should have the same content, we're going to symlink /etc/hiera.yaml to /etc/puppet/hiera.yaml.

First move the /etc/hiera.yaml file into /etc/puppet and then create a symlink, as seen in Listing 12-8.

Listing 12-8. Symlinking Hiera configuration files

```
$ mv /etc/hiera.yaml /etc/puppet/hiera.yaml
$ ln -s /etc/puppet/hiera.yaml /etc/hiera.yaml
```

■ **Note** The instructions for symlinking will be different if you are using PE.

Next is the content of the hiera.yaml file (Listing 12-9).

Listing 12-9. Default hiera.yaml file

```
---
:backends:
  - yaml
:hierarchy:
  - defaults
  - %{clientcert}
  - %{environment}
  - global

:yaml:
# datadir is empty here, so hiera uses its defaults:
# - /var/lib/hiera on *nix
# - %CommonAppData%\PuppetLabs\hiera\var on Windows
# When specifying a datadir, make sure the directory exists.
  :datadir:
```

■ **Note** This chapter makes extensive use of YAML. Before continuing, it would be beneficial to familiarize yourself with YAML at http://yaml.org/.

Notice that the file starts with three dashes (---). This is standard for a YAML file and must be present.

The first stanza is a YAML list of enabled backends. Hiera, rather than being itself a data store, has a pluggable backend system. By far the most common and generic backend is the YAML backend, which stores data in YAML text files. Later in this chapter we'll discuss enabling other backends.

The second stanza is the hierarchy configuration. This is read from top to bottom. When a lookup is performed, it will attempt to make the lookup on the first element. Then, if it fails to find anything, it will try again on the second, and continue until every element in the hierarchy has been hit or it has a successful lookup. Generally, if Hiera doesn't find anything at any level of the hierarchy it will return an error and the Puppet run will fail.

The third stanza is the configuration for the YAML backend. As you can see from the comment, it will use the directory /var/lib/hiera if no default is specified. Our first task will be to add a data directory to this configuration.

Configuring a Hiera Data Directory

First create the directory for data:

```
# mkdir /etc/puppet/data
```

Then change the YAML configuration option to look like Listing 12-10.

Listing 12-10. YAML backend configuration

```
:yaml:
  :datadir: /etc/puppet/data
```

Each backend that we load will have its own configuration stanza. We will now create our first datafile using the YAML backend and datadir.

The Hiera Command-Line Utility

Now that we have some base configuration, we can run through our first complete example with Hiera.

Populating a Hiera Datafile

Create the global.yaml file with the contents shown in Listing 12-11.

Listing 12-11. YAML data file

```
root@puppet-master-hiera-ubuntu:/etc/puppet# cat data/global.yaml
---
puppetmaster: 'puppetmaster.pro-puppet.com'
```

This sets the key puppetmaster to the value puppetmaster.pro-puppet.com.

Performing a Hiera Lookup

Once this code is in place, we can pull this data out using a Hiera lookup on the command line (Listing 12-12).

Listing 12-12. Using the hiera command for lookups

```
root@puppet-master-hiera-ubuntu:/etc/puppet# hiera puppetmaster
puppetmaster.pro-puppet.com
```

We can run it with the debug flag to see more of what's going on in Listing 12-13.

Listing 12-13. Using the hiera command with debugging enabled

```
root@puppet-master-hiera-ubuntu:/etc/puppet/data# hiera -d puppetmaster
DEBUG: Mon Sep 09 02:58:38 +0000 2013: Hiera YAML backend starting
DEBUG: Mon Sep 09 02:58:38 +0000 2013: Looking up puppetmaster in YAML backend
DEBUG: Mon Sep 09 02:58:38 +0000 2013: Looking for data source defaults
DEBUG: Mon Sep 09 02:58:38 +0000 2013: Looking for data source global
DEBUG: Mon Sep 09 02:58:38 +0000 2013: Found puppetmaster in global
puppetmaster.pro-puppet.com
```

Using Puppet to Perform a Hiera Lookup

We can also see the catalog run from Puppet in Listing 12-14.

Listing 12-14. Hiera lookup in Puppet

```
root@puppet-master-hiera-ubuntu:/etc/puppet# puppet apply -e '$foo = hiera("puppetmaster")
notify { $foo: }'
Notice: puppetmaster.pro-puppet.com
Notice: /Stage[main]//Notify[puppetmaster.pro-puppet.com]/message: defined 'message' as
'puppetmaster.pro-puppet.com'
Notice: Finished catalog run in 0.03 seconds
```

Note that the puppet apply command was introduced in Chapter 3.

Exploring the Hierarchy

Now let's create a new Hiera key, and put it in two places (Listings 12-15 and 12-16).

Listing 12-15. The /etc/puppet/data/global.yaml file

```
root@puppet-master-hiera-ubuntu:/etc/puppet/data# cat global.yaml
---
puppetmaster: 'puppetmaster.pro-puppet.com'
ntp_servers: clock4.pro-puppet.com
```

Listing 12-16. The /etc/puppet/data/defaults.yaml file

```
root@puppet-master-hiera-ubuntu:/etc/puppet/data# cat defaults.yaml
---
ntp_servers:
  - clock1.pro-puppet.com
  - clock2.pro-puppet.com
  - clock3.pro-puppet.com
```

We've created two data files that define the same key. Because defaults is ahead of global in the hierarchy, we see the behavior shown in Listing 12-17.

Listing 12-17. Hiera lookup of `ntp_servers`

```
root@puppet-master-hiera-ubuntu:/etc/puppet/data# hiera -d ntp_servers
DEBUG: Mon Sep 09 02:58:16 +0000 2013: Hiera YAML backend starting
DEBUG: Mon Sep 09 02:58:16 +0000 2013: Looking up ntp_servers in YAML backend
DEBUG: Mon Sep 09 02:58:16 +0000 2013: Looking for data source defaults
DEBUG: Mon Sep 09 02:58:16 +0000 2013: Found ntp_servers in defaults
["clock1.pro-puppet.com", "clock2.pro-puppet.com", "clock3.pro-puppet.com"]
```

The array of NTP servers from the `defaults.yaml` file was returned. This makes sense because Hiera's default behavior is to return the result of the first successful lookup. However, because both the default and global hierarchies are static, this is not very interesting. Let's use a dynamic hierarchy instead.

Building Dynamic Hierarchy

Recall our hierarchy:

```
:hierarchy:
  - defaults
  - %{clientcert}
  - %{environment}
  - global
```

The syntax for the `environment` variable means that the Puppet variable `$environment` will be used as a part of the hierarchy. Environments and the `environment` variable were first introduced in Chapter 3. Create two files for environments (Listings 12-18 and 12-19).

Listing 12-18. The `/etc/puppet/data/prod.yaml` file

```
root@puppet-master-hiera-ubuntu:/etc/puppet/data# cat prod.yaml
---
syslog_server: 'loghost.pro-puppet.com'
```

Listing 12-19. The `/etc/puppet/data/dev.yaml` file

```
root@puppet-master-hiera-ubuntu:/etc/puppet/data# cat dev.yaml
---
syslog_server: 'badlogs.pro-puppet.com'
```

What we see here is that the `syslog_server` variable is defined twice, once for the production environment and once for the development environment.

Hiera Lookups Using Variables

We can use simple command-line syntax with Hiera to explore the behavior of this configuration, as shown in Listings 12-20 and 12-21.

Listing 12-20. Hiera lookup of `syslog_server`

```
root@puppet-master-hiera-ubuntu:/etc/puppet/data# hiera -d syslog_server environment=prod
DEBUG: Mon Sep 09 03:37:42 +0000 2013: Hiera YAML backend starting
```

```
DEBUG: Mon Sep 09 03:37:42 +0000 2013: Looking up syslog_server in YAML backend
DEBUG: Mon Sep 09 03:37:42 +0000 2013: Looking for data source defaults
DEBUG: Mon Sep 09 03:37:42 +0000 2013: Looking for data source prod
DEBUG: Mon Sep 09 03:37:42 +0000 2013: Found syslog_server in prod
loghost.pro-puppet.com
```

Listing 12-21. Hiera lookup of syslog_server in a development environment

```
root@puppet-master-hiera-ubuntu:/etc/puppet/data# hiera -d syslog_server environment=dev
DEBUG: Mon Sep 09 03:37:46 +0000 2013: Hiera YAML backend starting
DEBUG: Mon Sep 09 03:37:46 +0000 2013: Looking up syslog_server in YAML backend
DEBUG: Mon Sep 09 03:37:46 +0000 2013: Looking for data source defaults
DEBUG: Mon Sep 09 03:37:46 +0000 2013: Looking for data source dev
DEBUG: Mon Sep 09 03:37:46 +0000 2013: Found syslog_server in dev
badlogs.pro-puppet.com
```

Hiera Lookups Using Puppet with Variables

As demonstrated in Listings 12-22 and 12-23, we can also use the Puppet client to perform lookups. In both listings we use Puppet apply to assign a variable with a value from hiera then print it out using the notify resource. The difference is the behavior of Hiera as it responds to Puppet running in different environments, as specified by the '--environment' command line argument.

Listing 12-22. Hiera lookup of syslog_server with puppet apply

```
root@puppet-master-hiera-ubuntu:/etc/puppet/data# puppet apply --environment=prod -e '$syslog =
hiera("syslog_server") notify { $syslog: }'
Notice: loghost.pro-puppet.com
Notice: /Stage[main]//Notify[loghost.pro-puppet.com]/message: defined 'message' as 'loghost.pro-
puppet.com'
Notice: Finished catalog run in 0.04 seconds
```

Listing 12-23. Hiera lookup of syslog_server with puppet apply in a development environment

```
root@puppet-master-hiera-ubuntu:/etc/puppet/data# puppet apply --environment=dev -e '$syslog =
hiera("syslog_server") notify { $syslog: }'
Notice: badlogs.pro-puppet.com
Notice: /Stage[main]//Notify[badlogs.pro-puppet.com]/message: defined 'message' as 'badlogs.pro-
puppet.com'
Notice: Finished catalog run in 0.04 seconds
```

Puppet agents that connect from the prod environment and run $syslog = hiera('syslog_server') will get the real syslog server running on loghost.pro-puppet.com. And Puppet agents that connect from the dev environment will end up with a $syslog that points to the non-prod log server running on badlogs.pro-puppet.com.

This, combined with some Puppet code like Listing 12-24, means that exactly the same code can run on both production and development servers, but have different results. This keeps the production logs clean and full of content and ensures that the Puppet code running in development is a good mock for the Puppet code running in production.

Listing 12-24. Hiera lookup of `syslog_server` in Puppet manifest

```
class { 'syslog-ng':
   loghost => hiera('syslog_server'),
}
```

Hierarchy Organization

We can split the hierarchy on any fact or variable available at catalog compilation time. It is very common to split on the $osfamily fact because of the massive differences between RedHat derivatives and Debian derivatives. You can see a very complex hierarchy in Listing.

```
:hierarchy:
  - environments/%{environment}/data/fqdn/%{fqdn}
  - environments/%{environment}/data/osfamily/%{osfamily}/%{lsbdistcodename}
  - environments/%{environment}/data/osfamily/%{osfamily}/%{lsbmajdistrelease}
  - environments/%{environment}/data/osfamily/%{osfamily}/%{architecture}
  - environments/%{environment}/data/osfamily/%{osfamily}/common
  - environments/%{environment}/data/modules/%{cname}
  - environments/%{environment}/data/modules/%{caller_module_name}
  - environments/%{environment}/data/modules/%{module_name}
  - environments/%{environment}/data/common
```

We've now seen how to create data files and get data out of them, and covered how the hierarchical backbone of Hiera can be useful. Let's now look at putting more structured data into Hiera.

Complex Data Structures

So far we've seen Hiera return strings and arrays of strings without giving much thought to type. But Hiera can return arbitrarily structured data as well. Arrays, hashes, and composite data structures can also be returned. These data structures can also be merged. This means we can configure Hiera to return an array for a key with elements of the array coming from different levels of the hierarchy. This is a very powerful feature and we will devote considerable time to it.

Returning Structured Data

Listing 12-25 provides an example of both an array and a hash type in the YAML format. Listing 12-26 shows lookups against both of these keys.

Listing 12-25. The `/etc/puppet/data/defaults.yaml` file

```
root@puppet-master-hiera-ubuntu:/etc/puppet/data# cat defaults.yaml
---
ntp_servers:
  - clock1
  - clock2
  - clock3
testuser:
```

```
gid: 1001
uid: 1001
gecos: Puppet Test User
shell: /bin/bash
```

Listing 12-26. Hiera lookup of ntp_servers

```
root@puppet-master-hiera-ubuntu:/etc/puppet/data# hiera ntp_servers
["clock1", "clock2", "clock3"]root@puppet-master-hiera-ubuntu:/etc/puppet/data# hiera testuser
{"uid"=>1001, "gecos"=>"Puppet Test User", "gid"=>1001, "shell"=>"/bin/bash"}
```

Array Merging

Hiera can also perform merges of arrays from multiple hierarchies. You must configure the :merge_behavior: of Hiera globally in hiera.conf as shown in Listing 12-27.

Listing 12-27. The /etc/puppet/hiera.yaml file

```
root@puppet-master-hiera-ubuntu:/etc/puppet/data# cat ../hiera.yaml  | grep merge
:merge_behavior: native
```

Make sure that global.yaml has the contents shown in Listing 12-28 and defaults.yaml has the contents from Listing 12-25. We can then show the merging behavior in Listing 12-29.

Listing 12-28. The /etc/puppet/data/global.yaml file

```
root@puppet-master-hiera-ubuntu:/etc/puppet/data# cat global.yaml
---
ntp_servers: clock4
```

Listing 12-29. Hiera lookup of ntp_servers with Hiera merging

```
root@puppet-master-hiera-ubuntu:/etc/puppet/data# hiera -a ntp_servers
["clock1", "clock2", "clock3", "clock4"]
```

The array has been merged from all levels of the hierarchy. Note that we are using the -a flag here to force an array lookup.

We can also use this for dynamic hierarchies. Listings 12-30 through 12-32 show how the data files must be configured. Listings 12-33 and 12-34 show the behavior of Hiera in different environments.

Listing 12-30. The /etc/puppet/data/prod.yaml file

```
root@puppet-master-hiera-ubuntu:/etc/puppet/data# cat prod.yaml
---
syslog_server: 'loghost.pro-puppet.com'
```

Listing 12-31. The /etc/puppet/data/dev.yaml file

```
root@puppet-master-hiera-ubuntu:/etc/puppet/data# cat dev.yaml
---
syslog_server: 'badlogs.pro-puppet.com'
users:
  - 'dev1'
  - 'dev2'
```

Listing 12-32. The /etc/puppet/data/global.yaml file

```
root@puppet-master-hiera-ubuntu:/etc/puppet/data# cat global.yaml
---
ntp_servers: clock4
users:
  - 'admin1'
  - 'admin2'
```

Listing 12-33. Hiera lookup of users in a production environment

```
root@puppet-master-hiera-ubuntu:/etc/puppet/data# hiera -a users environment=prod
["admin1", "admin2"]
```

Listing 12-34. Hiera lookup of users in a development environment

```
root@puppet-master-hiera-ubuntu:/etc/puppet/data# hiera -a users environment=dev
["dev1", "dev2", "admin1", "admin2"]
```

As you can see, we can to offload the question of "who is allowed on the machine" to the Hiera data service instead of implementing it in Puppet logic. The same trivial Puppet code can be used to handle both cases, as shown in Listing 12-35.

Listing 12-35. Hiera localusers Puppet class

```
class localusers {
  $users = hiera('users)

  localusers::user { $users: }

}
```

Hash Merges

Hiera can merge hashes by setting the merge_behavior in your hiera.yaml (Listing 12-36) and installing the RubyGem deep_merge (Listing 12-37).

Listing 12-36. The /etc/puppet/hiera.yaml file

```
root@puppet-master-hiera-ubuntu:/etc/puppet/data# cat ../hiera.yaml  | grep merge
:merge_behavior: deep
```

Listing 12-37. Installing the deep_merge Gem

```
$ gem install deep_merge
Fetching: deep_merge-1.0.0.gem (100%)
Successfully installed deep_merge-1.0.0
1 gem installed
Installing ri documentation for deep_merge-1.0.0...
Installing RDoc documentation for deep_merge-1.0.0...
```

Also make some further changes to your Hiera data (Listings 12-38 through 12-41).

Listing 12-38. The /etc/puppet/data/defaults.yaml file

```
root@puppet-master-hiera-ubuntu:/etc/puppet/data# cat defaults.yaml
---
ntp_servers:
  - clock1
  - clock2
  - clock3
backup_class:
  backup_server: 'backup.pro-puppet.com'
```

Listing 12-39. The /etc/puppet/data/dev.yaml file

```
root@puppet-master-hiera-ubuntu:/etc/puppet/data# cat dev.yaml
---
syslog_server: 'badlogs.pro-puppet.com'
users:
  - 'dev1'
  - 'dev2'
backup_class:
  backup_dirs:
```

Listing 12-40. The /etc/puppet/data/global.yaml file

```
root@puppet-master-hiera-ubuntu:/etc/puppet/data# cat global.yaml
---
ntp_servers: clock4
users:
  - 'admin1'
  - 'admin2'
backup_class:
  backup_dirs:
    - '/etc'
```

Listing 12-41. The /etc/puppet/data/prod.yaml file

```
root@puppet-master-hiera-ubuntu:/etc/puppet/data# cat prod.yaml
---
syslog_server: 'loghost.pro-puppet.com'
backup_class:
```

```
backup_dirs:
  - '/var/'
  - '/app/'
  - '/opt/app/'
```

And we can see the results of these lookups in Listings 12-42 through 12-44.

Listing 12-42. Hiera lookup of backup_class in some environment that is neither production nor development

```
root@puppet-master-hiera-ubuntu:/etc/puppet/data# hiera -h backup_class environment=dev
{"backup_dirs"=>["/etc"], "backup_server"=>"backup.pro-puppet.com"}
```

Listing 12-43. Hiera lookup of backup_class in a production environment

```
root@puppet-master-hiera-ubuntu:/etc/puppet/data# hiera -h backup_class environment=prod
{"backup_server"=>"backup.pro-puppet.com", "backup_dirs"=>["/"], "backup_dir"=>["/var/", "/app/", "/
opt/app/",
/etc/"]}
```

Listing 12-44. Hiera lookup of backup_class in a development environment

```
root@puppet-master-hiera-ubuntu:/etc/puppet/data# hiera -h backup_class environtment=development
{"backup_dirs"=>["/etc"], "backup_server"=>"backup.pro-puppet.com"}
```

Here we see that some keys to the hash, for example, backup_server, are set globally for all lookups. But backup_dirs array is set based on which environment is checking in. If a client checks in from an unaccounted-for environment, the default is to back up only /etc on that server. Notice that we are using the -h flag to force a hash lookup. If a client checks in from the production environment, additional directories are backed up.

Hiera lets us separate our configuration from our Puppet code, which has the effect of simplifying the Puppet code and focusing the data.

Additional Backends

Hiera has a pluggable backend system, which enables multiple backends to be loaded at the same time, but we'll only review a few of the most common ones in the following sections:

- file backend
- JSON backend
- MySQL backend
- gpg backend

These will affect how your lookups behave, but we'll explain that when we get there. Where putting strings into Hiera can help you get away from having site-specific strings in your Puppet modules, the file backend enables you to pull site-specific files out of the files directory in your modules.

Take, for example, an openvpn module. This module would have the things we expect from modules at this point—a templated configuration file, a package-file-service pattern, and so on. It would also include file resources for the private key and certificate. These files are usually stored on the filesystem as .pem files and are needed for establishing the crypto component of the VPN. An example of the manifests/init.pp file for this class is shown in Listing 12-45.

Listing 12-45. The modules/openvpn/manifests/init.pp file

```
class openvpn(
  $local_net   = '10.0.5.0/24',
  $full_tunnel = false,
){

# Package
package { 'openvpn-server':
  ensure => present,
}

# File
file { '/etc/openvpn/openvpn.conf':
  ensure  => file,
  content => template('openvpn/openvpn.conf.erb'),
  require => Package['openvpn-server'],
}


file { '/etc/openvpn/openvpn.crt':
  ensure => present,
  source => 'puppet:///puppet/openvpn/openvpn.crt',
}

file { '/etc/openvpn/openvpn.key':
  ensure => present,
  source => 'puppet:///puppet/openvpn/openvpn.key',
}

# Service
service { 'openvpn':
  ensure  => running,
  enabled => true,
  require => File['/etc/openvpn/openvpn.conf'],
}

}
```

Overall this class is good. It follows the package, file, service model. However, the private data files, the cert and key file to secure the VPN, are sitting in the files directory of the module. This means the module can never be shared outside the organization. Furthermore, the Puppet code now cannot be shared universally throughout the organization, since the private data must be kept secret. What we need to do is get the private data file into Hiera. We're going to use the file backend to do this.

The File Backend

First install the Gem as shown in Listing 12-46.

Listing 12-46. Installing the `hiera-file` Gem

```
root@puppet-master-hiera-ubuntu:~# gem install hiera-file
Fetching: json_pure-1.8.0.gem (100%)
Fetching: hiera-1.2.1.gem (100%)
Fetching: hiera-file-1.1.0.gem (100%)
Successfully installed json_pure-1.8.0
Successfully installed hiera-1.2.1
Successfully installed hiera-file-1.1.0
3 gems installed
```

Second, create a `global.d` directory to hold the files as shown in Listing 12-47.

Listing 12-47. Creating the directory layout for the `file` backend

```
root@puppet-master-hiera-ubuntu:/etc/puppet/data# mkdir global.d
root@puppet-master-hiera-ubuntu:/etc/puppet/data# ls
defaults.yaml  dev.yaml  global.d  global.yaml  prod.yaml
root@puppet-master-hiera-ubuntu:/etc/puppet/data# cd global.d/
root@puppet-master-hiera-ubuntu:/etc/puppet/data/global.d#
```

Now copy in the private data, as shown in Listings 12-48 and 12-49.

Listing 12-48. The openvpn private key

```
root@puppet-master-hiera-ubuntu:/etc/puppet/data/global.d# cat openvpn.key
-----BEGIN RSA PRIVATE KEY-----
MIIBOgIBAAJBAK1PvMB2d3hpusQiLiE+CITS9o9Bya3Mo4fFADlNqocp8mkbTve6
XFM4oQK6JQScNOISwyxlnamw9RozHyVQZXcCAwEAAQJBAIOx+7QkUVRmwOOWzAbm
pIKJ7GGflClFP16EDE9+/P4HWbyyFhAl8f4pCE8D/RVQpgHuJRoECwHjLGPb8yev
1YECIQDX+ENiRazDPRKdAimoOCyPUON4zNebx/OKcCvOmavdHwIhAM1vV+PNF6mY
82GRYf7o5+s4AWaK72fMfe3V8qJSyxSpAiBJORE3BZmHIdi6OYJrfMe+NGeLYnhP
Rou2haBzfRLBAQIgSzJndH4dHDpdVCh4O2ubgNEmShevHEqRCd7Xiq1NoskCIFBy
2d1c+mPqYP8LoOPxIUbeRbX3JxeDq9JIyMN+2AMp
-----END RSA PRIVATE KEY-----
```

Listing 12-49. The openvpn certificate

```
root@puppet-master-hiera-ubuntu:/etc/puppet/data/global.d# cat openvpn.crt
-----BEGIN CERTIFICATE-----
MIICODCCAnoCCQCtVdpdbMLF6DANBgkqhkiG9w0BAQUFADCB7jELMAkGA1UEBhMC
V2UxHDAaBgNVBAgME2FyZSBxdWlOZSBpbXByZXNzZWQxETAPBgNVBAcMCHRoYXQg
eW91MRowGAYDVQQKDBFhcmUgcmVhZGluZyB0aGlzLjEiMCAGA1UECwwZU2VyaW91
c2x5LCBoaGFOcyBhbWF6aW5nLjE9MDsGA1UEAwwOWW91IHNob3VsZCBlbWFpbCB1
cyBhbmQgdGVsbCB1cyBOaGFOIHlvdSBmb3VuZCBOaGlzLjEvMCOGCSqGSIb3DQEJ
ARYga3J1bS5zcGVuY2VyY2K3Byb3B1cHBldEBnbWFpbC5jb2OwHhcNMTMwOTEyMDA1
NjM5WhcNMjMwNjEyMDA1NjM5WjCB7jELMAkGA1UEBhMCV2UxHDAaBgNVBAgME2Fy
ZSBxdWlOZSBpbXByZXNzZWQxETAPBgNVBAcMCHRoYXQgeW91MRowGAYDVQQKDBFh
```

cmUgcmVhZGluZyBOaGlzLjEiMCAGA1UECwwZU2VyaW91c2x5LCBOaGF0cyBhbWF6
aW5nLjE9MDsGA1UEAwwOWW91IHNob3VsZCBlbWFpbCB1cyBhbmQgdGVsbCB1cyB0
aGF0IHlvdSBmb3VuZCBOaGlzLjEvMCoGCSqGSIb3DQEJARYga3J1bS5zcGVuY2Vy
K3Byb3B1cHBldEBnbWFpbC5jb20wXDANBgkqhkiG9w0BAQEFAANLADBIAkEArU+8
wHZ3eGm6xCIuIT4IhNL2jOHJrcyjh8UAOU2qhynyaRtO97pcUzjRArolBJwO4hLD
LGWdqbD1GjMfJVBldwIDAQABMAOGCSqGSIb3DQEBBQUAA0EAYBUxl8+372+odv+P
pLq8r3c6lTMNHuz6Mzz/6kUz5F+QmZ/L8g3kVR2xXZtH9y/OBGtnukRUB8OznlVY
A9xbQw==
-----END CERTIFICATE-----

Finally, let's modify our `hiera.yaml` to look like Listing 12-50.

Listing 12-50. Adding the `file` backend to `hiera.yaml`

```
root@puppet-master-hiera-ubuntu:/etc/puppet/data# cat ../hiera.yaml
---
:backends:
  - yaml
  - file

:hierarchy:
  - defaults
  - %{clientcert}
  - %{environment}
  - global

:yaml:
  :datadir: /etc/puppet/data

:file:
  :datadir: /etc/puppet/data

:merge_behavior: deep
```

We should also perform a couple of lookups, as shown in Listing 12-51.

Listing 12-51. Using the `file` backend

```
root@puppet-master-hiera-ubuntu:/etc/puppet/data# hiera openvpn.key
-----BEGIN RSA PRIVATE KEY-----
MIIBOgIBAAJBAK1PvMB2d3hpusQiLiE+CITS9o9Bya3Mo4fFADlNqocp8mkbTve6
...
root@puppet-master-hiera-ubuntu:/etc/puppet/data# hiera openvpn.crt
-----BEGIN CERTIFICATE-----
MIICODCCAnoCCQCtVdpdbMLF6DANBgkqhkiG9w0BAQUFADCB7jELMAkGA1UEBhMC
...
```

To bring things full circle, we can now revisit the file resources in our Puppet class and change them to the snippets presented in Listing 12-52.

Listing 12-52. The modules/openvpn/manifests/init.pp file

```
file { '/etc/openvpn/openvpn.crt':
  ensure  => present,
  content => template('openvpn.crt'),
}

file { '/etc/openvpn/openvpn.key':
  ensure  => present,
  content => template('openvpn.key)',
}
```

Note that the parameter has changed from source to content. We have successfully moved the private data files out of Puppet. Also, since Hiera is being leveraged, we can have different cert/key pairs for the production environment and the management/backend environments. Also note that the datadir used for hiera-file can be any directory; the only thing you can't do is specify more than one datadir.

When multiple backends and multiple hierarchies are configured, Hiera looks up keys by iterating over every level of the hierarchy for the first backend, and then every level of the hierarchy for the second backend, and so on.

The JSON Backend

Next we will install and use the JSON backend. Generally the JSON and YAML backends are essentially equivalent, and most sites should pick one and stick to it.

First create a new directory for just JSON data to keep it separate from YAML data, as shown in Listing 12-53.

Listing 12-53. Create the directory layout for the JSON backend

```
root@puppet-master-hiera-ubuntu:/etc/puppet# mkdir json_data
root@puppet-master-hiera-ubuntu:/etc/puppet# cd json_data/
root@puppet-master-hiera-ubuntu:/etc/puppet/json_data# ls
root@puppet-master-hiera-ubuntu:/etc/puppet/json_data#
```

Now install the hiera-json Gem as directed in Listing 12-54.

Listing 12-54. Installing the JSON backend

```
root@puppet-master-hiera-ubuntu:/etc/puppet/json_data# gem install hiera-json
Fetching: json-1.8.0.gem (100%)
Building native extensions.  This could take a while...
Fetching: hiera-json-0.4.0.gem (100%)
Successfully installed json-1.8.0
Successfully installed hiera-json-0.4.0
2 gems installed
```

Next modify hiera.yaml as shown in Listing 12-55.

Listing 12-55. Add the JSON backend to hiera.yaml.

```
---
:backends:
  - yaml
```

```
    - file
    - json

:json:
  :datadir: /etc/puppet/json_data
```

Next create a test JSON file as shown in Listing 12-56. The scoping, hierarchy, and merging behavior here are exactly the same as in the YAML examples earlier.

Listing 12-56. The /etc/puppet/json_data/global.json file

```
root@puppet-master-hiera-ubuntu:/etc/puppet/json_data# cat global.json
{
    "group_restrict": "yes",
    "groups": [
       "admin",
       "dev",
       "hr"
    ],
    "openvpn_server": "vpn.pro-puppet.com",
    "max_conns": 45

}
```

You can also use string interpolation with variables available to Hiera. Listing 12-57 shows what this looks like.

Listing 12-57. The /etc/puppet/json_data/defaults.json file

```
root@puppet-master-hiera-ubuntu:/etc/puppet/json_data# cat defaults.json
{
    "banner": "Welcome to %{hostname}"
}

root@puppet-master-hiera-ubuntu:/etc/puppet/json_data# hiera banner hostname=puppet-master-
hiera-ubuntu
Welcome to puppet-master-hiera-ubuntu
```

The same behavior also works for the YAML backend. It is recommended that you maintain your data directories in a version control system such as Git.

The MySQL Backend

Previously we have set up and used Hiera backends that live on the local file system. Now we will use MySQL as an example of an external Hiera backend.

First let's install the mysql-hiera Gem as shown in Listing 12-58. Note that you may have to install other packages on your system for the Gem to install successfully.

Listing 12-58. Installing the MySQL backend

```
root@puppet-master-hiera-ubuntu:/etc/puppet# gem install hiera-mysql
Building native extensions.  This could take a while...
Fetching: hiera-mysql-0.2.0.gem (100%)
```

```
Successfully installed mysql-2.9.1
Successfully installed hiera-mysql-0.2.0
2 gems installed
```

Configuring MySQL is beyond the scope of this book, but we will show an example with a MySQL server running on localhost with a database named hiera, a user puppet, a password puppet, a table puppet, and the data shown in Listing 12-59. We will also show the relevant portion of hiera.yaml (Listing 12-60)and an example of use(Listing 12-61.)

Listing 12-59. The MySQL puppet table

```
mysql> select * from puppet;
+-------------------+-------------+
| hiera_key         | hiera_value |
+-------------------+-------------+
| database_password | hunter2     |
| ldap_password     | hunter3     |
| root_password     | hunter4     |
+-------------------+-------------+
3 rows in set (0.00 sec)
```

Listing 12-60. Adding the MySQL backend

```
root@puppet-master-hiera-ubuntu:/etc/puppet# cat hiera.yaml
---
:backends:
  - yaml
  - file
  - json
  - mysql

...

:mysql:
    :host: localhost
    :user: puppet
    :pass: puppet
    :database: hiera

    :query: SELECT hiera_value FROM puppet WHERE hiera_key='%{key}'

:logger: console
```

Listing 12-61. Using the MySQL backend

```
root@puppet-master-hiera-ubuntu:~# hiera  database_password
hunter2
root@puppet-master-hiera-ubuntu:~# hiera ldap_password
hunter3
```

The MySQL backend can be configured to run multiple queries in sequence as well as other options. For full documentation, see https://github.com/crayfishx/hiera-mysql/blob/master/README.md.

So far we've discussed two ways to use plain text files with Hiera, the YAML and JSON backends. We've discussed the file backend as a way to move blobs of data regardless of content. And we've discussed using the MySQL backend to hit an external data source for configuration data. Next we are going to tackle the problem of securing data on disk using the hiera-gpg backend. This backend allows the data to exist on disk in an encrypted form and to be gpg-decrypted on the fly by the Hiera backend before it is fed to the Puppet master.

The gpg Backend

Let's install the Gem as shown in Listing 12-62.

Listing 12-62. Installing the GPG backend

```
root@puppet-master-hiera-ubuntu:~# gem install hiera-gpg
Fetching: gpgme-2.0.2.gem (100%)
Building native extensions.  This could take a while...
Fetching: hiera-gpg-1.1.0.gem (100%)
Successfully installed gpgme-2.0.2
Successfully installed hiera-gpg-1.1.0
2 gems installed
```

Then let's create a gpg key as shown in Listing 12-63. Make sure you run the following in the root user's home directory.

Listing 12-63. Generating a gpg key

```
root@puppet-master-hiera-ubuntu:~# gpg --gen-key
gpg (GnuPG) 1.4.11; Copyright (C) 2010 Free Software Foundation, Inc.
This is free software: you are free to change and redistribute it.
There is NO WARRANTY, to the extent permitted by law.


gpg: directory `/root/.gnupg' created
gpg: new configuration file `/root/.gnupg/gpg.conf' created
gpg: WARNING: options in `/root/.gnupg/gpg.conf' are not yet active during this run
gpg: keyring `/root/.gnupg/secring.gpg' created
gpg: keyring `/root/.gnupg/pubring.gpg' created
Please select what kind of key you want:
   (1) RSA and RSA (default)
   (2) DSA and Elgamal
   (3) DSA (sign only)
   (4) RSA (sign only)
Your selection? 1
RSA keys may be between 1024 and 4096 bits long.
What keysize do you want? (2048) 4096
Requested keysize is 4096 bits
Please specify how long the key should be valid.
         0 = key does not expire
      <n>  = key expires in n days
      <n>w = key expires in n weeks
      <n>m = key expires in n months
      <n>y = key expires in n years
```

```
Key is valid for? (0) 3y
Key expires at Mon 12 Sep 2016 04:15:13 AM UTC
Is this correct? (y/N) y

You need a user ID to identify your key; the software constructs the user ID
from the Real Name, Comment and Email Address in this form:
    "Heinrich Heine (Der Dichter) <heinrichh@duesseldorf.de>"

Real name: Puppet Master <puppet@pro-puppet.com>
Invalid character in name
Real name: Puppet Master
Email address: puppet@pro-puppet.com
Comment: Hiera-gpg
You selected this USER-ID:
    "Puppet Master (Hiera-gpg) <puppet@pro-puppet.com>"

Change (N)ame, (C)omment, (E)mail or (O)kay/(Q)uit? o
You need a Passphrase to protect your secret key.

We need to generate a lot of random bytes. It is a good idea to perform
some other action (type on the keyboard, move the mouse, utilize the
disks) during the prime generation; this gives the random number
generator a better chance to gain enough entropy.

Not enough random bytes available.  Please do some other work to give
the OS a chance to collect more entropy! (Need 278 more bytes)


..+++++
Not enough random bytes available.  Please do some other work to give
the OS a chance to collect more entropy! (Need 198 more bytes)
............+++++
gpg: /root/.gnupg/trustdb.gpg: trustdb created
gpg: key C5FBDE79 marked as ultimately trusted
public and secret key created and signed.

gpg: checking the trustdb
gpg: 3 marginal(s) needed, 1 complete(s) needed, PGP trust model
gpg: depth: 0  valid:   1  signed:   0  trust: 0-, 0q, 0n, 0m, 0f, 1u
gpg: next trustdb check due at 2016-09-12
pub   4096R/C5FBDE79 2013-09-13 [expires: 2016-09-12]
      Key fingerprint = 2C1A F200 9434 B823 31AC  2176 4601 6C41 C5FB DE79
uid                  Puppet Master (Hiera-gpg) <puppet@pro-puppet.com>
sub   4096R/51B40164 2013-09-13 [expires: 2016-09-12]
```

With the key in place we can use Listing 12-64 to fill out the hiera.yaml file.

Listing 12-64. Adding the gpg backend to hiera.yaml

```
---
:backends:
  - yaml
  - file
```

```
  - json
  - mysql
  - gpg

:gpg:
    :datadir: /etc/puppet/gpg_data
```

Next create a directory for the data as shown in Listing 12-65.

Listing 12-65. Creating the data directory for the GPG backend

```
root@puppet-master-hiera-ubuntu:/etc/puppet# mkdir gpg_data
root@puppet-master-hiera-ubuntu:/etc/puppet# cd gpg_data/
root@puppet-master-hiera-ubuntu:/etc/puppet/gpg_data# ls
```

And create a default.yaml with some data (note that we will be deleting this later) as in Listing 12-66.

Listing 12-66. The /etc/puppet/gpg_data/defaults.yaml file

```
root@puppet-master-hiera-ubuntu:/etc/puppet/gpg_data# cat defaults.yaml
---
very_secure_password: POnies!
```

Now we encrypt the file. First get the eight-character short-keyid using the commands from Listing 12-67.

Listing 12-67. Displaying the GPG short-keyid

```
root@puppet-master-hiera-ubuntu:/etc/puppet/gpg_data# gpg --list-keys
/root/.gnupg/pubring.gpg
------------------------
pub   1024R/3309614B 2013-09-13 [expires: 2016-09-12]
uid                  Puppet Master (Hiera-gpg) <puppet@pro-puppet.com>
sub   1024R/1C969AEE 2013-09-13 [expires: 2016-09-12]
```

Then encrypt the file for the key ID (Listing 12-68).

Listing 12-68. Encrypting the YAML file

```
root@puppet-master-hiera-ubuntu:/etc/puppet/gpg_data# gpg --encrypt -o defaults.gpg -r 3309614B
defaults.yaml
root@puppet-master-hiera-ubuntu:/etc/puppet/gpg_data# ls
defaults.yaml  defaults.gpg
root@puppet-master-hiera-ubuntu:/etc/puppet/gpg_data# mv defaults.yaml ..
root@puppet-master-hiera-ubuntu:/etc/puppet/gpg_data# hiera -d very_secure_password
```

In production you will want to remove defaults.yaml fully, perhaps even going to the extent of using the shred utility. The gpg command-line utility can also read data from STDIN, and so you might not have to write it to disk unencrypted ever. We only move it aside in Listing 12-68 because we think you might need a shot at debugging it.

Now let's perform a lookup in Listing 12-69.

Listing 12-69. Using the gpg backend

```
root@puppet-master-hiera-ubuntu:/etc/puppet/gpg_data# hiera -d very_secure_password
DEBUG: Fri Sep 27 00:48:37 +0000 2013: Hiera YAML backend starting
...
DEBUG: Fri Sep 27 00:48:37 +0000 2013: [gpg_backend]: Loaded gpg_backend
DEBUG: Fri Sep 27 00:48:37 +0000 2013: [gpg_backend]: Lookup called, key very_secure_password
resolution type is priority
DEBUG: Fri Sep 27 00:48:37 +0000 2013: [gpg_backend]: GNUPGHOME is /root/.gnupg
DEBUG: Fri Sep 27 00:48:37 +0000 2013: [gpg_backend]: loaded cipher: /etc/puppet/gpg_data/defaults.
gpg
DEBUG: Fri Sep 27 00:48:38 +0000 2013: [gpg_backend]: result is a String ctx
#<GPGME::Ctx:0x7fb29caaedc0> txt ---
very_secure_password: POnies!
DEBUG: Fri Sep 27 00:48:38 +0000 2013: [gpg_backend]: GPG decrypt returned valid data
DEBUG: Fri Sep 27 00:48:38 +0000 2013: [gpg_backend]: Data contains valid YAML
DEBUG: Fri Sep 27 00:48:38 +0000 2013: [gpg_backend]: Key very_secure_password found in YAML
document, Passing answer to hiera
DEBUG: Fri Sep 27 00:48:38 +0000 2013: [gpg_backend]: Assigning answer variable
POnies!
```

With this method, secrets can be committed to Git repositories and shared without leaking information. It is also possible to encrypt the file to multiple keys, by adding more key IDs to the -r flag. It is good practice to have different keys on each puppet Master, and to encrypt the file to each Puppet master as well as to the personal/work keys of the sysadmins who are allowed to know the secrets.

Now let's take a longer look at the Hiera function calls.

Hiera Functions in Depth

Hiera is used in Puppet as a function. Functions were covered in Chapter 2. The hiera() function has some deeper functionality we will explore now. From within Puppet, we can use the hiera() function call to make a Hiera lookup as shown in Listing 12-70.

Listing 12-70. A Hiera function call

```
class foo {
  $msg = hiera('msg')
  notify { $msg: }
}
```

The hiera() function actually takes three arguments. The first argument is the key to look up. The second argument is optional, a default value to use in case the lookup fails. Listing 12-71 shows what this looks like.

Listing 12-71. A Hiera function call with a default value

```
class foo {
  $msg = hiera('msg', "lookup on key failed")
  notify { $msg: }
}
```

Listing 12-72 makes it more concrete.

Listing 12-72 Hiera function with default value example

```
class ssh {
  $root_login = hiera('root_login', 'without-password')

  file { '/etc/ssh/sshd_config':
    ensure  => file,
    content => template('ssh/sshd_config.erb'),
  }
}
```

The ssh class here looks in Hiera for the rules on what to do with root logins (as implemented by the template later on); if it doesn't find a rule for this node, it defaults to 'without-password'. It can be good to provide sane defaults to Hiera lookups; by default, a failed Hiera lookup without a default value will abort the Puppet run. The abort happens during catalog compilation, which is before any resources are applied.

The third argument to the hiera() function is also optional; it is a hierarchy override. This means you can insert a hierarchy at the top of the list of hierarchies for exactly one lookup. It is not generally recommended to use this, as it reduces readability and expected behavior.

Other Hiera Functions

In addition to the hiera() function, there are a couple of other Hiera functions to look at. The hiera_array() function call returns an array type and is capable of using whatever merge behavior has been set in hiera.yaml; note that the default hiera() function call cannot perform merges, although it can return arrays and hashes. Similarly, the hiera_hash() function call returns a hash type and is capable of using whatever merge behavior has been set in hiera.yaml. All three functions take the same arguments as described earlier. There is also a hiera_include() function, which can be used to include classes; we'll talk about it in a more complete example in the "Hiera as an ENC" section. Note that hiera_array() and hiera_hash() will create datatypes from single results found at multiple levels.

```
root@puppet-master-hiera-ubuntu:/etc/puppet/data# cat defaults.yaml
---
foo: 'bar'

root@puppet-master-hiera-ubuntu:/etc/puppet/data# cat global.yaml
---
foo: 'baz'

root@puppet-master-hiera-ubuntu:/etc/puppet/data# puppet apply -e '$foo = hiera_array("foo")
notify { $foo: }'
Notice: Compiled catalog for puppet-master-hiera-ubuntu.green.gah in environment production in
0.21 seconds
Notice: baz
Notice: /Stage[main]//Notify[baz]/message: defined 'message' as 'baz'
Notice: bar
Notice: /Stage[main]//Notify[bar]/message: defined 'message' as 'bar'
Notice: Finished catalog run in 0.05 seconds
```

Module Data Bindings

One of the most important uses for Hiera inside Puppet doesn't involve the hiera() function at all. It's a technique called data bindings, and it sounds a bit scarier than it is. The concept of data bindings just means implicit key lookup in Puppet. Let's look at a parameterized class in Listing 12-73.

Listing 12-73. An example of module data bindings

```
class ssh(
  $root_login = 'without-password',
) {

  file { '/etc/ssh/sshd_config':
    ensure  => file,
    content => template('ssh/sshd_config.erb'),
  }

}
```

We have also seen this class presented as in Listing 12-74.

Listing 12-74. Another example of module data bindings

```
class ssh {
  $root_login = hiera('root_login', 'without-password')

  file { '/etc/ssh/sshd_config':
    ensure  => file,
    content -> template('ssh/sshd_config.erb'),
  }

}
```

Both of these classes are good for different reasons, but we can combine their functionality using data bindings. Binding data means that parameterized classes perform Hiera lookups on their parameters. This is especially useful because it removes the need for classes to accept parameters only to pass those parameters into other classes.

Listing 12-75 provides a very simple example.

Listing 12-75 A third example of module data bindings

```
root@puppet-master-hiera-ubuntu:/etc/puppet# cat modules/science/manifests/init.pp
class science(
  $param1 = 'default in module',
  $param2 = 'default in module',
  $param3 = 'default in module',
){
  notify { "param1: ${param1}": }
  notify { "param2: ${param2}": }
  notify { "param3: ${param3}": }
}

root@puppet-master-hiera-ubuntu:/etc/puppet# cat manifests/site.pp
```

```
class { 'science':
  param3 => 'passed in',
}
```

```
root@puppet-master-hiera-ubuntu:/etc/puppet# cat data/defaults.yaml
---
science::param2: 'looked up in hiera'
```

So what does all this mean? Well first we have a class that takes three parameters, all with defaults in the module. Second, we have a class instantiation stanza that specifically overrides the default of one parameter. Third, we have a Hiera data entry `science::param2: 'looked up in Hiera'`. This special Hiera syntax is part of module data bindings. The `science::` part namespaces the data and tells Puppet that we're defining a variable for the `science` class. The `param2` part is the name of the variable passed as a parameter to the class.

So what will happen? The order of precedence is, from highest to lowest:

1. Explicitly passed parameters

2. Hiera data bindings

3. Module defaults

Listing 12-76 shows the output.

Listing 12-76. Applying the module data bindings example from Listing 12-73

```
root@puppet-master-hiera-ubuntu:/etc/puppet# puppet apply manifests/site.pp
Notice: Compiled catalog for puppet-master-hiera-ubuntu.green.gah in environment production in
0.14 seconds
Notice: param2: looked up in hiera
Notice: /Stage[main]/Science/Notify[param2: looked up in hiera]/message: defined 'message' as
'param2: looked up in hiera'
Notice: param3: passed in
Notice: /Stage[main]/Science/Notify[param3: passed in]/message: defined 'message' as 'param3: passed in'
Notice: param1: default in module
Notice: /Stage[main]/Science/Notify[param1: default in module]/message: defined 'message' as
'param1: default in module'
Notice: Finished catalog run in 0.04 seconds
```

Hiera Examples

Next let's consider a larger example of using Hiera data to control configuration. In Listing 12-77 we see a node definition from the `openstack-infra` Puppet manifests.

Listing 12-77. Node definition from the Openstack manifests

```
node 'review.openstack.org' {
  class { 'openstack_project::review':
    github_oauth_token          => hiera('gerrit_github_token'),
    github_project_username     => hiera('github_project_username'),
    github_project_password     => hiera('github_project_password'),
    mysql_password              => hiera('gerrit_mysql_password'),
    mysql_root_password         => hiera('gerrit_mysql_root_password'),
```

```
    email_private_key            => hiera('gerrit_email_private_key'),
    gerritbot_password           => hiera('gerrit_gerritbot_password'),
    ssl_cert_file_contents       => hiera('gerrit_ssl_cert_file_contents'),
    ssl_key_file_contents        => hiera('gerrit_ssl_key_file_contents'),
    ssl_chain_file_contents      => hiera('gerrit_ssl_chain_file_contents'),
    ssh_dsa_key_contents         => hiera('gerrit_ssh_dsa_key_contents'),
    ssh_dsa_pubkey_contents      => hiera('gerrit_ssh_dsa_pubkey_contents'),
    ssh_rsa_key_contents         => hiera('gerrit_ssh_rsa_key_contents'),
    ssh_rsa_pubkey_contents      => hiera('gerrit_ssh_rsa_pubkey_contents'),
    lp_sync_key                  => hiera('gerrit_lp_sync_key'),
    lp_sync_pubkey               => hiera('gerrit_lp_sync_pubkey'),
    lp_sync_consumer_key         => hiera('gerrit_lp_consumer_key'),
    lp_sync_token                => hiera('gerrit_lp_access_token'),
    lp_sync_secret               => hiera('gerrit_lp_access_secret'),
    contactstore_appsec          => hiera('gerrit_contactstore_appsec'),
    contactstore_pubkey          => hiera('gerrit_contactstore_pubkey'),
    sysadmins                    => hiera('sysadmins'),
    swift_username               => hiera('swift_store_user'),
    swift_password               => hiera('swift_store_key'),
  }
}
```

The Openstack infrastructure team can make these Puppet manifests available to the public because there is no longer any secret data in the node definitions or Puppet manifests/modules. All of that data is passed in by hiera() calls in the node definition. Openstack-infra does not share their Hiera data with the larger public.

Note also the Puppet coding pattern here, where a single class openstack::review is included with many parameters. This role class will fire off whatever "get things done" classes (sometimes called profiles or bricks) are needed to create MySQL databases and set up Apache. The logic defining which parameters to pass to those brick modules is performed in the openstack::review class.

The sysadmins key is being looked up and is implied to be of an array type. Openstack passes this variable around a few times and then uses it to set the root@ email alias in Exim configs on every node.

The create-resources() Function

What if the sysadmins key returned a hash? Let's look at what that might look like in Listing 12-78.

Listing 12-78. Sysadmin hash in global.yaml

```
root@puppet-master-hiera-ubuntu:/etc/puppet# cat data/global.yaml
---
sysadmins:
  'spencer':
    uid: 1861
    gid: 300
    groups: root
  'william':
    uid: 11254
    gid: 300
    groups: root
```

Now let's confirm behavior with the Hiera command-line tool in Listing 12-79.

Listing 12-79. Hiera lookup of sysadmin hash

```
root@puppet-master-hiera-ubuntu:/etc/puppet/data# hiera sysadmins
{"spencer"=>{"uid"=>1861, "groups"=>"root", "gid"=>300}, "william"=>{"uid"=>11254,
"groups"=>"root", "gid"=>300}}
```

Now we can use a function called `create_resources()` to generate Puppet resources from this hash, as shown in Listing 12-80.

Listing 12-80. `create_resources` example

```
$sysadmins = hiera('sysadmins')

create_resources(user, $sysadmins)
```

Listing 12-81 shows the output.

Listing 12-81. Applying the `create_resources` example from Listing 12-80

```
root@puppet-master-hiera-ubuntu:/etc/puppet# puppet apply create_resources.pp
Notice: Compiled catalog for puppet-master-hiera-ubuntu.green.gah in environment production in
0.11 seconds
Notice: /User[spencer]/ensure: created
Notice: /User[william]/ensure: created
Notice: Finished catalog run in 0.32 seconds
```

Hiera as an ENC

Hiera can be used as an external node classifier through the use of the `hiera_include` function. Let's see what this looks like. Remember that our hierarchy looks like Listing 12-82.

Listing 12-82. Default hierarchy in `hiera.yaml`

```
:hierarchy:
  - defaults
  - %{clientcert}
  - %{environment}
  - global
```

We haven't used `%{clientcert}` yet. This variable is the common name field on the Puppet agent's client certificate. It is also the string used in node definitions. We can use `%{clientcert}` here to put per-node configuration into Hiera. Listing 12-83 shows what that looks like.

Listing 12-83. Hiera example files for ENC

```
root@puppet-master-hiera-ubuntu:/etc/puppet/data# cat global.yaml
---
classes:
  - sudo
  - ssh
  - updates
```

```
root@puppet-master-hiera-ubuntu:/etc/puppet/data# cat server01.yaml
---
classes:
  - ldap

root@puppet-master-hiera-ubuntu:/etc/puppet/data# cat server02.yaml
---
classes:
  - postgres
```

Let's use the command-line utility to investigate the behavior of these data. Note that we're using the -a flag to Hiera to force an array lookup and array merge behavior as seen in Listing 12-84.

Listing 12-84. Using Hiera as an ENC

```
root@puppet-master-hiera-ubuntu:/etc/puppet/data# hiera -a classes clientcert=server00
["sudo", "ssh", "updates"]

root@puppet-master-hiera-ubuntu:/etc/puppet/data# hiera -a classes clientcert=server01
["ldap", "sudo", "ssh", "updates"]

root@puppet-master-hiera-ubuntu:/etc/puppet/data# hiera -a classes clientcert=server02
["postgres", "sudo", "ssh", "updates"]
```

What we can see here is that some classes are put on all machines; and if a machine matches another Hiera lookup, it gets the union of the classes.

Finally, let's demonstrate use in manifests. Listing 12-85 contains the site.pp for the entire infrastructure.

Listing 12-85. site.pp when using Hiera as an ENC

```
node default {
  hiera_include('classes')
}
```

And we can see the behavior in a Puppet run in Listing 12-86.

Listing 12-86. Applying the site.pp from Listing 12-85

```
root@puppet-master-hiera-ubuntu:/etc/puppet# puppet apply manifests/site.pp
Notice: Compiled catalog for puppet-master-hiera-ubuntu.green.gah in environment production in
0.17 seconds
Notice: using sudo class
Notice: /Stage[main]/Sudo/Notify[using sudo class]/message: defined 'message' as 'using sudo class'
Notice: using updates class
Notice: /Stage[main]/Updates/Notify[using updates class]/message: defined 'message' as 'using
updates class'
Notice: using ssh class
Notice: /Stage[main]/Ssh/Notify[using ssh class]/message: defined 'message' as 'using ssh class'
```

How do we parameterize classes using this method? We fall back to using module data bindings, as shown in Listing 12-87.

Listing 12-87. Parameterized classes with Hiera ENC

```
root@puppet-master-hiera-ubuntu:/etc/puppet# cat data/server01.yaml
---
classes:
  - ldap
  - mysql
mysql::password: 'changeme'
```

This will set the `password` parameter of the `mysql` class to `changeme` for only the `server01` node.

Hiera-2

To close, let's briefly look at the future of Hiera. At the time of writing, Puppet 3.3.0 has just been released. This release contains an experimental release of Hiera-2. Hiera-2 brings Hiera data inside modules. Thus, public modules can be shared with their configuration embedded in Hiera, avoiding the much-maligned `params.pp` pattern. You can start using this experimental feature now by following the instructions at `https://github.com/pro-puppet/puppet-module-startrek`.

Summary

In this chapter we introduced the Hiera tool. We introduced the idea of separating data from code. You learned how to install Hiera and how to backport Hiera into your Puppet 2.7 infrastructure. You learned how to configure the `hiera.yaml` file; then you got comfortable writing data files and using the Hiera command-line utility. You learned about the hierarchical behavior of Hiera and its power. You learned about data structures beyond simple strings in Hiera and about merging schema to build them.

Then we discussed a slew of Hiera backends to store our Hiera data: YAML and JSON to store it easily, file to store raw files, MySQL to interact with an existing CMDB, and gpg to encrypt the configuration on disk. What we didn't cover was writing your own Hiera backend, which is out of this book's scope. This process is relatively straightforward for adept Ruby programmers. Right now the best resource for this is the source code of existing backends. Most of these are less than 200 lines of code.

Next we discussed the other optional arguments to the `hiera()` function, `default` and `override`. The `default` option is much more useful than the `override` argument. Then we talked about the other related Hiera functions.

After that, we discussed module data bindings, one of the most important concepts in Hiera. And finally we showed a few examples of Hiera use in Puppet manifests.

Resources

- Hiera Homepage: `http://projects.puppetlabs.com/projects/hiera`

- Hiera bug tracker: `http://projects.puppetlabs.com/projects/hiera/issues`

- Hiera source code: `https://github.com/puppetlabs/hiera`

- Puppet Labs Hiera docs: `http://docs.puppetlabs.com/hiera/1/index.html`

- JSON backend: `https://github.com/puppetlabs/hiera-json`

- gpg backend: `https://github.com/crayfishx/hiera-gpg`

- file backend: `https://github.com/adrienthebo/hiera-file`

- MySQL backend: `https://github.com/crayfishx/hiera-mysql`

- Data bindings: `http://docs.puppetlabs.com/puppet/3/reference/release_notes.html#automatic-data-bindings-for-class-parameters`

- More on data bindings: `http://docs.puppetlabs.com/hiera/1/puppet.html#automatic-parameter-lookup`

- Hiera-2: `https://github.com/pro-puppet/puppet-module-startrek`

- Data in modules: `https://github.com/hlindberg/misc-puppet-docs/blob/master/data-in-modules.md`

Index

■ A, B

ActiveMQ, 250
Autosign mode, 24

■ C

Custom facts
  external facts, 231
    executeable facts, 231
    structured facts, 232
  Puppet configuration, 227
    facts/plugins, 228
    lib directory, 228
    modules, 227–228
    pluginsync.setting, 228
    puppet.conf, 228
  testing facts, 231
    home fact, 231
    lib/ruby/facter, 231
  writing facts, 228
    case statements, 229
    complex fact, 230
    confine statement, 229
    Facter.add method, 228
    Facter method, 228
    operatingsystem fact, 230
    osfamily fact, 229
Custom functions, 245
  fail function, 245
  hexdigest method, 246
  lookupvar function, 246
  newfunction method, 246
  Puppet configuration, 232
    lib directory, 233
    pluginsync.setting, 233
  split function, 245
    pluginsync, 245

template function, 245
write functions
  validate_array, 245
  validate_bool, 245
  validate_hash, 245
Custom providers
  httpauth provider, 243
    ensurable method, 244
    exists? method, 245
    flush method, 245
    Webrick library, 244
  Puppet configuration, 232
    lib directory, 233
    pluginsync.setting, 233
  repo type, 238
  shells provider, 240
    cron type, 241
    default_target variable, 240
    desc method, 240
    ensure attribute, 241
  subversion provider
    creation, 236
    create method, 237
    delete method, 237
    ensurable statement, 237
    exists? method, 237
    fileutils, 237
    Git tool, 238
  testing
    HTTPAuth type, 245
    pluginsync, 245
Custom types
  httpauth type, 241–242
    defaultto method, 243
    ensurable method, 243
    newvalues, 243
    validate method, 243
  isnamevar method, 240

Custom types (*cont.*)
    Puppet configuration, 232
        lib directory, 233
        pluginsync.setting, 233
    repo type, 238
    shells type, 239
        default_target variable, 240
        ensurable statement, 239
        target parameter, 240
    testing
        HTTPAuth type, 245
        pluginsync, 245
    type creation, 234
        ensurable statement, 235
        isnamevar method, 236
        lib/puppet/type directory, 234
        munge hook, 236
        path parameter, 236
        repo type, 234
        source parameter, 235
        validate hook, 235–236

■ D

Debian packages (DEB), 169
Development and deployment, 73. *See also*
        Environments
    command and modes operation
        manifest files, 74
        printf, 74
        testing Puppet behavior, 74
    foreground Puppet master
        layout, 78
        output, 78
        puppet agent command, 79
    manifest files
        GitHub, 75
        modulepath, 75
        module testing environment, 76
        noop mode, 77
        Puppet module, 76
        ssh class, 77
        stdlib module, 75
        testing autorequires, 75
    overview, 73
    Vagrant (*see* Vagrant)

■ E

Environments
    branching and merging
        bare repository, 92
        benefits, 91
        central repository, 91
        individual changes, 92
        requires, 91

        clone creation, 86
        configure Puppet environments, 85
        development environment, 87
        example.com pty network, 84
        external modules, 84
        Git branches (dynamic environment) (*see* Git
            branches (dynamic environment))
        module maintenance, 84
        population, 85
        testing, 89
Exported resources
    load balancer worker, 163
        apache configuration, 163–164
        BalanceMember statements, 163
        balancermember resource, 164
        conf.d.members directory, 164
        front-end configuration, 163
        HTTP worker nodes, 163
        Include statements, 163–164
    nagios_service resources, 164–165
        check_command parameter, 166
        nagios_host resources, 165–166
        nagios::monitor class, 165, 167
        nagios::target class, 165–167
        ping command, 167
    SSH public host keys, 160
        host_aliases parameter, 161
        known_hosts file, 160–162
        puppet agent, 162
        ssh::hostkeys class, 161
        sshkey resources, 161–162
        ssh::knownhosts class, 161
External node carrier (ENC), 169
External node classification (ENC), 141
    back-end node classifier, 147
        MYSQL database, 148
        SQL statement, 148
        YAML data, 148
    configuring nodes, 143
        external_nodes, 143
        node_terminus, 143
        puppet.conf, 143
        puppet_node_classifier, 143
    foreman, 141
    Google, 141
    override node configuration, 148
    Perl-based node classifier, 146
        libyaml-perl package, 147
        perl-YAML package, 147
    ruby node classifier, 144–145
        production environment, 146
        puppetserver variable, 145
        YAML hash, 144, 146
    shell script, 143
        node statement, 144
        puppet_node_classifier, 143

$puppetserver, 144
simple node classifier, 143
YAML
database.yml, 142
indentation and syntax, 142
parameterized class, 144
three dashes (-), 142
YAML document, 142
YAML hash, 143
Zynga, 141

■ F

Facter package, 5, 8
Foreman
configuration, 173
connecting clients, 174
drilldown, 176
host page, 175
PuppetCA, 175
import data, 173
Puppet classes, 174
Puppet master, 174
installation, 169–170
debian packages (DEB), 170
disable TFTP, 170
file generated, 172
PuppetDB installation, 170
redHat packages (RPM), 170
running Puppet master, 170
save and exit, 171
welcome page, 172
reports, 178
eventful node, 179
eventful reports, 178
search facts, 179
using ENC, 176
adding classes, 176
parameterized classes, 177

■ G

Git branches (dynamic environment)
central repository, 94
Git hook, 95
Hiera configuration, 94
puppet.conf file, 93
workflow, 93

■ H

Hiera, 263
backends, 275
file backend, 277
gpg backend, 282

JSON backend, 279
manifests/init.pp file, 276
MySQL backend, 280
openvpn module, 275
command-line utility, 267
complex hierarchy, 271
dynamic hierarchy, 269
exploring hierarchy, 268
hiera lookup, 267
hiera lookup in puppet, 268
syslog_server, 269
syslog_server with puppet, 270
YAML data file, 267
configuration, 266
data directory, 267
hiera.yaml files, 266
create-resources() function, 289
data structures, 271
array merging, 272
hash merging, 273
return data, 271
external node classifier (ENC), 290
functions, 285
hiera_array() function, 286
hiera() function, 285
hiera_hash() function, 286
hiera_include() function, 286
ssh class, 286
Hiera-2, 292
installation, 265
list packages, 264
module data bindings, 287
mysql::db, 263
abstract parameters, 263
db_password, 263
hiera() function, 264
Openstack manifests, 288
Hierarchal data store. See Hiera
Hosts, 33. See also Modules
installation, 34
integration and bootstrapping (Kickstart file), 34
network, 33
node configuration (see Node configuration)
operating system, 33
role-specific applications, 34

■ I, J, K

Idempotency, 2
Inheritance, 37
Installation
agent and master server, 7
Apple Mac OS X, 14
command line, 18
facter installation, 15–16

Installation (*cont.*)
  Mac OSX pkg files, 15
  Verifyication, 17
  BIG-IP F5 devices, 18
  debian, 9
  Microsoft Windows, 11
    MSI file, graphics, 11
    using PowerShell, 13
  OpenIndiana, 9
  other platforms, 18
  puppetmaster package, 9
  Red Hat Enterprise Linux (RHEL), 8
    EPEL repositories, 8
    facter package, 8
    puppet labs repository, 8
    puppet package, 8
    RubyGems, 9
  solaris 10 and 10–11
  source tarballs, 10
  ubuntu, 9

■ L

LDAP server classification
  installing ruby libraries, 149
    ruby-ldap package, 149
    source package, 149
  openLDAP server, 149
  puppet.conf configuration, 150
    basenode, 153
    dapport option, 151
    environment attribute, 151
    ipHostNumber attribute, 152
    ldapbase option, 151
    ldappassword option, 151
    LDAP schema, 151
    ldapserver option, 151
    ldapuser option, 151
    LDIF nodes, 152
    node_terminus option, 151
    parentnode attribute, 151
    puppetclass attribute, 151
    puppetClient, 151
    puppetvar attribute, 151
  puppet schema document, 150
    include statement, 150
    openLDAP server, 150
    slapd.conf configuration, 150
  storing node configuration, 149
Lightweight directory access protocol (LDAP), 141
Load-balancing multiple Puppet masters
  configuration
    Apache setup working, 108
    directories creation, 110
    passenger.conf, 109

puppetmaster_proxy.conf file, 109
puppetmaster_worker_1.conf file, 110
worker processes, 108
front-end virtual host, 111
HTTP-based web services, 107
overview, 107
testing
  Apache front end load balancer error, 115
  disable back-end workers, 114–115
  enable both workers, 115
  front-end logging, 113
  passenger-status command, 115
  Puppet logs, 118
  puppetmaster.conf file, 116
  Puppet proxy group, 117
  request log, 114
  restart Apache and check, 113
  restart httpd, 117
  worker and test Puppet, 113
  worker logging, 113

■ M

Mail Transfer Agent (MTA), 28
Manifests, 20
Marionette Collective (MCollective), 249
  addressing hosts, metadata
    running mco package install, 260
    running mco service restart, 260–261
    service and package plug-ins, 260
  agent plug-in, 255
    installation, 255
    NRPE, 258
    running mco facts, 257
    running mco find, 257
    running mco help, 255
    running mco puppet runonce, 256
    running mco puppet status, 256
    running mco puppet summary, 257
  command and control tools, 249
  on GitHub, 261
  installation and configuration
    broker role, 251
    certificates, 252
    client node, 251
    mcollective daemon, 251
    mco-master node, 251
    permissions, 253
    testing, 254
    via puppet module, 250
    with RabbitMQ, 251
  messaging architecture, 250
  publish/subscribe messaging
    techniques, 250
STOMP, 250

Microsoft Windows, 11
  MSI file, graphics, 11
  using PowerShell, 13
Model
  client-server model, 2
  configuration/declarative language, 3–4
  resource abstraction layer, 5
  transactional layer, 6
Modules, 41
  Apache and websites
    Apache definitions, 63–64
    autoloading, 66
    ERB template, 65
    layouts, 62
    VirtualHost configuration file, 66
    VirtualHost template, 65
    website, 67
  file structure, 41
  functions, 50
  init.pp, 41
  manage SSH
    chaining exists, 52
    directory structure, 45–46
    ssh, 46, 50, 53
    stub ssh class, 44–45
  mysql module
    auditing mode, 61
    module structure, 58
    mysql, 59–61
  postfix
    files directory, 54
    postfix, 55, 57
    require function, 56
  puppet
    puppet, 68
    structure, 67
  sudo module, 41
  template, 42
  version control system (*see* Version control
    system (VCS))

■ N, O

Nagios Remote Plugin Executor (NRPE) plug-in, 258
Network Time Protocol (NTP), 24
Node configuration
  default node, 36
  external sources, 36
  inheritance, 37
  node defintions, 35
  Puppet style guide, 40
  similar hosts, 36
  variable scoping
    class inheritance, 38
    concepts, 37
    declarative language, 38
    parameterized classes, 39–40
    scope, 38
    ssh class, 38

■ P, Q

Package type, 5
Processors
  http report processor, 222
  log report processor, 219–220
    daemon facility, 220
    syslogfacility option, 220
  puppetdb report processor, 219, 222
  reports configuration, 220
  rrdgraph report processor, 219, 221
    rrddir directory, 222
    rrdtools package, 221
    RubyRRDtool, 221
  store report, 220
  tagmail report processor, 219–220
    puppet.conf configuration, 220
    tagmail.conf file, 220–221
    tagmap configuration, 220
Puppet, 1, 141
  3.1.x version, 6
  caveat, 7
  components, 24
  definition, 1
  external node classification (ENC), 141–142
  firewall configuration, 20
  first agent connection, 22
    node1.pro-puppet.com, 22
    puppetca binary/puppet cert, 23
    server option, 22
    sign option, 23
    test option, 23
    waitforcert, 23
  INI-style configuration, 19
  installation (*see* Installation)
  LDAP server classification, 141, 149
  main section, 19
  model, 2
    client-server model, 2
    configuration/declarative language, 3–4
    resource abstraction layer, 5
    transactional layer, 6
  node definition, 25
  puppet master, 21
  site.pp file, 20
  store node information, 141
  sudo module, 26
    catalog, 30
    file bucketing, 30
    files directory, 29

Puppet (*cont.*)
  init.pp file, 27
  metaparameter, 28
  module path, 26
  MTA, 28
  noop mode, 30
  $::osfamily fact, 28
  structure, 27
  sudo class, 28
Puppet and facter, 227, 232
  custom facts (*see* Custom facts)
  custom types, development
    (*see* Custom types)
  FACTER_datacenter, 227
  functions, development (*see* Custom functions)
  providers, development (*see* Custom providers)
Puppetboard, 169, 184
  dashboard (*see* Puppet DB)
  future advancements, 188
  installation, 185
Puppet configuration, 155
  expiring stale resources, 168
    PuppetDB, 168
    puppet node command, 168
  exported and stored configuration, 159
    puppetdb class, 159
    puppetdb log, 160
    puppetmaster, 159
  exported resources, 155, 160
  stored configuration, 155
  virtual resources, 155
Puppet consoles, 169
  foreman, 169
    connecting clients, 174
    import data, 173
    installion, 169
    reports, 178
    search facts, 179
    using ENC, 176
  Puppetboard, 184
    dashboard (*see* Puppet DB)
    future advancements, 188
    installation, 185
  Puppet enterprise console, 180
    add classes, 182
    connect PE agents, 181
    installation, 180
    inventory service, 182
    live management, 183
Puppet DB
  facts, 187
  nodes, 186
  query, 188
  reports, 187

Puppet forge, 191
  generating modules, 195
    cloned skeleton, 195
    demoapp module, 196
    generate action, 196
    params.pp file, 196
    puppet apply, 196
    puppet module tool, 195–196
  puppet librarian, 197
    apache module, 197
    librarian-puppet init, 197
    librarian-puppet install, 197
    Puppetfile.lock, 198
    puppetlabs/stdlib, 197
  puppet-lint, 199
    puppetlabs/rsync module, 199
    puppet-lint.rc., 200
  Puppet modules command, 192
  puppet modules, Geppetto, 210
    duplicate attribute, 211
    export module I, 213
    export module II, 214
    import project, 211
    invalid attribute, 212
    standalone application, 210
    tool tips, 212
    validate_bool, 212
  r10K, 198
    configuration, 199
    deploy command, 199
    GitHub, 198
    gitignore, 198
    Git repository, 199
    librarian-puppet, 198
    modules directory, 199
    RubyGems, 198
    support dynamic environment, 198
  search and install modules, 192
    mysql::db provider, 194
    MySQL module, 193–194
    mysql::server class, 194
    puppet module, 194
    README.md file, 194
    search command, 192
  testing modules, 200
Puppet master, 2, 21

■ R

RabbitMQ, 250
Red Hat Enterprise Linux (RHEL)
  EPEL repositories, 8
  facter package, 8
  puppet labs repository, 8

puppet package, 8
RubyGems, 9
RedHat packages (RPM), 169
Reporting puppet, 217, 225
    configuration, 219
        puppet.conf configuration, 219
        puppet master, 219
        report directory, 219
        reportdir option, 219
        store reports, 219
    custom reporting, 222, 224
        HTTP report processor, 223
        Puppet::Reports.register_report
          method, 223
        reportdir configuration, 224
        reports configuration, 223
        require puppet, 223
        self.host method, 224
        self.logs method, 224
        self.metrics method, 224
        YAML files, 222
    GitHub page, 225
    transcation report, 217
        events, 217, 219
        log messages, 217
        metrics, 217, 219
        Ruby, 219
        YAML file, 217, 219
Reporting processors, 219

▒ S

Scale Puppet
    anycast, 134
    Apache and Passenger
        configuration file, 101
        Debian/Ubuntu LTS, 98–99
        enterprise Linux, 99–101
        installation, 98
        server name, 105
    CA worker configuration
        configure Apache, 121
        endpoint certificates, 120
        HA configuration, 123
        sync CA data-CA hosts, 120
        testing, 124
    certificate requests
        CA worker configuration, 119
        hot standby, 127
        hot standby CA worker, 126
        HTTPS load balancing, 119
        primary CA directory, 129
    DNS round robin, 130
    DNS SRV records, 131

identification, 97–98
load-balancing multiple Puppet
    masters (*see* Load-balancing multiple
    Puppet masters)
masterless Puppet, 134
measuring performance, 137
splay time, 138
strategies, 97
TCP load balancer, 131
testing (Apache), 105
Splay time, 138
STOMP (Simple Text-Oriented
    Messaging Protocol), 250
Sudo module, 26
    catalog, 30
    file bucketing, 30
    files directory, 29
    init.pp file, 27
    metaparameter, 28
    module path, 26
    MTA, 28
    noop mode, 30
    $::osfamily fact, 28
    structure, 27
    sudo class, 28

▒ T, U

Testing modules
    rspec-puppet, 200
        collectd class, 205
        contain_package function, 203
        file_line resource, 205
        fixtures.yml file, 202
        Gemfile, 200
        pdxcat/collectd module, 200
        puppetlabs_spec_helper gem, 201
        purge_config parameter, 205
        raise_error check, 203
        Rakefile, 201
        spec_helper library, 203
        with_content file, 205
    rspec-system, 207
        collectd module, 208
        gitignore file, 208
        nodeset.yml file, 209
        puppetlabs_spec_helper gem, 210
        RSPEC_DESTROY
          variable, 210
    TravisCI, 205
        Markdown build image, 206
        README.md, 206
        rspec-puppet tests, 205
        travis.yml file, 205

■ V

Vagrant
    booting box, 81
    configuring Puppet, 82
    destroying and re-creating, 82
    initial setup, 80
    overall pattern, 80
    testing Puppet, 82
Version control system (VCS), 73, 233
    gitignore, 43
    Git package, 42
    Red Hat and Ubuntu, 42
    sudo module, 44
Vim package, 4
Virtual resources
    declaration errors, 155
    declare and realize, 156
        accounts::virtual class, 156
        realize() function, 157
        realizing spaceship operator, 156
        webapp class, 157
    duplicate resource, 155
    mysql class, 156

parameters collection
        specified, 157
realize() function, 156–157
realizing spaceship operator, 157
    realize() function, 157
    webapp package, 157
relationship-chaining syntax, 158
    apache account, 158
    arrow relationship syntax, 158
    parameters, 158
    syntax arrows, 158
    tilde arrows, 158
resource declaration, 156
spaceship syntax, 156
webapp class, 155

■ W, X

Waitforcert, 23

■ Y, Z

Yet ain't markup language (YAML), 142

Get the eBook for only $10!

Now you can take the weightless companion with you anywhere, anytime. Your purchase of this book entitles you to 3 electronic versions for only $10.

This Apress title will prove so indispensible that you'll want to carry it with you everywhere, which is why we are offering the eBook in 3 formats for only $10 if you have already purchased the print book.

Convenient and fully searchable, the PDF version enables you to easily find and copy code—or perform examples by quickly toggling between instructions and applications. The MOBI format is ideal for your Kindle, while the ePUB can be utilized on a variety of mobile devices.

Go to www.apress.com/promo/tendollars to purchase your companion eBook.

Apress®

THE EXPERT'S VOICE™

Made in the USA
Lexington, KY
07 May 2014